WILKES AND LIBERTY

A Social Study

WILKES AND LIBERTY

A Social Study

GEORGE RUDÉ

LAWRENCE AND WISHART
London

Lawrence and Wishart Ltd
39 Museum Street
London WC1A 1LQ

First published by Clarendon Press, 1962,
this edition with new Preface
first published by Lawrence and Wishart, 1983

Printed and bound in Great Britain at
The Camelot Press Ltd, Southampton

FOR DOREEN

PREFACE

THE present volume was written in 1960–61 and was first published in 1962. My purpose at the time was not so much to carry further forward or to enrich upon the work previously done by John Wilkes's biographers, who had been mainly concerned with his life, opinions and political career, as to focus on the nature and social background of his followers and to attempt to trace the course and outcome of the popular movements in which they became engaged. It was in fact in the sociology rather than in the politics — and still less in the bedroom scandals — of the Wilkite episode that I was primarily concerned. In this, if I am to accept the opinions of my reviewers, I appear to have had some success. But much water has flowed under the bridges in the last twenty years and it would be absurd to imagine that scholarship in this field, any more than in any other aspect of social history, has stood still. Little further attention has been given, it is true, to the narrower biographical aspects of Wilkes's career unless it be such additions as afforded by the further development of *The History of Parliament* under the direction of Professor John Brooke. Hard on the heels of my own book (such is the luck of the draw) followed Ian Christie's analytical *Wilkes, Wivill and Reform* (1962), which certainly gave more breadth to the political reform movement whose study I had confined to the career and impact of Wilkes.

But far more important as an extension of my own and others' work in this field has been the outcome of recent work in the symbols and ritual of popular politics and crowd behaviour; this provides a new dimension that may help to enrich the study of the crowd. In this sense, I would recommend John Brewer's *Party, Ideology and Popular Politics at the Accession of George III* (1976), all the more because it focuses in an original way on the whole episode of 'Wilkes and Liberty' in a chapter entitled 'Personality, Propaganda and Ritual'. This book has of course been added, together with half-a-dozen others, to the short, and highly selective, Bibliography at the end of this volume.

A few words of acknowledgement need to be added. In the first place, my book owes a great deal to the patience, forbearance and generous help afforded to me over a number of years by archivists, librarians and assistants in the British Library, the Public Record Office, the Guildhall Library, the Corporation of London, Middlesex and Surrey Record Offices,[1] and a number of other libraries and archives in London, the Home Counties, the North and West Country. Among them, I am indebted, above all, to Miss E. D. Mercer, F.S.A., then County Archivist of Middlesex, and to Dr. A. E. J. Hollaender, F.S.A., former librarian and custodian of London records at the Guildhall Library: in fact, the researcher could not hope to find a more faithful friend and wiser counsellor than I found in Dr. Hollaender in the course of my various incursions into London's eighteenth-century history in the 1950s and 1960s.

Among other scholars whose advice I sought at this time, I should like to acknowledge a particular debt to Professor Ian Christie, then of University College, London, and to Professor Thomas Copeland and Dr. John Wood, then at a comparatively early stage in the construction of their fine edition of the Burke Correspondence, for helping me to gain such easy and fruitful access to the Wentworth Woodhouse MSS. in the Sheffield Central Library. In this respect, my thanks are also due to Earl Fitzwilliam and the Trustees of the Wentworth Woodhouse Settled Estates for allowing me to publish certain extracts from the Burke and Rockingham MSS. in that collection. I also wish to thank the Librarian of the University of Edinburgh Library for permission to refer to Dr D. G. D. Isaac's unpublished Ph.D. thesis, 'A Study of Popular Disturbances in Britain, 1714–1754', in chapter I, and the Editor of *The English Historical Review* for allowing me to reproduce in chapter V the substance of my article of October 1960, entitled 'The Middlesex Electors of 1768–1769'.

Beckley, Sussex,
20 January, 1983. G. R.

[1] The two first are now incorporated in the newly constituted Greater London Council Record Office at Clerkenwell, EC1.

CONTENTS

	Introduction	xi
I	London Background	1
II	'Wilkes and Liberty!'	17
III	The 'Massacre' of St. George's Fields	37
IV	Wilkes *v.* Luttrell	57
V	The Middlesex Electors	74
VI	Industrial Unrest	90
VII	The Petitions of 1769	105
VIII	The Petitioners of 1769	135
IX	The City of London	149
X	Wilkes and his Supporters	172
	Epilogue	191

APPENDIXES

I	Eyewitnesses' Accounts of the Attack on Edward Russell's House in Southwark on the Night of 10–11 May 1768.	199
II	The Marquess of Rockingham and the Middlesex Petition of 29 April 1769	200
III	Industrial Unrest 1768–69: persons arrested and convicted	203
IV	Industrial Unrest, 1768–69: journeymen weavers' letters to Peter Auber, weaver of Spital Square, August 1769	205
V	Middlesex Electors, 1768–69: voting and value of properties	206

VI Middlesex Electors, 1768–69: voting record of M.P.s and clergy 208

VII Petitions of 1769: signatures and signatories 211

VIII London Livery Companies: membership, livery fines, support for Wilkes in 1768 212

IX Wilkes Supporters on the Court of Common Council, 1768–71 214

X City of London Aldermen, 1768–74 217

XI Persons suspected, arrested, and convicted in Wilkite disturbances in London, 1763–74 220

Bibliography and Abbreviations 224

Index 229

INTRODUCTION

This is not another biography of John Wilkes. Since Horace Bleackley's work appeared over forty years ago,[1] a great deal has been added to our knowledge of Wilkes and his times — not so much by his later biographers as by those, who, in recent years, have been closely associated with the late Sir Lewis Namier in compiling the History of Parliament. When those parts of the History are published that deal with the 1760s and 1770s we shall no doubt know more than we do at present about the political origins of the Wilkite movement and about Wilkes's political associates in both London and the provinces. We already have a glimpse of what such inquiries may reveal in Mr. John Brooke's work on the Chatham government of 1766 to 1768,[2] and a fuller picture in Dr. Lucy Sutherland's annotations to the second volume of the Burke *Correspondence* and in her Creighton Lecture on the metropolitan radical movement of 1768–74.[3] With further research of this kind in progress, we may perhaps look forward to the publication, in the not too distant future, of that 'definitive' biography of Wilkes that is already overdue.

The present volume makes no claim to meet this purpose, nor even to develop the study of John Wilkes along the lines traced by Bleackley and, after him, by O. A. Sherrard and Raymond Postgate.[4] It glosses over, or treats in the barest outline, much that must be of endless fascination to the student of so colourful a character as Wilkes — a man who not only aroused the deepest personal antipathy of George III and of many of his most devoted servants, but was dismissed by as liberal-minded an observer as Benjamin Franklin as 'an outlaw and exile of bad personal character, not worth a farthing', was considered by Edmund Burke to be 'a lively agreeable man, but of no prudence and no principle', and

[1] H. Bleackley, *Life of John Wilkes* (1917).

[2] J. Brooke, *The Chatham Administration 1766–1768* (1956)

[3] *The Correspondence of Edmund Burke*, vol. ii: July 1768–June 1774, ed. Lucy S. Sutherland (Cambridge and Chicago, 1960); L. S. Sutherland, *The City and the Opposition to Government, 1768–1774* (1959).

[4] O. A. Sherrard, *A Life of John Wilkes* (1930); Raymond Postgate, *That Devil Wilkes* (1930). W. P. Treloar's *Wilkes and the City* appeared in 1917.

wrung from Horace Walpole the solemn jibe that 'Despotism will for ever reproach Freedom with the profligacy of such a Saint'. Indeed, a man who so neatly balanced a reputation for wanton extravagance, frivolity and undiscriminating gallantry with the fervent loyalty and devotion of many of the most God-fearing citizens in the country, is clearly no hero cast in the conventional mould, and cannot fail to be an attractive subject for the biographer. Yet in this volume little is said of Wilkes's private life or of his vices or virtues, his personal conduct is neither condemned nor condoned, and no more attempt is made to justify the epithets showered on him by his enemies and critics than the adulation heaped on him by his friends and admirers. Such matter, while of intimate concern to the biographer, has little place in a study whose object is not so much to portray the life, career and opinions of Wilkes in themselves as to relate them to their social background and to trace the nature, course and outcome of the movements that sprang up in their wake.

It is, in fact, 'Wilkes and Liberty' rather than John Wilkes himself that is the central theme of this volume. 'Wilkes and Liberty' was, in the first place, a slogan adopted by Wilkes's supporters in London; but it became far more than a mere slogan and, in a wider sense, the term may properly be applied to the whole series of political movements, petitions, demonstrations and more violent outbreaks – of merchants, craftsmen, journeymen, freeholders and others – with which his name became associated between the spring of 1763, when the affair of *The North Briton* first brought him fame and notoriety, and the autumn of 1774, when he became Lord Mayor of London and was able to assume his seat as Member for Middlesex. What was the social appearance of London in Wilkes's day? Who were the Middlesex freeholders? Who composed the London crowds that demonstrated for Wilkes and shouted 'Wilkes and Liberty!'? Who were the petitioners – 60,000 in all – that, in 1769, demanded that Wilkes be recognized by Parliament as the lawful M.P. for Middlesex? What were the causes of Wilkes's popularity among such widely differing social classes? How far did his influence extend? What have been the ultimate results and the historical significance of the Wilkite movement? These are some of the questions that have been largely neglected by Wilkes's biographers and that the present volume makes some attempt to answer.

Such an approach is a new one; yet it is set in a biographical framework and the story of Wilkes himself, though shorn of much of its trappings, remains an essential part of the picture. It has, therefore, been necessary to refer once more to sources already consulted by Wilkes's biographers. Among these, considerable use has been made of the Hardwicke, Liverpool, Newcastle and Place MSS. in the British Museum; of parts of the Chatham MSS. in the Public Record Office, and of the printed correspondence (or memoirs) of George III, Edmund Burke, the Duke of Grafton, the Grenvilles, the Marquess of Rockingham, Horace Walpole, the First Earl of Malmesbury and the Earl of Chatham. In addition, a limited use has been made of the Burke and Rockingham MSS. among the Wentworth Woodhouse MSS. now available in the Sheffield Central Library. For the important Commons debates of January-February 1770 and of February-March 1771 reference has mainly been made to the Cavendish MS. Diary (Eg. 3711) in the British Museum and the Parliamentary Diary of Matthew Brickdale in the Bristol University Library.[1]

Among sources specifically relating to John Wilkes, the most valuable have proved to be the four manuscript volumes in the Guildhall Library in London, containing the Crown Solicitor's papers in the affairs of *The North Briton* and the *Essay on Woman*: these, though already used to good effect by Mr. Postgate, have been well worth a fresh examination. The same cannot be said, however, of the thirty-two volumes of Wilkes Papers (Add. MSS. 30865–96) in the British Museum and of John Almon's edition of Wilkes's correspondence. These, though providing the necessary starting-point for Wilkes's biographers, are almost exclusively concerned with personal affairs and have proved of little value for a study of this kind.

It has, of course, been found necessary to extend the range of inquiry far beyond these traditional sources. Fuller use has been made than hitherto of London and metropolitan records — the Minutes of Wards and Vestries; records of the London Livery and City companies; Rate Books; Land Tax registers; Episcopal Visitation Books; lists of merchants and Common Council men in the *Royal Calendar*, Baldwin's *Guide to London*, the *Court and City Register* and the *London Directory*; Freeholders' Books and Poll Books. Commissions of the Peace have been studied in a dozen

[1] For fuller details, see Bibliography.

counties. A more liberal use has been made of the press — not only of the London press but of a fair range of provincial newspapers. The town and county petitions of 1769 have been consulted in the Public Record Office. Above all, extensive use has been made of judicial records, which are an essential source for the study of popular movements of the period and of their participants. These include the printed *Proceedings* of the Old Bailey for 1763–75, the sessions papers (rolls, minutes, files and bundles) and Process Books in the London, Middlesex, and Surrey Record Offices; and the Surrey Assizes records, Home Office papers and Calendars, the correspondence and Entry Books in the State Papers Domestic, and the Treasury Solicitor's papers in the Public Record Office.[1]

The picture that emerges will perhaps bring little that is new to the informed reader or student concerning Wilkes's life, personality, opinions and public activities, but it is hoped that it will add something to his understanding of the society in which Wilkes lived, of the impact that he made on it, and of the contribution that he and his associates made to the nation's further political development.

1962

[1] For fuller details, see Bibliography.

I

LONDON BACKGROUND

JOHN WILKES was a Londoner and it was in London that the cry of 'Wilkes and Liberty!' was first heard, was most persistently voiced, and left the most enduring echoes. It was in the years that Wilkes grew to manhood that the metropolis of London was beginning to assume something of its present shape and definition. The component parts of this metropolis — the Cities of London and Westminster, the 'out'-parishes of Middlesex, the boroughs of Bermondsey and Southwark — still clung to their separate entities, their own forms of administration and their traditional electoral patterns; but by the middle of the eighteenth century it would have been possible to define this whole area as metropolitan London — an urban agglomeration whose combined population was estimated at 676,250 in 1750 and at 900,000 fifty years later.[1]

Yet, though increasingly unified by geography, economic life and common pursuits, London's population lay scattered over the widest diversity of streets, squares, gardens, courts, lanes and alleys. Extremes of wealth and poverty continued to rub shoulders within the same parish; yet the tendency was now the other way, and new fashionable areas of residence were growing up in Westminster and on the approaches to the City to respond to the social needs and ambitions of courtiers, politicians, the wealthy gentry and financial magnates. Though Buckingham House was acquired by George III in 1762, the Royal residence continued to be St. James's Palace. It was a time when Closet and Treasury were still the twin fountains of preferment and when vacant posts in Church and State were solicited by eager contenders with an obsequiousness and persistence — and often a lack of delicacy —

[1] See M. Dorothy George, *London Life in the XVIIIth Century* (1925), p. 329. In using the terms 'metropolis' and 'metropolitan area' I have generally followed the boundaries suggested by Dr. George, who includes within them the City within the Walls, the City without the Walls, the Borough (5 parishes of old Southwark), the City of Westminster, the 'out'-parishes of Middlesex and Surrey, and the five parishes of Chelsea, Kensington, Paddington, St. Marylebone and St. Pancras — the latter not included within the so-called Bills of Mortality (ibid., pp. 329, 409).

that would have done credit to the Court of Louis XIV.[1] It is, therefore, not surprising that the Court of St. James's should have drawn within its orbit, in the neighbouring parishes of St. George's and St. James's, the great landowners, Cabinet Ministers, party leaders and aspirants to office, whose political life was divided between Whitehall, the Palace of Westminster and the town and country houses of the aristocracy.

In St. James's Square, planned by the Earl of St. Alban's in 1663 as a *piazza* and let out in lots at annual rents of £80 and more, George III had been born and the Duke of Norfolk built a new residence in 1756. At the height of his political career as the Great Commoner, William Pitt lived in the Square in 1759 before retiring to Hayes in the '60s; and Sir Charles Asgill, Lombard Street banker and alderman of Candlewick Ward, was established there in 1774. Suitably adjacent lay St. James's Street with its notorious trio of fashionable gaming clubs — Boodle's, Crockford's and the Old Club at White's; among its wealthier residents in 1763 was Lady Elizabeth Germaine, holder of £25,000 of East India stock. Some of the statelier residences lay along or off Piccadilly, where land-values had begun to soar in the '60s. Lord Chesterfield's house, for example (before his move to Grosvenor Square), lay behind Shepherd's Market, with Lord Eglington's, Boswell's patron, close by in Queen Street; Devonshire House lay off Berkeley Street and farther east was Burlington House, whose new porch and colonnade were much admired. The Duke of Queensberry's mansion was in the Gardens behind, while in adjoining New Burlington Street, Alderman John Sawbridge, M.P. for Hythe, had, in 1769, a house assessed for the Watch Rate at £90 a year. Behind Devonshire House, in Berkeley Square, Robert Adam built for the Earl of Bute in 1765 what later became known as Lansdowne House. A few doors away, Robert Clive took his life in 1774; while Horace Walpole moved into the Square from Arlington Street in 1779 and, three years later, had his windows smashed by the over-zeal of crowds celebrating Lord Rodney's victories. Farther north, in Grosvenor Square, lay the residences of Lord North, the Earl of Hardwicke and the Marquess

[1] See a great part of the correspondence of Charles Jenkinson, Secretary to the Treasury, in the Liverpool Papers in the 1760s — e.g. a request for the vacant post of Dean of Windsor in September 1763, and one 'for the reversion of an office abroad' (accompanied by the offer of £1,000 in the event of satisfaction) in November; Add. MSS. 38201, ff. 134, 254.

of Rockingham, with Lord Bute's at no. 73 South Audley Street close by.[1]

Some aristocrats, however, either from choice or circumstance, lived outside the immediate orbit of the Court. In the first half of the century, Leicester House, built for the Prince of Wales, the future George II, in Leicester Fields, had been the centre of opposition to the King's government. The Duke of Northumberland resided at Charing Cross: it was here that he skilfully warded off the Wilkite rioters of March 1768 by promptly 'putting out lights' and ordering the Ship Ale-House to fill them with beer. On the same occasion, the Duke of Newcastle's house off Lincoln Fields did not escape so lightly.[2] Round Oxford Street, too, there had grown up pockets of residence owned by men of birth and of the monied interest. Soho Square, built in 1681, had earlier housed the Duke of Monmouth and the Dutchman Riperdà; in the 1760s, it counted among its residents the notorious Chevalier d'Eon, General Conway, James Adair, and William Beckford, twice Lord Mayor of London.[3] By 1780, this tendency to move outwards from the centre had grown apace; among the most distinguished of the victims of the Gordon Riots of that year was the Earl of Mansfield, whose house in Bloomsbury Square, with its fine library of books and prints, was rented for £230.[4] The same year, in St. Marylebone, lying on the northern fringe of the built-up area of the metropolis, the nobility and principal inhabitants, having decided to form a voluntary association for self-protection against future riots, appointed a committee composed of the Dukes of Portland and Manchester, the Earls of Macclesfield, Harcourt, Sussex and Bessborough, Viscounts Townshend, Cranbourne and Mahon, Lord de Ferrers, Lord Duncannon, the Dean of Windsor, seven baronets and forty other notables.[5]

While a few wealthy City men like Asgill, Beckford and Sawbridge

[1] H. B. Wheatley and P. Cunningham, *London Past and Present* (3 vols., 1891), ii. 164, 296, 298–301, 303–4, 381; Add. MSS. 32948, f. 332; Jack Lindsay, *1764* (1959), p. 162; *Boswell's London Journal 1762–1763*, ed. F. A. Potter (1950), p. 353; W. Crawford Snowden, *London 200 Years Ago* (1946), p. 20; Westminster Lib., St. James, West., Watch Rate, 1769, D 595, p. 27.

[2] See pp. 43–44 below.

[3] Wheatley and Cunningham, iii. 264–5. Beckford's house was assessed for rates at £68 p.a. (West. Lib., St. Ann, West., Scavengers' Rate, 1769, A 1234, p. 6).

[4] Holborn Lib., St. George, Bloomsbury, Poor Rate, June 1769, p. 18.

[5] St. Marylebone Lib., Proceedings of the Vestry of St. Marylebone, 1778–82, pp. 292–5.

might share the amenities of St. James's, St. George's or St. Ann's with courtiers, gentry and aristocrats, the solid core of the 'middling people' — professional men, merchants and the more prosperous craftsmen — lived farther east or south: in the Westminster parishes of St. Margaret's or St. Martin's in-the-Fields; in Holborn, the City of London, the Boroughs of Bermondsey and Southwark, or in the Middlesex 'out'-parishes that sprawled east and north of the City. If we followed Boswell too closely as our guide to eighteenth-century London, we might derive an exaggerated impression of the importance in contemporary London life of the *piazzas* of Covent Garden, the eating-houses of the Strand, and the coffee-houses of Fleet Street and Drury Lane. Yet these, of course, had their place in the world of letters, entertainment and political gossip: Boswell had his first view of Wilkes, Charles Churchill and the Earl of Sandwich when he dined with Lord Eglington at the rooms of the Sublime Society of Beefsteaks in Covent Garden; Samuel Johnson had chambers in the Temple and held court in the taverns around Fleet Street; and, at this time, the Sheridans lived in Henrietta Street, Covent Garden, David Garrick off the Strand, and Sir Joshua Reynolds at 47 Leicester Fields.[1]

The main bulk of the 10,000 or more merchants and 'principal tradesmen' of the metropolis were spread over a wider field. Tanners and leather-dressers were confined to the misty wasteland of Bermondsey. Brewers and distillers also tended to set up shop outside the Cities of Westminster and London; and, in 1769, we find Henry Thrale, Johnson's friend, established in Park Street, Southwark; Sir Joseph Mawbey, M.P., in Vauxhall; Sir Ben Trueman in Brick Lane, Spitalfields; and Samuel Whitbread in Chiswell Street, St. Luke's.[2] In the Gordon Riots, a dozen years later, it is true, a principal victim was Thomas Langdale, Roman Catholic distiller, who received a compensation of nearly £19,000 for damage done by fire to his extensive premises at nos. 26 and 81 Holborn.[3] But the areas in which trade and manufacture were extending most rapidly were those spreading out southwards and eastwards from the City — into Surrey and the 'out'-parishes of

[1] *Boswell's London Journal*, pp. 44, 51–52, 355; Wheatley and Cunningham, ii. 383. Swift lodged in Leicester Fields in 1711 and Hogarth came to live there, in a house rated at £60, in 1733 (ibid., ii. 382–3).

[2] Baldwin's *Guide to London*, 1770.

[3] Corp. London R.O., CR 13A ('Riots 1780').

Middlesex. These were also centres of rapidly rising population during the latter half of the century, areas, too, in which we find the main concentration of sundry manufacturers, wharfingers, lightermen, warehousemen, importers, sugar-refiners and coal-merchants, whose warehouses, shops, offices and goods-yards lay scattered over the riverside parishes of Shadwell, Wapping, Limehouse and St. George-in-the-East. It was in these districts and among such 'new' trading and manufacturing elements that Wilkes was to win his most solid body of support in the Middlesex elections of 1768 and 1769.[1]

But the City of London, with a population of some 150,000, remained the main centre of banking, insurance, overseas trade, and of the ancient crafts. The Bank of England, the principal insurance offices and the great merchant companies, like the East India and the South Sea Companies — the so-called 'monied interest' — were almost a law unto themselves and played a more significant part in national than in City politics;[2] their governors and directors were as likely to live in the fashionable parishes of Westminster or on rural freeholds in Surrey or Middlesex as in the 'out'-parishes or within the confines of the City itself. But the real backbone of the City's commercial and political life was formed by the 8,000 liverymen and 12,000–15,000 freemen attached to the sixty-odd City companies.[3] Though aldermen were not bound by a residential qualification and might be found serving as justices in widely scattered counties,[4] the 236 members of the Common Council were obliged to be freemen householders within the wards that appointed them, and we find that a fair number of those who played a leading part in City politics during Wilkes's heyday were bound to the City by residence as well as by occupation.[5]

[1] See pp. 80–81 below.

[2] Lucy S. Sutherland, 'The City in Eighteenth-Century Politics,' in *Essays presented to Sir Lewis Namier*, ed. R. Pares, and A. J. P. Taylor (1956), pp. 49–53. But there were several bankers among aldermen engaged in City politics (see p. 150–51 below).

[3] See *A List of the Liverymen of the several Companies of the City of London* (1756).

[4] Thus, Beckford, James Townsend and Thos. Harley were justices in Middlesex; Sawbridge and Barlow Trecothick in Kent; Beckford in Wiltshire; Serjeant John Glynn in Cornwall; and Brass Crosby, Brackley Kennet, and Trecothick in Surrey.

[5] E.g. Richard Oliver, West India merchant, of Fenchurch Street; William Nash, wholesale grocer, of Cannon Street; Frederick Bull, tea-merchant, of Threadneedle Street; and Rt. Hon. Thomas Harley, merchant (and later banker), of Aldersgate Street (*London Directory*, 1771).

Some Common Council men may, of course, have used a City residence purely as an electoral qualification, but comparatively few of them — and indeed few of the liverymen that elected them to office — were Middlesex freeholders and voted as such in the elections of 1768 and 1769.[1] It seems, in fact, probable that the great majority of the freemen and liverymen, merchants and craftsmen of the City lived within its boundaries and confined their political energies to debating and voting in its twenty-six wards and 100 vestries — a concentration of energy that goes a long way to explain the power of the City of London as a political force.[2]

Sharply distinct, no less in manners than in dress, outlook, residence and living standards, from these citizens of the upper and 'middling' sort were the majority of the people of London —'the lower orders', or those whom Wilkes, on an historic occasion, termed 'the inferior set of people'. These were, by no means, all of one social class: even the wage-earners among them had not yet acquired, as they acquired in the nineteenth century, the attributes of a more or less distinctive class. They ranged from the shop-keepers and stallholders of Westminster, the Boroughs and street-markets, and the skilled craftsmen of the City, whose incomes might be no lower than those of many within the 'middling' groups, to the domestic workers and that great mass of unskilled and undernourished whom Sir John Fielding wrote of as 'the infinite number of chairmen, porters, labourers and drunken mechanics' — of whom many crowded into the filthy courts and alleys and insalubrious garrets and tenements of St. Giles-in-the-Fields, Chick Lane, Field Lane and Black Boy Alley.[3] Between these extremes were the many thousands of journeymen, apprentices and 'servants' in skilled or semi-skilled occupations — tanners and fellmongers of Bermondsey; silk-weavers of Spitalfields, Shoreditch and Bethnal Green; riverside workers, sailors and coal-heavers of Shadwell, Wapping and Limehouse; Thames-side watermen and lightermen; watchmakers of St. Luke's and Clerkenwell, and tailors and hatters of Charing Cross, Tottenham Court Road and Oxford Street.[4]

[1] See p. 79 below.

[2] It is no doubt significant that of 16,000 'inhabitants of London, Westminster, and Southwark' listed in 1793 only 300 appear as freeholders of Middlesex (*Universal British Directory*, 1793, i (London), 49-341).

[3] Cit. Francis Place, Add. MSS. 27825, ff. 243, 211.

[4] See M. D. George, op. cit., pp. 155–213.

These together composed, for all their diversity, what Henry Fielding termed 'that very large and powerful body which forms the fourth estate in the community and has long been dignified by the name of the Mob'.[1]

For the mass of these citizens life was hard, brutal and violent and a constant struggle against disease, high mortality and wretched economic conditions. 'The waste of life', writes Dr. George, 'was at its worst since the days of the plague between 1727 and 1750.'[2] The rate of mortality was particularly high among young children: in the seven years 1728 to 1734, of 188,208 burials within the so-called Bills of Mortality of London, 72,853 were of children under the age of two. The most common causes of death were 'convulsions', 'consumption', 'fevers or purple', and small-pox.[3] A newspaper advertisement of 1771, when the chances of survival had long since begun to improve, illustrates the persistence of certain types of illness and of popular faith in quack remedies:

> Dr. James's Powder, for Fevers, the Small Pox, Measles, Pleurisies, Quinsies, Acute Rheumatism, Colds, and all Inflammatory and Epidemical Disorders, as well as for those which are called Nervous, Hypochondriac and Hysteric.[4]

Wages varied according to occupation, sex and skill; but, in terms of the cost of food and lodging, they were generally low and changed little in the course of the century. During the middle years, labourers' weekly wages ranged between 9s. and 12s. and those of journeymen in the lower-paid trades between 12s. and 15s.; and, in 1768, we find a Member of Parliament complaining to the Duke of Newcastle of the 'impudence' of tailors in 'set[ting] forth their inability to live on two shillings and sevenpence a day, when the common soldier lives for under six pence'. On the other hand, a compositor might earn 22s. to 27s. a week, a jeweller or chair-carver as much as £3 or £4, and the East London coal-heavers, whose riotous proceedings will feature in a later chapter, were reputed to earn up to 10s. a day. But such earnings were exceptional. Least favoured of all were women domestic workers: we read of a silk-winder being hired at Spitalfields Market in 1760 for a mere 3s. a week. Working hours were long. Tailors worked from six in the morning till seven or eight in the evening;

[1] Cit. J. P. de Castro, *The Gordon Riots* (Oxford, 1926), p. 249.
[2] M. D. George, op. cit., p. 25.
[3] *Gent's Mag.*, 1735, p. 165; 1736, p. 750.
[4] *Public Advertiser*, 27 March 1771.

bookbinders, until 1785, worked from six to nine; building workers from six to six, or as daylight permitted; workers in handicrafts from six to eight; and a journeyman shipwright, sentenced in the Gordon Riots, said he worked from five in the morning till eight at night.[1]

Matters of prime concern to the wage-earners and all small consumers were the price of bread and the price of lodgings. The weekly rent of a furnished room in the poorer London districts varied between 2s. and 3s. 6d. We find a £50-a-year clerk paying 2s. 6d. a week for lodgings in a mean part of the town in 1767,[2] and Francis Place tells us that, twenty-five years later, he paid 3s. 6d. for his lodgings near Butcher Row, behind St. Clement's Church, at a time when he was earning 14s. a week as a journeyman tailor.[3] But the price of bread was a matter of even more serious moment, as it took up a larger part of the poor man's budget and fluctuated far more sharply. In the middle years of the century, at least, the average Londoner — man, woman or child — consumed a quarter of wheat per year, or eight lb. of bread per week, and, in 1779, we hear of a journeyman saddler with a wife and three children, who, out of a weekly wage of 20s., spent 4s. 11d., or nearly a quarter of his income, on bread.[4] This proportion might, of course, become much greater in times of bad harvests or national emergency, when rising bread-prices would leave the small consumer correspondingly short of the other necessities of life. In the first half of the century, the price of wheat was low and might, in a normal year, fluctuate between 30s. and 36s. a quarter and the price of bread between 1¼d. and 1½d. a pound. There were only three bad seasons — in 1727, 1728 and 1740; but between 1756 and 1773 crops tended to be poor;[5] prices were high again in 1775 and 1777; and after 1793 the French wars brought prolonged inflation and shortage. So we find the price of bread in London rising to 2d. a pound in 1768, 1773 and 1777; while, in 1795, it rose to the then fantastically high price of over 3d. a pound, or to 4s. 6d. for the wheaten

[1] M. D. George, op. cit., pp. 163 ff., 206–7; Jas. West, M.P., to Duke of Newcastle, 16 May 1768, Add. MSS. 32990, ff. 77–8; O.B. *Proceedings*, 1780 (Surrey Commission), pp. 11–13, 112–15.

[2] M. D. George, op. cit., p. 192.

[3] Add. MSS. 35142, f. 197.

[4] 'Observations humbly submitted to the Consideration of the Honourable Committee of the House of Commons appointed to enquire into the Assize of Bread' (1768) [Guildhall Lib., MS. 7799]; D. G. Barnes, *A History of the English Corn Laws from 1660 to 1846* (1930), p. 109; M. D. George, op. cit., p. 167.

[5] Ibid., p. 27; Barnes, op. cit., p. 32.

peck-loaf of 17 lb. 6 oz.[1] It may be readily imagined what catastrophic effects such sharp increases in the cost of living had on the incomes and budgets of the wage-earners, street-sellers and other small consumers. To the thousands of women domestic workers, the aged, infirm and parish poor who, even in normal times, lived on the border-line of bare subsistence, it meant utter destitution and, often, starvation and death.[2] But, at such times, even journeymen and labourers of settled occupation found it impossible to make ends meet and, in order to maintain their standards, resorted to riots, strikes and violent disputes with their employers.[3]

There were, of course, other means of seeking compensation or an escape from poverty, drudgery and destitution, and most historians and commentators have agreed that the seamier side of eighteenth-century London life, which so outraged the sensibilities of the virtuous Francis Place,[4] sprang as much from the social conditions of the day as from the settled policy, indifference or bad example of the governing classes. Crime, drunkenness, prostitution and violence thrived during the greater part of this period, though they appear to have diminished, with the fall in the mortality rate, in the latter years of the century.[5] Gin had come in from Holland with William of Orange, had taken firm roots among the London poor and, for sixty years, became both a source of profit to farmers and distillers and a social evil of incalculable consequences. This was the age when every fourth house in St. Giles's was a dram-shop and when a working man or woman could get into a drunken stupor for 1d. or 2d. The sale of spirits rose from 3½ million gallons in 1727 to nearly 5½ million gallons in 1735 and to over 8 million in 1743; while, by the latter date, more than 7,000 shops, both licensed and unlicensed, were selling gin and brandy in the metropolitan area of Middlesex alone.[6] As late as 1751, after the

[1] Prices are calculated from the monthly returns recorded (with some gaps) in the *Gent's Mag.*, 1735–95.

[2] In 1779, Saunders Welsh, the London Magistrate, told Dr. Johnson that more than twenty such persons died every week of starvation in the streets and garrets of London (*The Life of Samuel Johnson* (Edinburgh, 1876), p. 410).

[3] See chapter VI below.

[4] For the 'low morals' of the eighteenth century and for Francis Place's estimation of the improvement in manners and morals that took place between the 1790s and 1830s, see Add. MSS. 27825–30.

[5] Add. MSS. 27827, ff. 48–49; M. D. George, op. cit., pp. 3, 56–61.

[6] Add. MSS. 27826, ff. 27–42; *East London Observer*, 22 May 1915; M. D. George, op. cit., pp. 31 ff; Lord Kinross, 'Prohibition in Britain', *History Today*, July 1959; G. Rudé, '"Mother Gin" and the London Riots of 1736', *The Guildhall Miscellany*, no. 10, September 1959.

still-born Gin Act of 1736 and another attempt by Parliament in 1743 to stamp out the grosser excesses of gin-drinking, Henry Fielding wrote in his *Enquiry*:

> A new kind of drunkenness, unknown to our ancestors, is lately sprung up amongst us, and which if not put a stop to, will infallibly destroy a great part of the inferior people. The drunkenness I hear intend is . . . by this poison called Gin . . . the principle sustenance (if it may be so called) of more than a hundred thousand people in this Metropolis.[1]

Soon after, with the aid of Hogarth's pictorial propaganda and a further Gin Act, the London of *Gin Lane* was beginning to be a thing of the past; yet, in 1780, at the height of the Gordon Riots, Horace Walpole was able to write, with reasonable accuracy, in relating the drunken orgies performed outside Thomas Langdale's gutted distilleries in Holborn, that 'as yet there are more persons killed by drinking than by ball or bayonet'.[2]

The increase in crime was a constant complaint of magistrates. In a pamphlet published in 1758, Sir John Fielding pointed to the Sessions Papers and Calendars for 1755 and 1756, 'when gangs of friendless boys, from 14 to 18 years of age, were transported, indeed, I may say by wholesale, for picking of pockets and pilfering from shops'; and he added that scarcely a session passed 'without indictments being found against porters and such low sort of men for ravishing the infants of the poor'.[3] The Old Bailey *Proceedings* of December 1762 to October 1763 record the trials of 433 persons for murder, burglary, robbery and theft: of 243 persons convicted, 42 men and 5 women were sentenced to death, 122 men and 49 women were sentenced to transportation, 10 men and 2 women were branded and 5 women whipped. By 1770, the number of capital convictions in a year had risen to 91. A parliamentary Report of 1812 illustrates from the findings of a committee of inquiry set up forty years before the remarkable increase in burglaries and robberies committed in London and Westminster between 1766 and 1770: whereas 13 houses were broken into

[1] Henry Fielding, *An Enquiry into the Causes of the late Increase of Robbers* (1751), p. 18.

[2] *The Letters of Horace Walpole, Fourth Earl of Orford*, ed. P. Cunningham (9 vols., 1906), vii. 392.

[3] John Fielding, Introduction to *A Plan for the Asylum for Orphans and other deserted Girls of the Poor of this Metropolis* (1758), pp. 3, 6. Fielding adds: 'And as the deserted boys were thieves from necessity, their sisters are whores from the same cause; and having the same education with their wretched brothers, generally join the thief to the prostitute' (p. 3).

between Michaelmas 1766 and Lady-Day 1767, 36 houses were broken into between Lady-Day and Michaelmas 1767, 52 in 1767–78, 63 in the middle months of 1769, and 104 between Michaelmas 1769 and Lady-Day 1770. Four years later, the *Gentleman's Magazine* reported: 'The papers are filled with robberies and breaking of houses, and with recitals of the cruelties committed by the robbers, greater than ever known before.'[1] It was a time, too, when fashionable society was amazed and scandalized by the daring deeds of armed footpads and highwaymen often carried out in the very heart of the metropolis. In 1773, a mounted highwayman robbed Sir Francis Holburne and his sisters in their coaches in St. James's Square; the Lord Mayor was held up at pistol-point at Turnham Green before all his retinue a few years later, and, in the 1780s, the Prince of Wales and the Duke of York were the victims of robbers in Hay Hill, Berkeley Square. Some were inclined to blame the Irish, who were among the poorest of London's poorer citizens, for this increase in crime, and a newspaper report of 1763 runs:

> It is remarkable that of 19 or more footpads and street-robbers now in custody, at least 15 of them are Irishmen, and all lately discharged from His Majesty's ships.[2]

The violence of crime was matched by the violence of popular entertainment. It was the age of women prize-fighters, such as the redoubtable Bruising Peg who, when battling with an opponent in Spa Fields for a new shift, 'beat her antagonist in a terrible manner'.[3] It was an age, too, of bear-baiting, cock-fighting and fantastic wagers lightly undertaken, but often ending in mutilation or death.[4] Another pastime was to pelt the poor wretches sitting in the stocks at Charing Cross, though on occasion the victim might win the sympathy of the crowd and elicit a cheer rather than a rotten apple or egg. But the greatest sport of all was to watch the hangings at 'Tyburn Fair' or to toast the victims in beer or gin as they were carried along Holborn, St. Giles's and Oxford Street to the place of execution. 'Within my recollection,' wrote Place, 'a

[1] O.B. *Proceedings*, 1763; *Lond. Chron.*, 3–5 Nov. 1772, p. 440; *Parliamentary Papers*, 1812, vol. ii, appendices 7–8 (there was a slight decrease between Lady-Day 1768 and Lady-Day 1769); *Gent's Mag.*, 1774, p. 443.

[2] Wheatley and Cunningham, ii. 299; Add. MSS. 27826, f. 110; *Gent's Mag.*, 1776, p. 433; *Read. Merc.*, 2 May 1763. For the high rate of crime among the Irish poor in London, see M. D. George, op. cit., pp. 119–21.

[3] *Daily Advertiser*, 22 June 1768.

[4] See J. Lindsay, op. cit., pp. 210–11, 260.

hanging day was to all intents and purposes a fair day. The streets from Newgate to Tyburn were thronged with people, and all the windows were filled.' Some victims were enormously popular — none more so than the fabulous John Rann, alias Sixteen-String Jack, who, a showman to the last, was hanged in a pea-green coat with a huge nosegay in his button-hole. The onlookers on such 'brutalizing occasions' were, added Place with pardonable exaggeration, composed of 'the whole vagabond population of London, all the thieves, and all the prostitutes, and all those who were evil-minded and some, a comparatively few, curious people'.[1] Fashionable society might deplore or smile condescendingly at these excesses and seek their own more elegant diversions in regattas and suppers at Ranelagh[2] or in the gaming clubs of St. James's, but the violence of the poor was, in part at least, but a reflection of the violence of their rulers and social betters. It was a time when the desiccated heads of the executed rebels of the 'Forty-Five' still grinned down from the Temple Bar, a stone's throw from Dr. Johnson's chambers; one of the last two of these trophies fell from its perch on 31 March 1772.[3] Public hangings at Tyburn were, until 1783, maintained by Parliament as an instrument of public policy; Johnson, to Francis Place's disgust, commended them.[4] Affairs of honour were settled by gentlemen with sword or pistol — sometimes ending in farcical anti-climax, but often in death or injury. Sons of the gentry were schooled in violence from an early age: Mrs. Harris, mother of the First Earl of Malmesbury, describes a drunken brawl followed by a riot at Winchester College, in the course of which the young gentlemen broke out of Hall, sallied forth 'with weapons of all kinds', and fought the townsmen with such vigour that the magistrates were compelled to read the Riot Act.[5] Cock-fighting was also a fashionable pastime and gentlemen might wager as much as forty guineas a battle on the success of their birds at the Royal Cockpit. Boswell, on one occasion, 'was sorry for the poor cocks' and 'looked round to see if any of the spectators pitied them when mangled and torn in a most

[1] Add. MSS. 27826, f. 107. For further, and more lurid, details of public executions in eighteenth-century London, see Alfred Marks, *Tyburn Tree, its History and Annals* (n.d.), pp. 221–68.

[2] F. H. W. Sheppard, 'An Eighteenth-Century Regatta on the Thames', *History Today*, Dec. 1959.

[3] Wheatley and Cunningham, iii. 359.

[4] Add. MSS. 27826, ff. 94–102.

[5] Mrs. Harris to her son James, 23 Feb., 3 March 1770, *Letters of the First Earl of Malmesbury from 1745 to 1820* (2 vols., 1870), i. 194–5, 197.

cruel manner'. But, he adds, 'I could not observe the smallest relenting sign in any countenance'.[1] High wagers, too, were placed by gentlemen on the outcome of prize-fights. In July 1764, runs a press-report, chairman Brooker and Brick-Street Jack fought it out in a field near Knightsbridge. 'The battle was the most desperate ever known, the combatants having fought successively for 48 minutes, and, during the contest, several hundred pounds were won and lost.'[2]

But in one activity at least the 'mobbish part of the Town' had nothing to learn from their superiors. Popular rioting was endemic throughout the eighteenth century. In country districts and market towns, riots took place against rising food prices, against turnpikes, enclosures, work-houses, Smuggling and Militia Acts, and against Methodists' and Dissenters' chapels; above all, they broke out in years of shortage, when the prices of wheat, flour and bread were appreciably above the average. In London, too, the century was punctuated by periodic rioting; here, too, riot-'captains' would, as occasion demanded, marshal their followers of a day or a week to assail the houses of their intended victims; but food-rioting in London was the exception rather than the rule. Though there were deeper social under-currents, the ostensible targets of these riots were more often Roman Catholics, Jews, Scots, Irish, Dissenters, and other 'alien' or non-conforming (or even wage-cutting) elements;[3] the Englishman's cult of 'freedom' and his detestation of 'Popery and wooden shoes' also played a considerable part in such disturbances; or they might be staged in order to promote the cause of some popular hero of the day — men like William Pitt, John Wilkes, Admiral Keppel or Lord George Gordon.[4] Yet, for a brief period after 1714, London's 'lower orders' were swept by a wave of yearning for Jacobite 'utopias', and in 1715 and 1716, 'High Church' crowds paraded the streets of the City, Holborn and Whitechapel to shouts of 'High Church and Ormonde', smashed the windows of government supporters, and attacked a Presbyterian Meeting House in Highgate.[5] More characteristic was the riot of 1733, when London crowds, in

[1] *Boswell's London Journal*, p. 87. [2] Cit. J. Lindsay, op. cit., p. 188.

[3] For eighteenth-century Londoners' hostility to Irish, Jews and foreigners, see M. D. George, op. cit., pp. 117–34.

[4] See my article, 'The London "Mob" of the Eighteenth Century', *The Historical Journal*, II, i (1959). 1–18.

[5] D. G. D. Isaac, 'A Study of Popular Disturbance in Britain, 1714–1754' (Ph.D. Thesis, Edinburgh, 1953), pp. 143–85.

league with City interests, besieged Parliament to cries of 'No slavery — no excise — no wooden shoes!' and compelled Sir Robert Walpole to withdraw his Excise Bill.[1] In July 1736, the dismissal of English workmen and the employment of cheaper Irish labour by building contractors and master weavers touched off violent rioting in East London. Shouting 'Down with the Irish!' bands of rioters attacked, or 'pulled down', Irish dwellings and ale-houses in Shoreditch, Spitalfields and Whitechapel. Similar disturbances threatened in Holborn and Westminster, a few weeks later, when the new Gin Act came into operation, and a letter sent to Sir Robert Walpole by one of his informants suggests that there were other issues, too, involved in the riots of that year:

> It is evident that there are great discontents and murmurings through all the mobbish part of the Town. The Gin Act and the Smuggling Act stick hard in the stomachs of the meaner sort of people, and the Bridge Act greatly exasperates the watermen insomuch as they make no scruple of declaring publicly that they will join in any mischief that can be set on foot.[2]

In the 1760s, too, there were various causes of public disorder; and the London crowds who, in 1768, gaily smashed their opponents' windows and assaulted their property to shouts of 'Wilkes and Liberty!' may have been as filled with anger at the high price of bread and hatred of the Scots as with enthusiasm for the cause of John Wilkes.[3] Most widespread and most destructive of all the London outbreaks were the Gordon Riots of June 1780, when 'No Popery' crowds held the streets of a great part of the metropolis for nearly a week, burned or pulled down 100 houses or more, and did damage assessed at over £100,000.[4] The fears aroused by these riots in government circles and among property-owners were revived by the last great outbreak of the century — when, in August 1794, 'a mixed multitude of men, women, boys and children' (to quote one of the Lord Mayor's dispatches) defied the Militia and Guards for three days and attacked and destroyed 'crimping houses', or houses used for Army-recruiting, in Holborn, the City, Clerkenwell and Shoreditch.[5]

[1] R. R. Sharpe, *London and the Kingdom* (3 vols., 1895), iii. 36.

[2] See my article, ' "Mother Gin" and the London Riots of 1736', *Guild. Misc.*, Sept. 1959.

[3] See chapter III below.

[4] See my article, 'The Gordon Riots: a Study of the Rioters and their Victims', *Trans. Royal Hist. Soc.*, 5th series, vi (1956), 93–114.

[5] P.R.O., H.O. 42/33; O.B. *Proceedings*, 1793–94, pp. 1326–32; *Gent's Mag.*, 1794, pp. 721–3; *Ann. Reg.*, 1794, p. 25.

No doubt the feelings prompting or underlying such demonstrations were shared by even the most debased and wretched of the denizens of St. Giles's or Saffron Hill, or of those who (according to Francis Place) flocked most eagerly to Tyburn; but historians have too readily assumed that the 'mobs' that rioted were of this species and were of necessity drawn from 'criminal elements', the slum population, or from 'the inhabitants of the dangerous districts . . . who were always ready for pillage'.[1] Yet this was not the case. Rioters were certainly drawn from what Henry Fielding termed 'the Mob' and they tended to be wage-earners rather than self-employed craftsmen, peddlars or small proprietors, but they were rarely criminals, vagrants or the poorest of the poor, and in so far as any parts of the metropolis may be said to have been more riotous than others, they were the City, the Strand, Southwark, Shoreditch and Spitalfields rather than St. Giles-in-the-Fields or the shadier alleys of Holborn. Nor need this surprise us. The ideas underlying or accompanying the violent actions of 'the inferior set of people' were often those more lucidly and decorously expressed by the 'middling sort' — the merchants, tradesmen and master craftsmen — who composed the vestries and wards of the City, Westminster, and the Surrey or Middlesex 'out'-parishes. Nowhere did the opinions of these elements find such vocal and consistent expression as in the Common Hall or Common Council (though less frequently in the Court of Aldermen) of the City of London. Far from working in close co-operation with Court and Administration, the City prided itself on its independence and was, more often than not, in opposition to the policies of Whitehall and St. James's.[2] Having acclaimed George I and led the country in denouncing Jacobite conspiracies, the City settled down to steady opposition to Walpole's administration. Led by the redoubtable Sir John Barnard, it headed the campaign against the Excise Bill of 1733, both in and outside Parliament; and when Walpole was 'mobbed' on leaving the Commons, the City was charged with responsibility for the outrage.[3] The Common Council equally voiced the mood of those insisting on war with Spain over Jenkins' Ear and continued to harass Walpole over the insufficiency of convoys, and when the Minister was finally driven out of office,

[1] M. D. George, op. cit., pp. 118–19.
[2] Lucy S. Sutherland, op. cit., pp. 53–55.
[3] Ibid., pp. 62–63; R. R. Sharpe, op. cit., iii. 4–9, 36–38.

the City celebrated the victory over 'corruption' by urging Parliament to promote a Place Bill and a Pensions Bill and to repeal the Septennial Act. In 1756, the Common Council clamoured for war and for Byng's execution after the surrender of Minorca, and William Pitt, newly appointed Secretary of State, aroused their enthusiasm by reorganizing the Militia and sending Hanoverian and Hessian conscripts out of the country. On Pitt's dismissal a few months later, he was presented by the City with its Freedom. The City subscribed enthusiastically to the war and honoured Pitt by naming after him what later became known as Blackfriars Bridge. On his retirement from office in October 1761, the Common Council ostentatiously voted him their thanks, and when Pitt and his brother-in-law, Earl Temple, accompanied George III to the Guildhall on a ceremonial visit a few days later, it was for them and not for the King that the loudest ovations were reserved, while Bute, the Favourite, was pelted and booed. Previously, the Common Council had already laid down its terms for what it considered would be an honourable peace by instructing its M.P.s to ensure that there should be no surrender of Guadaloupe or of any of the North American possessions.[1] Even more significant of things to come was a speech by William Beckford, champion of the 'middling people' and Pitt's principal henchman in the City, who, in standing for election to Parliament in March 1761, denounced the importance accorded to 'little, pitiful boroughs' and thus fired the opening shot in the City's campaign for parliamentary reform.[2]

Soon after, there burst on London that remarkable phenomenon, John Wilkes. It is with the impact that he made on the various classes of society — above all in the metropolis — and the echoes and reactions that it stirred among them that this book is largely concerned.

[1] R. R. Sharpe, op. cit., pp. 38, 48, 58–65, 69–70.

[2] Lucy S. Sutherland, *The City of London and the Opposition to Government, 1768–1774*, pp. 10–11.

II

'WILKES AND LIBERTY!'

JOHN WILKES was born, the second son of pious and well-to-do parents, in St. John's Square, Clerkenwell, on 17 October 1725.[1] His father, Israel Wilkes, was a prosperous distiller, and his mother, Sarah, having attempted to instil in him her own principles of unbending nonconformity, did not fail, in later years, to upbraid him for the laxity of his private life.[2] At the age of nine, he was sent to study Latin and Greek at a boarding-school at Hertford; his love of the classics was never to leave him. Ten years later, after a brief spell in the charge of a private tutor, he was sent to complete his education at the University of Leyden. Among his fellow-students were two future Chancellors of the Exchequer, William Dowdeswell and Charles Townshend; but, strangely enough in view of later proclivities, his closest friends at this time were Scots — the philosopher Andrew Baxter and Alexander Carlyle of Inveresk.[3]

After two years at Leyden, Wilkes was recalled to Clerkenwell to celebrate his twenty-first birthday and was, shortly afterwards, provided by loving parents with a rich wife in the person of Mary Meade of Aylesbury. Apart from her substantial endowments, the lady had few charms for him and the marriage was soon to break up, but not before it had brought him two durable assets — a daughter, Polly, to whom he remained deeply devoted, and the Manor of Aylesbury, where he soon established himself as an improving squire and a member of the county bench. The friends and supporters that he won at this time included such local dignitaries as John Stephens, the vicar; John Dell, gentleman farmer and surveyor; Robert Neale, vestryman and church-warden; Edward and Richard Terry, brewers; Henry Sheriff, proprietor of the George Inn; Robert Patten, innholder; and John

[1] Bleackley, pp. 5–6, 445–6. I have followed Bleackley's general narrative of events in the course of this chapter, unless otherwise stated.
[2] R. Postgate, *That Devil Wilkes* (1930), p. 1.
[3] See *The Autobiography of Dr. Alexander Carlyle of Inveresk 1722–1805* (1910).

Perkins, merchant and landowner.[1] These men of the 'middling sort' were not only to prove an invaluable asset in helping to return Wilkes to Parliament a few years later; they were also to give proof of continued loyalty at a time when more substantial and highly placed supporters deserted him on his return from exile in 1768.[2]

His range of acquaintances, however, soon extended into more urbane and influential circles than those formed by the townsmen of Aylesbury. He became a close friend of Thomas Potter, dissolute son of an Archbishop of Canterbury, Member for a Cornish borough but anxious to exchange it for the parliamentary seat of Aylesbury. Potter both launched Wilkes on a life of fashionable pleasure and dissipation and helped him on to the first rung of his political career. Through Potter, he was presented to Earl Temple of Stowe, his brother George Grenville, and his brother-in-law-to-be William Pitt: the introduction was to have momentous consequences for Wilkes's future. Its first-fruits were that, with George Grenville's support, he was appointed High Sheriff of Buckingham for the year 1754. In breaking the news to his friend John Dell, he wrote: 'You see, I declare myself throughout a friend of liberty and will act up to it.'[3] It was a title that he obstinately clung to for the rest of his days and that was finally inscribed on his tombstone forty-three years later.

Even with the powerful backing of Stowe, Wilkes's first attempt to enter Parliament proved costly and still-born. In the General Election that followed Henry Pelham's death in 1754, he presented himself, at Temple's suggestion, at Berwick-on-Tweed as a candidate pledged to support the Duke of Newcastle. He was handsomely beaten at a cost of nearly £4,000. But a new opportunity arose in 1757: Pitt consented to become member for Bath and resigned his borough of Oakhampton to Potter, thus leaving the field clear for Wilkes at Aylesbury. Yet, even with Pitt's support, votes had to be paid for and he wrote to Dell in June:

> I will give two guineas per man, with the promise of whatever more offers. If you think two guineas not enough I will offer three or even five.[4]

[1] R. Gibbs, *A History of Aylesbury with its Boroughs and Hundreds* (Aylesbury, 1885), chap. xxv. Wilkes-Dell correspondence, Aylesbury Museum. Bucks R.O., Sir William Lee correspondence; Land Tax duplicates, Aylesbury (Town), 1780, Q/RPC 1/1; Wills, W 289 (1769); Jury Books, 1769, JB/1.

[2] See page 67 below.

[3] Wilkes to Dell, 15 Jan. 1754.

[4] Ibid., 22 June 1757.

The electors responded and, on 6 July, Wilkes became Member for Aylesbury at a cost of some £7,000.

A seat in Parliament, though it at first did little to establish Wilkes's political reputation, brought added social connexions and responsibilities. In Covent Garden, he began to frequent the fashionable Sublime Society of Beefsteaks, where Boswell saw him some years later dining under a canopy inscribed *Beef and Liberty*.[1] He became an officer in the Buckinghamshire militia, serving under Sir Francis Dashwood as colonel and Earl Temple as Lieutenant-General. Dashwood, who had a taste for spicy anecdote and the macabre, soon found in Wilkes a kindred spirit and enrolled him as one of a closed circle of twelve Monks of St. Francis, whose nightly orgies on the site of Medmenham Abbey, compounded of debauchery and mock Devil-worship, earned them the title of the Hell-Fire Club.[2] The Monks included such distinguished, though tarnished, figures as Bubb Dodington and the Earl of Sandwich, but they did little for John Wilkes other than add to his already considerable reputation as a wit and libertine. Of far greater importance was his growing intimacy with Earl Temple. He became a frequent visitor to Stowe and Temple's letters from the autumn of 1761 onwards reveal a genuine affection and mutual respect between the two men. On 22 October, Temple writes: 'I shall ever be happy, my good, though wicked, friend, if I can contribute in any way to the giving you the least degree of satisfaction.'[3] A letter of 27 December is addressed to 'that prodigy of reformation, Miss Wilkes's most honoured father, honoured by all and much beloved by his most truly devoted Temple'.[4] In the spring of 1762, Wilkes was promoted to the rank of colonel in succession to Dashwood, who had accepted office as Chancellor of the Exchequer under Bute; *The North Briton* was in the making, and the correspondence became largely concerned with militia affairs and the political state of the nation. Yet, despite differences over the policy of the new paper, Temple retained his regard for Wilkes, not least for his loyalty and disinterested support. On 7 October 1762 he wrote to Colonel Berkeley:

[1] *Boswell's London Journal 1762–1763*, pp. 51–52.

[2] D. McCormick, *The Hell-Fire Club* (1958).

[3] Temple to Wilkes, 22 October 1761, *Grenville Papers*, ed. W. J. Smith (4 vols. 1852–53), i. 406.

[4] Temple to Wilkes, 27 Dec. 1761, 'The King *v*. Wilkes. Original Papers connected with the Prosecution of John Wilkes Esq., M.P.' (3 manuscript vols., 1761–65, Guildhall Lib. MSS. [cited below as Guild MSS.], 214/1).

'I never had it in my power to do him the least favour. I have indeed frequently recommended to him as well as to others of my friends to sail with the new current . . . and avail themselves of the tide of the Court favour before it was spent.'[1]

The 'new current' was indeed flowing strongly. George III had succeeded his grandfather in October 1760 and, guided by his 'dearest friend' the Earl of Bute, had begun to edge out the trusted counsellors of the old régime. The General Election of 1761 was jointly manipulated by Newcastle and Bute;[2] but, soon after, the Ministry was reconstituted and Pitt and Temple resigned office over their colleagues' refusal to declare war on Spain. Wilkes, for whom Pitt's retirement marked the end of any hopes of an office under the Crown,[3] made his first effective speech in the Commons on 13 November 1761 in defence of his fallen leader. Temple was utterly despondent and wrote to Wilkes in December: 'I can weep over this minion-minded country as well at Stowe as in Pall Mall.'[4] But the apprehensions of those who, in the City of London and elsewhere, feared an early peace and a restoration of conquests in North America and the West Indies, were temporarily allayed when war with Spain broke out in January 1762, and was attended by rapid victories in the Caribbean. The hopes thus aroused were, however, soon defeated when it became known that the Duke of Bedford was conducting negotiations for an early peace in Paris — a peace that, by surrendering Guadaloupe and other conquests, bitterly disappointed the merchants of London and Liverpool.[5]

It was against this background of ministerial reshuffling and peace preliminaries that *The North Briton* was born on 6 June 1762, with John Wilkes and Charles Churchill as joint editors. For some weeks Lord Bute's administration had been running a weekly paper — *The Briton*, edited by Tobias Smollett — whose purpose it was to justify and win support for the government's policies.

[1] Temple to Col. Berkeley, 7 Oct. 1762, *Grenville Papers*, i. 479.
[2] L. B. Namier, *England in the Age of the American Revolution* (1930).
[3] See Bleackley, p. 57.
[4] Temple to Wilkes, 29 Dec. 1761, Guild. MSS. 214/1.
[5] For the City's reactions, see Sharpe, *London and the Kingdom*, iii. 70–73. For a memoir of the town of Liverpool urging the retention of Guadaloupe in the interests of the slave trade, presented by Sir William Meredith in Oct. 1762, see Liverpool Papers, Add. MSS. 38200, ff. 47–50. For the hostility that such views aroused among government supporters, see Edward Richardson to Charles Jenkinson, 17 April 1763, Add. MSS. 38200. f. 311: the corporation of London is referred to as 'an incorporated set of City sharpers'.

The North Briton, as its name suggests, was both a direct ripost to this publication and a satirical commentary on the widely-held belief that the new administration was over-heavily staffed with Scots and over-tender to Scottish interests. The forty-five numbers that appeared between June 1762 and April 1763 are more remarkable for the brilliance and audacity of Wilkes's journalism than for any originality of ideas or for any positive declaration of new policies. Its practice, rather, was negative: to expose and ridicule the new government's conduct of affairs; to harry the Scots on each and every occasion; to heap all manner of abuse and ridicule on the government and its friends — on Lord Bute in particular, whose alleged intimacy with the King's mother, the Princess Dowager, was a subject of constant comment. All this was vastly entertaining and heartening to some, while it roused the passionate anger and resentment of others. One injured party, Earl Talbot, Lord Steward of the Household, challenged Wilkes to a duel; but, by his good-natured handling of the affair, Wilkes turned the incident to his advantage and won more friends from it than enemies.[1] Yet Burke was surprised to find him, about this time, at the Cockpit with other Members of Parliament and thought it 'rather impudent of him to appear there'.[2] The opposition leaders viewed *The North Briton* with mixed feelings. Pitt was hostile from the start, while the Duke of Devonshire considered its author 'the life and soul of the Opposition'.[3] Temple himself, though he financed the paper throughout, was torn between admiration for Wilkes's debating skill and audacity and disapproval of the violence of his diatribes. On the first day of publication, he hoped 'to live to see Mr Monitor and Mr N. Briton treated as they deserve'.[4] A week later, he expresses disapproval of the wholesale attacks on the Scottish nation and on Bute in particular and voices his conviction 'that the sooner this scene of indiscriminate and excessive personality is closed, the better'. After further instalments of anti-Scottish abuse, he regrets that 'the N. Briton does not mend from sage advice'.[5] Even more forthrightly, he complains to his sister, the future Lady Chatham, on 10 October:

[1] See Temple to Wilkes, 14 Sept. 1762, *Grenville Papers*, i. 471.

[2] Burke to Charles O'Hara, 25 Nov. 1762, *The Correspondence of Edmund Burke*, ed. Thos. W. Copeland (Chicago, 1958), i. 158.

[3] Bleackley, pp. 75–76.

[4] Temple to Wilkes, 6 June 1762, Guild. MSS. 214/1.

[5] Temple to Wilkes, 14 and 27 June 1762, *Grenville Papers*, i. 456–7, 460–1.

Mr. Pitt and I disapprove of this paper war, and the daily abominations which are published; though, because Wilkes professes himself a friend of mine, I am ever represented infamously as a patron of what I disapprove and wish I could have put an end to.[1]

Yet, in November, commenting on No. 25's stalwart support of Pitt's war policy, he 'cannot sufficiently admire the North B— of this week: it is unanswerable, as it is founded on stubborn facts, which cannot be controverted'.[2]

Meanwhile the government, though urged to take action against Wilkes and his collaborators, awaited a more favourable opportunity.[3] At one time, it seemed as if the occasion might never arise, as the news of Bute's resignation on 11 April 1763 and of his replacement by George Grenville prompted the editors of *The North Briton* to suspend publication. No. 44 had appeared on 2 April and looked like being the last. But, on 19 April, the King's Speech at the opening of Parliament commented on the preliminary articles of peace in terms which goaded Wilkes — and probably Pitt and Temple, too — to fury. The result was the appearance on 23 April of the famous No. 45 that set Britain by the ears.

There was nothing in this latest number of *The North Briton* that would seem to our generation to warrant a charge of seditious libel. Its references to the King were couched in terms of the profoundest respect. The opening sentence even carefully stated that 'the King's Speech has always been considered by the Legislature, and by the public at large, as the speech of the Minister'. The writer went on:

The *Minister's speech* of last Tuesday is not to be parallelled in the annals of this country. I am in doubt whether the imposition is greater on the Sovereign, or on the nation. Every friend of this country must lament that a prince of so many great and admirable qualities, whom England truly reveres, can be brought to give the sanction of his sacred name to the most odious measures and the most unjustifiable public declarations from a throne ever renowned for truth, honour, and an unsullied virtue.[4]

Nevertheless, at a time when the principle of 'ministerial responsibility' was not yet fully evolved, it seemed to many — and not

[1] Temple to Lady Hesta Pitt, 10 Oct. 1762, *Correspondence of William Pitt, Earl of Chatham*, ed. W. S. Taylor and J. H. Pringle (4 vols. 1838–40), ii. 192–3.

[2] Temple to Wilkes, 21 Nov. 1762, *Grenville Papers*, ii. 4.

[3] A general warrant for the apprehension of the authors, printers, etc., of *The North Briton* was actually drawn up on 4 Nov. 1762, but withdrawn (Guild. MSS. 214/3).

[4] *The North Briton* (1763), 228, 231.

least to George III himself — that, despite Wilkes's disclaimers, the King was being accused of being a liar. Furthermore, the ministers were being provided with what appeared a heaven-sent opportunity for strangling the opposition to the government's peace proposals, both by diverting public attention from that issue and by discrediting the opposition leaders for their overt or implied association with the scandalous Wilkes.[1]

At all events, George Grenville and the two Secretaries of State, Lords Egremont and Halifax, proceeded with commendable speed, though it was tempered with caution. On 24 April, the day after publication, Philip Carteret Webb, the solicitor to the Treasury, was summoned to meet his superior, Charles Jenkinson, and George Grenville himself.[2] On the next day the law officers of the Crown, Charles Yorke and Sir Fletcher Norton, were asked for their opinion as to whether proceedings might be opened against the editors, publishers and printers of No. 45 for seditious libel. The answer (at first verbally given) being in the affirmative, the two Secretaries issued jointly on 26 April a general warrant for the arrest of 'the authors, printers and publishers of a seditious and treasonable paper, entitled *The North Briton*, Number XLV, Saturday, April 23rd, 1763, printed by G. Kearsley in Ludgate-Street, London'. A slight delay now followed while further legal opinion was sought. The written report of the Attorney-General and Solicitor-General was received and studied, and, on 26 April, P. C. Webb dined with the Earl of Hardwicke, whose advice in such matters, though he was a supporter of the Duke of Newcastle, no government could afford to neglect. Thus armed, the Secretaries felt strong enough to order the four Messengers, to whom the warrant had been issued, to proceed on the morrow to arrest the publisher, George Kearsley, and the presumed printer, Dryden Leach. As it soon appeared, however, that the latter had ceased connection with *The North Briton* since printing No. 26 some months before, a fresh start had to be made and, in place of Leach, Richard Balfe was taken and brought before the Secretaries of State. Under cross-examination,

[1] This was certainly the view of the Duke of Newcastle who, a month later, wrote to the Duke of Devonshire: 'This unlucky affair of Wilkes . . . has given, or is made, a pretence for the Ministers to stand upon new ground. We hear little of Peace now, all turns upon Faction, and the personal affront to the King' (Newcastle to Devonshire, 21 May 1763, Add. MSS. 32948, ff. 344–5).

[2] Grenville to Webb and Jenkinson to Webb, 24 April 1763, Guild. MSS. 214/3.

Kearsley and Balfe formally acknowledged that Wilkes had edited No. 45, and, the same evening, further advice was sought from the law officers as to what might be done about Wilkes who, as a Member of Parliament, might be considered immune from arrest in such cases. The law officers, however, replied that 'the publication of a libel, being a breach of the peace, is not a case of privilege and that Mr Wilkes might be committed to prison for the same'.[1] And so it was decided, the same evening, to instruct the Messengers to take Wilkes into custody by means of the same general warrant that had already done service in the case of Kearsley, Leach and Balfe, and was later to do service in the case of forty-five others![2]

The Messengers duly appeared at 13 Great George Street, but, for some unaccountable reason, made no attempt to arrest Wilkes until the next day. When he emerged at six in the morning, his pursuers were easily persuaded to let him pass and waited while he raided Balfe's printing-shop in the Old Bailey, removed No. 46 from the press and tore up the original manuscript of No. 45. On his return, he invited the Messengers into his house, engaged them in lengthy argument on the validity of general warrants, and sent word to Lord Temple to apply in the Court of Common Pleas for a writ of *habeas corpus* to secure his release. Finally he agreed to accompany the officers — in a sedan-chair — to Lord Halifax's house a few doors down the street. But, having arrived, he refused to answer questions and exasperated the Secretaries by his cheerful evasions and studied insults. Meanwhile, Chief Justice Pratt had granted the required writ in the Common Pleas, but it proved invalid as the prisoner had by now passed out of the custody of the Messengers into that of the Secretaries. A further writ had to be applied for, while Wilkes's house was ransacked for incriminating evidence and he himself was committed on a new warrant to the Tower where, on the personal instruction of Lord Egremont, he was kept a close prisoner.[3] Even a letter that he wrote next day to his daughter Polly was stopped by his gaolers and is to be found among the papers of the solicitor to the Treasury:

Be assured that I have done nothing unworthy a man of honour who has

[1] Guild. MSS. 214/1.

[2] According to Webb's own notes, it was formally decided not to issue a new warrant mentioning Wilkes by name (Guild. MSS. 241/3). Webb himself may have been the moving spirit behind this decision (Bleackley, p. 96).

[3] Guild. MSS. 214/3.

the happiness of being your father . . . As an Englishman I must lament that my Liberty is so wickedly taken from me; yet I am not unhappy for my honour is clear, my health good, my spirits unshaken, I believe indeed invincible.[1]

The news of Wilkes's arrest and commitment placed the opposition leaders in a considerable dilemma. Earl Temple showed no hesitation and, much to the annoyance or embarrassment of his fellow-peers, both busied himself on his friend's behalf in the Court of Common Pleas and attempted to gain access to him in the Tower. The Dukes of Bolton and Grafton also paid a visit to the Tower in order to demonstrate their disapproval of the manner of Wilkes's arrest and confinement, but the latter refused, much to Temple's annoyance, to stand bail for him when requested.[2] The Duke of Newcastle, very conscious of his responsibilities as a party leader and believing that he could 'see the end of Charles the Second's reign coming on very fast', sought advice where he might and found himself, in consequence, subjected to opposing pressures. On the one hand, his nephews, George Onslow and Lord Middleton ('the zealous young gentlemen', as Hardwicke termed them), urged him to make some public gesture in support of Wilkes. Lord Middleton was the more insistent: he declared his intention to visit Wilkes in the Tower, as there was no suggestion of his having 'committed treason against a King of the House of Brunswick', and he begged Newcastle to consider carefully 'shewing Wilkes that he will not abandon him unconvicted to the fury of an insolent Minister'. Hardwicke, on the other hand, without revealing the part he had himself played in the affair, wrote of No. 45 that he was 'amazed at that paper when I read it, as being the most unguarded and audacious I had ever seen'. He added that 'the libel is certainly not only unjustifiable but inexcusable', condemned Lord Temple for being 'quite so forward in this affair', and concluded that 'we should not to too hasty to make cause commun (sic!) with Mr. Wilkes'. Pitt, too, it appeared, was 'very cool & moderate in Wilkes's affair', and Newcastle was inclined to take the advice of his older, rather than of his younger, friends: 'I doubt,' he wrote to the Duke of Devonshire, 'our friend Lord Temple is

[1] Ibid.

[2] *Autobiography and Political Correspondence of Augustus Henry Fitzroy, Third Duke of Grafton*, ed. Sir William Anson (1893), pp. 189–92; Grafton to Temple, 3 May 1763, *Grenville Papers*, ii. 53.

too warm; I cannot think it would be right for us all to make this parade of going to the Tower to see Wilkes.'[1]

Meanwhile, after some delay, a second writ of *habeas corpus* had been granted in the Court of Common Pleas and, on 3 May, Wilkes was brought from the Tower by coach to Westminster Hall. The day before, Newcastle had been assured by the numerous company that gathered at his house 'that the whole City of London would attend Wilkes to Westminster Hall'.[2] So indeed it seemed, and when, on arrival in court, he addressed the judges in carefully chosen words, protesting that the liberty of an Englishman should 'not be sported away with impunity', he was cheered to the echo by a large and sympathetic audience. Wilkes's counsel, Serjeant Glynn, who followed, argued that his client had been wrongfully committed but did not raise the question of the validity of general warrants. In the first place, he objected that Wilkes had not been charged by any evidence before the Secretaries of State with being the author of the libel in question; secondly, that the warrant committing him to the Tower did not charge him with any specific offence; and, thirdly, that there was no legal ground for committing his client anyway in view of his privilege as a Member of Parliament — a privilege that applied in all cases except in those of treason, felony and a breach of the peace.[3] The proceedings were adjourned until Friday, 6 May. As Wilkes left the court-room he was greeted with thunderous shouts of 'Liberty! Liberty! Wilkes for ever!'[4]

On his reappearance in Westminster Hall three days later, Wilkes prefaced his remarks to his judges with words that were carefully calculated to evoke a response among the varied throng of gentlemen, shopkeepers and craftsmen that crowded the galleries and approaches to the court-room. 'My Lords,' he cried, 'the liberty of all peers and gentlemen, and, what touches me more sensibly, that of all the middling and inferior set of people, who stand most in need of protection, is in my case this day to be finally decided upon a question of such importance as to determine

[1] Newcastle to Hardwicke, 1 May; G. Onslow to Newcastle, Middleton to Newcastle, 2 May; Hardwicke to Newcastle, 30 April, 1 May; Newcastle to Hardwicke, 2 June; Newcastle to Devonshire, 2 May 1763; Add. MSS. 32948, ff. 188–9, 199, 201, 204, 207–9; 32949, ff. 9–10.

[2] Newcastle to Lincoln, 2 May 1763, Add. MSS. 32948, f. 211.

[3] 'A Justification of the issuing and execution of the Warrant for taking the Author of the North Briton into Custody', by P. C. Webb, Guild. MSS. 214/2.

[4] Bleackley, p. 85.

at once whether English Liberty shall be a reality or a shadow.'[1] In giving the judges' opinion, Chief Justice Pratt dismissed the first two of Serjeant Glynn's objections: Secretaries of State must, in such cases, have the powers enjoyed by any justice of the peace; the warrant committing Wilkes to the Tower was therefore, good both in form and substance. But the question of privilege was quite another matter. The prosecution had argued that a libel was 'an actual breach of the peace'. This view the judges contested, and Pratt concluded:

> The person of a Member ought to be sacred; even if he should commit a misdemeanour, unless it is absolutely necessary to confine him to prevent further mischief. We are therefore all of opinion that Mr. Wilkes is entitled to the privilege of Parliament, and therefore he must be discharged.[2]

When Wilkes rose to thank his judges, 'the mob', as the Duke of Portland reported to Newcastle, 'could no longer refrain expressing their approbation in the loudest & strongest terms; though I am told [he added] that the better kind of people who were in the galleries above the Court endeavoured as much as possible to prevent any improper behaviour'.[3] George Onslow, however, who sent his uncle an enthusiastic account of the proceedings, described 'the many thousands that escorted Wilkes home to his house' as being 'of a far higher rank than common Mob'. From all accounts the common cry of 'Whigs for ever, no Jacobites!' – a cry that gave particular pleasure to George Onslow[4] – merged with the new slogan of militant radicalism, 'Wilkes and Liberty!'[5]

The first round had gone to Wilkes, but it was clear that matters could not remain where they were. The government were at least able to draw a modicum of comfort from the fact that the court's judgement had not raised the larger issue of the legality of general warrants; but the reputation of ministers and, by implication, of

[1] *English Liberty: being a collection of Interesting Tracts from the Year 1762 to 1769, containing the Private Correspondence, Public Letters, Speeches and Addresses of John Wilkes Esq.* . . . (2 vols. bound in one, 1770), i. 87; cit. Bleackley, pp. 105-6, and Postgate, p. 64.

[2] 'Some Observations on the late determination for discharging Mr. Wilkes from the Tower of London . . . By a Member of the House of Commons' (manuscript by P. C. Webb), Guild. MSS. 214/1.

[3] Portland to Newcastle, 6 May 1763, Add. MSS. 32948, f. 238. Portland added piously that this showed 'that moderation & steadiness are distinguishing characteristics of *the good cause*'.

[4] G. Onslow to Newcastle, 6 May 1763, Add. MSS. 32948, ff. 234–6.

[5] Bleackley, pp. 107, 113.

the King himself, had been injured by Wilkes's release. Something must therefore be done, and that quickly, to bring him to justice and, in order that he might be suitably dealt with, to expel him from Parliament. But the government's legal advisers were divided on the advisability of reopening proceedings in the Court of King's Bench,[1] where Lord Mansfield might be presumed to be more favourable to the Treasury's case than Chief Justice Pratt, so that Wilkes, who was eager to follow up his advantage, struck first. At first, he wrote to the Secretaries of State, insisting that they should return to him forthwith the papers 'stolen' from his house. On receiving an angry reply, he instituted proceedings against Halifax, Egremont and Robert Wood, under-Secretary of State, for theft and against P. C. Webb for perjury. The case against Webb was dismissed, possibly because the Attorney-General argued that attempts had been made to prejudice the jury against him: 'He could prove that there were bonfires & rejoicings made when the Bill was found & people invited to share therein.'[2] Similar attempts by the Crown to prove undue pressure on juries by Wilkes's supporters and by the press did not prevent Wilkes himself and the numerous printers and others involved in the production of *The North Briton* from receiving substantial damages for wrongful arrest or wrongful seizure of papers in the course of the next months. In July, William Huckle and thirteen other printers were awarded damages totalling £2,900; in December, Wilkes himself recovered £1,000 against Wood; and, a few days later, Dryden Leach, wrongfully arrested as the printer of No. 45, recovered £400 in his action against the Messengers.[3]

But, though the amount of damages to be awarded was hotly disputed between the contestants, the real issue in all these cases, as in Wilkes's original hearing before Chief Justice Pratt, was whether general warrants were legal or not. The Secretaries of State undoubtedly considered that they were and we have seen how careful they were to consult their legal advisers at every step before committing themselves too deeply in their prosecution of Wilkes. They certainly had a case, which rested, as P. C. Webb cogently

[1] Newcastle to Rockingham, 24 May 1763, Add. MSS. 32948, f. 350; Newcastle to Hardwicke, 2 June 1763, Add. MSS. 32949, ff. 6–7; P. C. Webb's notes in Guild. MSS. 214/3; Bleackley, p. 114.

[2] E. Langton to Hardwicke, 22 May 1763, Hardwicke Papers, Add. MSS. 35607, ff. 56–57.

[3] P. C. Webb's 'Justification' (see p. 26, n. 3 above), Guild. MSS. 214/2.

argued, on common usage. From the 'Glorious Revolution' onwards, Secretaries of State had, for nearly a hundred years, been issuing similar warrants in cases of persons suspected of seditious libel and, until April 1763, their validity had never been challenged in a Court of law. In fact, as recently as November 1762, a general warrant had been issued by Lord Halifax himself for the apprehending of Beardmore, Entick and others concerned in the editing, publishing and printing of the Whig journal, *The Monitor*, and, at the time, no formal objection had been raised.[1] The first counter-blast came from Chief Justice Pratt who, in granting a writ of *habeas corpus* in the case of Wilkes on 30 April, was reported as observing: 'The warrant I think a very extraordinary one, I know no law that can authorize it, nor any practice that it can be founded on.'[2] Yet this was only a random remark and the issue was not raised by either Glynn or Pratt in the proceedings at Westminster Hall in May. Hardwicke, though not a government supporter in most matters, shared Webb's view and Newcastle wrote on 2 May to Devonshire: 'Temple and Pratt are (I fancy) a little mistaken, when they call this warrant illegal & unprecedented. If I remember, I have signed many in the same form & words.'[3] However, the public at large refused to be fobbed off with constitutional niceties and insisted, against all legal evidence, that Wilkes had in fact been discharged from the Tower on the grounds of the illegality of general warrants, so the matter was bound to be further ventilated. On 6 July, when hearing Huckle's case against Money, Pratt attacked once more, on an even wider front, and declared it as his opinion 'that both these kinds of warrants, as well the particular one which named the offenders, as the general one which described them as the authors, printers and publishers, were both void and illegal'. At the same time, he conceded that he stood alone and hoped that the matter would soon be more fully debated by his colleagues on the Bench. Though he urged restraint on the jury in assessing damages, there can be little doubt that this opinion of Pratt's weighed heavily with the London juries who, in this and other cases, awarded damages considered by the Crown to

[1] Ibid. Subsequently, both Beardmore and Entick, encouraged by the outcome of the printers' actions, instituted proceedings and recovered substantial damages. Entick's case (*Entick* v. *Carrington*) has become famous in legal history (see p. 30 below).

[2] Add. MSS. 32948, ff. 169–70.

[3] Hardwicke to Newcastle, 30 April; Newcastle to Devonshire, 2 May 1763; Add. MSS. 32948, ff. 189, 204.

be 'grievous' and 'oppressive'.[1] The subsequent history of general warrants may be briefly added. Two years after Pratt's pronouncements, the whole Bench of judges concurred in his view; the same year, the case of *Entick* v. *Carrington*, heard before Chief Justice Pratt (now Lord Camden), declared such warrants to be null and void; and, finally, in April 1766, a resolution of the House of Commons condemned the whole practice as illegal and obnoxious.[2]

Meanwhile, Wilkes had been basking in the popularity showered on him from various quarters by friends old and new. From Aylesbury, where he was hailed on arrival by shouts of 'Wilkes and Liberty!',[3] he wrote to Temple on 5 June: 'I have most successfully got through the fine list of patriotic toasts, and the nasty wine of the borough . . . I had the honour of being escorted into the town by every man who had, or could hire, a horse, and if I have the honour of being expelled, the declaration is universal that I shall be re-chosen.' On 11 June, he assures Temple that with all this, he has 'never lost sight of the great object of the liberty of the subject at large'. When Huckle's action came up three weeks later, he 'found almost as much difficulty to get to the King's Arms, where we dined, as I did to get from Westminster Hall to Great George Street, and the people were almost as loud in their applause. The two days have been most propitious for liberty, most honourable to me'. Commenting, two days later, on the outcome of the case, he wrote: 'The trials of Wednesday and Thursday have demonstrated to me where the strength of our cause really lies; for the merchants, as I had ever the honour of submitting to your Lordship, are firm in the cause of liberty . . . The City are firmly my friends and talk of 20,000 l. damages to me . . . North Briton and Wilkes will be talked of together by posterity.' On 23 July, after a further visit to Aylesbury, he described his 'happiness of finding that the City of London and County of Surrey are almost unanimous in the great cause of Liberty'. And, having decided that things were going well enough for him to visit Polly in Paris, he wrote on 2 August: 'I was received at Canterbury and Dover with many marks of regard, and I found the true glory and stability of our country, the English sailors, no enemies to *Wilkes and Liberty*.'[4]

[1] Webb's 'Justification . . . ', Guild. MSS. 214/2.
[2] Guild. MSS. 214/3.
[3] *St. James's Chronicle*, 4–7 June 1763; Bleackley, p. 119.
[4] Wilkes to Temple, 5, 11 June; 7, 9, 23 July; 2 August 1763; *Grenville Papers*, ii. 59, 61, 70, 71–72, 75, 78, 82–83.

He returned to London in late September to find that he had stirred up another hornet's nest and that his tribulations were by no means over. Soon after his release from the Tower, he had decided to set up a printing-press of his own at 13 Great George Street and had hired as his foreman Michael Curry, who had been one of the many journeymen printers arrested for their presumed connection with *The North Briton*. Wilkes had two main tasks in mind. One was to re-print *The North Briton* in volume form, a project of which Temple heartily disapproved, as it might provide the government with the direct proof that he was the author of No. 45, the evidence for which at the moment rested on remarkably flimsy grounds. The other project was to print for private circulation (possibly among his former Medmenham associates?) an obscene and blasphemous parody on Pope's *Essay on Man*, entitled *An Essay on Woman* and fictitiously ascribed to Dr. Warburton, Bishop of Gloucester. This poem, and a number of lesser parodies that were to be printed with it, had been composed in the 1750s, at the time of Wilkes's intimacy with Thomas Potter. It seems likely that Potter (since deceased) had been mainly responsible for the poem, while Wilkes had contributed the commentary and notes and, possibly, some additional lines on Bute and Hogarth.[1] Curry was instructed to print twelve copies, but the poem was a long one and, after a month, only nine pages, each containing ten or eleven lines with footnotes, had been struck off when Wilkes decided to turn the press over to the more urgent operation of re-printing *The North Briton* of which he hoped to sell 2,000 copies at half a guinea each, thus helping to pay off his debts.[2] Four new journeymen were engaged and the new work was completed in a little over a month. But, meanwhile, the type of the *Essay* had to be distributed and Wilkes went off lightheartedly to Paris on a prolonged visit. It would not be surprising if the government had wind of these proceedings before his departure, but his long absence certainly made things easier for them. Their object was, of course, to obtain a copy of the *Essay*, ascribe its authorship to Wilkes, and use this fact both to proceed against him for publishing obscene and blasphemous libels and to blast his reputation among his more respectable followers.

The upshot was that, by early October, P. C. Webb had obtained

[1] Bleackley, pp. 36–38; Postgate, pp. 76–81.
[2] Wilkes to Temple, 9 July 1763, *Grenville Papers*, ii. 75.

from Curry a proof-copy of the first ninety-four lines of the *Essay*. The steps leading to this result were spread over a number of months and mystery still surrounds certain of the details, though it seems reasonably certain, despite Webb's emphatic denials, that Curry was bribed and probably intimidated. The most certain evidence for this is a letter of 24 September from a master printer, William Faden, to Webb and still to be seen, among other 'cloak-and-dagger' correspondence, in Webb's papers:

I should have sent you an account of my proceedings before if I could have completed the business, which there is no other way that I can conceive, but by getting some gentleman that can appear with me in company and tendering down the money to Michael Curry, who I believe will not resist the temptation. He is the principal person that can do every thing in the affair, being the manager entirely of Wilkes' business. Enclosed is the list of the men employed at George Street during the time his presses were at work there.[1]

The government's own version of what took place, pieced together by Webb from a number of individual accounts, is fantastic enough. According to this, Samuel Jennings, one of Wilkes's compositors, picked up a part of the proof from the workshop floor, showed it to Thomas Farmer, another printer, who showed it to his foreman, Lionel Hassall, who, in turn, took it to his employer, William Faden. Faden happened to have staying in his house the Rev. John Kidgell, Rector of Godstone and Horne in Surrey and chaplain to the Earl of March. March, having seen the sheet and appreciating its possibilities as a means of discrediting Wilkes, put Kidgell into touch with Webb and Charles Jenkinson at the Treasury. These three then devised a plan for persuading Curry to part with a set of revised proofs that he was known to have in his possession. This Curry was persuaded to do after quarrelling with Wilkes on the latter's return from Paris in late September. At this point, a real 'cloak-and-dagger' element enters the story: it was considered advisable to lodge Curry a few days at Webb's house and then to spirit him out of London — ostensibly to save him from Wilkite vengeance, but, in fact, no doubt, to prime him as a key witness before the House of Lords.[2]

For, in the middle of these proceedings, Lord Egremont had

[1] William Faden to P. C. Webb, 24 Sept. 1763, Guild. MSS. 214/3.

[2] 'A genuine Account of the Proceedings against Mr. Wilkes for being the Author, Printer and Publisher of the Essay on Woman', by P. C. Webb, Guild. MSS. 214/2.

died and been succeeded in office by the Earl of Sandwich, who had consented to play the principal role in bringing Wilkes to book. 'I wish to play a forward part in this business', he wrote to Webb on 22 October, and, for the next three weeks, his correspondence with the solicitor to the Treasury shows how wholeheartedly the ex-Monk of Medmenham entered into his new role of inquisitor-general.[1] On 15 November, when Parliament reassembled, Curry, Jennings and others were duly examined by the Lords, but the great moment came when the reprobate Earl of Sandwich read in hushed tones, though with evident relish, the printed text of the *Essay on Woman* to their scandalized Lordships. Even Temple was only lukewarm in Wilkes's defence, and the House unanimously condemned the *Essay* as 'a most scandalous, obscene, and impious libel'. 'Nobody', wrote Halifax the same evening to the King, 'spoke against the motions or seem'd desirous of protecting Mr Wilkes.'[2] Fashionable society was outraged, or professed to be so. Mrs. Harris, mother of the future Earl of Malmesbury, wrote that day to her son at Oxford, expressing the hope that Wilkes might 'be made an example of . . . for a more wicked wretch never lived in any age. His blasphemy with regard to our Saviour is enough to shock even those who never think of religion'.[3] And in the Commons, a week later, Pitt, while defending Wilkes's right to privilege, denounced him as 'the blasphemer of his God and the libeller of his King'.[4]

But Wilkes's supporters among 'the middling and inferior set of people' were not to be so easily swayed from their loyalties. While the Lords were condemning the *Essay*, the Commons debated *The North Briton* and, by 273 to 111 votes, resolved that No. 45 was 'a false, scandalous, and seditious libel' and ordered it to be burnt by the Common Hangman at the Royal Exchange. A fortnight later, the Lords joined with the Commons in this verdict and it was ordered that the ceremony take place in the presence of the sheriffs on 3 December. At the appointed time, however, a large crowd of Londoners, 'to the number of 500 and more', gathered at the entrance to Cornhill, pelted the sheriffs, Thomas

[1] Sandwich-Webb correspondence (13 letters), 22 Oct.–14 Nov. 1763, Guild. MSS. 214/1.

[2] Halifax to George III, 15 Nov. 1763, *The Correspondence of King George III*, ed. Sir John Fortescue (6 vols. 1927–28) (cited below as Fortescue), i. no. 29.

[3] *Letters of the First Earl of Malmesbury from 1745 to 1820* (2 vols. 1870), i. 101.

[4] Bleackley, p. 137.

Harley and Richard Blunt, with 'hard pieces of wood and dirt', smashed the glass of Harley's coach, rescued *The North Briton* from the bonfire, and made it impossible for both hangman and sheriffs to discharge their duties. Later, at the Old Bailey, John Franklin, a ship's steward, was fined 6s. 8d. for his part in the affair.[1] The Commons duly voted the sheriffs their thanks for attempting to carry out their wishes, but the Common Council of the City pointedly refused to do so.[2]

Wilkes might well feel encouraged by such demonstrations of support, as by the handsome sum of £1,000 damages awarded to him, the same month, by a London jury — a verdict that was greeted by the attendance of great crowds at Westminster Hall and in Great George Street to shouts of 'Wilkes and Liberty!' and with cheers for Chief Justice Pratt and groans for their ministerial opponents.[3] But other considerations prompted him to retire, temporarily at least, from the political scene. In mid-November, he had been seriously wounded by a bullet in the groin, sustained in the course of a duel with a political opponent, Samuel Martin, M.P.[4] He was still recovering from its effects when summoned by Parliament to attend in order to answer further charges relating to *The North Briton*. He pleaded sickness and requested a postponement. The idea that he might go abroad and so elude the justice that was being prepared for him was already concerning his opponents. The day of his duel with Martin, Lord Halifax wrote to the King:

> It is Lord Halifax's duty further to acquaint his Majesty that Lord Sandwich, Ld Holland, Dr Marchant and Lord Halifax have had some conversation since dinner on the propriety of preventing Mr Wilkes's escape, to the prevention of his trial for his infamous performance; and that it is hoped an effectual method may be found to prevent the criminal's escape from justice.[5]

On 11 December, while Wilkes was still convalescing in Great George Street, one of Charles Jenkinson's more forthright

[1] O.B. *Proceedings*, 1764, pp. 128–30; London R.O., Sessions Minute Books, 1763–64; Sessions Files, Dec. 1763. Webb was informed by Grenville's private secretary that 'the Mob in the City rose & prevented the North Briton's being burnt & wounded Harley & were very tumultuous' (Charles Lloyd to Webb, 3 Dec. 1763, Guild. MSS. 214/3).

[2] *Gent's Mag.*, 1763, p. 615.

[3] *Public Advertiser*, 8 Dec. 1763; *Ann. Reg.*, 1763, p. 145.

[4] There are grounds for believing that this was a case of premeditated intent to kill rather than of a simple 'affair of honour' (Walpole, *Memoirs*, i. 252–3).

[5] Fortescue, i. no. 34.

correspondents wrote to him: 'It is a pity that squinting rascal can't yet be produced. I suspect he will be gone before you meet again after the holidays.'[1] He was right. On Christmas Eve, having evaded the attentions of the Treasury's spies, Wilkes slipped down to Dover by post-chaise and crossed to France the next day. His immediate concern was to see Polly and to complete his recovery, and he may well have intended, at this stage, to return to face his enemies when Parliament reassembled; at least, he wrote to Temple from Calais that he would be back on 14 January.[2] But, on the 13th, he sent the Speaker from Paris a doctor's certificate and begged further indulgence. The government, however, decided to proceed and, on the 20th, he was expelled from Parliament. A month later, a Middlesex Grand Jury in the Court of King's Bench found him guilty of printing the *Essay on Woman* and of re-publishing No. 45, and issued a writ for his arrest. On 1 November following, as he still failed to make an appearance, the same court formally pronounced him an outlaw. These proceedings finally decided Wilkes to stay on abroad. After hearing of his first conviction in the Court of King's Bench, he wrote to Temple: 'I owe what I suffer to the neglect of your Lordship's advice. I foresee all the consequences of being entirely at the mercy of an abandoned Administration and vindictive judge, and intend never to put myself in their power, though I leave my dear native country, and all the charms that it ever had for me.'[3]

Though their victim had escaped them, the Court party had reasonable grounds for satisfaction. The opposition had, by its divisions and hesitations, made remarkably little capital out of 'the unlucky affair of Wilkes', and it seemed as if public opinion, even in the turbulent southern counties, might rally more firmly to the side of Administration.[4] Wilkes would soon be forgotten. 'The unfortunate gentleman', wrote a journalist, might now be regarded as irrevocably ruined.[5] Yet such hopes proved to be too sanguine. Two years after his departure, Wilkes received word that, on Edmund Burke's election as Member for Wendover, the toasts had

[1] Thos. Ramsden to Jenkinson, 11 Dec. 1763, Add. MSS. 38201, f. 312. The same correspondent had, in an earlier letter of 11 August, in referring to Wilkes's previous visit to Paris, expressed pleasure that 'the grand Incendiary is marched abroad' (f. 61).

[2] Wilkes to Temple, 25 Dec. 1763, *Grenville Papers*, ii. 185–6.

[3] Wilkes to Temple, 25 Feb. 1764, ibid., ii. 269.

[4] A. Fall to Jenkinson, 29 Jan. 1764, Add. MSS. 38202, f. 67.

[5] P. Quennell, *Four Portraits* (1945), p. 224.

been 'Wilkes and Liberty!', 'Burke and Wilkes!', 'Freedom and Wendover!'[1] The *Essay on Woman*, though it had not finally discredited Wilkes, had proved disastrous to the reputation of his pursuers. The Earl of Sandwich was henceforth to enjoy the unflattering sobriquet of 'Jemmy Twitcher'. Michael Curry was blacklisted by the master printers and wrote pathetic letters to Webb begging him to find him work. William Faden pursued Webb for several years with bills that were never honoured, while his foreman, Lionel Hassall, complained that he had been 'made contemptible by the odious name of informer'. The Rev. Kidgell became involved in a financial scandal, was driven from the country by his creditors, and, for years to come, pestered the Earl of March with his unwelcome correspondence from Utrecht, where he had taken refuge under the name of Kidgell de Horne. P. C. Webb himself lost his post at the Treasury in July 1765, felt that he had been harshly treated, and wrote a lengthy *apologia* to justify his conduct.[2] Meanwhile, the constant object of their attentions was spending some years of not unenjoyable travel in France and Italy. To many — and certainly to George III — it must have seemed that the Devil knew how to take care of his own.

[1] L. Macleane to Wilkes, 24 Dec. 1765, Add. MSS. 30868, f. 221.
[2] Guild. MSS. 214/1, 3; Walpole, *Memoirs*, i. 245–9.

III

THE 'MASSACRE' OF ST. GEORGE'S FIELDS

NEVERTHELESS, exile proved a mixed blessing and creditors abroad were becoming as pressing as those at home.[1] Besides, the retirement of Grenville and Halifax in July 1765 and their replacement by Rockingham and Grafton seemed to improve the political climate for a royal pardon and an early return. But, first, there were to be a number of false starts. The new Ministry were willing to make Wilkes a small pension and to pay his debts but were not at all anxious to see him back in England. In the New Year, however, there were rumours of his arrival in London and Edmund Burke wrote apprehensively to his brother Richard: 'He [Wilkes] ought to be sensible that though the true *motives* for his prosecutions were political, the prosecution he actually labours most under is not at all political, but for an offence against the ordinary laws . . . Between ourselves Lord R. is extremely averse from asking anything for him from the K. at the same time that he is willing to do almost anything for him from his private pocket, and to avow it to the K. or to any person.'[2] Wilkes, however, was in a hurry and made his first reappearance in London in early May; it was short-lived and he was soon back in Paris, having failed to persuade Rockingham to receive him. Further approaches made through Burke proved abortive.[3] Grafton succeeded Rockingham and, in late October, Wilkes proceeded once more to London to plead his case. By this time, Pitt (newly created Earl of Chatham) had become the effective head of the administration and met the 'patriot' 's overtures with a stony refusal.[4] Back in Paris, Wilkes was able to make some capital out of this by his violent strictures on Chatham ('this marble-hearted friend') in a widely publicized letter to the Duke of Grafton. Though its publication estranged him temporarily from his 'late valuable friend' Temple,[5] it won him support in other quarters,

[1] Bleackley, pp. 175, 181, 184.
[2] E. Burke to R. Burke, 14 Jan. 1766, *Burke Correspondence* i. 230–1.
[3] Wilkes to Burke, 12 June 1766; Burke to Wilkes, 4 July 1766; ibid., i. 256, 259.
[4] Grafton, *Autobiography*, pp. 192–3.
[5] Wilkes to Temple, 1 Feb. and 16 Nov. 1767, *Grenville Papers*, iv. 1–4, 188.

and his brother Heaton wrote enthusiastically in May 1767 that the letter 'has done you infinite service in the City and on the Exchange'.[1] Wilkes was certainly not downhearted and wrote the same day to Temple that he looked forward 'with a gleam of hope, not I own from the public, which is too corrupt, too selfish, too unfeeling, but from some private advantages I still enjoy'.[2] Some further months went by and, in November, it was the persistence of his Paris creditors rather than the prospects of a favourable reception at home that precipitated another visit to London. Once more, after consulting friends, he decided to retreat and this time, withdrew to Leyden to await there the dissolution of Parliament, which now was imminent. He set out for the Hague in the New Year and, soon after, crossed over from Ostend to Dover, arriving in London on 6 February, his exile at last completed.

Some of his more fashionable friends and patrons might not welcome his return with any degree of enthusiasm; even Lord Temple was at first distinctly cool and made no serious attempt to receive him. But, in other quarters, Wilkes had chosen his moment well for making a considerable impression. For some months past, it had been rumoured that he would stand as a parliamentary candidate in the City of London and his return was, from the start, the subject of widespread comment and speculation in the press — most of it favourable to himself and hostile to the administration.[3] Other factors favoured his return to political life. The winter had been exceptionally severe. The Thames had been frozen over and the Common Council of the City had been obliged to open a subscription for the destitute.[4] There was considerable economic distress. The price of wheat and bread, having fallen in the last months of 1767, had risen sharply again in the New Year: in February, the quarter of wheat sold at 47s. 6d. and the wheaten peck-loaf (17 lb. 6 oz.) at 2s. 9d.[5] The Spitalfields weavers and the coal-heavers of Shadwell and Wapping had already embarked on a series of protracted disputes with their employers over wages and conditions of work, the first of a succession of industrial disputes

[1] H. Wilkes to J. Wilkes, 11 May 1767, Add. MSS. 30866, f. 121; cit. Bleackley, p. 180.

[2] Wilkes to Temple, 11 May 1767, *Grenville Papers*, iv. 17.

[3] Bleackley, pp. 183–5.

[4] O. A. Sherrard, *A Life of John Wilkes*, (1930), p. 170.

[5] *Read. Merc.*, 15 Feb. 1768; *Gent's Mag.*, 1768, p. 50.

that were to cause Lord Grafton and his colleagues considerable concern.[1] An instruction to the Middlesex magistrates drafted in the Earl of Shelburne's office and dated 26 January speaks of 'disorderly persons [having] lately assembled, in a riotous manner and committed many outrages in and about Spitalfields', and, while hoping that 'the power of the civil magistrates will be sufficient to quell any disturbances which may arise' adds that 'orders have been, however, given, in case of absolute necessity, for a proper number of soldiers to be marched from the Tower for the support and assistance of the magistrates when required by them'.[2] In fact, a popular movement of considerable proportions was already under way before Wilkes's return to the political scene. His own activities and subsequent events were undoubtedly to spread and to intensify this movement, but he can in no sense be held responsible for its origins.

Nevertheless, Wilkes's intervention was dramatic enough and had startling consequences. He did not wait long before drawing the attention of the authorities to his return; on 4 March, a footman was sent to the Palace with a letter, respectfully craving His Majesty's pardon. This remained unanswered: the King seemed no more anxious than his Ministers to repeat the over-hasty zeal previously displayed by Grenville and Halifax. So Wilkes was, for the time being, left free to go where he pleased and to take the necessary steps to qualify as a candidate for election in the City of London. This he proceeded to do by enrolling as a member of the Joiners' Guild, whose minutes record that

> On the 10th March 1768 at a Private Court of that Guild held at Joiners' Hall, present Mr. Wm. Hopkins, Master, and others, John Wilkes Esq. (of the Royal Exchange) was admitted into the freedom of this Company by redemption.
> Co 10/-, fees and duty 17/8d, on enrolment 3/4d . . . and he paid the Renter Warden Mr. John Sage the sum of Twenty pounds for both his said fines, and paid the fees, and was thereupon excused from serving the office of Steward and admitted on the Livery and took the cloathing of the Company on him accordingly.[3]

The next day, his election address to the London livery appeared in the papers; in it particular stress was laid on 'the two important questions of public liberty, respecting *General Warrants* and the

[1] Grafton, *Autobiography*, pp. 188–9. See chapter VI below.
[2] P.R.O., S.P. Dom., 37/6, no. 80/2, ff. 186–7.
[3] Cit. W. P. Treloar, *Wilkes and the City* (1917), p. 63.

Seizure of Papers'. One observer wrote that 'some had laid [bets] that Mr Wilkes will be certainly chosen, others that he will be in *durance vile* before the expiration of the week'.[1] Neither prophecy was to be fulfilled, but when he presented himself with six other candidates at the City Guildhall on 16 March, 'in dark blue with metal buttons',[2] he was cheered to the echo as he declaimed: 'I stand here, Gentlemen, a private man, unconnected with the Great, and unsupported by any Party. I have no support but you, I wish no other support. I can have none more certain, none more honourable.'[3] The enthusiasm was particularly great among the small City masters and craftsmen who, on a first 'show of hands', gave him a resounding, though unofficial, majority.[4] But when it came to the official poll, which extended over a whole week, the outcome was not in doubt: too many 'patriot' votes had been pledged to William Beckford and Barlow Trecothick — soon themselves to become occasional Wilkites. Yet the enthusiasm of his supporters remained undiminished. On the third day of polling, according to a press report,

> the master of a Public House by the side of the Fleet-Market hired the hackney coach no. 45 & six black horses with long tails, on the top of which was a man with a flag, another behind the coach, who held the end of it, with blue cockades in their hats; and in this manner he was carried to Guildhall, accompanied in the coach by a fruiterer in the Fleet-Market and other friends, and each of them gave a single vote to John Wilkes Esq. From Guildhall they proceeded in the same manner over London and Westminster Bridges, on their return home followed by a number of people, huzzaing and crying *Wilkes and Liberty*.

On the same occasion, as Wilkes's sedan-chair was hoisted on eager shoulders and carried to his headquarters at the King's Arms Tavern in Cornhill, an enthusiast shouted, 'By G—, Master Wilkes, we'll *carry* you, whether you *carry* your election or not.' The next morning, a Sunday, a printed paper appeared on the walls of several City churches with the message: 'The prayers of this congregation are earnestly desired for the restoration of Liberty, depending on the election of Mr. Wilkes.'[5]

Despite all this, Wilkes emerged bottom of the list of seven

[1] *Glos. J.*, 14 and 21 March 1768.
[2] *Brist. J.*, 19 March 1768.
[3] *Trewman's Exeter Flying Post*, 18–25 March 1768.
[4] *Gent's Mag.*, 1768, p. 139.
[5] *Exeter Flying Post*, 18–25 March 1768; *Read. Merc.*, 28 March 1768.

candidates. Top of the poll were the two 'courtiers', Thomas Harley, the Lord Mayor, and Sir Robert Ladbroke, closely followed by the two 'patriots', Beckford and Trecothick.[1] Wilkes, however, was quite undaunted and, having ascribed his lack of success to his late entry into the field,[2] gaily announced his intention to contest one of the Middlesex seats. 'And now, Gentlemen, permit me to address you as Friends of Liberty and Freeholders of the County of Middlesex, declaring my intention of appearing as a candidate to represent you in Parliament.' After which, we are told, a large crowd seized his carriage, unharnessed the horses, 'and dragged the carriage themselves, with Mr. Wilkes and another gentleman in it, from the Mansion House to the George and Vulture tavern in Cornhill'.[3]

The Middlesex election opened at Brentford Butts on the morning of 28 March. Wilkes's opponents were the two sitting Members, George Cooke, a Chathamite and Joint Paymaster of the Forces,[4] and Sir William Beauchamp Proctor, a prosperous lawyer and occasional 'courtier'.[5] Though Wilkes lacked the support of influential backers, he was well served by his two closest associates of the time, Serjeant John Glynn and the Rev. John Horne of Brentford.[6] According to one account, nearly 250 coaches, filled with Wilkite supporters and bedecked with blue favours, set out for the hustings, every passenger having been given a blue cockade

[1] The votes were cast as follows: Harley, 3,729; Ladbroke, 3,678; Beckford, 3,402; Trecothick, 2,957 (*elected*); Sir Richard Glyn Bart., 2,823; John Paterson, Esq., 1,769; John Wilkes, Esq., 1,247. None of the other six candidates voted for Wilkes, though he received the votes of two aldermen: W. Bridgen (Farringdon Within) and Sir W. Baker (Bassishaw); also those of Frederick Bull, salter, of Leadenhall Street, and a later Lord Mayor, and of 13 out of 236 Common Council men. Wilkes himself did not vote. (*The Poll of the Livery of London*, 1768; A. B. Beaven, *The Aldermen of the City of London* (2 vols., 1908), i. 292; *Royal Calendar*, 1768.)

[2] Benjamin Franklin, who described Wilkes at this time as 'an outlaw and exile of bad personal character, not worth a farthing', shared this opinion (J. Grego, *A History of Parliamentary Elections and Electioneering from the Stuarts to Queen Victoria* (1892), p. 168).

[3] *Brist. J.*, 26 March 1768; *Glos. J.*, 28 March 1768.

[4] John Brooke, *The Chatham Administration 1766–1768* (1956), pp. 107, 252. Cooke also received the support of the Newcastle interest (Thos. Greening to Newcastle, 28 March 1768, Add. MSS. 32989, ff. 268, 271). It is not clear why Mr. Brooke should call him a 'radical' (p. 252) — even less why Grego should label him a 'Conservative' (op. cit., p. 167).

[5] Proctor held three Middlesex freeholds — one at Edmonton assessed at £24 p.a., a second at Tottenham assessed at £70, and a third in Bruton Street, St. George's Westminster, assessed at £92 (Middlesex R.O., Land Tax Assessments, 1767, nos. 18, 188; Westminster Lib., Poor Rate, 1768, St. George's Hanover Square, C 311).

[6] Parson of New Brentford vicarage and the future John Horne Tooke.

and a 'Wilkes and Liberty' card.[1] 40,000 hand-bills had been distributed, requesting Wilkes's supporters 'to preserve peace and good order . . . to convince the world that Liberty is not joined with licentiousness'.[2] Wilkes himself rode to Brentford 'in a coach drawn by six long-tail horses' and attended, wrote an observer, 'by an amazing number of people'; but, wrote another, 'no riot or disturbance happened on the Acton Road [a most private road] by which Mr. Wilkes's friends went'.[3] At Hyde Park Corner, however, through which the main body of his opponents passed, the proceedings were not so peaceful. According to Horace Walpole, the Spitalfields weavers — as always champions of the 'patriot' party — had mustered in strength in Piccadilly, giving out blue cockades and papers inscribed 'No. 45, Wilkes and Liberty';[4] and objection was raised to two blue silk standards carried by Proctor's supporters, bearing the provocative inscriptions, 'No Blasphemer' and 'No French Renegade', which (it was said) 'raised an unhappy resentment in the populace'. A scuffle ensued in the course of which the glass on one of Proctor's coaches was broken and a Mr. Cooke, son of the City Marshal, was pelted and knocked off his horse and had the wheels stripped off his carriage and his harness slashed.[5]

At Brentford itself, the election was conducted in a perfectly orderly manner, though Wilkes's supporters noisily demonstrated their allegiance, waving banners inscribed 'No. 45' and 'Wilkes and Liberty', while others bore the motto, 'More Meat and fewer COOKS'.[6] George Cooke was laid up with gout and failed to appear, but Sir William Proctor bore his ordeal manfully. The London livery were well represented and, it was reported, many of those 'who lately voted against Mr. Wilkes at Guildhall were the first to poll in his favour at Brentford'.[7] At all events, Wilkes headed the poll from the start and it was only some doubt as to which of his opponents should have second place that delayed the result until late in the evening. The final count gave 1,292 votes to Wilkes, 827 to Cooke and 807 to Proctor. Commenting on the

[1] Bleackley, pp. 189–90.
[2] *Read. Merc.*, 4 April 1768.
[3] *Glos. J.*, 4 April 1768; *Read. Merc.*, 4 April 1768.
[4] Walpole, *Letters*, v. 91–92. See also Sherrard, pp. 175–6.
[5] *Read. Merc.*, 4 April 1768; *Ann. Reg.*, 1768, p. 86; Bishop of Norwich to Newcastle, 29 March 1768, Add. MSS. 32989, f. 272.
[6] *Glos. J.*, 4 April 1768.
[7] Ibid.

whole proceedings, the *Annual Register* added the curious observation:

> There has not been so great a defection of inhabitants from London and Westminster to ten miles distant, in one day, since the lifeguardsman's prophecy of the earthquake, which was to destroy both those cities in 1750.[1]

There had been also a considerable 'defection' of magistrates and constables to cope with the crowds that had gathered at Brentford and its approaches, and the peace officers remaining in London and Westminster were quite insufficient to deal with the riots that followed.[2] For two days, notwithstanding Wilkes's appeal for peace and good order, his supporters of 'the inferior set' held the streets and noisily celebrated his victory. Citizens were obliged to light up their windows at night, every door from Temple Bar to Hyde Park Corner (so it was reported) was chalked with 'No. 45', and the Austrian Ambassador was even dragged from his coach and had the slogan chalked on the soles of his boots![3] At night, wrote the *Annual Register*,

> the rabble was very tumultuous; some persons who had voted for Mr. Wilkes having put out lights, the mob paraded the whole town from east to west, obliging every body to illuminate and breaking the windows of such as did not do it immediately. The windows of the Mansion-house, in particular, were demolished all to pieces, together with a large chandelier and some pier glasses, to the amount of many hundred pounds. They demolished all the windows of Ld Bute, Lord Egmont, Sir Sampson Gideon, Sir William Mayne, and many other gentlemen and tradesmen in most of the public streets of both cities, London and Westminster. At one of the above gentlemen's houses, the mob were in a great measure irritated to it by the imprudence of a servant, who fired a pistol among them. At Charing Cross, at the Duke of Northumberland's, the mob also broke a few panes; but his Grace had the address to get rid of them by ordering up lights immediately into his windows, and opening the Ship ale-house, which soon drew them to that side.[4]

An eyewitness spoke of 'a Mob of about 100 men and boys' setting out from Charing Cross about nine o'clock in the evening on 29 March and smashing windows in Leicester Fields, Covent Garden, Russell Street, the Strand, Long Acre, Oxford Street and

[1] *Ann. Reg.*, 1768, p. 86.
[2] Sir John Fielding to Robert Wood, 28 March 1768, S. P. Dom., Entry Books, 44/142, p. 103.
[3] Walpole, *Memoirs*, iii. 130–1.
[4] *Ann. Reg.*, 1768, p. 86. See also *Brist. J.*, 2 April 1768.

Piccadilly. Before becoming lost to view in Southampton Street, they had broken the Duke of Newcastle's windows off Lincoln's Inn Fields and the lamp over Sir John Fielding's door in Bow Street, and drunk two gallons of beer to 'Wilkes and Liberty' at the Six Cans Tavern in Turnstile, Holborn. Among those arrested as the result of this incident was one Matthew Christian, a 'gentleman of character and fortune', late of Antigua, who was alleged to have spent £6 or £7 on filling the rioters with beer in a number of ale houses.[1] The same evening, according to a newspaper report, there was a riot in Wood's Close, Clerkenwell; 'and while a laundress in that place was putting out lights, some of the villains went into the yard, and carried away upwards of forty ruffled shirts, the property of divers persons'.[2]

Meanwhile, during the previous night's disturbances, 'a vast number of people, some thousands' (it was said), had gathered before the Mansion House to settle accounts with Thomas Harley, the Lord Mayor. To shouts of 'Wilkes for ever!', they had broken every lamp and window in the building.[3] We learn from the Mansion House Committee's minutes that the accounts later submitted by City glaziers for the repair of the damage amounted to £30 4s. for lighting lamps and £174 for window-panes — including an account for £25 5s. submitted by John Monk of Finch Lane 'to 136 Sash sqrs of the Best Crown Glass cont. 270 Ft. . . . at 1s. 6d. per foot'.[4]

The government were naturally much alarmed and sent the usual instructions to the parties most concerned to cope with the situation as best they might. In a letter of 29 March, Lord Weymouth requested Lord Barrington, Secretary at War, to hold troops in readiness and urged the Duke of Northumberland as Lord Lieutenant of Middlesex to ensure 'that every proper and prudent precaution be taken to prevent a continuation of these riotous proceedings', adding 'that you should call for Military

[1] S. P. Dom., 37/6, no. 80/13, ff. 225–6: 'The King ag'st Christian. A State of the Evidence ag'st the Def't touching his being concerned in a Riot on the 29th March 1768.' According to Sir John Fielding on 30 March: 'We yesterday discovered that Mr Robert Chandler, a Tea-Broker in the City, headed a Mob in Westminster' (S.P. Dom., Entry Bks., 44/142, p. 107).

[2] W. J. Pinks, *The History of Clerkenwell* (1881), pp. 645–6.

[3] O.B. *Proceedings*, 1768, pp. 192–5.

[4] Corp. Lond. R.O., Mansion House Committee Papers, 1768. These accounts include the cost of repairing further (though less extensive) damage incurred in the riots of 9–10 May of the same year.

Force to support the Civil Magistrate, if you find it absolutely necessary to the keeping up good order'.[1] In consequence, considerable pressure was put on Sir John Fielding, the presiding magistrate at Bow Street, to meet the numerous demands for assistance made upon him by despairing householders, whose windows were being broken in different parts of the capital.[2] But the available peace officers and constables were far too few to deal effectively with such an emergency and, after strenuous efforts, only six persons were taken into custody, and of these only three were convicted.[3]

Meanwhile, a Common Council, meeting at the City Guildhall on 30 March, heard a report on the riots and the extent of the damage, and resolved 'to prosecute with the utmost rigour such persons who [have] been active in the said Riots', to pay a £50 reward upon conviction, and 'to prosecute with the utmost vigour all persons who shall hereafter be guilty of any such Riots and Disorders'. It was further resolved that the order be published in the press and posted in all public places within the City, and to appoint a committee of aldermen and Common Council men under the presidency of the Lord Mayor 'to carry on such prosecutions as may arise from the above Resolution'.[4] But the results proved decidedly meagre and the Crown prosecutor in a later case was to comment sadly on these measures in the following terms:

> Notwithstanding the above advertisement and his Lordship's care and vigilance to suppress the Riots and Disturbances, they still continued almost every night from the 28th of March to ye 12th or 13th May last.[5]

By this time, the political leaders had had some opportunity of taking stock of the new situation arising from Wilkes's return to active political life. Lord Camden, now Lord Chancellor under Chatham, was indignant that 'a criminal should in open daylight thrust himself upon the country as a candidate, his crime unex-

[1] Weymouth to Barrington and Northumberland, 29 March 1768, S. P. Dom., Entry Bks., 44/142, pp. 42–43.

[2] S.P. Dom. 37/6, no. 80/16, ff. 223–4. S.P. Dom., Entry Bks., 44/142, pp. 44–45.

[3] For fuller details of arrests and convictions of rioters of 1768–69, see G. Rudé, 'Wilkes and Liberty, 1768–69', *The Guildhall Miscellany*, no. 8, July 1957. See also chapter X and Appendix XI below.

[4] Corp. Lond. R.O., *Journals of the Court of Common Council*, lxiv (1765–69), ff. 247vo–248vo.

[5] Guild. Lib., MS. 3724: 'Wilkes Riots, 1768; the King *v.* John Williams, to be tried at the Old Bailey on Saturday 25th of Feby 1769.'

purgated'.[1] Burke, while confessing that he had not expected Wilkes to win a seat in Middlesex, shrewdly observed that 'the crowd always want to draw themselves from abstract principles to personal attachments'; and that 'since the fall of Ld Chatham, there has been no hero of the Mob but Wilkes'.[2] Richmond welcomed the news of Wilkes's election, 'for whatever men may think of Mr. Wilkes's private character', he wrote to Newcastle, 'he has carried his election by being supposed a friend to Liberty, and I think it will shew the Administration that, though they may buy Lords & Commons & carry on their measures smoothly in Parliament, yet they are not so much approved of by the Nation'. Newcastle shared his view: 'Wilkes's merit is being a friend to Liberty; and he has suffered for it; and, therefore, it is not an ill symptom that it should appear that that is a merit with the Nation.'[3] Lord Chatham, it was reported to Newcastle, refused to express an opinion on 'Wilkes's affair'; whereas Temple, though not anxious to restore their old relationship, considered that 'tho' his faults were enormous, he had suffered abundantly' and must be protected against Ministerial injustice.[4] The Cabinet were for the moment divided between those who wished to take strong measures to bring Wilkes to justice and those who preferred to temporize; Lord Grafton was known to favour moderation, an attitude that aroused the King's deep displeasure.[5]

So Wilkes was once more allowed to take the initiative and publicly announced that he would surrender to his outlawry at the Court of King's Bench after the Easter recess. Anticipating further disturbances, Lord Weymouth sent out precise and detailed instructions to the Lord Mayor and the Surrey and Westminster magistrates as to how to dispose their forces and as to what calls might be made, in the event of an emergency, on the troops stationed at the Tower, the Savoy, the War Office and the Tilt Yard in Whitehall. In reply, the magistrates assured him of their

[1] Camden to Grafton, 3 April 1768, Grafton, *Autobiography*, p. 199. Nevertheless, on 20 April, the day of Wilkes's surrender to his outlawry at the Court of King's Bench, Camden wrote: 'As the times are, I had rather pardon W. than punish him' (ibid. pp. 199–201).

[2] E. Burke to Chas O'Hara, *Burke Correspondence*, i. 349.

[3] Richmond to Newcastle, 3 April; Newcastle to Richmond, 4 April 1768; Add. MSS., 32989, ff. 294, 299.

[4] James West, M.P., to Newcastle, 24 April 1768, Add. MSS. 32989, f. 377.

[5] Id. to id., 23 April; Newcastle to Rockingham, 13 April 1768; Add. MSS. 32989, ff. 375, 329. Thomas Whateley to Grenville, 18 April 1768, *Grenville Papers*, iv. 267–71. See also Walpole, *Memoirs*, iii. 137–9, 142.

preparedness. Sir John Fielding, who was particularly anxious not to be caught off his guard, divided his justices into groups, stationed variously at the Westminster Guildhall, the vestry rooms of St. Martin's and St. Clement Dane's churches, at St. James's Coffee House, in Litchfield Street and 'near Buckingham Gate.'[1] After all this, Wilkes's appearance in court on 20 April was something of an anti-climax. After the defendant had complained of various irregularities attending his conviction and the case had been argued between Serjeant Glynn and the Attorney-General, Lord Mansfield surprised some and disappointed others by declaring that Wilkes might go free until such time as a writ of *capias ut legatum* had been served on him. Describing these proceedings, James West wrote jubilantly to Newcastle that 'there has not been the least riot, tumult or Mob more than is usual on the first day of the Term'.[2] The same evening, however, in Shadwell, Wilkes's temporary release was celebrated by a large band of Irish coal-heavers, who had mustered to settle accounts with an unpopular coal-'undertaker'. Before making an armed assault on his public house in New Gravel Lane, they were heard to shout, 'Wilkes and Liberty, and coal-heavers for ever!' So much appears from the subsequent trials at the Old Bailey of John Green, the 'undertaker', and his principal assailants. There were further cries of 'Damn you, light up your candles for Wilkes', and soon every house along the Ratcliffe Highway was lighted up in his honour. The immediate cause of celebration seems to have been clear enough, yet there was some confusion as to what would happen next. On inquiring 'what they had done with Mr. Wilkes', a witness was told, 'he is cleared till the parliament sits, then he is to be tried by the House of Lords'. Nor were they entirely unanimous; in one group an argument took place between Wilkes's supporters and opponents.

> They said, who are you, to one another; one said I am for Wilkes; damn you, said others, I am for Bute; after that, they began to swagger with sticks at one another, and then over their heads.[3]

Wilkes's freedom, however, was not to last long. A week later, the writ had been duly served and he appeared once more — and for the last time — in Westminster Hall. Lord Mansfield refused

[1] S.P. Dom., Entry Bks., 44/142, pp. 55–71; Add. MSS. 32989, f. 356.
[2] West to Newcastle, 20 April 1768, Add. MSS. 32989, ff. 363–5.
[3] O.B. *Proceedings*, 1768, pp. 204–14, 247; *Brist. J.*, 23 April 1768. For the coal-heavers' dispute, see pp. 95–98 below.

bail and committed him to the custody of the Marshal of the King's Bench prison. As he left the court at 6.30 in the evening, accompanied by the tipstaff and the faithful 'Parson' Horne, crowds formed in Palace Yard and along Westminster Bridge. Sir John Fielding sent urgent messages to the Surrey magistrates across the water warning them of the prisoner's approach, but to no avail. As the procession drew near to the Surrey side, 'a number of persons took off the horses, turned the coach round and, with expedition beyond conception, drew the coach through the Strand, and through Temple Bar, and into the City' — with Sir John Fielding and his clerk in hot pursuit![1] And so on to the Three Tuns Tavern by Spitalfields Church, where Wilkes appeared at an upper window and was acclaimed by his supporters before vanishing in disguise and under cover of dark to surrender to his jailers at the King's Bench prison.[2] Temple was delighted with Wilkes's display of moderation and his 'wise and humane discouragement of all tumult and disorder', and immediately wrote him a warm letter of sympathy offering to visit him in prison.[3] The authorities, however, had been caught badly napping; no single rioter had been arrested; and Lord Weymouth angrily described the incident to his subordinates as 'a disgrace to civil government'.[4]

But worse was to come: from now on riots were continuous for almost a fortnight. 'The next day', writes a local chronicler,

> the prison was surrounded by a prodigious number of persons, but no disturbance happened till night, when the rails which enclosed the footway were pulled up to make a fire, and the inhabitants of the Borough were obliged to illuminate their houses, but a Captain Guard arriving soon after 12 the Mob dispersed.[5]

Two labourers and a lighterman were arrested and charged with 'assembling riotously' before the gates of the prison and with 'breaking, spoiling, demolishing, burning and destroying sundry wooden posts belonging thereto'; of these, one was subsequently

[1] S.P. Dom., Entry Bks., 44/142. pp. 144–6.

[2] *Gent's Mag.*, 1768, p. 197; G. Onslow to Newcastle 27 April; J. West to Newcastle, 28 April 1768; Add. MSS. 32989, ff. 397, 402.

[3] Temple to Wilkes, 28 April 1768, *Grenville Papers*, iv. 279–80.

[4] S.P. Dom., Entry Bks., 44/142, pp. 143–6.

[5] 'Historical Notices of the Borough of Southwark' (manuscript account by Richard Corner, Gentleman (d. 1820), preserved in Southwark Library), pp. 134–5.

fined 13s. 4d. and committed to prison for twelve months.[1] A week later, Wilkes's affairs were further argued in his absence by counsel in the Court of King's Bench; 'a vast crowd' gathered in the expectation of seeing him and 'went away greatly dissatisfied at Mr. Wilkes not being there'.[2] The next day, 8 May, the press reported that 'a numerous Mob assembled about the King's Bench prison exclaiming against the confinement of Mr. Wilkes, and threatened to unroof the Marshal's house.' Wilkes, who was watching these proceedings, made a brief speech from his window and persuaded them to disperse — but not before 'a well-dressed man, said to be a North Briton', had been thrown into the pond for speaking offensively of Wilkes and made to get down on his knees and shout 'Wilkes and Liberty!'[3] The next evening, a watchman was manhandled and the prison lobby was demolished to further shouts of 'Wilkes and Liberty!' On this occasion, one Robert Hall was committed for the offence, while a certain Jane Murray was taken into custody for 'comforting and aiding and abetting divers persons unknown' who had taken a hand in it.[4]

The next day, 10 May, witnessed the far more violent affray known as 'the Massacre of St. George's Fields', an event that was to cause the government considerable embarrassment and to provide the Wilkite cause with its first martyrs. It was the day of the opening of Parliament and the authorities, fearing that great crowds might assemble in the Fields, had ordered a troop of Horse and 100 men of the Third Regiment of Foot Guards to support the Surrey magistrates at the King's Bench prison.[5] The Lord Mayor, too, had taken certain precautions: having received information 'that great numbers of young persons, who appear to be apprentices and journeymen, have assembled themselves together in large bodies in different parts of this City . . . for several evenings last past', he had called on master tradesmen to keep their journeymen and apprentices off the streets and reminded Freemen of the City of their pledge to keep their journeymen 'from

[1] Surrey R.O., Sessions Rolls, 1768 (Midsummer); Sessions Bundles, 1768 (Midsummer); Process Register Books of Indictments (1761–69); QS. 3/5/9, p. 25; QS. Order Books (1767–71); QS. 2/1/22, pp. 166–7. See also chapter X and Appendix XI below.

[2] West to Newcastle, 7 May 1768, Add. MSS. 32990, f. 25.

[3] *Read. Merc.*, 16 May 1768.

[4] *Gent's Mag.*, 1768, pp. 323–5; P.R.O., T.S. 11/443/1408; Assizes 35/208. Surrey Summer Assizes. 8th Geo. 3rd 1768.

[5] S.P. Dom., Entry Bks., 44/142, pp. 76, 81–2; Add. MSS. 30884, f. 70.

going abroad' in times of disorder.[1] Yet, from ten o'clock in the morning, crowds gathered in the Fields from every part of the capital.[2] Various rumours had spread: one was that Wilkes would be escorted to the Commons to take his seat; another that he would be taken for trial; a third (and this was plausible enough) 'that an attempt would be made to break open the prison doors & set Mr. Wilkes & all the prisoners there at Liberty'.[3] So, whether as idle spectators or as active participants in a Wilkite demonstration, large numbers had gathered, these numbers swelling from one thousand in the early morning to 15,000 or 20,000 — some said even 40,000 — in the course of the afternoon.[4]

Between ten and eleven o'clock, the Southwark magistrates, who were meeting in the Rotation Office on St. Margaret's Hill, received word from the prison Marshal that the crowds were becoming unruly and requesting their assistance. Hurrying to the Fields, Samuel Gillam and three other justices found that demonstrators had broken through the ranks of the Foot Guards drawn up inside the railings surrounding the prison, and had pasted to the wall a paper bearing the doggerel:

Venal judges & Ministers combine
Wilkes and English Liberty to confine;
Yet in true English hearts secure their fame is,
Nor are such crowded levies at St. James's.
While thus in Prison Envy dooms their stay,
Here, O grateful Britons, your daily homage pay.
Philo Libertatis no. 45.[5]

When, on the magistrates' orders, the paper was torn down, the crowd became more restive. There were shouts of 'Give us the paper' and 'Wilkes and Liberty for ever!'; and even — so a hostile, and probably unreliable, witness reported — 'No Wilkes, no King!' 'Damn the King, damn the Government, damn the Justices!' and 'This is the most glorious opportunity for a Revolution that ever offered!'[6] At all events, Justice Gillam felt obliged to read the

[1] *Lloyd's Evening Post*, 11–13 May 1768.
[2] Among some 25 persons arrested in Southwark as the result of the events of 10–11 May, 2 were from Bermondsey, 3 from the City of London, 3 from Westminster and 6 from other parts of Middlesex (Surrey R.O., Sessions Rolls, 1768 (Midsummer)).
[3] *Read. Merc.*, 16 May 1768; *Ann Reg.*, 1768, p. 129; Add. MSS. 30884, f. 69; T.S. 11/946/3467.
[4] O.B. *Proceedings*, 1768, pp. 276–7; *English Liberty*, i. 170.
[5] T.S. 11/946/3,467; Add. MSS. 30884, f. 72 (for a slight variant, see *English Liberty*, i. 170).
[6] Add. MSS. 30884, f. 72.

Riot Act, which was met with jeers and a volley of stones. At this point 'a man in a red waistcoat' flung a stone that wounded Gillam in the head and stung him to order the guards to pursue his assailant. Accordingly, Captain Murray and three grenadiers chased him off the Fields, lost sight of him and, in Blackman Street near by, entering a cow-house annexed to the Horse Shoe Inn, shot dead William Allen, the publican's son, whom they appear to have mistaken for their quarry.[1] More casualties followed. After the Riot Act had been read a second time, the foot-soldiers, by now reinforced by Horse Guards, were ordered to fire into the crowd and '5 or 6 were killed on the spot & about 15 wounded'.[2] Some of these were casual bystanders, the victims of stray bullets. 'Several of His Majesty's subjects,' noted Burke, 'returning to Town from *the most useful occupation of husbandry*, were killed on ye high road on the way to market, some on hay carts, others in waggons & dung carts &c. Eleven lives were lost in this manner.'[3] *English Liberty* lists 'some of the persons killed and wounded' as follows:

Mr. *William Allen*, shot to death in his father's cow-house.
Mr. *William Redburn*, weaver, shot through the thigh, died in the London Hospital.
William Bridgman, shot through the breast as he was fitting a hay-cart in the Haymarket, died instantly.
Mary Jeffs, of St. Saviour's, who was selling oranges by the Haymarket, died instantly.
Mr. *Boddington*, baker, of Coventry, shot through the thigh-bone, died in St. Thomas's hospital.
Mr. *Lawley*, a farrier, shot in the groin, died the 12th of May.
Margaret Walters, Mint, pregnant, died the 12th of May.
Mary Green, shot through the right-arm bone.
Mr. *Nichols*, shot through the flesh of his breast.
Mrs. *Egremont*, shot through her garment under her arm.
Mr. ———in Kent-Street, stabbed with a bayonet in his loin.
Mr. ———, unknown, stabbed with a bayonet.[4]

One constable, at least, blamed the Horse Guards for this holocaust, as he later testified at the Old Bailey:

[1] T.S. 11/946/3467. For an attempt to justify the shooting, see T.S. 11/443/1408.

[2] *Ann. Reg.*, 1768, p. 108.

[3] From Edmund Burke's notes for a speech (of 8 March 1769?) on the 'massacre' of St. George's Fields, Sheffield Central Library, W[entworth] W[oodhouse] MSS., Bk 8b.

[4] *English Liberty*, i. 172–3. Mary Jeffs and William Bridgeman were the subject of later petitions (S.P. Dom., Entry Bks., 44/142, pp. 203–4; Burke's notes [see n. 3 above]).

The horse occasioned a great disturbance, and the whole disturbance, I believe; the people huzzaed and hissed, but no further riot. The soldiers [he added] fired at random. A great number of them loaded three times, and seemed to enjoy their fire; I thought it a great cruelty.[1]

More disturbances were to follow. That evening, between nine and ten o'clock, while the justices were still attempting to disperse the crowds from St. George's Fields, 'some hundreds of disorderly persons', to quote from the Treasury Solicitor's notes, 'detached themselves from the Mob in the Fields'[2] and proceeded to take their revenge for the shootings by attacking and 'pulling down' the houses of two of the Southwark magistrates, Edward Russell, a distiller of Borough High Street, at the foot of London Bridge, and Richard Capel of Bermondsey Street. According to the *Gentleman's Magazine*, 'the activity of the two gentlemen . . . in suppressing the tumults, occasioned the outrage'.[3] It was even said that Justice Capel had claimed to have 'an order from the Ministry to kill twenty-five of the people'.[4]

Russell's family were in bed, but quickly rose to light up candles, thinking that another Wilkite celebration was being called for. The rioters, however, were not appeased and smashed in windows, frames and panels, stove in the front door, and removed a twenty-gallon cask of spirits which they drank or spilled, 'to the amount of several £100s'.[5] Soon after, Russell arrived to read the Riot Act and Capel, after driving away the rioters from his own house, came round with a body of Life Guards to give support. Here, according to Capel's own account of these events,

. . . one John Percival took him by the collar and said 'Damn you, I'll mark you'; and accordingly he did mark him with large figures No. 45 on the cape of his great coat. He then immediately took him into custody and deliver'd him to the care of the sentinels then and there on duty. After which several well-dressed persons, and in particular one Richard Gilbert, came up to him and demanded to know by what authority he took the said John Percival into custody. He told them he was a magistrate and came there to preserve the peace. He then insisted on seeing his authority and otherwise insulted him. He [this deponent] then took hold

[1] O.B. *Proceedings*, 1768, p. 278. Nevertheless, a soldier outside the prison was heard to say: 'We are all ready to fire on our enemies, the French and the Spaniards, but never will on our countrymen' (*English Liberty*, i. 110).

[2] T.S. 11/443/1408.

[3] *Gent's Mag.*, 1768, p. 243.

[4] O.B. *Proceedings*, 1768, p. 281.

[5] T.S. 11/443/1408. See also Appendix I below.

of him [the said Richard] and deliver'd him into the custody of the sentinels on duty. Soon after which the Mob dispersed, and return'd with the Horse Guards into Bermondsey Street.[1]

Meanwhile, the riots had spread to other parts of the capital. In Fore Street, Limehouse, a band of five hundred sawyers, having given previous notice of their intentions, pulled down a brand-new saw-mill recently built for Charles Dingley, a prosperous City merchant, at a cost of 'near 5000 l'.[2] Political motives do not appear to have played any part in this assault, though Charles Dingley, described by one writer as 'a creature of the Duke of Grafton',[3] was some months later to distinguish himself by contesting Wilkes's candidature in Middlesex and by organizing a demonstration of 'loyal' City merchants against him.[4] On 9 and 10 May, too, further disturbances took place at the Mansion House and more windows, lamps and furniture were broken. On the first occasion, a gibbet was carried along Cornhill, bedecked with a boot and petticoat, the current opposition symbol for Lord Bute and the Princess Dowager. 'There were great hissing and hallooing', stated a witness, 'and cries of "Wilkes and Liberty"'. On the 10th, crowds threw stones and 'damned the Lord Mayor', and a demonstrator, later convicted at the Old Bailey, was said to have collected stones for breaking the Mansion House windows 'at the Borough or King's Bench.'[5] The same day, the Westminster magistrates found it difficult to prevent 'the hallooing of the common people in Palace Yard',[6] and there was a riot outside the House of Lords, in the course of which some cried 'Wilkes and Liberty', others 'that bread and beer were too dear & that it was as well to be hanged as starved'.[7]

These events were not quickly forgotten. On 13 May, the House of Commons passed a vote of thanks to Thomas Harley, Lord Mayor of London,

[1] Surrey R.O., Sessions Bundles, 1768 (Midsummer): 'Rich'd Capel Esq. ag't Percival & Gilbert, Inform^{n} dated 16th June 1768.' See also Appendix 1.

[2] O.B. *Proceedings*, 1768, pp. 256–7; *Read. Merc.*, 16 May 1768. See also pp. 93–94 below.

[3] Grego, op. cit., p. 193.

[4] See pp. 62–65 below.

[5] O.B. *Proceedings*, 1768, pp. 285–8.

[6] S.P. Dom., Entry Bks. 44/142, p. 85.

[7] Rockingham to Newcastle, 10 May 1768, Add. MSS. 32990, ff. 35–36; cit. J. Brooke, op. cit., pp. 357–8. See also Midd. R.O., Sessions Rolls (Westminster), no. 3202, 17 June 1768, for the case of John Biggs, committed for 'disturbing the Peace of the Rt. Hon. House of Lords'.

for his vigilance and active conduct, in support of the Laws, and for the preservation of the public Peace, during the late Disturbances.

The Commons also resolved, *nem. con.*,

That an humble Address be presented to His Majesty, that he will be graciously pleased to order Compensation to be made to Mr. Russell, Mr. Capell, and other Magistrates, for those losses which they have suffered, by exerting themselves to suppress the late seditions and dangerous Riots in this Capital, and the neighbourhood thereof; and to assure His Majesty that this House will make good the expenses thereof to His Majesty.[1]

Accordingly, we find the following Treasury Minute of 16 August:

Read the account of the damages done by the rioters in Southwark to the House and Warehouse of Edward Russell Esq[re] on the 10th of May last amounting to £491-5-6.
Read the account of the damages done . . . to the dwelling-house of Richard Capell Esq[re] on the 10th of May last amounting to £69-4-7.
Read an Address of the House of Commons to His Majesty of the 13th of May last on the subject.
Prepare Warrants for paying to Mr. Russell and Mr. Capell the amount of the damages they have respectively suffered according to the above accounts.[2]

This time, too, the zeal of the magistrates was reflected in a fair toll of arrests and commitments. The names of thirty-four persons of varying occupations — though predominantly of 'the inferior set' — and committed on a variety of charges appear in the numerous judicial records relating to these incidents. Most of these, however, were discharged and a mere half-dozen seem to have been sentenced to fines or terms of imprisonment.[3]

One way or another, the authorities were not permitted to draw much satisfaction from the outcome of this affair. A coroner's inquest into the death of William Allen found that Captain Murray and two of the grenadiers (unhappily for the government, all three Scots!)

feloniously, wilfully and of their malice aforethought, did kill and murder, against the peace of our said Lord the King, his Crown and dignity.[4]

[1] *Commons Journals*, xxxii. 11.
[2] P.R.O., Treasury Minutes, T. 29/39, p. 200.
[3] For details, see Appendix XI below.
[4] *English Liberty*, i. 173–5. In all other cases verdicts of 'chance medley' were returned (ibid. i. 185–8).

Subsequently, at Guildford, on 8 August, a Grand Jury, having heard nineteen witnesses (including John Wilkes), returned a true bill against Donald McLane, one of the grenadiers, while discharging his comrades, Alexander Murray and Donald M'Laury. On the day following, in the face of conflicting evidence, the jury at the Surrey Assizes, could not do other than return a verdict of Not Guilty against McLane. Yet it was widely believed that another grenadier, Peter MacLaughlin, had done the actual shooting and been allowed to 'desert' by his superiors.[1] Meanwhile, a Middlesex Grand Jury, on 7 July, found a bill for wilful murder against Justice Gillam, who had given the order to fire that resulted in the death of William Redburn, a weaver; but he was acquitted at the Old Bailey a few days later.[2]

The parliamentary opposition were in their usual state of confusion. On the one hand, they prepared to condemn the government for the shootings in St. George's Fields and to draw the maximum political advantage from their embarrassment; on the other, they had no sympathy whatsoever with the rioters and little with Wilkes, they were deeply apprehensive of the prevailing public mood, and were anxious to keep 'Wilkes's affair' in cold storage as long as the government would allow. Newcastle, while approving Parliament's action in thanking the Lord Mayor for his conduct, dolefully reflected: 'We must be either governed by a mad, lawless Mob, or the peace be preserved only by a Military Force; both of which are unknown to our Constitution.' As for Wilkes, if only Bute's and Bedford's supporters would leave him alone, he would be 'half forgot' before the winter![3] The government's own supporters had their qualms as well. 'The death of the apprentice of the Borough by the soldiers', wrote West to Newcastle, 'makes ill-blood among many warm friends, otherwise, of Administration.'[4] Public alarm was, therefore, hardly appeased by the publication in the press on 12 May of a letter sent by Lord Barrington to the officer in charge of the Foot Guards, commending his men for their conduct in St. George's Fields.[5] Wilkes himself,

[1] Add. MSS. 30884, ff. 65–76: 'The King ag't McLane [for murder]'; *Gent's Mag.*, 1768, pp. 394–5.

[2] Ibid. p. 346; O.B. *Proceedings*, 1768, pp. 374–83.

[3] Newcastle to Rockingham, 13 May and 12 May 1768, Add. MSS. 32990, ff. 53, 39. See also West to Newcastle, 15 May: 'The situation of the public is alarming to the last degree, and, unless something is done very soon, there is much to fear' (ibid., f. 69).

[4] West to Newcastle, 12 May 1768, ibid., f. 49.

[5] *Gent's Mag.*, 1768, p. 244.

though under lock and key, was not slow to take advantage of the government's follies, and, a few weeks later, he was able to publish, with suitable comments, the instructions sent by Lord Weymouth to magistrates in April, enjoining them to make full use of the military in the event of riots.[1] Thus the 'massacre' was made to appear among a wider public not merely as the mishandling of a difficult situation by a weak though well-intentioned administration, but as an affair deliberately staged by a brutal and tyrannical executive which would not even scruple, in order to impose its will and to trample on Englishmen's liberties, to hire the muskets of an alien soldiery!

The stronger this mood, of course, the stronger the sympathy that the public — including many who had little sympathy for the riotous 'inferior set'— felt for the cause and person of John Wilkes.

[1] *St. James's Chronicle*, 8–10 December 1768.

IV

WILKES *v.* LUTTRELL

When Wilkes appeared once more at the Court of King's Bench on 8 June, it seemed at first that he had won another triumph. On somewhat obscure technical grounds Lord Mansfield decided that his outlawry should be reversed. The verdict was received with acclaim. 'Lord Mansfield,' wrote Rockingham to Newcastle, 'by all accounts did exceeding well. I hear the Mob had a mind to draw his coach home.'[1] But the rejoicing was premature; ten days later, the same court, supported by an imposing display of Foot and Horse Guards,[2] sentenced Wilkes to a fine of £1,000 and a total of twenty-two months imprisonment for his various misdemeanours.[3]

The sentence did not prove to be a great material hardship. Wilkes was housed in comfortable seclusion in a first-floor room of the prison with windows overlooking St. George's Fields. Gifts, food-parcels, delicacies, money, commemorative medallions and other tokens of respect and affection poured in from every part of England and even from the Sons of Liberty at Boston and the House of Assembly of South Carolina.[4] His friends, Horne, Glynn, Sawbridge, Townsend, Beckford, Oliver and others had easy access to his conversation and his table — not to mention a steady succession of well-wishers from the other sex. Among the latter (so it was reported) were two of his fellow-prisoners: a certain 'Black Bess' collected £100, flung them at Wilkes's feet and cried: 'If Squire Wilkes wants money, by G—, he shall have my all'; another, Lucy Cooper by name, having no material gifts to bring, is reputed to have offered to share her prison quarters with him.[5] Among other supporters were the King's Bench debtors who, we read in a newspaper account of June 1769,

[1] Rockingham to Newcastle, 9 June 1768, Add. MSS. 32990, f. 186. He added: 'It would have been droll and would have half killed the Proprietor of Hayes & perhaps a Chancellor.' The verdict had been foreseen by Hardwicke (see Philip Yorke to Hardwicke, 8 May 1768, Add. MSS. 35608, f. 171).

[2] S.P. Dom., Entry Bks., 44/142, pp. 151–3.

[3] Bleackley, pp. 202–3.

[4] Ibid., pp. 233–48.

[5] *Brist. J.*, 14 May 1768.

this morning . . . marched with music playing before them to the Town Hall at St. Margaret's Hill to be cleared; they gave Mr. Wilkes three cheers at coming out of the prison, and the cavalcade cut a very droll appearance.[1]

His popularity with the London 'inferior set' remained undiminished. A news item of 4 July 1768 reads:

At the sessions of the peace at Guildhall, a woman was tried for assaulting Mr. Emmerton, a constable, at St. Bride's parish. He had taken her into custody for bawling *Wilkes and Liberty*, when for his folly, she said, she would take the liberty to break his head, which she accordingly did. The jury found her guilty, and the court fined her one shilling.[2]

His birthday on 28 October was the occasion for further demonstrations of Wilkite supporters, and 'a great number of disorderly persons went in a body through the principal streets, breaking windows on pretence of their not being illuminated'.[3] One of the victims was James Pearson, a linen-draper, of 106, Cheapside, opposite Bow Church Yard, whose house was attacked by one James Jacob, servant to John Mills of Great St. Helen, London, 'with 40 other persons'. Jacob was charged with

making a noise and disturbance before the house of . . . James Pearson with a lighted candle in his hand at eleven o'clock last Friday night . . . and throwing a great quantity of dirt and stones against his house and windows and violently knocking at his door;

and, on 20 February 1769, was sentenced at General Quarter Sessions to a fine of £5 and to provide surety for his good behaviour for one year.[4]

Meanwhile, Wilkes's fellow-Member for Middlesex, George Cooke, had died in June. Sir William Beauchamp Proctor, already secure in the favour of the Court,[5] wrote to the Duke of Newcastle to solicit support for his candidature, and received an encouraging reply:

I most heartily wish you success and will do everything in my power to promote it, & will be sure to send, without delay, to all my tenants, tradespeople, & friends to give you all the assistance they can.[6]

[1] *Read. Merc.*, 6 June 1769.
[2] *Gent's Mag.*, 1768, p. 346.
[3] Ibid., p. 539. See also Thos. Whately to G. Grenville, 28 October 1768, *Grenville Papers*, iv. 392–3.
[4] Corp. London R.O., Sessions Files, 5 Dec. 1768; Sessions Minute Bks. vol. xvii (Dec. 1768–Nov. 1769).
[5] See Grenville to Whately, 13 April 1768, *Grenville Papers*, iv. 267.
[6] Proctor to Newcastle, 17 July; Newcastle to Proctor, 18 July 1768; Add. MSS. 32990, ff. 313, 315. See also Chas. Yorke to Newcastle, 20 October 1768, Add. MSS. 32991A, f. 289. See also p. 77, n. 3 below.

But even this dual support of Court and opposition was not to secure him election in a contest with the Wilkite candidate, Serjeant John Glynn.

The election took place at Brentford Butts on Thursday, 8 December, and was attended by violent disturbances. From the welter of pamphlets, newspaper reports, acrimonious correspondence, sworn affidavits and criminal proceedings that followed this extraordinary affair, it appears beyond reasonable doubt that it was Proctor's supporters, and not Glynn's, that provoked the disorders. Mindful of his uncomfortable experience at Brentford at the previous election, Proctor had instructed his agents to recruit a number of persons both to serve as a personal bodyguard and — so he later claimed — 'as *assistants* to the civil magistrates'.[1] Whatever his own intentions, his agents appear to have hired a body of distinctly riotous Irish chairmen, one of whose leaders, Edward McQuirk (also know as The Infant), was later alleged to have stated that

> he was hired by a person, whose name was Tetam, or Chetham, and he was to have the same wages as at Northampton election; he said he was hired to go down there; that this Tetam was agent to Lord Halifax,[2] that the wages was two guineas a week, victuals and drink for himself, and as many men as he brought should have the same.[3]

'This mob', wrote Horace Walpole, 'seems to have been hired by Sir William Beauchamp Proctor for defence, but by folly or mismanagement proved the sole aggressors.'[4]

The poll opened at eleven o'clock, but before this, wrote the *Oxford Magazine*

> One of the narrow avenues leading to Brentford Butts was occupied very early by a hired mob, with bludgeons, bearing favours in their hats, inscribed 'Proctor and Liberty' . . . A much larger, but very compact body armed as the former, and with the same distinctions, were planted near the hustings, on an eminence, and in a disposition which was

[1] Proctor's address to the Middlesex freeholders, 10 Dec. 1768, *Ox. Mag.* (9 vols., July 1768–Dec. 1772), i. 227–8.

[2] According to H. Walpole, 'Tatum' was an agent of the Duke of Northumberland (*Memoirs*, iii. 225).

[3] Evidence of Robert Jones Esq., J.P., of Fonmon Castle, Glamorganshire, who claimed to have extracted this admission from McQuirk at the Shakespeare Tavern in Covent Garden (O.B. *Proceedings*, 1769, p. 69). For sworn affidavits to a similar effect by three Irish chairmen — Boyce, Davies and Wheeler — see *Ox. Mag.* i. 240

[4] *Letters*, v. 140.

evidently the arrangement of an experienced sergeant. The rest of these banditti were stationed in different quarters of the town, to strike a general terror into the honest part of the freeholders; there were besides a corps de reserve which was to sally forth on a sign given.

When these dispositions were secured, a chosen party of butchers, in the same interest, traversed the town, and insulted the hustings with marrow-bones and cleavers.[1]

The proceedings seem, however, to have been relatively peaceful until two o'clock when, at a given signal, a band of twenty-five to thirty persons, armed with bludgeons and bearing the device 'Liberty and Proctor' in their hats, appeared from the direction of the Castle Inn and drove the startled freeholders from the hustings.[2] 'The sheriffs, the candidates, the clerks and the poll-books,' added the *Oxford Magazine*, 'all vanished in a moment.' The poll was suspended by the sheriffs and the books removed for examination to the Crown and Anchor Tavern in the Strand; at this stage, Glynn was leading by 147 votes. Meanwhile, the Brentford riots continued till nightfall, when 'the inhabitants of the town', moved 'by a general indignation', and doubtless fearing for the safety of their property, 'sallied out, attacked the rioters with great spirit, and drove them out of the town'.[3] Further clashes between Glynn's and Proctor's supporters followed in Covent Garden and at the Angel, Islington.[4] The poll was resumed in good order five days later and, on Wednesday, 14 December, Glynn was declared elected with 1,542 votes against his opponent's 1,278. The usual round of illuminations followed in the Strand and City to celebrate another Wilkite victory.[5]

Some of the more lurid accounts of the bloodthirsty behaviour of the Irish chairmen and other hired ruffians must no doubt be taken with a pinch of salt — as, for example, the report in the *Reading Mercury* that, on the night of 8 December,

as a linen-draper at Hammersmith was standing at his door, with his children, to see the company return from Brentford, the mob of Irish chairmen came by and attacked him with their sticks, beat out his brains, and he fell over the children, dead in his own shop.[6]

[1] *Ox. Mag.*, i. 238–9. See also *Ox. J.*, 17 Dec. 1768; *Read. Merc.*, 12 Dec. 1768; and Grego, op. cit., pp. 178–89.

[2] At the subsequent Old Bailey trial it was admitted by some of Proctor's witnesses that the 'desperate sort of ruffians' that caused the disturbance wore this insignia, though it was claimed that they did so to incriminate Proctor and that they shouted 'Glynn for ever!' (O.B. *Proceedings*, 1769, pp. 66–84, 87–100).

[3] *Ox. Mag.*, i. 238–9.

[4] Ibid. i. 240; Harris to Hardwicke, 9 Dec. 1768, Add. MSS. 35608, f. 303.

[5] *Gent's Mag.*, 1768, p. 587.

[6] *Read. Merc.*, 12 Dec. 1768.

Nevertheless, at least one death followed the disturbances — that of George Clarke, a young Wilkite lawyer, who died from head wounds received in the course of the fighting at Brentford. Proceedings were opened against two of the Irish chairmen, Lawrence Balfe and Edward McQuirk — both for causing Clarke's death and for assaulting 'one William Beale' and Samuel Clay, a High Constable of the Hundred of Ossulston. They came up for trial at the Old Bailey on the former count in January 1769, and the jury, having heard the case debated at length, took only twenty minutes to find them guilty of murder.[1] They were sentenced to death but, after a number of respites, the case was allowed to drop.[2] The atmosphere of suspicion engendered by this affair may well have contributed to Wilkes's first electoral success in the City of London, when, on 27 January, at a Wardmote Court held in the parish church of St. Bride's, he was returned unopposed as alderman of the ward of Farringdon Without.[3]

It was at about this time that, urged by John Horne, some of Wilkes's wealthy and influential friends in Southwark, Middlesex and the City of London decided to appeal to a wider public to contribute to the payment of his political expenses and outstanding debts. After numerous preliminary meetings called in his support by Westminster and Middlesex freeholders, the Society of the Supporters of the Bill of Rights was formed at a meeting at the London Tavern in Bishopsgate Street on 20 February. Among its founders were such prominent public figures and men of wealth as Alderman John Sawbridge, M.P. for Hythe; James Townsend, M.P. for West Looe; Richard Oliver, later M.P. for London; Sir Joseph Mawbey, malt-distiller and M.P. for Southwark; Sir Cecil Wray Bart., M.P. for East Retford; and Samuel Vaughan, merchant of Mincing Lane.[4] The Society's published objects were 'to defend and maintain the legal, constitutional liberty of the subject'

[1] Middlesex R.O., Process Register Bks. of Indictments, xvii (1761–69), 837–8; Sessions Rolls (Middlesex), no. 3211 [(a)], 9 Jan. 1769; O.B. *Proceedings*, 1769, pp. 66–84, 87–100.

[2] *Gent's Mag.*, 1769, pp. 53, 166–7, 212, 269; R. Wood to Hardwicke, no date, Add. MSS. 35608, f. 352.

[3] Guild. Lib., St. Bride's Fleet Street, Vestry Minute Book, 1767–1810, MS. 6554/6, pp. 32–34; St. Dunstan in the West, Wardmote Inquest, 1558–1823, MS. 3081/1, pp. 253–4.

[4] For further details, see my article in *The Guildhall Miscellany*, no. 8, July 1957, pp. 20–21, and chapter IX below. For other members of the Society, see Lucy S. Sutherland, *The City of London and the Opposition to Government, 1768–1774*, pp. 19–20, 20 n. 1.

and to support 'Mr. Wilkes and his cause'. These wider aims were to find expression in the political campaign conducted over the Middlesex election issue a few months later;[1] but the more immediate purpose was to raise money to settle 'Mr. Wilkes's affairs' and, on 7 March, it was decided 'that £300 be sent to Mr. Wilkes for his immediate use'. This was only a first instalment, soon to be followed by an annuity of £1,000, and, eventually, before winding up its business in April 1770, the Society had raised and paid out on Wilkes's behalf some £20,000, or two-thirds of his outstanding debts.[2]

It was no doubt in direct response to the early activities of the Society that City 'loyalists', led by Charles Dingley, decided to organize an address to the King. The first meeting called to launch this ill-starred venture was held at the King's Arms Tavern in Cornhill on 1 March; City merchants, tradesmen, stockbrokers and other inhabitants were invited to attend on payment of an entrance fee of 1s. A draft address was produced and signatures invited.[3] When several 'considerable merchants' refused to sign they were asked to leave the hall, but declined. Pandemonium broke loose in the course of which Samuel Vaughan, a Wilkite merchant, was voted into the chair after John Reynolds, a Wilkite attorney, had floored Charles Dingley, who attacked him, with a blow in the face. 'It is extraordinary,' observed the *St. James's Chronicle*, in reporting this incident, 'that the first disorder or indecency that has happened at these meetings should be committed by the gentlemen who exclaim so loudly against Riot and Tumult; and that they should come armed with sticks for the sake of Quiet, and give blows to keep the Peace.' A week later, a counter-meeting called by Vaughan and his supporters, and attended by 300 merchants, deplored the 'arbitrary' and 'factious' behaviour of Dingley and his associates. Nevertheless, the 'loyalists' were able to muster nearly 600 signatures for their address and decided to go ahead.[4]

[1] See pp. 108 ff. below.

[2] *Ann. Reg.*, 1769, pp. 74–75, 79; Postgate, pp. 162–4; Bleackley, pp. 240–2.

[3] The address, as finally adopted, ended: '. . . and we beg leave to express our concern and abhorrence of every attempt to spread sedition, to inflame the minds, and alienate the affections of a free and loyal people from the best of Kings and his Government, which we apprehend has of late been encouraged, without the least shadow of foundation, by some ill-designing persons to answer sinister and selfish purposes' (*St. James's Chronicle*, 21–23 March 1769).

[4] Ibid. 9–11, 16–18 March 1769.

In publishing the names of 576 signatories in a subsequent series of 'Black Lists', the *Middlesex Journal* interspersed among the occupations of linen-draper, merchant, watchmaker, soap-manufacturer and other tradesmen that formed the bulk of the addressers such prejudicial labels and epithets as 'fictitious', 'can't be found', 'a Scotch peddlar', 'a Spaniard resident in England' and 'a Popish recusant': all this, of course, was part of the political game.[1] The signatories, or a part of them, formed, none the less, a substantial and solid body of City opinion that Wilkes and the radicals, including the men of wealth and substance among them, were never able to win over even at the height of their electoral influence. Besides Dingley himself, who was of no particular account, they included Chauncy Townsend, father of the radical James Townsend, a government contractor and former Member for Westbury;[2] Lewis Chauvet, wealthy textile merchant and manufacturer of Crispin Street, Spitalfields;[3] Nathaniel Bishop, Proctor of Doctors' Commons; Edward Elcott, Commissioner of Trade; eight directors of the East India Company, including two M.P.s; a Governor and two directors of the Bank of England; a director of the South Sea Company; a director of London Assurance, and the Secretary and two directors of the Royal Exchange Assurance Company.[4]

Yet, whatever their solidity and substance in the world of trade and finance, they cut a sorry figure as political petitioners. Of the 130 that set out in their coaches on the morning of 22 March, a mere mud-bespattered dozen got through with their address to St. James's Palace,[5] for Wilkes's supporters had chosen the moment to stage a counter-demonstration of considerable scope and violence in the streets of London and Westminster. The merchants' cavalcade, reported the *Annual Register*,

[1] *Middlesex Journal*, nos. 18–28 (11 May to 3–6 June 1769).

[2] J. Brooke, *The Chatham Administration*, pp. 251, 358 n. 3.

[3] See pp. 101–2 below.

[4] These directors etc. were as follows: *E.I.C.* Henry Crabb Boulton (M.P. for Worcester), John Stephenson (M.P. for St. Michael), Robert James, Luke Scrafton, John Harrison, John Woodhouse, John Pardoe, William James; *Bank of England.* Matthew Clarmont (Governor), James Sperling, Benjamin Hopkins; *South Sea Co.* G. Girardot; *London Assurance.* A. Mellor; *Royal Exchange Assurance Co.* J. Bell (Secretary), Christopher Puller, P. J. Fremeaux.

Benjamin Hopkins had a freehold in Finchley assessed at £20 p.a., voted for Proctor against Glynn in December 1768, became M.P. for Great Bedwin in 1771 and alderman for Broad Street in 1773, and was elected City Chamberlain in preference to Wilkes in 1776.

[5] Duke of Chandos to G. Grenville, 23 March 1769, *Grenville Papers*, iv. 417.

[was] interrupted by a desperate mob on passing through the City, who insulted, pelted and maltreated the principal conductors, so that several coaches were obliged to withdraw, some to return back, others to proceed by bye-ways, and those who arrived at St. James's were so daubed with dirt, and shattered, that both masters and drivers were in the utmost peril of their lives.[1]

Among the other eyewitness accounts of this colourful event[2] none is more vivid, more detailed and more humorous than that sent by Mrs. Harris to her son, the future first Earl of Malmesbury, at Madrid:[3]

About noon [she wrote], a hearse attended by an immense Mob came down Pall Mall;[4] the hearse was decorated with prints and two pictures, one of which represented the killing of Allen in St. George's Fields, the other the killing of Clarke in the riot at Brentford; it was drawn by one black, and one white horse, the coachman dressed in black, with a fur cap and and a quantity of blue ribbon. This hearse, amid the acclamation of the mob, went close to Palace Gate, and then up St. James's Street. It had taken its place just before the procession of merchants,[5] who came up with their address, and who, when they arrived, appear to have been pelted with dirt and stones, all their glasses and many wooden blinds broken in, the coachman and footmen covered with dirt as well as the masters. The same insults continued when the merchants alighted; on which a party of Grenadiers were placed at the gate of St. James's, Lord Talbot as Lord Steward with his staff, Lord Despencer and some others of the Court came down and assisted the merchants and kept off the rabble, advancing some paces before the gate for that purpose. One rioter was seized by Justice Walsh,[6] but was soon rescued by his friends and carried off in triumph. One coach with the addressers was stopped, not being allowed to put down company. The Duke of Northumberland was severely pelted, as he went back to the Palace;[7] the ammunition of these rioters consisted chiefly of dirt, but many stones were seen to be thrown, and one glass bottle. The Riot Act was read without any effect, Lord Talbot harangued at the gate, one Mr. Whitworth (not Sir Charles) was haranguing from St. James's coffee-house, and a drunken woman in a third place: they each had their

[1] *Ann. Reg.*, 1769, p. 84. This account is quoted in full by S. Maccoby, *English Radicalism 1762–1785* (1955), p. 114.

[2] See also Walpole's *Letters*, v. 148–9, 151; Chandos to Grenville, 23 March 1769, *Grenville Papers*, iv. 415–17; Whately to Grenville, 25 March 1769, ibid. iv. 417–18; *Gent's Mag.*, 1769, pp. 165–6, 210; Grego, op. cit., pp. 202–6.

[3] Mrs. Harris to Jas. Harris junr., 24 March 1769, *Letters of the First Earl of Malmesbury*, i. 176–9.

[4] According to Chandos, 'the mob' first assembled at the King's Bench prison (Chandos to Grenville, loc. cit.).

[5] In the Strand (*Ann. Reg.*, 1769, p. 84).

[6] Presumably Saunders Welch, J.P.

[7] Chandos adds: 'The Dukes of Kingston and Northumberland had their chariots broke to pieces.'

audiences, but the Wilkism and obscenity of the woman proved the greatest attraction. The tumult still continued at its height, when from the Palace Yard issued the Horse Guards and Horse Grenadiers, with their swords drawn, and commanded by three officers. The rabble, whose spirit of mischief is only equalled by their timidity, immediately retired and left a large vacancy before the Palace. The Horse formed into two fronts, one up St. James's Street, the other up Pall Mall; soon after the Horse came, several rioters were seized and carried into custody.

During this period all the shops in the neighbourhood were shut. The merchants, when they got to St. James's, could not find their address. The gates of Temple Bar having been shut against them, a most infamous riot took place there. Mr. Boheme, the chairman, was insulted and forced to quit his coach, and got into a coffee-house; in the bustle he left the address in the coach, which was carried back to his coach-house; this was made known to His Majesty, who said he *would wait for it, if it was till the next day*. At last, I believe, it was brought privately by water from Whitehall; it was four o'clock before it could be presented. The Guards patrolled the streets that afternoon and evening. It was said that, amongst the mob, there were men of better appearance, supposed to be their leaders, but this is not certain.

Your father was in St. James's coffee-house all the morning, so saw the whole. Your sisters and I were at Clapham in the morning, and came down to Pall Mall in the midst of the mob. We let down our glasses, they cried Wilkes and Liberty enough to us, but did not insist on our joining them, so we got safe home, though I was a great deal flurried at the time. Many of the mob cried Wilkes, and no King,[1] which is shocking to think on.

'Tis reported some of these rioters are sent to Newgate, and that seventeen are taken.

Of the prisoners five only came up for trial; they included a bottle-merchant of Thomas Street, London, and a shoemaker and three 'labourers' of St. James's.[2] Their indictments read

that they unlawfully, riotously, routously and tumultuously did assemble & meet together to disturb the peace of the said Lord the King before the Palace, or usual place of residence of our said Lord the King, commonly called Saint James's Palace.

These, too, were discharged by a Grand Jury meeting, a week later, at the New Guildhall, Westminster[3] — a decision that infuriated George III who, on hearing the news, wrote angry notes to Lord North demanding an inquiry; he roundly condemned the 'partial conduct' of the jury and added:

[1] 'Some had the impudence to sing *God save great Wilkes, our King*' (Chandos).

[2] See Appendix XI.

[3] Middlesex R.O., Sessions Rolls (Westminster), no. 3212, 28 March 1769; Whately to Grenville, 30 March 1769, *Grenville Papers*, iv. 419–20; T.S. 11/443-1408.

It therefore behoves every honest man with vigour to stand forth . . . I am ready to take any forward path that the present crisis may require & I trust that every man not absorbed in Faction will now firmly unite to crush this Party that aim at the very vitals of all Government.[1]

The King's feelings on the matter were no doubt shared by those witnesses of the riotous events of 22 March who, standing at the Palace gates, had talked of 'authority and licentiousness' and argued 'that absolute government was better than mob government'.[2] They were echoed, too, in the spate of loyal messages and addresses, deploring the insult to the King and condemning the practices of Wilkite rioters and the Bill of Rights Society, that came pouring into the Palace: one journal reported the reception of such addresses from Coventry, Norwich, Lancaster, Linlithgowshire, the freeholders of Haddington and the Chancellor and professors of the University of St. Andrews.[3]

In the meantime, the Commons had at last taken the bull by the horns and expelled Wilkes from his seat in Parliament. It was certainly not the outcome of any sudden impulse: it had been on the agenda of Cabinet discussion almost since the day of his election for Middlesex. By 20 April of the previous year, the Cabinet appear to have reached a decision;[4] on the 22nd, the Duke of Grafton reported to the King 'the desire of His Majesty's principal servants jointly expressed that Mr. Wilkes should not be allowed to sit in Parliament if it could be avoided by any means justifiable by law and the Constitution & conformable to the proceedings of Parliament'.[5] The King, for his part, entered into the business with enthusiasm and wrote to Lord North on the 25th: 'I think it highly proper to apprize you that the expulsion of Mr. Wilkes appears to be very essential and must be effected.'[6] Further meetings of government supporters favoured the project, though some doubts remained as to the grounds on which the expulsion should be urged: should it be on the grounds of Wilkes's outlawry (which the courts were expected to reverse) or on those of the two old misdemeanours for which he had already been expelled? Meanwhile, the government's intentions had spread abroad and,

[1] The King to North, 31 March 1769, Fortescue, ii. nos. 706–7.
[2] Whately to Grenville, *Grenville Papers*, iv. 417–18.
[3] *Read. Merc.*, 27 March 1769.
[4] Camden to Grafton, 20 April 1768, Grafton, *Autobiography*, pp. 200–1; cit. J. Brooke, op. cit., p. 354
[5] Grafton to the King, 22 April 1768, Fortescue, ii. no. 612.
[6] The King to North, 25 April 1768, Fortescue, ii. no. 613.

on 30 April, Wilkes's old friends in Aylesbury wrote to their two Members, John Durand and Anthony Bacon, urging them, 'should an attempt be made to deprive him of his seat in Parliament', to use their 'utmost endeavour to prevent the success of such a measure'. The letter was signed by John Dell, John Stephens, Robert Neale, Henry Sheriff and thirty other townsmen.[1]

When Parliament reassembled for a short session in May, Wilkes's outlawry had not yet been reversed and public business was largely taken up with measures to repress disorder following the riots in Southwark and the City. Attempts by Sir Gilbert Elliot and the Duke of Bedford's supporters to force an early decision were resisted by the majority and the matter was left over till the winter.[2] By this time, a new pretext for Wilkes's expulsion had arisen in the shape of his violent denunciation of Lord Barrington's congratulatory message to the troops that had fired in St. George's Fields. George III took up the cudgels with renewed vigour and, on 27 January, in a letter to Lord Hertford, hoped that his sons would

> support the measure, for I should be sorry that anyone could say that in a measure whereon almost my Crown depends, his family should not have taken an active part.[3]

The measure was duly carried and, to the King's intense satisfaction, Wilkes was declared expelled from Parliament on 3 February by 219 votes to 137.[4]

The expulsion was met with riots in Drury Lane, 'where a number of persons riotously assembled' and pulled down some old houses, before being dispersed by the Guards summoned by the Westminster peace officers.[5] But far more significant was the effect the 'measure' had on the Middlesex freeholders, 2,000 or more of whom promptly readopted Wilkes as their candidate for the next election.[6] There followed in quick succession his unopposed return on 16 February; his further disqualification by the Commons on the 17th; his second unopposed election, after the

[1] *Brist. J.*, 14 May 1768; Gibbs, *A History of Aylesbury*, p. 232.
[2] Brooke, op. cit., pp. 354–60.
[3] The King to Hertford, 27 Jan. 1769, Fortescue, ii. no. 693.
[4] Fortescue, ii. nos. 696–8; Harris to Hardwicke, various reports: 23 Jan.–10 Feb. 1769, Add. MSS. 35608, ff. 328–36. The names of the minority (including 2 tellers) of 139 gentlemen, 'whose healths . . . are drank in most public companies, being enemies to oppression and friends to the Liberties of Englishmen', appear in *Ox. Mag.*, ii. 97–98.
[5] *Gent's Mag.* 1769, p. 106.
[6] *Ann. Reg.*, 1769, pp. 74–75; Maccoby, op. cit., p. 105.

withdrawal of Charles Dingley (who failed to find a nominator at the hustings) on 16 March; its annulment by Parliament on the 17th; and Wilkes's further readoption by the Middlesex electors on the 20th.[1]

A short lull followed, while the Court selected and briefly groomed a candidate who might be relied upon not only to seek nomination, but to stand for election against Wilkes in Middlesex. The chosen candidate was Henry Lawes Luttrell, son of Lord Irnham and a young army colonel of the lowest reputation; he resigned his seat, the pocket borough of Bossiny in Cornwall, to take on the assignment. Two further candidates came forward, Serjeant William Whitaker, who had vague hopes of gaining the support of the Rockinghamite opposition, and a swashbuckling captain, David Roach, who may have been put up to it by Wilkes's own friends in order to split the vote of the official Court candidate. But, to all intents and purposes, it was a straight contest between Luttrell and Wilkes — between the Court party and the rising force of radicalism.[2]

The poll opened at Brentford on 13 April at eleven in the morning. Urged by Lord Weymouth, who feared a repetition of the riots of three weeks before, Sir John Fielding had made ample provision to guard against another round of disorders. The Middlesex justices were to accompany Sir John himself to Brentford; their Westminster colleagues were to assemble at the Guildhall; the constables were variously assigned — some to Hyde Park Corner, others to St. James's Street to watch the Palace, others again to the Haymarket, to Charing Cross, to Buckingham Gate and the Westminster Guildhall. The High Constable was to parade on horseback, make a round of inspection and report back to the Westminster justices who would, in turn, report proceedings to the Treasury. In the evening, the justices would be dispersed between the Guildhall and St. James's Palace, while the constables would man the Round Houses of their respective parishes. Meanwhile, parties of Grenadier and Horse Guards would patrol the different parts of the capital and, in case of riots, would report to the magistrates at the Guildhall and the Palace.[3]

[1] *Gent's Mag.*, 1769, pp. 108, 165; J. Harris to Hardwicke, 17 March 1769, Add. MSS. 35608, f. 348.

[2] See p. 78 below.

[3] Sir John Fielding to William Fraser (secretary to Lord Weymouth), 13 April 1769, S.P. Dom., Entry Bks., 44/142, pp. 201–2; William Fraser to Fielding, ibid., pp. 202–3.

In the event, the precautions proved to be more than sufficient to cope with the minor disturbances that attended the election. Wilkes's supporters formed themselves into various cavalcades that paraded peacefully through the streets of London before proceeding to Brentford to cast their votes. One of these 'set out from the Prince of Orange in Jermyn Street, before whom were carried 6 or 7 flags (Bill of Rights, Magna Carta etc.), all badges of the different societies of which Mr. Wilkes had been made a member'. Another 'great body of freeholders'

> preceded by a band of music, with colours flying, marched along Pall Mall, and stopped fronting the Palace, where they gave 3 loud huzzas, and the music began to play. This alarmed the Guards, who marched out of the gate with their bayonets fixed; but the company marched on peaceably for Brentford, and the soldiers returned into barracks.

A third party, composed of three hundred horsemen, started out, with music playing and colours flying, from Poplar, Mile End and other 'out'-parishes, joined up with a further contingent at the London Tavern in Bishopsgate Street, and rode to Brentford via the Old Bailey and Fleet Street, some stopping on the way to 'hail' Charles Dingley at the Royal Exchange, others to serenade the Lord Mayor at the Mansion House — and all this 'amidst the acclamations of a vast concourse of people, who expressed their wishes that their choice this time might be final'. That day, it was reported, 'the publicans all the way from Knightsbridge to Brentford sold their beer at 3d. per pot, which they said was in honour of Mr. Wilkes', while one enterprising publican of Fleet Street, 'known by the title of Lord Mills', rode to Brentford in a coach and six with flags displayed and accompanied by a large covered waggon carrying forty-five persons to the hustings.[1] Meanwhile, Serjeant Whitaker had failed to turn up at Brentford, being detained by legal business at Westminster Hall.[2] Captain Roach made a brief appearance, but withdrew, after some arguments with the sheriffs, at midday.[3] Luttrell was held up at Grosvenor Gate in Hyde Park as he rode to the Butts, was pelted by 'the mob' and had his hat knocked off; at Brentford, he only got through to the hustings by the courtesy of Wilkes' supporters:

[1] *Ox. Mag.*, ii. 155–7; *Mid. J.*, 13–15 April 1769; *Read. Merc.*, 17 April 1769.
[2] J. Claxton to Sir William Lee Bart., 13 April 1769, Bucks R.O., Sir William Lee Correspondence.
[3] According to the *Mid. J.*, it was due to a dispute over his qualifications (loc. cit.)

Horne, Beckford and Townsend formed a bodyguard to hustle him through hostile crowds.[1] But the election itself was peaceful enough. The poll closed at 3.30 in the afternoon and Wilkes was declared returned, for the fourth time, with 1,143 votes against Luttrell's 296; Whitaker received five votes and Roach none. The result was hailed with illuminations and the ringing of church bells, while

> a number of horsemen . . . attended by several thousand people went through St. James's Street, the Strand and over London Bridge to the King's Bench, to congratulate Mr. Wilkes on his success.[2]

To the majority in the House of Commons, however, this marked and repeated display of popular favour was no argument for reversing their previous decisions regarding Wilkes. On 15 April, George Onslow, who had become one of Wilkes's most implacable opponents, moved that Luttrell be admitted. And so, 'after a long and tedious debate', with 'the Lobby full of dirty people',[3] it was resolved in an historic and provocative phrase, by 197 to 143 votes, 'that Henry Lawes Luttrell Esq. ought to have been returned a member for Middlesex and not John Wilkes Esq'.[4] George III was delighted and wrote to thank Lord North for his 'spirit and good conduct . . . during the whole of this unpleasant business';[5] but it was by no means the end of the affair. The very same day, the King was expressing alarm at protest meetings being held by Middlesex freeholders at the London Tavern and the Mile End Assembly Room and calling for a record to be kept of resolutions passed and 'of those who are the most active in framing them'.[6] On 17 April, the number of freeholders attending the main

[1] J. Claxton to Sir Wm. Lee Bart., 13 April 1769; *Ox. Mag.*, ii. 156.

[2] Ibid.; *Gent's Mag.*, 1769, pp. 212–13. *The Middlesex Journal* noted that, this time, Wilkes's own 'particular friends' abstained from voting 'so that the election was the free and genuine desire of the people'; also that the joyful celebrations that followed were greater than ever before, 'because [it might be presumed] the people of Middlesex now look upon the gaining of such an election as carrying their own cause more than that of Mr. Wilkes' (loc. cit.).

[3] Harris to Hardwicke, 15 April 1769, Add. MSS. 35608, f. 358.

[4] Lists of voters in this division — both of the 197 'who preferred 296 to 1143' and of the 143 'who voted 1143 in preference to 296' — appear in the *Ox. Mag.*, ii. 183–4, 184–7; *The North Briton*, 6 May; and the *Mid. J.*, 4, 6, 9 May 1769. The *Ox. Mag.* notes, in addition, the placemen among the majority (pp. 184–7). For the Middlesex voters among these, see p. 77 n. 4, below.

[5] The King to North, 16 April 1769, Fortescue, ii. no. 711.

[6] The King to Lord Rochford, 16 April 1769, ibid., no. 709.

meeting at Mile End had risen to 1,750 — one report said 2,500 — with a further 5,000 people gathered in the road outside. Sawbridge presided, James Townsend spoke and, on 'Parson' Horne's proposal, it was decided to set up a committee of a hundred freeholders, with Walpole Eyre as chairman and George Bellas as deputy, to prepare a Bill of Grievances and Apprehensions for submission to Parliament.[1] Further popular demonstrations followed. On 20 April, Wilkes was escorted from the King's Bench prison to Lord Mansfield's chambers in Serjeant's Inn to surrender his bail to a number of civil actions that had been brought against him. As he emerged into Chancery Lane after the interview, crowds followed him into the Strand 'with loud huzzas', and 'at St. Clement's Church they took the horses from the coach in order to draw it themselves'; to escape their attentions (it was almost a repetition of April 1768!), he had to take refuge in the Crown and Anchor Tavern and change coaches in Arundel Street near by. The next day, crowds escorted the King to the House of Lords and chanted, as he drove back to St. James's, 'Wilkes for ever, no Luttrell!'[2] Nor were such demonstrations confined to London. On 6 May, when the King and Queen attended the races at Epsom, it was reported that

> a fellow who stood near His Majesty had the audacity to hallow out, 'Wilkes and Liberty for ever!'[3]

Meanwhile, the Middlesex Bill of Grievances and Apprehensions had grown into an immoderate length; and, at a further meeting of freeholders on 27 April at the Mile End Assembly Room, where James Adair presided in the absence of Walpole Eyre, it was decided to present a petition to Parliament. 'Upwards of 500' signed forthwith, and it was agreed that the petition should be presented by Serjeant Glynn, the County Member, attended by nine other gentlemen — including George Bellas, Walpole

[1] *Mid. J.*, 16–18 April 1769; *Ox. Mag.*, ii. 156; *Political Register*, iv. 296. Other meetings were held, on 15 April, at the Swan Tavern at Westminster Bridge and, on 17 April, at the Prince of Orange's Head in Jermyn Street; but these merely endorsed the decisions taken at Mile End (*Mid. J.*, 18–20 April 1769).

Walpole Eyre owned land in Marylebone; George Bellas, one of Wilkes's most active City supporters, was a liveryman of the Carpenters' Guild, a Common Council man, Proctor of the Admiralty Court, and owned a freehold in St. Margaret's Westminster. Both voted for Wilkes or Glynn in the three Middlesex contests of 1768–69.

[2] *Ox. Mag.*, ii. 157.

[3] *Gent's Mag.*, 1769, p. 268.

Eyre, John Sawbridge and James Townsend.[1] This plan, however, appears to have been modified after discussions with the Rockingham Whigs — probably through the intermediary of James Adair, the acting chairman of the freeholders' committee. The final form of the petition was drafted by Rockingham himself after consulting with Edmund Burke and Dowdeswell; it was confined to a protest against the admission of Luttrell in the place of Wilkes and was presented to the Commons on 29 April by Sir George Savile, Member for Yorkshire and one of Rockingham's most highly respected supporters.[2] The business was deferred until 8 May, when the Court lawyers' argument was upheld that, in view of the omnicompetence of the House of Commons in matters relating to elections, Wilkes's 'incapacity' to sit in Parliament was legal and beyond challenge,[3] and it was decided, by 221 to 152 votes, 'that Henry Lawes Luttrell is duly elected a Knight of the Shire to serve in the present Parliament for the County of Middlesex'.[4]

The King had insisted that 'with firmness . . . this affair will vanish into smoke'.[5] Yet this first Middlesex petition, though

[1] *Mid. J.*, 27–29 April 1769; *Pol. Reg.*, iv. 298. The five other gentlemen were: James Adair, Recorder of London, with chambers in Lincoln's Inn and a house in Soho Square, an associate of the Marquess of Rockingham; Francis Ayscough, who owned land in Hammersmith; George Prescot, merchant of 10, Coleman Street, and owner of a messuage assessed at £58 p.a. in Enfield; Arnold Wallinger, who owned a messuage and land at North End; and the Rev. Dr. Thomas Wilson, Prebendary of Westminster. Of the ten, neither Glynn nor Wilson appears to have held Middlesex freeholds; George Prescot voted for Proctor in December 1768 and abstained in the two other elections; the rest voted for Wilkes or Glynn in at least two of the three Middlesex contests. One should perhaps only look on three of the ten — Bellas, Glynn and Wilson — as firm Wilkites.

[2] Sheffield Central Lib., Wentworth Woodhouse MSS., R 87 1 (1–2); Earl of Albemarle, *Memoirs of the Marquis of Rockingham* (2 vols. 1852), ii. 110. For a discussion of this incident, see Appendix II.

[3] 'The lawyers for the Court,' wrote Edmund Burke to the Earl of Charlemont on 9 May, 'were, as they have generally been for some time past, bold and profligate. The chief arguments that they insisted upon were that when a court having competent jurisdiction in a cause has determined its determination is the law of the land, until it is reversed; that we had already determined this point; it was therefore against order to debate it again; and against law to contradict the determination of a court from whence no appeal lay' (Burke to Earl of Charlemont, [9] May 1769, *Burke Correspondence*, ii. 23). Luttrell himself had earlier, in a maiden speech, used the even more specious argument 'that 1143 voters out of above 4,000' had no right to claim to be a majority! (*Mid. J.*, 22–25 April 1769.)

[4] *Commons Journals*, xxxii (1769), 447, 451.

[5] The King to Rochford, 16 April 1769, Fortescue, ii. no. 709. It is true that he added: ' . . . but if this is omitted no one can answer to what lengths Faction may not go'.

quickly disposed of, was but the opening shot in a prolonged political conflict over the rights of electors – a conflict that was only resolved when the motion first declaring Wilkes's 'incapacity' was, thirteen years later, expunged from the Journals of the House of Commons.[1]

[1] This was the resolution of 17 February 1769, which declared Wilkes 'incapable of being elected a Member of the present Parliament'.

V

THE MIDDLESEX ELECTORS

Up to now, we have seen something of the political behaviour of the Middlesex freeholders — how they voted in three consecutive contested elections, and how they acclaimed Wilkes's victories at the polls, and prepared to protest against his exclusion from Parliament and against the Commons' decision to admit Luttrell in his place as the Member that 'ought to have been returned'. We have seen, too, that considerable numbers of freeholders became involved in these activities: that the votes cast for Wilkite candidates in these elections ranged from 1,143 in April 1769 to 1,542 in December 1768; that over 2,000 voted to readopt Wilkes after his exclusion from the Commons in February 1769; and that a number variously estimated at 1,750 and 2,500 voted, in the following April, for measures that led to a protest petition to Parliament.[1] These are impressive figures when it is realized that the number of freeholders entitled to vote — that is, those owning freeholds of an annual value of 40s. — probably did not exceed 3,500 to 4,000.[2]

So far, so good; but the reader is still left with only the most general impression of the political sentiments of the Middlesex electors. We know that in each of three consecutive elections they returned Wilkes or a Wilkite candidate with a substantial majority; but did these majorities reflect a consistent pattern of radical opinion, or were they arrived at by a more or less fortuitous addition of votes? Were they evenly distributed over the county as a whole, or did certain parishes, or groups of parishes, prove to be more Wilkite in tendency than others? When Wilkes presented himself for election in Middlesex for the first time, a newspaper commented:

[1] See pp. 42, 60, 70, 71 above.

[2] Contemporary estimates ranged from 'between 2,000 and 3,000' (*St. James's Chronicle*, 24–26 March 1768) and Luttrell's 'over 4,000' (see p. 70, n. 72 above). The first is too low while it paid Luttrell at the time, in support of his argument, to inflate the number. In fact, a little under 3,500 names appear in the Poll Books for the three contested elections of 1768–69 and some allowance must be made for abstentions.

The talk is that Mr. Wilkes is sure of a very extensive interest in the Eastern Division of the County of Middlesex and which alone contains, it is said, considerably more than one third of the electors.[1]

Was this forecast to prove correct? Were the urban parts of the county (including this 'Eastern Division') more Wilkite than the rural? Did the larger freeholders or more prosperous voters, or the clergy and office holders, tend to vote for Proctor or Luttrell rather than for Wilkes or Glynn? Among what sort of freeholders — the *larger*, the '*middling*', or the *lesser* — did Wilkes find his most consistent support? Such questions have their importance both for the study of Wilkes himself and for that of his supporters and opponents; yet they have never been seriously considered by historians. In this chapter, some attempt will be made to answer them — mainly with the aid of the Middlesex Poll Books for 1768–69,[2] the Freeholders' Book,[3] and the Land Tax assessments or Poor Rate Books for the period.[4]

To answer the first question — how far these majorities reflected a more or less consistent pattern of political opinion — we must consider the elections both individually and collectively.[5] In those of December 1768 and April 1769 there is no special problem, as, in each case, there were, for practical purposes, only two candidates contesting for a single seat — Glynn and Proctor in the first and Wilkes and Luttrell in the second. In the General Election of March 1768, the picture is not so simple, as there were three candidates — Proctor, Cooke and Wilkes — contesting for two seats. Nevertheless, the pattern of voting is fairly consistent throughout: those voting for Proctor had a strong tendency to vote for Cooke and those voting for Wilkes, while they might in some cases vote for Cooke (who enjoyed the Duke of Newcastle's favour), very rarely voted for Proctor. Though to Wilkes's supporters Cooke might appear as a less obnoxious candidate than Proctor, who is constantly labelled a 'courtier', he was a junior Minister in Lord Chatham's administration, and the pattern of

[1] *St. James's Chronicle*, loc. cit. It added: 'It is certain that Mr. Cooke, in his former strong contest with Mr. Honeywood, greatly availed himself of *this numerous body of little freeholders*.' (My italics.)

[2] Middlesex R.O., Middlesex Poll Books, 1768–69 (undated transcript in 1 volume).

[3] Middlesex R.O., Freeholders' Book, no. 12, 1767–71.

[4] I have consulted some 50 Land Tax assessments and Poor Rate Books in respect of 44 Middlesex parishes. For details of these, see my article, 'The Middlesex Electors of 1768–1769', *The English Historical Review*, Oct. 1960, pp. 601–17, which this chapter in large part reproduces.

[5] For what follows, see Middlesex Poll Books.

voting suggests that he was more frequently seen as a 'running partner' for Proctor than as a more or less neutral third party — still less, of course, as a suitable team-mate for Wilkes. Yet, even so, by taking the elections in isolation from one another, we cannot be certain whether electors in voting for a candidate were drawn to support him by virtue of his personal qualities or known record of public service, or by virtue of the political principles that he was believed to represent. It is only by comparing the votes of the same electors in three consecutive elections, when confronted with a different set of candidates, that we can begin to see whether there is, in fact, a clear-cut division between those voting Proctor-Cooke-Luttrell on the one hand and those voting Wilkes-Glynn on the other.

At first sight, this is not so evident. On the one hand, we find Glynn polling considerably more votes than Wilkes: whereas Wilkes polled 1,292 votes in March 1768 and 1,143 votes in April 1769, Glynn polled no less than 1,542 votes in December 1768, when the number of voters was said to exceed by forty-two 'the greatest number ever known to poll at any previous election'.[1] This can no doubt be largely accounted for by the particular circumstances of the election which also increased Proctor's poll far above that of the three-cornered contest of March 1768; but a study of the Poll Books also reveals that Glynn had a following of his own, and one that was considerably greater than that of Wilkes himself, not only in the Inns of Court — where it might be expected — but in Kensington, St. Luke Old Street and the parishes of Westminster.[2] This discrepancy, however, is quite insignificant when contrasted with the failure of Proctor's supporters of March and December to muster in support of Luttrell in the following April: whereas Proctor polled 807 votes in March (when he shared the anti-Wilkite poll with Cooke) and 1,248 votes in December, Luttrell received a mere 296 votes in April 1769. In fact, as a candidate of somewhat doubtful repute and one who had so clearly been imported — and at such short notice — to

[1] Grego, *A History of Parliamentary Elections*, p. 184. The combined votes of the two candidates amounted, on this occasion, to 2,820, compared with 1,439 in April 1769 and 2,926 (for three candidates contesting for two seats) in March 1768.

[2] In these places, the comparative figures were: *Inns of Court* — Glynn, 53; Wilkes, 18 and 15. *Kensington* — Glynn, 29; Wilkes, 20 and 14. *Westminster* (all parishes) — Glynn, 233; Wilkes, 152 and 150. *St. Luke Old Street* — Glynn, 90; Wilkes, 60 and 67.

promote a purely Ministerial advantage, he had not been able to build up a sizeable following in any single one of the 160 parishes, liberties and hamlets of the county; in only three places (and these were all parishes of 75 voters or more) did he attract 10 or more votes[1] and his vote only exceeded Proctor's of December 1768 in two tiny hamlets.[2] This reluctance of respectable freeholders, though evidently anti-Wilkite in interest or sympathy, to vote for Luttrell even in a straight contest with Wilkes is perhaps best illustrated by the lukewarm reception given to him by clergymen, Members of Parliament and other persons most likely to rally in support of a Ministerial candidate. Of 30 M.P.s holding freeholds in Middlesex who had voted for Proctor in March or December 1768, only 7 voted for Luttrell on 13 April 1769[3] – and (perhaps even more significant) only 8 of them voted with the majority in Parliament, two days later, for Luttrell's adoption as the lawful Member for the county in the place of Wilkes, while 7 voted in opposition and the rest were absent or abstained.[4] Similarly, of 38 clergymen and ministers voting for Proctor in one or both of the two preceding elections, only 9 voted for Luttrell in his contest with

[1] These were Brentford (16 votes), St. Luke Old Street (15) and St. Margaret Westminster (10).

[2] These were Ascot (Proctor 0, Luttrell 1) and Stanmore (Proctor 2, Luttrell 3).

[3] Only 5 of these voted for Proctor in March (see Appendix VI), but at this election he had not received the Duke of Newcastle's blessing (see p. 58 above).

[4] The 30 freeholder-M.P.s voting for Proctor in one or both of the two previous elections [(?) denotes some doubt as to identification] were:— (?) Edward Bacon (Norwich), Thos. Brand (Oakhampton), Chas. Brett (Lostwithiel), Henry C. Boulton (Worcester), Sir Chas. Bunbury Bart. (Suffolk), George Byng (Wigan), Sir George Colebrooke (Arundel), Sir John Cotton (Cambridgeshire), Sir William Dolben (Northants), John St. L. Douglas (Hindon), John Eames (Newport, Hants), (?)William Fitzherbert (Derby), Sir Thos. Frankland (Thirsk), Lord Gage (Seaford), Philip Jennings (Totnes), Sir Robert Ladbroke (London), Benjamin Lethuillier (Andover), Sir Roger Newdigate (Oxford Univ.), (?)William Plumer (Herts), Isaac M. Rebow (Colchester), Hans Sloane (Newport, Hants), John Stephenson (St. Michael), William Strode (Yarmouth, Hants), Sir Simeon Stuart (Hants), Richard Vernon (Bedford), (?)Nathaniel Webb (Taunton), Samuel Whitbread (Bedford), Robert Wood (Brackley), Hon. Chas. Yorke (Cambridge Univ.), Hon. John Yorke (Reigate).

The 8 voting with the majority in the parliamentary division of 15 April 1769 were: (?)E. Bacon, Sir J. Cotton, Sir W. Dolben, John Douglas, J. Stephenson, Sir S. Stuart, R. Vernon and (?)N. Webb. There were, in addition, 4 placemen voting with the majority who, as freeholders of Middlesex, had voted only for Luttrell: Hon. Charles Fitzroy, vice-chamberlain to the Queen and brother of the Duke of Grafton; Stephen Fox, son of Lord Holland; Sir James Lowther, son-in-law of Lord Bute; and Viscount Palmerston, a Lord of the Admiralty (see *Ox. Mag.*, ii. 184–7).

The 7 voting with the minority were: G. Byng, Sir G. Colebrooke, Sir T. Frankland, P. Jennings, B. Lethuillier, (?) W. Plumer and Hon. John Yorke.

Wilkes; only 19 justices of the peace voted for Luttrell where 55 had voted for Proctor; while not one of 9 Common Council men of the City of London, with freeholds in Middlesex and whose voting record in 1768 suggests that they were supporters of Proctor rather than of Wilkes, thought fit to vote for the new Court candidate in April 1769.[1]

Yet, while such evidence points to the very different degree of support enjoyed among the more 'respectable' freeholders by the two Court candidates in consecutive elections, it does not show any appreciable movement of votes away from the Court candidate to his radical opponent. In the cases just quoted, no single clergyman, one solitary M.P., and only two justices and two Common Council men transferred their vote to Wilkes in the latter election; the rest simply abstained. Taking the voting as a whole and allowing for the divergencies in the pattern that we have noted, there is, in fact, a close concordance among those voting Proctor-Cooke and Luttrell on the one hand and among those voting Wilkes and Glynn on the other. In examining the lists of voters parish by parish we find a remarkable consistency in the voting pattern: those voting Proctor-Cooke in March tend to vote Proctor in December and to vote Luttrell or to abstain in April; similarly, those supporting Wilkes in March tend to support Glynn in December and Glynn again in April. It seems, therefore, reasonable to conclude that a considerable proportion of the voters were perfectly well aware of the issues at stake: the supporters of Administration or of the Newcastle interest voted for Proctor-Cooke, for Luttrell or abstained; those favouring the radical challenge to Administration associated with Wilkes (though not necessarily promoted by him) voted for Wilkes himself or for Serjeant Glynn. There were undoubtedly pockets of private and particular loyalties, but, by and large, these played an altogether secondary part.

While this conclusion appears to be valid for the Middlesex voters as a whole, the radical majority that emerged in all three elections was by no means evenly spread over the numerous parishes, liberties and hamlets of the county. Nor need this surprise us. Unlike the cities of London and Westminster and certain predominantly rural counties, eighteenth-century Middle-

[1] Middlesex R.O., Commission of the Peace, no. 133, 24 Jan. 1769; *Royal Calendar*, 1768.

sex was as lacking in uniformity in its political as in its economic or administrative aspects. No doubt, the county as a whole felt, to a greater or lesser extent, the 'pull' of the metropolis, and the freeholders as a body were remarkably free of any settled county interest.[1] There were, moreover, important electoral links between different parts of the county: thus, several London merchants held freeholds in the 'out'-parishes adjoining the City — though fewer in the rural parishes beyond — and some 500 Westminster freeholders, in these elections at least, exercised their right to vote in Middlesex.[2] Yet the Poll Books for these elections do not bear out the contention that the Middlesex freeholders were at this time 'mostly Londoners living outside the City itself and Westminster'.[3] At any rate, twenty-five years later, in a list of 16,000 London 'inhabitants' (mainly merchants and tradesmen), we find only 300 described as owning freeholds in Middlesex.[4] The view, however, seems to have been held by some contemporaries. Wilkes himself, as we saw, though with perhaps greater optimism than conviction, exhorted the London liverymen, after his General Election defeat in the City, to vote for him at his pending contest in the county 'as freeholders of the County of Middlesex',[5] and a witness of the election that followed actually reported that 'it was remarked that several of the Livery of London who lately voted against Mr. Wilkes at Guildhall were the first to poll in his favour at Brentford'.[6] This may have been strictly true, though it probably did not amount to very much, as only a dozen of the 236 Common Council men and four of the twenty-six Aldermen of 1768 are listed among the county voters of 1768–69.[7] Leaving aside the exceptions that we have noted, the great bulk of the 40s. freeholds in respect of which votes were cast at these elections were

[1] M. Robbins, *Middlesex* (A New Survey of England, 1953), p. 25.

[2] This is a small number compared with the 9,000 or more householders who, at this time, regularly voted for Westminster's own parliamentary candidates (Westminster Poll Books, 1749, 1774, 1780); but Westminster was an area of large and relatively few freeholds.

[3] Robbins, op. cit., p. 99

[4] *The Universal British Directory* (1793), i. 49–347.

[5] *Glos. J.*, 28 March 1768.

[6] Ibid., 4 April 1768. See pp. 41–42 above.

[7] In any case, the press was inclined to exaggerate. In the *Gloucester Journal's* account of the proceedings at Brentford on 28 March 1768 we find, for instance, among those listed as being present at the hustings, the names of William Beckford, Sir George Colebrooke, Sir Richard Glyn, Sir Francis Blake Delaval and Alderman Shakespear (*Glos. J.*, 4 April 1768); and yet we learn from the Poll Books that, in this election, only two of these — Colebrooke and Glyn — voted (in both cases, for Proctor).

distributed, more or less evenly, over two sharply distinct and dissimilar areas — the so-called 'out'-parishes of Middlesex,[1] with their urban concentration, dwelling houses, messuages, warehouses, wharves and tenements straggling along the river to the east of the City or adjoining it to the north, and the more decidedly rural parishes with their scattered hamlets, market towns, grasslands and arable, and unenclosed commons and waste, lying to the north and west of the cities of London and Westminster.[2] As might be expected, there were important variations in the pattern of voting between these two main groups of parishes and between the predominantly urban area (Westminster and the 'out'-parishes combined) and the predominantly rural part of the county in the elections of 1768–69.

Taking the three elections together, the geographical distribution of voters was approximately as follows: Westminster, 14 per cent.; Middlesex 'out'-parishes, 47 per cent.; rural parishes, 39 per cent.[3] Thus the combined urban area accounted for some 61 per cent. of the total vote. We may see how far the votes cast for each candidate within each of the main areas corresponds to or departs from these 'norms' by tabulating votes, candidates and areas as follows:

TABLE I

DISTRIBUTION OF VOTES CAST FOR EACH CANDIDATE IN MAIN AREAS

Candidate	*Westminster*		*'Out'-parishes*		*Rural parishes*	
	(*a*) *Votes*	(*b*) % *Candidate's poll*	(*a*) *Votes*	(*b*) % *Poll*	(*a*) *Votes*	(*b*) % *Poll*
In March 1768						
Proctor	92	11.4	308	38.2	407	50.4
Cooke	92	11.1	301	36.4	434	52.5
Wilkes	152	8.5	681	52.8	459	38.7
In Dec. 1768						
Proctor	170	13.3	534	41.8	574	44.9
Glynn	233	15.5	801	52.0	508	32.5
In April 1769						
Luttrell	56	18.9	95	32.1	145	49.0
Wilkes	150	13.1	566	49.5	427	37.4

[1] These are the 22 Middlesex parishes listed in the Bills of Mortality and the liberties and hamlets lying within the Finsbury, Holborn and Tower Divisions of the Hundred of Ossulston (M. D. George, *London Life in the XVIIIth Century*, pp. 405, 412–14).

[2] See Robbins, op. cit., pp. 25, 35 ff; J. Middleton, *Agriculture of Middlesex* (1798), *passim*.

[3] For practical purposes, I have included with the 'out'-parishes proper the 5 parishes of Chelsea, Kensington, Paddington, St. Marylebone and St. Pancras, which are not listed in the Bills of Mortality (George, op. cit., p. 405).

In the first place we see that, in each of these contests, the predominantly rural parishes of the county were less inclined to vote for the radical candidate than the predominantly urban. In the election of March 1768, it is perhaps surprising that the proportion of votes cast for Wilkes in Westminster should have been so small, but the distribution of his votes, and of those of his opponents, as between urban and rural districts shows a clear enough trend: whereas Proctor and Cooke polled a majority of their votes (50.4 and 52.5 per cent. respectively) in the rural parishes, Wilkes polled a little over one-third of his votes in these parishes and nearly two-thirds in the urban area. In December, a similar pattern is repeated: while Proctor, in this case, polled a distinctly higher proportion of his votes in the urban area (55.1 per cent., compared with the previous 49.6 per cent.), he actually out-voted Glynn in the rural parishes, where the latter scored less than one-third of his total poll. In April 1769, the same general trend is maintained — though Wilkes, faced, on this occasion, with a far less redoubtable opposition than in March 1768, won considerably larger majorities in both urban and rural areas.[1] That the Court candidates should obtain a higher proportion of the votes cast in the rural area than in the urban is perhaps not unexpected; what is more remarkable is the decisive majority gained by both radical candidates in the Middlesex 'out'-parishes. In Westminster, as we saw, Wilkes's vote was relatively low, particularly in March 1768; and Luttrell's vote in these parishes was, proportionately, even higher than in the rural area. But in the 'out'-parishes the Court candidates were, on each occasion, overwhelmingly defeated. In the first election, Wilkes's vote here more than exceeded the combined votes of his two opponents; in the second, Glynn's vote exceeded Proctor's by 50 per cent.; while, in the third, Wilkes's vote, though considerably lower than in the far more closely contested election of March 1768, was nearly six times that of Luttrell. It is evident, therefore, that the mainstay of Wilkite support lay not so much in the urban area as a whole — still, less, of course, in the rural districts — as in the populous commercial parishes lying to the east and north of the City.

[1] In March 1768, a number of considerable rural parishes — Uxbridge, Hillingdon, Twickenham and Harrow — voted overwhelmingly against Wilkes; in April 1769, his combined vote in these strongly anti-Wilkite parishes was slightly higher than Luttrell's; Proctor's previous supporters for the most part abstained.

So much for the geographical pattern. Can we now find a pattern based on the social status or occupations of the voters? From what we have already learned of Wilkes's history we should hardly expect him, at this stage of his career at least, to have been received with enthusiasm by a significant number of placemen, county gentry, parsons, Members of Parliament, justices of the peace, or even of City dignitaries – by many, in fact, of those who might be considered to be part of the 'Establishment'. Even so, the almost unrelieved consistency of the opposition to the radical candidates from these quarters is perhaps surprising. Of 39 M.P.s who, as Middlesex freeholders, voted in one or more of these contests, only 2 voted for Wilkes and Glynn in two consecutive elections, and these were two of the founder-members of the Society of Supporters of the Bill of Rights, John Sawbridge, Member for Hythe, and James Townsend, Member for West Looe; another, George Byng, Member for Wigan, having voted for Proctor against Glynn, voted for Wilkes against Luttrell. Of 32 peers, sons of peers, baronets and knights voting in these elections, only 3 voted for the radical candidate on any occasion: the Hon. John Scott, who owned land in Ealing, voted for Wilkes in March 1768; Sir John Danvers of Hanover Square voted for Glynn in December; and Sir Ben Trueman, Quaker and brewer of Brick Lane, Spitalfields, voted for Glynn in December and for Wilkes against Luttrell in April. Justices of the peace showed considerable reluctance to support the radical candidates: of 66 justices selected at random from those voting as Middlesex freeholders, only 11 – once more including Byng and Townsend – voted for Wilkes and Glynn in any election.[1] Equally solid was the opposition of the churches: of 42 clergymen, ministers and doctors of divinity whose votes are recorded, only 4 voted, in any contest, for Wilkes or Glynn. One of these was the Rev. John Horne, Wilkes's most energetic election agent, the others were the Rev. Joseph Williamson, of the vicarage in the Liberty of the Rolls; William Prior, curate of St. John, Wapping; and the Rev. Martin Justice of St. George, Hanover Square. Against these, however, Proctor could muster the votes of a dozen vicars, ten rectors and two curates – in addition to those of other clergy.[2] The leaders of the City

[1] Middlesex R.O., Commission of the Peace, no. 133, 24 Jan. 1769.

[2] Poll Books; Guildhall Lib., London Diocese. Episcopal Visitation Bks., (General Clergy), 3 May 1769, MS. 9537/42. See Appendix VI.

upporters. In the seventeen 'out'-parishes and liberties n is similar. In this case, the 'Wilkites' numbered 664 roctorites' 296. The total annual value of properties held 6 and £5,167 respectively, yet the average annual value of tes' ' property exceeded that of the 'Proctorites' in only shes and equalled it in one other. Taking the parishes as a average annual value of properties held was £34 in the roctor's and a little over £23 in the case of Wilkes's s. Finally, in the twenty-two selected rural parishes, there 'Wilkites' and 329 'Proctorites', and the total annual heir properties amounted to £7,199 in the first case and 3 in the second. In five parishes only did the average lue of 'Wilkite' properties exceed that of the 'Proctorite'. age annual value of properties held in all twenty-two vas £53 10s. od. in the case of 'Proctorites' and £36 in the Vilkites'.

TABLE II

S OF 1768–69 CLASSIFIED ACCORDING TO THE ANNUAL VALUE OF PROPERTIES

	Annual value	*'Proctorite' voters:* *Number*	*% voters*	*'Wilkite' voters* *Number*	*% voters*
al	£100 and over	53	7.2	26	2.3
	£50–£99	100	13.7	70	5.9
':	£40–£49	23	3.1	18	1.6
	£30–£39	33	4.5	39	3.3
	£20–£29	67	9.1	81	6.9
	£10–£19	90	12.3	198	16.9
	Under £10	368	50.1	739	63.1
	Totals	734	100.0	1,171	100.0

ends and conclusions emerging from these figures are l when we classify the supporters of the rival groups of s according to the annual value of their properties. From npanying table it will be seen that a fairly large majority ore substantial voters — here taken to be those whose s are valued at £50 or above — were supporters of r Luttrell. Of 79 electors owning or occupying properties nual value of £100 and above, 52 voted for Proctor or nd 26 for Wilkes or Glynn, and of 170 whose properties ed at £50–£99, 100 voted for Proctor or Luttrell and 70

administration and of its financial community were also, in the earlier elections at least, predominantly hostile to the Wilkite candidates. Of 12 Common Council men voting in Middlesex in March and December 1768, 9 voted consistently for Cooke or Proctor and only 2 for Wilkes and Glynn; yet, in April 1769, 5 voted for Wilkes and not a single one for Luttrell.[1] Of 4 London aldermen voting in these elections, 3 voted for Proctor or Cooke[2] and 1 for Glynn;[3] one of the former, Sir Richard Glyn, Bart., of Dowgate ward, banker and president of the Society for Equitable Assurance in Lives and Survivorship,[4] also voted for Luttrell in April 1769.[5] Other bankers voting for Proctor in 1768 were Sir George Colebrooke, M.P. for Arundel, and Benjamin Hopkins, director of the Bank of England. Proctor also received the support of the chairman, vice-chairman and two directors of the East India Company[6] and of Benjamin Way, a director of the South Sea Company; but Wilkes, also, counted among his supporters a South Sea Company director — Abraham Hake, who held a freehold in Spitalfields. Not surprisingly, too, Proctor attracted the votes of a number of eminent lawyers and legal placemen, among them Sir Thomas Sewell, Master of the Rolls, and four Masters in Chancery.[7] Finally, both rural and urban gentry tended to support Proctor and Luttrell rather than Wilkes and Glynn: of 84 persons bearing the suffix of 'Esquire' among the voters in forty-four parishes and liberties, less than one-quarter voted for the radical candidates in these elections.[8]

It is evident, then, that the great majority of office-holders,

[1] They were George Lewis Carr (Aldersgate), George Bellas (Castle Baynard), Luke Young (Cordwainer), William Rogers (Portsoken) and Lawrence Holker (Vintry).

[2] Sir Robert Ladbroke (Bridge Without), Sir Richard Glyn, Bart. (Dowgate), and Sir James Esdaile (Cripplegate).

[3] William Bridgen (Farringdon Within), who also voted for Wilkes in the City contest in March 1768.

[4] *Court and City Register*, 1769.

[5] For party allegiance in the City, see pp. 151–52 and Appendixes IX–X below.

[6] These were Sir George Colebrooke (see also p. 88 below); Henry Crabb Boulton, M.P. for Worcester; John Stephenson, M.P. for St. Michael (also a Luttrell-supporter); and John Pardoe of Catharine Street. See also p. 63, n. 4 above.

[7] Edward Montague (Lincoln's Inn); John Eames, M.P. for Newport, Hants. (Court of Chancery); Thomas Anguish and Thomas Cudden (Liberty of the Rolls).

[8] Proctor also had the support of the majority of parish officers owning Middlesex freeholds: of 22 churchwardens of 18 parishes (15 rural), 13 voted for Proctor and 9 for Wilkes; of 10 parish clerks (7 rural), 6 voted for Proctor and 4 for Wilkes (Episcopal Visitation Bks. (Churchwardens), 3 May 1769, MS. 9537/43).

clergy and the socially more substantial voters favoured the Court candidates and showed a marked hostility to Wilkes and Serjeant Glynn. Judging, however, by the latters' particular success in the commercial 'out'-parishes, where warehouses, workshops and business premises abounded, we should hardly expect the same to be true of the bulk of the voters engaged in trade or manufacture. The evidence on this point is distinctly slender, as neither Middlesex Poll Books nor Land Tax registers give occupations; for these we have to rely on the incomplete and inadequate lists of those qualifying for jury service in the Freeholders' Book, the Westminster Poll Book of 1774, and the occasional names of Middlesex electors among the annual lists of London merchants.[1] But, meagre as they are, these sources give eloquent enough proof that these voters of the 'middling sort' tended to support the radical candidates. There are, indeed, exceptions: brewers, distillers and maltsters, for instance, tended, on the whole, to vote for Proctor;[2] more decisively Proctorite were the shopkeepers, bakers, victuallers, publicans, farmers, craftsmen and undefined 'yeomen' of the rural parishes.[3] But the great majority of merchants, tradesmen and manufacturers of every kind — particularly those owning freeholds in the Middlesex 'out'-parishes — showed an unmistakable preference for Wilkes and Glynn. Thus, of 180 urban voters engaged in such occupations, 130 gave their support to the radical candidates; and, of these, no less than 94 were among the wharfingers, lightermen, warehousemen, importers, coal-merchants, shopkeepers and victuallers of Shadwell, Wapping, St. George-in-the-East, Limehouse and St. Luke's, Old Street.

The general social pattern of the voters, therefore, emerges fairly clearly. But can we carry our analysis further and determine a pattern of voting according to the size or value of the property held? To be more precise, were Wilkes's, or Proctor's, supporters to be found among the substantial, the 'middling', or the lesser

[1] Freeholders' Book, no. 12, 1767–71; Westminster Poll Book, 1774; Baldwin's *Guide*, 1770. In addition, I have consulted the Registers for Births, Burials and Marriages of a number of parishes, but these have proved disappointing.

[2] Brewers voting for Proctor/Luttrell were: Richard Hare (Limehouse), James Keeling (Clerkenwell), Samuel Whitbread (St. Luke Old Street), and William Wilson (St. George Middlesex); those voting for Wilkes/Glynn were: Thomas Allen (Wapping), John and Samuel Curteis (Wapping), John Hill (Sunbury) and Sir Ben Trueman (Spitalfields).

[3] Of rural tradesman and craftsmen 2 in 3 (44 out of 64 in 44 parishes) voted for Proctor/Luttrell. Their supporters included also 6 farmers out of 10 and 11 'yeomen' out of 16.

freeholders or occupiers of lands, te
of the county? To attempt an answ
Tax registers or Poor Rate Books,
find the annual value of the propert
sentative sample has been taken by
case of 17 'out'-parishes and libe
parishes, and 5 of the parishes o
accounting in all for the freeholds of
3,500 electors voting in one or more
fact, owing to a number of deficienc
values of only a little over 1,000 hav
affecting the properties of some 30
no means claim to be exact in every
error is not great enough to rob it
that emerges is accurate enough t
determined the annual value of the
divided the voters concerned accordi
we find that, on balance, the more su
of property tended to vote Proctor
those owning or occupying property
Wilkes rather than Proctor. While th
is not true of every parish, and, in t
clearly defined as when the voters
status or occupation.

Thus, in the five selected parishes
138 'Wilkite' and 109 'Proctorite' vot
properties owned or occupied was £
£2,260 in the latter. In four parishe
annual value of property held by
exceeded that held by the 'Wilkites';
of the property held by the 'Proctori
little over £38, compared with £25

[1] For full details of sources consulted, see
on p. 75 n. 4 above. See also Appendix v.

[2] For a fuller explanation of this point, see

[3] i.e. according as to whether their votes
Proctor/Cooke/Luttrell or for Wilkes/Glynn.
who has for a voted Court candidate only in on
has voted more frequently for a Court cand
Similarly, a 'Wilkite' is one who has either
Glynn, or who has voted more frequently f
Proctor, Cooke or Luttrell. This, of course,
voters of whom no account has been taken in

Glynn's
the patt
and the
was £7,
the 'Wi
three pa
whole,
case of
support
were 3
value o
to £12,
annual
The av
parishe
case of

vo

substa

'midd

lesser

The
confir
candid
the ac
of the
prope
Procto
of an
Luttre
were

for Wilkes or Glynn. Between them, these two groups of substantial voters accounted for 20.9 per cent. of 'Proctorite' supporters and for only 8.2 per cent. of 'Wilkites'. Turning to the 'middling' group — here assumed to be those the annual value of whose properties range between £10 and £49 — we find that the 'Wilkites' begin to catch up in the lower ranges and, that, taking this group of voters as a whole, they are, in proportion to the votes cast, almost equally divided between Proctor's and Wilkes's supporters; 29 per cent. of 'Proctorite' voters and 28.7 per cent. of 'Wilkite' voters are drawn from these 'middling' freeholders. At the bottom of the scale, however, among the lesser freeholders — those whose properties are assessed for Land Tax at less than £10 — the 'Wilkite' tendency is clearly pronounced. While Proctor and Luttrell draw 50.1 per cent. of their votes from this section, they account for no less than 63.1 per cent. of the total radical vote. Moreover, the 'Wilkite' vote from this group alone is actually higher than the 'Proctorite' vote as a whole. These facts illustrate both the strength of Wilkes's appeal for the smaller property-owners of the county and the decisive part that these lesser freeholders played in determining the outcome of the Middlesex elections.

But it would be a mistake to imagine that the more prosperous freeholders of the county, though showing an unmistakable preference for Proctor, were as solidly hostile to Wilkes or Glynn as the pensioners, placemen, justices and clergy, from whom they could count on only the most exceptional support. Among the most substantial of all the substantial freeholders voting in these elections were two of Wilkes's most consistent and devoted supporters of this period: John Sawbridge, M.P., sheriff for London and Middlesex, who rented a house in New Burlington Street at £90 per year and owned land in Edmonton and Tottenham, the latter of an annual value of £480, and James Townsend, also M.P. and sheriff, owner of Bruce Castle, Tottenham, which was assessed for Land Tax at £806 per annum.[1] There was also the 'patriotic gentleman, possessed of 18,000 l. per annum in Wales', who, the press reported, though riddled with gout, made the journey to Brentford in order to vote for Wilkes against Luttrell.[2]

[1] Townsend had further property in Tottenham assessed at £55 p.a. and in Edmonton assessed at £26 p.a.

[2] *Mid. J.*, 16–18 April 1769.

There were, besides, other substantial Wilkite supporters in the business community — such as two brewers of St. John, Wapping: Thomas Allen of Messrs Allen and Ambrose and John Curteis of John & Samuel Curteis, whose properties had an annual value of £206 and £121 respectively; Hugh Hunston, coal-merchant and wharfinger of Burr Street; Allen Spenceley of Spenceley & Co., warehousemen of Aldermanbury, whose freehold in Islington was assessed at £162 p.a.; James Minestone, shipbuilder, and David Trinder, timber-merchant, both owners of numerous tenements and warehouses in St. Paul's, Shadwell; and Sir Ben Trueman, brewer of Spitalfields, whose extensive properties in Brick Lane were assessed at a combined annual value of £358. Moreover, among Proctor's own more substantial supporters of March and December 1768 were some who were by no means consistent upholders of Administration or of Court candidates. There was, for example, Sir George Colebrooke, M.P. for Arundel, banker and East India Company vice-chairman, whose manor at Stepney was assessed for land tax at £200 per annum, and who, having voted for Proctor and Cooke in the General Election, abstained from voting at the two subsequent elections, voted with the minority in the parliamentary division of 15 April 1769 (and again on 25 January 1770) and was one of ten gentlemen instructed by the Surrey freeholders in June of that year to present a petition of protest to the King.[1] There was, also, George Byng, M.P. for Wigan, whose estates — including the family seat of Wrotham Park — in the parish of South Mimms were assessed at £475, who voted for Proctor against Glynn in December but supported Wilkes against Luttrell in April, and became, like Colebrooke, a vigorous upholder of Wilkes's claim to retain his seat in Middlesex.[2] Such men should, of course, not be mistaken for Wilkites — their aversion to Luttrell did not convert them into more than occasional supporters of Wilkes — but cases like these, added to those already cited, serve to emphasize the point that Wilkes did not lack the sympathy of some and the active support of others among the wealthier property-owners of both rural and urban parishes.

The support, or even the benevolent neutrality, of such men could not but be of advantage to the radical candidates in the parishes where they owned property and carried influence, but, of

[1] *Ox. Mag.*, ii. 183; *Pol. Reg.*, v. 50–52; vi. 113.
[2] *Ox. Mag.*, ii. 183; *Pol. Reg.*, vi. 113.

administration and of its financial community were also, in the earlier elections at least, predominantly hostile to the Wilkite candidates. Of 12 Common Council men voting in Middlesex in March and December 1768, 9 voted consistently for Cooke or Proctor and only 2 for Wilkes and Glynn; yet, in April 1769, 5 voted for Wilkes and not a single one for Luttrell.[1] Of 4 London aldermen voting in these elections, 3 voted for Proctor or Cooke[2] and 1 for Glynn;[3] one of the former, Sir Richard Glyn, Bart., of Dowgate ward, banker and president of the Society for Equitable Assurance in Lives and Survivorship,[4] also voted for Luttrell in April 1769.[5] Other bankers voting for Proctor in 1768 were Sir George Colebrooke, M.P. for Arundel, and Benjamin Hopkins, director of the Bank of England. Proctor also received the support of the chairman, vice-chairman and two directors of the East India Company[6] and of Benjamin Way, a director of the South Sea Company; but Wilkes, also, counted among his supporters a South Sea Company director — Abraham Hake, who held a freehold in Spitalfields. Not surprisingly, too, Proctor attracted the votes of a number of eminent lawyers and legal placemen, among them Sir Thomas Sewell, Master of the Rolls, and four Masters in Chancery.[7] Finally, both rural and urban gentry tended to support Proctor and Luttrell rather than Wilkes and Glynn: of 84 persons bearing the suffix of 'Esquire' among the voters in forty-four parishes and liberties, less than one-quarter voted for the radical candidates in these elections.[8]

It is evident, then, that the great majority of office-holders,

[1] They were George Lewis Carr (Aldersgate), George Bellas (Castle Baynard), Luke Young (Cordwainer), William Rogers (Portsoken) and Lawrence Holker (Vintry).

[2] Sir Robert Ladbroke (Bridge Without), Sir Richard Glyn, Bart. (Dowgate), and Sir James Esdaile (Cripplegate).

[3] William Bridgen (Farringdon Within), who also voted for Wilkes in the City contest in March 1768.

[4] *Court and City Register*, 1769.

[5] For party allegiance in the City, see pp. 151–52 and Appendixes IX–X below.

[6] These were Sir George Colebrooke (see also p. 88 below); Henry Crabb Boulton, M.P. for Worcester; John Stephenson, M.P. for St. Michael (also a Luttrell-supporter); and John Pardoe of Catharine Street. See also p. 63, n. 4 above.

[7] Edward Montague (Lincoln's Inn); John Eames, M.P. for Newport, Hants. (Court of Chancery); Thomas Anguish and Thomas Cudden (Liberty of the Rolls).

[8] Proctor also had the support of the majority of parish officers owning Middlesex freeholds: of 22 churchwardens of 18 parishes (15 rural), 13 voted for Proctor and 9 for Wilkes; of 10 parish clerks (7 rural), 6 voted for Proctor and 4 for Wilkes (Episcopal Visitation Bks. (Churchwardens), 3 May 1769, MS. 9537/43).

clergy and the socially more substantial voters favoured the Court candidates and showed a marked hostility to Wilkes and Serjeant Glynn. Judging, however, by the latters' particular success in the commercial 'out'-parishes, where warehouses, workshops and business premises abounded, we should hardly expect the same to be true of the bulk of the voters engaged in trade or manufacture. The evidence on this point is distinctly slender, as neither Middlesex Poll Books nor Land Tax registers give occupations; for these we have to rely on the incomplete and inadequate lists of those qualifying for jury service in the Freeholders' Book, the Westminster Poll Book of 1774, and the occasional names of Middlesex electors among the annual lists of London merchants.[1] But, meagre as they are, these sources give eloquent enough proof that these voters of the 'middling sort' tended to support the radical candidates. There are, indeed, exceptions: brewers, distillers and maltsters, for instance, tended, on the whole, to vote for Proctor;[2] more decisively Proctorite were the shopkeepers, bakers, victuallers, publicans, farmers, craftsmen and undefined 'yeomen' of the rural parishes.[3] But the great majority of merchants, tradesmen and manufacturers of every kind — particularly those owning freeholds in the Middlesex 'out'-parishes — showed an unmistakable preference for Wilkes and Glynn. Thus, of 180 urban voters engaged in such occupations, 130 gave their support to the radical candidates; and, of these, no less than 94 were among the wharfingers, lightermen, warehousemen, importers, coal-merchants, shopkeepers and victuallers of Shadwell, Wapping, St. George-in-the-East, Limehouse and St. Luke's, Old Street.

The general social pattern of the voters, therefore, emerges fairly clearly. But can we carry our analysis further and determine a pattern of voting according to the size or value of the property held? To be more precise, were Wilkes's, or Proctor's, supporters to be found among the substantial, the 'middling', or the lesser

[1] Freeholders' Book, no. 12, 1767–71; Westminster Poll Book, 1774; Baldwin's *Guide*, 1770. In addition, I have consulted the Registers for Births, Burials and Marriages of a number of parishes, but these have proved disappointing.

[2] Brewers voting for Proctor/Luttrell were: Richard Hare (Limehouse), James Keeling (Clerkenwell), Samuel Whitbread (St. Luke Old Street), and William Wilson (St. George Middlesex); those voting for Wilkes/Glynn were: Thomas Allen (Wapping), John and Samuel Curteis (Wapping), John Hill (Sunbury) and Sir Ben Trueman (Spitalfields).

[3] Of rural tradesman and craftsmen 2 in 3 (44 out of 64 in 44 parishes) voted for Proctor/Luttrell. Their supporters included also 6 farmers out of 10 and 11 'yeomen' out of 16.

freeholders or occupiers of lands, tenements, houses or messuages of the county? To attempt an answer, we must refer to the Land Tax registers or Poor Rate Books, where alone we may hope to find the annual value of the properties held. In this case, a representative sample has been taken by consulting such records in the case of 17 'out'-parishes and liberties, 22 of the largest rural parishes, and 5 of the parishes of the City of Westminster – accounting in all for the freeholds of rather more than 2,000 of the 3,500 electors voting in one or more of the elections of 1768–69.[1] In fact, owing to a number of deficiencies in the records, the annual values of only a little over 1,000 have been traced, and this sample affecting the properties of some 30 per cent. of the voters can by no means claim to be exact in every detail.[2] Even so, the margin of error is not great enough to rob it of all value and the pattern that emerges is accurate enough to serve our purpose. Having determined the annual value of the freeholds in our sample and divided the voters concerned according to their electoral allegiance,[3] we find that, on balance, the more substantial owners and occupiers of property tended to vote Proctor rather than Wilkes and that those owning or occupying property of a lesser value tended to vote Wilkes rather than Proctor. While this pattern is fairly constant, it is not true of every parish, and, in this case, the pattern is not so clearly defined as when the voters were distributed by social status or occupation.

Thus, in the five selected parishes of Westminster, there were 138 'Wilkite' and 109 'Proctorite' voters. The total annual value of properties owned or occupied was £1,924 in the former case and £2,260 in the latter. In four parishes out of the five, the average annual value of property held by the 'Proctorites' appreciably exceeded that held by the 'Wilkites'; and the average annual value of the property held by the 'Proctorites' in all five parishes was a little over £38, compared with £25 in the case of Wilkes's and

[1] For full details of sources consulted, see my article in the *E.H.R.* mentioned on p. 75 n. 4 above. See also Appendix v.

[2] For a fuller explanation of this point, see my article in the *E.H.R.*

[3] i.e. according as to whether their votes had been cast predominantly for Proctor/Cooke/Luttrell or for Wilkes/Glynn. A 'Proctorite', in this sense, is one who has for a voted Court candidate only in one or more of these elections, or who has voted more frequently for a Court candidate than for Wilkes or Glynn. Similarly, a 'Wilkite' is one who has either voted consistently for Wilkes or Glynn, or who has voted more frequently for one or other of them than for Proctor, Cooke or Luttrell. This, of course, leaves a fair number of 'neutral' voters of whom no account has been taken in our calculations.

Glynn's supporters. In the seventeen 'out'-parishes and liberties the pattern is similar. In this case, the 'Wilkites' numbered 664 and the 'Proctorites' 296. The total annual value of properties held was £7,196 and £5,167 respectively, yet the average annual value of the 'Wilkites'' property exceeded that of the 'Proctorites' in only three parishes and equalled it in one other. Taking the parishes as a whole, the average annual value of properties held was £34 in the case of Proctor's and a little over £23 in the case of Wilkes's supporters. Finally, in the twenty-two selected rural parishes, there were 369 'Wilkites' and 329 'Proctorites', and the total annual value of their properties amounted to £7,199 in the first case and to £12,123 in the second. In five parishes only did the average annual value of 'Wilkite' properties exceed that of the 'Proctorite'. The average annual value of properties held in all twenty-two parishes was £53 10s. 0d. in the case of 'Proctorites' and £36 in the case of 'Wilkites'.

TABLE II

VOTERS OF 1768–69 CLASSIFIED ACCORDING TO THE ANNUAL VALUE OF PROPERTIES

	Annual value	*'Proctorite' voters:* Number	% voters	*'Wilkite' voters* Number	% voters
substantial	£100 and over	53	7.2	26	2.3
	£50–£99	100	13.7	70	5.9
'middling':	£40–£49	23	3.1	18	1.6
	£30–£39	33	4.5	39	3.3
	£20–£29	67	9.1	81	6.9
	£10–£19	90	12.3	198	16.9
lesser:	Under £10	368	50.1	739	63.1
	Totals	734	100.0	1,171	100.0

The trends and conclusions emerging from these figures are confirmed when we classify the supporters of the rival groups of candidates according to the annual value of their properties. From the accompanying table it will be seen that a fairly large majority of the more substantial voters — here taken to be those whose properties are valued at £50 or above — were supporters of Proctor or Luttrell. Of 79 electors owning or occupying properties of an annual value of £100 and above, 52 voted for Proctor or Luttrell and 26 for Wilkes or Glynn, and of 170 whose properties were valued at £50–£99, 100 voted for Proctor or Luttrell and 70 for Wilkes or Glynn. Between them, these two groups of substantial voters accounted for 20.9 per cent. of 'Proctorite' supporters and for only 8.2 per cent. of 'Wilkites'. Turning to the 'middling' group — here assumed to be those the annual value of whose properties range between £10 and £49 — we find that the 'Wilkites' begin to catch up in the lower ranges and, that, taking this group of voters as a whole, they are, in proportion to the votes cast, almost equally divided between Proctor's and Wilkes's supporters; 29 per cent. of 'Proctorite' voters and 28.7 per cent. of 'Wilkite' voters are drawn from these 'middling' freeholders. At the bottom of the scale, however, among the lesser freeholders — those whose properties are assessed for Land Tax at less than £10 — the 'Wilkite' tendency is clearly pronounced. While Proctor and Luttrell draw 50.1 per cent. of their votes from this section, they account for no less than 63.1 per cent. of the total radical vote. Moreover, the 'Wilkite' vote from this group alone is actually higher than the 'Proctorite' vote as a whole. These facts illustrate both the strength of Wilkes's appeal for the smaller property-owners of the county and the decisive part that these lesser freeholders played in determining the outcome of the Middlesex elections.

But it would be a mistake to imagine that the more prosperous freeholders of the county, though showing an unmistakable preference for Proctor, were as solidly hostile to Wilkes or Glynn as the pensioners, placemen, justices and clergy, from whom they could count on only the most exceptional support. Among the most substantial of all the substantial freeholders voting in these elections were two of Wilkes's most consistent and devoted supporters of this period: John Sawbridge, M.P., sheriff for London and Middlesex, who rented a house in New Burlington Street at £90 per year and owned land in Edmonton and Tottenham, the latter of an annual value of £480, and James Townsend, also M.P. and sheriff, owner of Bruce Castle, Tottenham, which was assessed for Land Tax at £806 per annum.[1] There was also the 'patriotic gentleman, possessed of 18,000 l. per annum in Wales', who, the press reported, though riddled with gout, made the journey to Brentford in order to vote for Wilkes against Luttrell.[2]

[1] Townsend had further property in Tottenham assessed at £55 p.a. and in Edmonton assessed at £26 p.a.

[2] *Mid. J.*, 16–18 April 1769.

There were, besides, other substantial Wilkite supporters in the business community — such as two brewers of St. John, Wapping: Thomas Allen of Messrs Allen and Ambrose and John Curteis of John & Samuel Curteis, whose properties had an annual value of £206 and £121 respectively; Hugh Hunston, coal-merchant and wharfinger of Burr Street; Allen Spenceley of Spenceley & Co., warehousemen of Aldermanbury, whose freehold in Islington was assessed at £162 p.a.; James Minestone, shipbuilder, and David Trinder, timber-merchant, both owners of numerous tenements and warehouses in St. Paul's, Shadwell; and Sir Ben Trueman, brewer of Spitalfields, whose extensive properties in Brick Lane were assessed at a combined annual value of £358. Moreover, among Proctor's own more substantial supporters of March and December 1768 were some who were by no means consistent upholders of Administration or of Court candidates. There was, for example, Sir George Colebrooke, M.P. for Arundel, banker and East India Company vice-chairman, whose manor at Stepney was assessed for land tax at £200 per annum, and who, having voted for Proctor and Cooke in the General Election, abstained from voting at the two subsequent elections, voted with the minority in the parliamentary division of 15 April 1769 (and again on 25 January 1770) and was one of ten gentlemen instructed by the Surrey freeholders in June of that year to present a petition of protest to the King.[1] There was, also, George Byng, M.P. for Wigan, whose estates — including the family seat of Wrotham Park — in the parish of South Mimms were assessed at £475, who voted for Proctor against Glynn in December but supported Wilkes against Luttrell in April, and became, like Colebrooke, a vigorous upholder of Wilkes's claim to retain his seat in Middlesex.[2] Such men should, of course, not be mistaken for Wilkites — their aversion to Luttrell did not convert them into more than occasional supporters of Wilkes — but cases like these, added to those already cited, serve to emphasize the point that Wilkes did not lack the sympathy of some and the active support of others among the wealthier property-owners of both rural and urban parishes.

The support, or even the benevolent neutrality, of such men could not but be of advantage to the radical candidates in the parishes where they owned property and carried influence, but, of

[1] *Ox. Mag.*, ii. 183; *Pol. Reg.*, v. 50–52; vi. 113.
[2] *Ox. Mag.*, ii. 183; *Pol. Reg.*, vi. 113.

course, it was a relatively minor factor in the county as a whole when set against the solid and consistent weight of support that Proctor, and even Luttrell, enjoyed among men of wealth and, far more, among men of social substance and authority. Wilkes and Glynn, as we have seen, could, on the other hand, count on the solid backing of the 'middling' type of tradesman, merchant and manufacturer in the Middlesex 'out'-parishes, where the political influence of justice, squire and parson must long since have become negligible. In addition, they could rely, in the county as a whole, to a considerably greater extent than their opponents, on the backing of the lesser freeholders who, according to our calculations, outnumbered all other groups of voters.[1] In modern terms, this would seem in itself to be the guarantee of a candidates' electoral success, but this was by no means the case in the eighteenth century, and when we consider the overwhelming weight thrown into the electoral scales on behalf of the Court candidates in almost every rural parish by justices, substantial landowners, gentry and ministers of religion — all potent forces for guiding and moulding opinion — it is all the more remarkable that Wilkes and Serjeant Glynn should have carried the day in all three elections. Apart from the particular qualities of the radical candidates and their election agents, it is, of course, a remarkable tribute to the exceptional vigour and political independence of the Middlesex freeholders.

[1] According to our sample, they accounted for 58 per cent. of all voters.

VI

INDUSTRIAL UNREST

APPARENTLY linked with the Wilkite political movement of this time was a remarkable series of industrial disputes involving workers in a wide variety of London trades. Mention has already been made of the weavers' and coal-heavers' disputes of early 1768 and we have noted that the coal-heavers, along the Ratcliffe Highway, combined their own particular form of industrial action with shouts of 'Wilkes for ever!'[1] But the weavers' and coal-heavers' disputes were only the most violent and protracted of a great crop of workers' strikes, demonstrations, marches and petitions to Parliament that marked the spring and summer of 1768 and thoroughly alarmed both Ministers and magistrates. In mid-May, as the price of wheat at the London Corn Exchange rose to 56s. a quarter,[2] the authorities were faced with almost simultaneous demands and demonstrations by sailors, watermen, coopers, hatters, glass-grinders, sawyers, tailors, weavers and coal-heavers. To contemporaries it seemed that the movement would inevitably spread though the wage-earning population as a whole. Reporting on the sailors' strike to the Duke of Newcastle on 13 May, James West added the comment: 'So the evils, if not suppress'd, will go through all the inferior orders of men'.[3] Thomas Harley, the Lord Mayor, believing that such gatherings were a grave danger to the public peace, took, as we have seen, extraordinary precautions at this time to keep the journeymen and apprentices from assembling in the streets of the City.[4] And the Duke of Grafton, commenting in his *Autobiography* on the series of disorders that marked the year 1768, could hardly fail to see a connexion between these journeymen's and labourers' disputes and the great popular political movement that had arisen in the wake of Wilkes's election in Middlesex.

Artisans of almost every denomination [he wrote] . . . combined for an advance of wages, and their discontents, and disobedience to the laws led

[1] See pp. 38–39, 47 above.
[2] *Read. Merc.*, 9 and 16 May 1768.
[3] West to Newcastle, 13 May 1768, Add. MSS. 32990, f. 62.
[4] *Lloyd's Evening Post*, 11–13 May 1768. See also pp. 49–50 above.

them to join often, in numbers, those mobs which the consequence of the elections for Middlesex frequently produced.[1]

Historians have also generally surmised that there must have been some sort of connexion between these movements,[2] but one biographer of Wilkes, at least, has carried the argument further and actually characterized the industrial disputes as 'an outbreak of political strikes'.[3] To this point we must return after looking at these movements more closely.

Apart from the coal-heavers and weavers, whose activities will be discussed later, the sailors appear to have been first in the field. On 5 May, the *Gentleman's Magazine* reported that

a great body of sailors assembled at Deptford, forcibly went on board several ships, unreefed the top-sails, and vowed no ships should sail till the merchants had consented to raise their wages.[4]

Sailors' disputes had been endemic since the discharge of many thousands from the Royal Navy at the end of the wars with France in the spring of 1763.[5] That autumn, the justices of the Tower Division were ordered by the Secretaries of State 'to take proper measures for suppressing the riots of sailors and others at Shoreditch'.[6] The agitation of May 1768 arose over wages and spread to London from northern ports. In April, sailors rioted at Newcastle, Tinmouth, Sunderland and Shields 'upon the pretence of demanding an advance of wages' and compelled the ship-owners to sign agreements with their representatives.[7] The London seamen, for their part, demanded a wage of 35s. a month, 'alleging that their families would be starving in their absence'; till this was conceded, 'they would neither engage, nor suffer any ship to sail'.[8] All outward-bound ships were visited by the sailors' committees ('for the sailors have their committees')[9] and, by 9 May, the Navy Office had to report that every single ship on the Thames had been

[1] Grafton, *Autobiography*, pp. 188–9.
[2] See, e.g., S. Maccoby, *English Radicalism 1762–1785*, p. 456: '. . . an unrest not altogether to be dissociated from the political excitements of the year on the score of Wilkes.'
[3] Postgate, p. 181.
[4] *Gent's Mag.*, 1768, p. 242.
[5] For a letter to the press suggesting that 'numbers of them, for want of employment, have turned thieves', see *Read. Merc.*, 2 May 1763.
[6] *Cal. H. O. Papers*, 1760–65, no. 1168.
[7] S.P. Dom., Entry Bks., 44/142, pp. 47–49, 50–51, 54.
[8] Grafton, *Autobiography*, p. 188.
[9] Sir Matthew Fetherstonehaugh, Bart., to Duke to Newcastle, 19 May 1768, Add. MSS. 32990, ff. 107–8.

disabled from sailing; one vessel had escaped, but was boarded at Limehouse Hole and made to toe the line. Meanwhile, a mass meeting of 5,000–6,000 sailors assembled at Stepney Fields to devise further measures.[1] Some proposed to go to Richmond to see the King: 'One who has a flag', Lord Weymouth reported to George III, 'mounted on the rails before the Queen's House & hollowed out *for Richmond.*'[2] Others assembled in St. George's Fields and marched to St. James's Palace 'with colours flying, drums beating and fifes playing', and presented a petition to the King.[3] This was followed on the 10th by a petition to Parliament, when 'a great body of sailors' — estimates varied between 5,000 and 15,000 — marched to Palace Yard, where, having been addressed by two gentlemen 'mounted on the roof of a hackney-coach', they 'gave three cheers and dispersed'.[4] A week later, the strike seemed to be settled. Several ship-owners, concerned for their loss of trade, had come to terms with the sailors' committees and their ships had been allowed to sail; the Hudson's Bay Company had even been compelled, for this privilege, to pay 'the exorbitant wages of 40s. per month', though they claimed that their own sailors were 'well disposed in themselves to accept of moderate wages'.[5] But further disturbances followed, and it was not until July, wrote Grafton, 'that the sailors took fairly to their work'.[6]

Meanwhile, the Thames watermen had gone into action. On 9 May, two thousand of them demonstrated before the Royal Exchange and the Mansion House. Five hundred were admitted to place their demands and grievances before the Lord Mayor. These, ran a press report, were that provisions were too dear; that private persons were permitted to keep boats on Thames-side that competed with the watermen's craft; and that they were not allowed to work on Sundays. Thomas Harley, despite his other preoccupations, is said to have given them a friendly reception and advised them to appoint a 'proper person' to draw up a petition, which he undertook to present to Parliament on their behalf. Whereupon, having given three huzzas, they went away peacefully.[7]

1 S.P. Dom., Entry Bks., 44/142, pp. 79–80.
2 Weymouth to the King, 6 May 1768, Fortescue, ii. no 616.
3 *Gent's Mag.*, 1768, p. 242.
4 Ibid., p. 243. See also Entry Bks., 44/142, pp. 88–89.
5 Ibid., pp. 128–9.
6 Ibid., pp. 162–6; *Cal. H.O. Papers*, 1766–69, p. 371; *Gent's Mag.*, 1768, p. 442; 1769, p. 162; Grafton, *Autobiography*, p. 189.
7 *St. James's Chronicle*, 7–10 May 1768; *Gent's Mag.*, 1768, p. 242.

The same day, 'the hatters struck and refused to work till their wages had been raised'.[1] The dispute, though not mentioned in the State Papers, must have lasted for some weeks, for, according to the information of John Dyer, hatmaker of St. Olave's, Southwark, taken on oath on Tuesday, 21 June:

> On Thursday last, a Mob or Gang of Hatters to the number of thirty came to his house in the Maze in the Parish of St. Olave's, Southwark, about one o'clock at noon, in a riotous manner, and insisted on this Informant turning off the men he then had at work, which he refused; and, upon such refusal, the said Mob or Gang of Hatters threatened to pull his house down and take this Informant thereout. And this Informant saith they would have begun to execute such threats if it had not been for one Mr. Phillips who accidentally was at this Informant's house, and did prevail on them to omit it. And this Informant saith that there was one Thomas Fitzhugh present and aiding & assisting among ye sd Mob, and came & asked this Informant whe^{r} he wo^{d} turn off his men which he refused; and upon that the said Fitzhugh declared, if he wo^{d} not, 'damn them that wo^{d} not have you out (meaning this Inform't) & the house down'.[2]

On 10 May, the day of the St. George's Fields 'massacre', Charles Dingley's mechanical saw-mill in Limehouse was attacked and partially destroyed by five hundred sawyers.[3] Despite Dingley's political pretensions and hostility to the radical movement the motive does not appear to have been political; this was rather an early instance of 'Luddism', or machine-wrecking, by men threatened with the loss of work. 'The reason given for this outrage,' ran a press report, 'is that it deprived many persons in that branch from being employed.'[4] This view of the dispute is confirmed by the evidence later given at the Old Bailey by Christopher Robertson, Dingley's principal clerk, who stated that, when he asked 'the mob of sawyers and other people' what they wanted,

[1] Ibid.

[2] Surrey R.O., Sessions Bundles, 1768 (Midsummer). A recognisance for Thomas Fitzhugh, hatter of Holland's Leagues, Christ Church, Surrey, appears in the Surrey Sessions Roll for 1768 (Midsummer), according to which he is charged with 'a breach of the peace and a misdemeanour', released on a bail of £50 and required to appear at Guildford Quarter Sessions on 12 July; then he disappears from the records. In February 1770, there was a strike of journeymen hat-dyers in Southwark and 'at all shops they came to they obliged the men to strike in order to have their wages raised' (*Ann. Reg.*, 1770, p. 74). For further disputes involving hatters in 1775, see S. and B. Webb, *An History of Trade Unionism* (1869), p. 46.

[3] See p. 53 above.

[4] *Read. Merc.*, 16 May 1768.

They told me the saw-mill was at work when thousands of them were starving for want of bread. I then represented to them that the mill had done no kind of work that had injured them, or prevented them receiving any benefit. I desired to know which was their principal man to whom I might speak. I had some conversation with him and represented to him that it had not injured the sawyers. He said it partly might be so, but it would hereafter if it had not; and they came with a resolution to pull it down, and it should come down.[1]

A week later, glass-grinders, coopers and journeymen tailors all assembled to present their various petitions to Parliament.[2] Lord Weymouth seems to have been less sanguine than the Lord Mayor about the peaceful outcome of such demonstrations: he commended the Westminster magistrates' efforts 'to dissuade the tailors from proceeding to the House of Commons with a petition' and hoped the coopers would disperse peacefully. If not, his secretary, William Fraser, wrote to Fielding, 'you are already informed where to meet with support whenever you shall find it necessary to call for it'.[3] No more is heard of the glass-grinders and coopers, but the tailors were more persistent and their past history was such as to cause the government more particular concern. It was, in fact, the London journeymen tailors who, as far back as 1720, had made one of the first attempts in modern history to form a stable trade union, and, in that year, the master tailors had complained to Parliament about their journeymen's 'combinations' over the past two years to raise wages and reduce working hours:

and for the better carrying on their design [they] have subscribed their respective names in books prepared for that purpose, at the several houses of call or resort [being public-houses in and about London and Westminster][4]

According to a later petition by the masters,

they had formed into a kind of republic, holding illegal meetings at 42 different public-houses and appointing from each 2 persons to represent the body, and form the 'Grand Committee for the Management of the Town', which made rules and orders for the direction of the masters and the whole body of journeymen.[5]

[1] O.B. *Proceedings* 1768, p. 256.
[2] *Gent's Mag.*, 1768, p. 245.
[3] William Fraser to Sir John Fielding, Entry Bks., 44/142, pp. 92–94.
[4] *Commons Journals*, xix, 416, 424, 481; cit. S. and B. Webb. op. cit. p. 27.
[5] *Cal. H.O. Papers*, 1760–65, no. 1389.

In 1744, 15,000 of them had combined again to advance their wages beyond the maximum fixed by Parliament.[1] In January 1764, they petitioned the Middlesex justices to increase their wages beyond the statutory limit and won a minor concession: wages were now to be 2s. 6d. a day all the year round and hours to be reduced by one hour in the winter half-year. A further concession followed: summer and winter hours were to be equalized; but some of the masters refused to accept the award and, in July, a strike broke out, leading to a number of convictions to short terms of hard labour.[2] The movement of 1768 was simply a further instalment in this long-protracted engagement. 'The tailors intend', wrote Weymouth to the Lord Mayor, 'to assemble tomorrow evening and to go round to the several masters in London to compel their journeymen to join them, in order to oblige the trade to raise their present wages.'[3] These appear, by this time, to have risen to 2s. 7d., for we find James West writing waspishly to the Duke of Newcastle: 'They impudently set forth their inability to live on two shillings and sevenpence a day, when the common soldier lives for under sixpence.' But, this time, it proved to be a perfectly orderly movement. Two thousand tailors assembled, marched to Parliament and presented their petition. After receiving a few reassuring words, 'they went away very quickly & peaceably'.[4]

The coal-heavers' dispute was a far more violent, complex and protracted affair. The East London trade of coal-heaving (or unloading of coals) was, in the mid-eighteenth century, pursued by some 670 persons, resident in Shadwell and Wapping, of whom the majority were Irish Roman Catholics. They were viewed with the utmost suspicion by the authorities. 'A few . . . are quiet laborious men,' wrote the Treasury Solicitor in preparing a brief against a number of them, 'the rest are of a riotous disposition and ready to join in any kind of disorders; and from 70 to 100 are the very dregs of mankind and capable of all kinds of mischiefs and barbarities.'[5] The disturbances of 1768 arose essentially from a dispute over wages, but they were complicated by a 'war' between two groups of agents operating rival schemes for registering coal-

[1] Sir Walter Besant, *London in the Eighteenth Century* (1902), pp. 223–4.
[2] *Cal. H.O. Papers*, 1760–65, no. 1389; M.D. George, *London Life in the XVIIIth Century*, p. 206; J. Lindsay, *1764*, pp. 240, 329–30.
[3] Weymouth to the Lord Mayor, Entry Bks., 44/142, p. 92.
[4] West to Newcastle, 16 May 1768, Add. MSS. 32990, ff. 77–8.
[5] P.R.O., T.S. 11/443/1408.

heavers. Up to Christmas 1767, the recognized rate for unloading Thames-side colliers had been 16d. a score of 'chauldrons', or sacks, but, in face of a steeply rising cost of living, the men's leaders demanded 20d. per score and later raised their claim to 2s. Strikes followed and, when the masters refused to comply with the men's terms, the coal-heavers 'unanimously determined to desist from their labour; whereby a total stop was put to the business of unloading coals in the port of London'.[1] The other aspect of the dispute was more complex and had a longer history. The coal-heavers had traditionally had their affairs run for them by different groups of 'undertakers' — generally local publicans, who also lodged and fed them and provided them with liquor. In 1758, after the men had complained of being robbed by their 'undertakers', an official scheme was set up by Act of Parliament, whereby work-gangs were organized by recognized foremen, and all coal-heavers who registered and paid 2s. in the £ from their wages became eligible for sick and funeral benefits and for benefits for their widows and orphans. The administration of the scheme was entrusted to William Beckford, alderman of Billingsgate Ward, who appointed a deputy to organize the fund and Francis Reynolds, an attorney, to keep the register. Unfortunately, Reynolds converted some £500 or £600 of the coal-heavers' contributions to his own use and was imprisoned for debt. Beckford momentarily lost interest, but after the wages dispute had started, he reopened his office — possibly with a view to break the strike — and appointed John Green, publican of the Round About Tavern in Shadwell and a former 'undertaker', as one of his principal agents. Meanwhile, a Middlesex justice, Ralph Hodgson of Shadwell, taking advantage of the temporary eclipse of the official scheme, had decided to operate a scheme of his own, which he appears to have run on trade-union lines; wages were pushed up to 20d. a score of chauldrons, and the coal-heavers began to flock into the new organization.[2] Hodgson seems to have made himself all the more popular with these men by flattering their national sentiments: on St. Patrick's Day, it was reported, he had headed a demonstration of four hundred of them — the great majority being

[1] Middlesex R.O., Sessions Papers (Middlesex), Sept. 1768: 'To the Hon. the Lord High Chancellor of Great Britain. The Representation of His Majesty's Justices of the Peace for the County of Middlesex in the General Sessions assembled at Hicks Hall on Thursday the 8th of Sep'r 1768.'

[2] T.S. 11/443/1408.

Irishmen — parading with shamrocks in 'the high streets and public highways of Shadwell, Ratcliffe and the parish of Stepney . . . with drums beating and colours flying'.[1]

To win back their members and to break the strike, Beckford's agents now advertised in the press in early April, inviting men willing to work to report to their office. John Green's public house in New Gravel Lane was besieged by angry coal-heavers, armed with cutlasses and bludgeons, who demolished his windows and a panel of his front door, but were repulsed by musket-fire. The next day, Hodgson's men in Billingsgate threatened that 'they would do for [him] if [he] did not desist in [his] proceedings'. On the night of 20 April, news of Wilkes's temporary discharge by the Court of King's Bench reached the riotous coal-heavers who, to shouts of 'Wilkes and coal-heavers for ever!', called for illuminations to celebrate the victory.[2] They then proceeded to make an armed assault on Green's house, taunted him with shouts of 'Green, you bougre, why don't you fire?', and swore that 'they would have his heart and liver, and cut him in pieces and hang him on his sign'. Green defended himself stoutly and, before escaping over the roof-tops to a neighbouring ship-yard, shot dead two of assailants — Thomas Smith, a cobbler, and William Wake, a coal-heaver.[3] Subsequently, seven coal-heavers — John Grainger, Daniel Clare, Richard Cornwall, Thomas Murray, Peter Flaherty, Patrick Lynch and Nicholas McCabe — were sentenced to death at the Old Bailey and hanged at the Sun Tavern Fields in Stepney before a crowd of 50,000, attended by three hundred soldiers and 'a prodigious number of peace officers'.[4]

A week after the riot in New Gravel Lane, there appears to have been a temporary settlement, when the coal-heavers' foremen, after meeting Alderman Beckford and other justices, agreed to register

[1] Middlesex R.O., Sessions Papers (Middlesex), Sept. 1768.

[2] See p. 47 above.

[3] T.S. 11/443/1408; O.B. *Proceedings* 1768, pp. 204–7, 207–14, 244–56. Green was subsequently tried, but acquitted, on two charges of murder at the Old Bailey on 18–21 May 1768 (O.B. *Proceedings*, 1768, pp. 204–14). For an attack by coal-heavers on another public house — that of James Marsden of the Ship and Shears in Shadwell — on 20 April 1768, see T.S. 11/443/1408.

[4] Ibid.; O.B. *Proceedings*, 1768, pp. 244–56; *Ann. Reg.*, 1768, pp. 139–40. It appears that 6 of the convicted men were Roman Catholics; but 'one, being a Protestant, [was] attended by a gentleman of Mr. Wesley's persuasion (ibid. p. 140). In September 1769, another coal-heaver, David Creamer, was sentenced to 7 years in Newgate for firing at John Green (Middlesex R.O., Sessions Rolls (Middlesex), no. 3217a, 26 June 1769; Process Register Bks. of Indictments, xviii (1769–75). 8).

their gangs and return to work; but, on 12 May, having failed to win their masters' consent in writing to a rise in wages, the coal-heavers marched to the Mansion House. Thomas Harley, however, having doubtless had a trying week, 'very prudently declined intermeddling with their affairs'.[1] A series of violent affrays followed between coal-heavers and sailors who had, meanwhile, been engaged to man the colliers on the Thames. On 23 May, coal-heavers boarded the *Thomas and Mary*, lying in Shadwell Dock, and threatened to murder any sailor who continued to load; on the next day, sailors coming ashore from another collier, the *Free Love*, were attacked with bludgeons and cutlasses, two were wounded and a young sailor, John Beatty, was stabbed to death.[2] Again, on 1 June, two captains of colliers, who had come ashore at King James's Steps, Wapping, to purchase provisions, were beaten up by fifty coal-heavers. A further clash was reported on 6 June, but after the military had been called in to assist the magistrates, twenty more 'desperadoes' were taken into custody,[3] and the movement seems to have collapsed.

Even more protracted was the weavers' dispute, which formed but an episode in the stormy history of the silk-weavers of Spitalfields, Moorfields, Stepney and Bethnal Green with their long tradition of action — both industrial and political — to promote their trade interests.[4] On some such occasions, masters and journeymen combined their forces in common protest, as when, in May 1765, angry weavers marched to Parliament with black flags and besieged Bedford House, because the Duke had defeated a Bill designed to protect the London silk-weavers' livelihood by excluding French silks from the English market.[5] Again, in January 1768, masters and journeymen joined in a great march from Spitalfields to St. James's to thank the King for reducing

[1] *Ann. Reg.*, 1768, pp. 101–2; *Gent's Mag.*, 1768, p. 243.

[2] T.S. 11/443/1408. For the Old Bailey trial of 9 coal-heavers charged with the murder — Thomas Carnan (or Kearns), James Murphy, James Dogan, John Castello, Thomas Davis, James Hammond, Hugh Henley, Michael (Malachi) Doyle and Thomas Farmer alias Terrible — see O.B. *Proceedings*, 1768, pp. 264–74. Seven were acquitted; Murphy and Dogan were hanged at Tyburn on 11 July (*Gent's Mag.*, 1768, p. 347).

[3] *Ann. Reg.*, 1768, pp. 119, 121, 124. The names of 10 of these appear in Middlesex R.O., Process Register Bks. of Indictments, xvii (1761–69). 799; 4 were subsequently sentenced at Hicks Hall to 3 or 7 years' imprisonment for rioting and 'going armed' (T.S. 11/443/1408).

[4] D. M. George, op. cit., pp. 176–95; Maccoby, op. cit., pp. 453–5.

[5] Albemarle, *Memoirs of the Marquis of Rockingham*, i. 198–200, 207; Maccoby, loc. cit.

the period of Court mournings.[1] But such joint demonstrations in support of common interests were more frequently overshadowed by disputes over journeymen's wages. In October 1763, in the course of such a dispute, two thousand journeymen weavers disguised themselves as sailors and, armed with cutlasses, broke into the houses of journeymen who had refused to join them, broke their looms, wounded several, and threatened further reprisals.[2] In fact, the 'cutting' and destroying of looms and the silk being woven in them had become the usual form of reprisal against both wage-cutting masters and journeymen hesitant to join the 'combination'. An Act of Parliament of 1765 had, in addition to excluding French silks, sought to remedy the abuse by making 'cutting' a criminal offence, but the journeymen,

> knowing their fate, if apprehended, . . . disguised themselves and performed all their exploits in the dead of night, procured arms and offensive weapons of all kinds, cut, beat and abused persons of all ranks & denominations, whom they thought fit to visit for the purpose of cutting their looms and work.[3]

So it was in the weavers' outbreaks of 1768–69. Early in January of the former year, the masters reduced the price of work by 4d. a yard;[4] this provoked a dispute which was further complicated by the long-standing hostility of the single-hand ribbon-weavers to those operating the engine-loom, originally brought in from Holland. The same month, there were three cases of assault by single-hand weavers on their opponents' looms in Stepney, leading to a capital conviction a year later.[5] It was at this time that the Earl of Shelburne offered military support to magistrates who were unable to suppress the 'outrages' committed by 'disorderly persons . . . in and about Spitalfields';[6] while the Archbishop of Canterbury, in a letter to Charles Jenkinson, expressed sorrow

> for every instance of unreasonableness & wildness in a body of men to whom I most heartily wish well.[7]

[1] *Ann. Reg.*, 1768, pp. 59–60. [2] *Cal. H.O. Papers*, 1760–65, no. 1029.

[3] T.S. 11/818/2696: 'The case against Daniel Murphy for the wilful murder of Adam McCoy.'

[4] *Ann. Reg.*, 1768, pp. 57, 68.

[5] This was the case of Peter Perryn, sentenced to death at the Old Bailey in October 1769 for forcibly entering the house of John Clare in Stepney in January 1768, with intent to destroy 4 looms (O.B. *Proceedings*, 1769, pp. 446–7), See also *Public Advertiser*, 8 Jan. 1768; *Ann. Reg.*, 1768, p. 68.

[6] S.P. Dom., 37/6, no. 80/2, ff. 186–7; see p. 39 above.

[7] Archbishop of Canterbury to Chas. Jenkinson, 28 Jan. 1768, Add. MSS. 38206, f. 22.

A lull followed; and then, on 26 July, it was reported that

> a great number of evil-disposed persons, armed with pistols, cutlasses and other offensive weapons, and in disguise, assembled themselves together about the hour of twelve in the night . . . and entered the houses and shops of several journeymen weavers in and near Spitalfields . . . and . . . cut to pieces and destroyed the silk works then manufacturing in nine different looms there, belonging to Mr. John Baptist Herbert, of Stewart-Street, Spitalfields, the damage of which is very considerable.[1]

Again, on 20 August, we read that the Spitalfields weavers 'rose in a body', broke into the house of Nathaniel Farr in Pratt's Alley, cut to pieces the silk in two looms and, in the house of Elizabeth Farr, shot dead Edward Fitch, a lad of seventeen. Rewards were offered, but no prosecution followed.[2]

Soon after, there appears to have been an agreement reached between the master weavers and their journeymen, and price-lists were drawn up by certain firms, at least, allowing for earnings of 12s. to 14s. weekly and more. But as the Middlesex justices refused to confirm the agreement, it was soon broken by some of the masters and journeymen, and reprisals began again. To support their cause, the journeymen weavers had formed themselves into committees for the different branches of the trade, called themselves the Bold Defiance, and levied a monthly contribution of 2s. to 5s. a loom to build up a strike fund and meet all expenses. These contributions were collected in conspiratorial fashion at a number of public houses in the weaving districts, to which committee members came in disguise and armed with pistols, swords and cutlasses. Summonses were sent out to masters and journeymen couched in such terms as:

> Mr. Hill, you are desired to send the full donation of all your looms to the Dolphin in Cock Lane. This from the Conquering and Bold Defiance, to be levied 4s. per Loom;

and contributors were handed receipts made out as follows:

> Independent and Bold Defiance
> Received . . . shillings . . . Looms.
> Success to Trade.

Among these places of collection were the Duke of Northumberland's Head, Gun Street; the White Horse, Wheeler Street; the

[1] *Ann. Reg.*, 1768, p. 139.
[2] Ibid., p. 157; *Gent's Mag.*, 1768, p. 442.

White Hart, Vine Court, Spitalfields; the Dolphin, New Cock Lane; the Crown in Hare Street; and the Angel in the parish of St. Agnes le Clere.[1] Correspondence was maintained with Ireland, and a letter sent by seventeen Dublin weavers, thanking the London Committee for its 'unwearied diligence' and proposing joint action by the London and Dublin journeymen, was intercepted by Lord Weymouth.[2]

The 'cutters' reopened their campaign in the spring of 1769 — both, it would seem, to bring wage-cutting employers to heel and to intimidate those defaulting on their subscriptions. On 10 March, we read that Spitalfields throwsters had 'extorted money from the masters and committed many outrages'.[3] On 10 April, William Tilley of St. Leonard, Shoreditch, cut and destroyed a loom 'and a warp of thread therein of the value of ten shillings', the property of Lydia Fowler.[4] Further attacks followed in the summer and autumn. During the night of 7 August, Thomas Poor, self-employed journeyman weaver of Stocking-Frame Alley, Shoreditch, was visited by a number of 'cutters', headed by two of their leaders and committeemen, John Doyle and John Valline. Though Poor protested that he had paid his weekly contribution of 3s. 6d. for the seven looms that he worked with his journeymen for the master weavers, the intruders 'cut a large quantity of bombazine silk in the loom', his looms were 'cut' again on two subsequent occasions and, for fear of more serious reprisals, he was eventually compelled to leave his house and seek nightly refuge 'under hedges in the fields'.[5] Another target of the 'cutters'' animosity was Peter Auber, weaver of Spital Square, who refused to pay the weekly levy demanded. He had his windows broken and was left a number of threatening letters, one of which was phrased in almost lyrical terms:

> Mr. Obey, we give you now an Egg Shell of Honey, but if you refuse to comply with the demands of yesterday, we'll give you a Gallon of Thorns to your final Life's End.[6]

A more substantial victim was Lewis Chauvet of L. Chauvet & Co., silk handkerchief weavers, of 39, Crispin Street, Spitalfields

[1] T.S. 11/818/2696.
[2] *Cal. H.O. Papers*, 1766–69, pp. 509–10.
[3] *Ann. Reg.*, 1769, p. 164.
[4] Middlesex R.O., Sessions Rolls (Middlesex), no. 3214, 9 May 1769; Process Register Bks. of Indictments, xvii (1761–69). 874.
[5] T.S. 11/818/2696; O.B. *Proceedings*, 1769, pp. 438–42; ibid., 1770, pp. 31–46.
[6] T.S. 11/818/2696. See also Appendix IV.

Market.[1] Chauvet, who had signed the 'loyal' merchants' address a few months previously, was accused by John Valline and a crowd of 1,500 weavers of failing to contribute to the committee's funds. Seventy-six of his looms were 'cut' and the work in them destroyed, and it was only after he had given his assailants a written undertaking to pay his contribution and £2 2s. for beer-money that the crowds dispersed.[2] A number of other outrages, leading to capital convictions, followed.[3]

Meanwhile, the authorities had decided to take more vigorous action. At the end of September, the magistrates, supported by military, made an armed raid on the Dolphin Ale-House in New Cock Lane, in the course of which a soldier was shot dead by the weavers, two 'cutters' were killed in the tap-room and one of their leaders, Daniel Murphy, found in the landlord's bed, was arrested and later sentenced to death.[4] Publicans who put their houses at the disposal of the 'cutters'' committees were threatened with the loss of their licences. Troops were quartered in Spitalfields, and Lewis Chauvet and 150 other master weavers undertook to lodge the officers at their own expense and to feed their men at the Three Tuns Tavern at a cost of 9d. per head per day. The City 'patriots' were incensed and the sheriffs, James Townsend and John Sawbridge, protested energetically and held a meeting with Sir John Fielding.[5] The 'patriots'' anger was further aroused by the decision, promoted by 'some principal people about Spitalfields', to terrorize the weavers by hanging two of their leaders, Doyle and Valline, in the neighbourhood of their crimes. The sheriffs, who had raised no protest against the execution of the coal-heavers in Stepney, at first refused (advised, it is said, by Serjeant Glynn) to execute the warrant.[6] Nevertheless, on 6 December, Doyle and Valline were hanged before great crowds of weavers near the Salmon and Ball, Bethnal Green.[7]

[1] *Survey of London*, xxvii (1957). 140.
[2] T.S. 11/818/2696. See Appendix III.
[3] For details of assaults and convictions, see my article, 'Wilkes and Liberty, 1768–69', *The Guildhall Miscellany*, no. 8, July 1957, p. 19, and Appendix III below.
[4] T.S. 11/818/2696.
[5] *Cal. H.O. Papers*, 1766–69, pp. 540–3.
[6] John Shebbeare to James Harris, M.P., 22 Nov. 1769, *Letters of the First Earl of Malmesbury*, i. 180–2.
[7] *Ann. Reg.*, 1769, pp. 159–60. The same day. Lewis Chauvet's house was again attacked, and his windows broken, by Simon Rawlings and 'others unknown' (Middlesex R.O., Sessions Rolls (Middlesex), no. 3222, 8 Jan. 1770; Process Register Bks. of Indictments, xviii (1769–75), 43–4).

On 18 December, Sir John Fielding was able to report on 'the quiet state of the weavers',[1] but the agitation for the release of other convicted 'cutters' went on and received support in the City of London. The same day, we read of John Sawbridge advising a weavers' deputation to appoint a committee and to present a petition to the King 'in favour of their unfortunate brethren now under sentence of death'.[2] Horne also claimed later to have paid £20 out of his own pocket to procure counsel for Baker, an indicted journeyman weaver.[3] Yet Wilkes and his closest associates do not appear to have played any significant part in the agitation — any more than in the weavers' movement as a whole — and Horne wrote to Wilkes in July 1771 that he 'never did receive any subscription for the affair of the weavers of Spitalfields'.[4]

There is, in fact, little evidence to support the view that any of these disputes were other than movements of wage-earners in furtherance of purely economic demands. The coal-heavers, it is true, on one riotous occasion among many, responded to the prevailing enthusiasm over Wilkes and called for illuminations in Shadwell. The Spitalfields weavers, so Horace Walpole assures us, gathered at Hyde Park Corner in March 1768 in order to acclaim Wilkes and to heckle his opponents, but there is no suggestion that these were journeymen rather than masters.[5] Again, the 'patriot' sheriffs, Sawbridge and Townsend, concerned themselves with the fate of the condemned 'cutters' and, in accordance with traditional 'Revolution principles', objected to the drafting of troops into the weaving districts and to public executions being held, with full military support, in any other place but Tyburn. But neither piece of evidence suggests that there was any continuous political direction — either by Wilkites or anyone else — of these complex and protracted disputes, both of which had their own particular history. In the case of the sailors, the evidence is even slighter. While the Newcastle dispute was in full swing, a London newspaper reported:

[1] *Cal. H.O. Papers*, 1766–69, p. 543.

[2] *Ann. Reg.*, 1769, p. 161.

[3] *Controversial Letters of John Wilkes Esq., the Rev. John Horne, and their principal Adherents* (1772), p. 21.

[4] Ibid.

[5] For further evidence of radical trends among Spitalfields weavers, see their petition of May 1773, attributing their 'present distress' to the 'insatiable venality' of Ministers and to the bad relations existing between England and the American colonies — due to the 'same spirit of rapacity' (*Gent's Mag.*, 1773, p. 247); but this was almost certainly inspired by the masters and not the journeymen.

At Newcastle the cry for Wilkes and Liberty is said to be as loud among the sailors as at London, and attended with the same violence.[1]

And yet, according to Walpole, the London sailors petitioning the Commons on 10 May 'declared for the King and drove away Wilkes's mob',[2] and this is confirmed by Lord Weymouth who, in reporting to George III a few days earlier, wrote: 'They cry for redress & seem to disclaim Wilkes.'[3] As for the other half-dozen disputes of the period — those of the tailors, the watermen, the glass-grinders, the hatters and the sawyers — here we cannot find even this minimum element of political intrusion. There can therefore be little justification for treating these movements, either in whole or in part, as 'an outbreak of political strikes'.

Grafton may, of course, have been on more certain ground in contending that the 'discontents' and unruliness of workers engaged in industrial disputes 'led them to join often, in numbers, those mobs which the consequences of the elections for Middlesex frequently produced'. It might indeed seem likely that such workers, being temporarily without employment and already aroused over wages or working conditions, might the more easily be stirred by the pervasive slogan of 'Wilkes and Liberty' and drawn into such great crowds as gathered at Hyde Park Corner, at Brentford or in St. George's Fields, and we have noted the measures taken by the Lord Mayor to meet just such a contingency. Yet such evidence as there is does not give the view much support: of forty-four persons whose occupations are known out of sixty-four arrested in the course of Wilkite disturbances, we find one cooper and two weavers; and none may have been a journeyman.[4] Admittedly, this does not prove very much, but, for lack of other evidence, it might be wisest to conclude that it was only in exceptional circumstances that the industrial disputes of the period 'merged' (as, for a brief moment, in the case of the Shadwell coal-heavers) with the 'Wilkes and Liberty' movement. In general, the two movements ran side by side and, though they must have had some common origins,[5] they were virtually independent and unrelated.

1 *Gent's Mag.*, 1768, p. 241.

2 *Walpole Letters*, v. 100. See also Walpole, *Memoirs*, iii. 141–2.

3 Weymouth to the King, 6 May 1768, Fortescue, ii. no. 616. On 27 March 1771, during the debates on the City-Commons dispute over the London printers, James Townsend even made the charge that 'the sailors' mob was hired and paid by government' (Bristol Univ. Lib., The Parliamentary Diary of Matthew Brickdale, v. 50).

4 See p. 183 and Appendix XI below.

5 See pp. 188–90 below.

VII

THE PETITIONS OF 1769

FAR from 'vanishing into smoke', as George III had hoped, the agitation aroused by the Commons' recognition of Luttrell as Member for Middlesex led to an extensive campaign of protesting petitions to the King, involving nearly a score of counties and a dozen towns and cities all over England; Scotland and Wales remained discreetly outside the movement. In some cases, these petitions were a sequel to the 'instructions' that a number of counties and boroughs had already, in the early months of 1769, sent to their representatives at Westminster to protest against Parliament's previous actions against Wilkes: such 'instructions' were drawn up in Middlesex and Westminster in January, in the City of London in February and in Bristol in March, and aroused a varying response in a number of other constituencies.[1] The petitions that followed were, however, considerably more widespread, more highly organized, they raised more pertinent political and constitutional issues and, above all, though reflecting the varying aims of competing groups of politicians, they were more solidly and directly founded on the deeper sentiments of the mass of the county freeholders and the freemen and householders of the larger trading cities. The 60,000 petitioners must, indeed, have accounted for something more than a quarter of the total voting population and certainly far outnumbered the subscribers to the loyal counter-addresses to the King that they provoked.[2] Sir William Meredith, opposition Member for Liverpool, was, in fact, guilty of merely pardonable exaggeration when he claimed in a widely circulated pamphlet of the day that

> The Middlesex election was a cause in which not only the freeholders of that county were interested, but every other freeholder in the Kingdom, every owner of a franchise, and every other person who, though not

[1] Lucy S. Sutherland, *The City of London and the Opposition to Government, 1768–1774*, pp. 22–3, 24 and n. 1. Newcastle-on-Tyne sent 'instructions' as late as April (*Mid. J.*, 2–4 May 1769).

[2] For G. Grenville's Commons speech of 25 Jan. 1770, see Journal of Debates in the House of Commons, 9–31 January 1770, by Sir Henry Cavendish, Bart., B.M., Eg. 3711, pp. 129–51. For further details see p. 135 and n. 2 below.

immediately represented himself, shares the benefits of our Constitution in common with those who send their representatives to Parliament.[1]

These words betray, of course, the limited objects of the the campaign — it was in no sense a movement for the extension of the parliamentary franchise — and it would be wrong to infer from them that it was a purely spontaneous movement of angry freeholders and citizens. At a time when, in county elections, 'not more than one in every twenty voters . . . could freely exercise his statutory rights',[2] the petitions could hardly be the product of a spontaneous outburst of public alarm and irritation: they had to be organized, and in the counties, at least, their promoters had to be drawn from the county gentry, or even from territorial magnates, whose influence was generally decisive in matters relating to elections or political campaigning. The movement of 1769 was no exception, and, while the petitions voiced a common alarm at the threat to electors' rights implied in the Commons' adoption of Luttrell, they also differed considerably in detail and reflected both the aims of their promoters and occasional local interest. Though there was some overlap between them, these promoters fall into three main groups. There were the metropolitan radicals connected with the Society of Supporters of the Bill of Rights, whose influence was paramount in Middlesex, the City of London, Westminster and Southwark, considerable in Surrey and extended, by personal connection, into Essex and into the western and south-western counties of Wiltshire, Devon and Cornwall and the cities of Bristol and Exeter. There were the Rockingham Whigs, the leading group within the parliamentary opposition since the death of Newcastle, whose interest was paramount in Yorkshire, considerable in such northern counties as Derby, Durham, Lancashire and Cumberland and in the commercial city of Liverpool, and infiltrated via William Dowdeswell into the western counties of Worcester and Hereford. Finally there were the 'three brothers' — Chatham, Temple and George Grenville — temporarily reunited, whose effective influence, on this occasion at least, was largely confined to the counties of

[1] *The Question Stated whether the Freeholders of Middlesex lost their Right by voting for Mr. Wilkes at the last Election. In a letter from a Member of Parliament to one of his Constituents* . . . (1769). An answer to Meredith appears in *A Letter to the Author of the Question Stated* (1769).

[2] Sir Lewis Namier, *The Structure of Politics at the Accession of George III* (2nd. edition, 1957), p. 73.

Buckinghamshire and Kent.[1] Yet attempts were made from the start, and with some success, to narrow the differences between them. George Grenville and William Dowdeswell, Rockinghamite leader in the House of Commons, held discussions with some of the City leaders in early May, and, a week later, a dinner at the Thatched House Tavern was attended by all members of the opposition groups in the Commons and some sort of programme of joint action was agreed upon.[2]

But differences persisted and left their mark on both the content of the petitions and the conduct of the campaign in a number of counties and cities. The Supporters of the Bill of Rights and City radicals (here at variance with Wilkes himself) wanted to make Wilkes's disqualification and the adoption of Luttrell the occasion for a general onslaught on the government's policies, in the course of which freeholders and freemen should be called upon to air a long list of grievances for presentation to the King: this, as we shall see, was the pattern set by the Society's leaders in Middlesex and London, though it was later modified under the influence of the parliamentary opposition groups. The Rockingham Whigs, on the other hand, insisted on limiting the field of agitation to the single issue of the Middlesex election: they had no desire whatever either to advance the personal cause of Wilkes or to promote the radical aims of the Middlesex freeholders and the London livery. For long, they hesitated between petitioning and drafting 'instructions', and it was only Edmund Burke's persistence, supported by Dowdeswell, that overcame the objections of the other Rockinghamite leaders to the course of petitioning the Crown for a redress of grievances.[3] Even Dowdeswell, though accepting Burke's arguments, was to complain that 'the injudicious list of grievances which filled the first petitions . . . disinclined the

[1] There was considerable overlapping between the three groups: Sawbridge and Townsend, both Middlesex freeholders and Supporters of the Bill of Rights, were parliamentary Chathamites and Sawbridge promoted Chatham's interest in Kent; Beckford was a City radical (though not a Supporter of the Bill of Rights), an intimate of Chatham's and had personal influence in Wilts and Somerset (see Sutherland, op. cit., pp. 21, 27); and James Adair, while co-operating with Rockingham in promoting the first Middlesex petition of April 1769, was the first to sign the distinctly non-Rockinghamite petition of 24 May. In addition, Chatham, Rockingham and Temple all had their own particular interest in City politics (see pp. 151–2, 167 below).

[2] Sutherland, op. cit., p. 25. Dr. Sutherland's account of the petition campaign (pp. 24–32) is by far the best that has appeared.

[3] Burke to Rockingham, 2 and 30 July, 6 and 13 Sept. 1769; Burke to Thos. Whately, 21 Aug. 1769; *Burke Correspondence*, ii. 40–1, 50–1, 56, 73, 79.

sober part of the people to signing petitions which they concluded must partake of the same spirit'.[1] Sir George Savile was distinctly lukewarm,[2] and Rockingham himself, ever mindful of the opinion of 'the sober, large-acred part of the nation' (Burke's phrase), hesitated almost up to the last moment before accepting Burke's repeated advice to recommend this course to his supporters and retainers in Yorkshire: 'I *must say* [he wrote] that the thing which weighs most against adopting the mode of petitioning the King is *where* the example was first set.'[3] Finally, Temple and Chatham, though their interest in City politics inclined them to follow London's lead,[4] eventually took Burke's advice; and the draft of the Buckinghamshire petition was actually submitted by Temple to Burke for his approval.[5]

The Supporters of the Bill of Rights and the metropolitan radicals suffered less than their political rivals from divided counsels and it was they who took the initiative and set the pace. As soon as the Commons had resolved, on 15 April, to accept Luttrell in the place of Wilkes, James Townsend had invited the Middlesex freeholders to see 'the necessity of seeking out some new remedy for a new grievance'.[6] The first Middlesex petition was, as we saw, adopted on 27 April and presented to Parliament a few days later.[7] In London, a demand was voiced, almost simultaneously, for a Common Hall of the livery to discuss the Middlesex election, but, owing to differences within the Common Council,[8] the meeting was deferred for two months. Meanwhile, on 8 May, the Supporters of the Bill of Rights had appointed a committee of four

> to take into consideration and to make use of the best means to redress the grievances of the electors of this Kingdom and to restore to them the privileges which they ought to enjoy by the Bill of Rights and the Constitution of England.[9]

[1] Dowdeswell to Burke, 5 Sept. 1769, ibid. ii. 70.
[2] Savile to Rockingham, 24 Sept. 1769, *Rockingham Memoirs*, ii. 132–6.
[3] Rockingham to Burke, 1, 3 Sept. 1769, *Burke Correspondence*, ii. 65.
[4] See Rockingham to Burke, 17 July 1769, ibid, ii. 48: 'Lord Temple will try to include all the matters mentioned in the City and Livery petition . . . I even should scarce be surprised if annual or triennial Parliaments were recommended.'
[5] See p. 117 below.
[6] *Lond. Chron.*, 15–18 April 1769; cit. Sutherland, op. cit., p. 24.
[7] See pp. 71–72 above. Historians do not appear to have noted that there were *two* Middlesex petitions — the first (29 April) presented to Parliament, the second (24 May) presented to the King.
[8] See p. 153 below.
[9] *Ox. Mag.*, ii. 197.

It was this committee — composed of Sawbridge, Townsend, Bellas and Horne — that played the main part in promoting the Society's aims in the course of the petition campaign. Not content with this, the Society further decided to attempt to set up a more permanent form of electoral machinery based on its local support, and, three weeks later, it sent out letters to parliamentary constituencies, inviting them to form corresponding societies with the parent body and 'to promote its political principles'; this more ambitious appeal appears, however, to have evoked but a limited response.[1] In the meantime, the Middlesex freeholders had gone ahead with remarkable speed and, by 24 May, a second petition was ready for presentation to the King and had been signed by 1,565 freeholders. This time, it was the moving spirits of the Bill of Rights Society and not the Rockingham Whigs that decided both its form and its contents. The King was urged 'to banish from [his] royal favour, trust and confidence for ever those evil and pernicious counsellors . . . ' This final request was preceded by an impressive array of over a score of grievances, including arrests by general warrant, neglect of *habeas corpus* and trial by jury, failure to consider petitions, attacks on freedom of the press, the outlawry and imprisonment of Wilkes, excessive use of the military, the murder of peaceful citizens, the reprieve of Balfe and McQuirk, the violating of the rights of electors, the squandering of public funds, and the mismanagement of the American colonies.[2]

A month later, the long-delayed meeting of the London livery took place at the Guildhall. It had been called ostensibly for the election of new sheriffs; but even before Townsend and Sawbridge were elected[3] — itself a triumph for the 'patriot' party — there was a loud cry (so Richard Burke reported to his brother Edmund) of 'Petition, Petition!' The Lord Mayor, Samuel Turner, promised that it should be considered and a petition was duly read by Mark Lovell, a West India merchant of Mark Lane, which, after

[1] Sutherland, op. cit., p. 28 and n. 1. In Norwich, a Society of Correspondence was set up in early June and a subscription opened (*Read. Merc.*, 12 June 1769). In Liverpool, a local paper advertised the Society's aims (*Williamson's Liverpool Advertiser*, 2 June 1769). A further circular, dated 6 June, was received by William Dowdeswell, who decided not to reply and was complimented on this by Rockingham (Dowdeswell to Burke, 10 Aug. 1769; Rockingham to Burke, 1, 3 Sept. 1769; *Burke Correspondence*, ii. 53–4, 65).

[2] P.R.O., H.O. 55/4; *Pol. Reg.*, iv. 347–9; *Ann. Reg.*, 1769, pp. 197–200; *Read. Merc.*, 5 June 1769.

[3] Only 3 or 4 votes were cast for their opponents, John Kirkman and Samuel Plumbe (E. Langton to Hardwicke, 24 June 1769, Add. MSS. 35608, ff. 373–4).

speeches by Beckford and Trecothick, was adopted with only one dissentient.[1] Like the Middlesex petition, it took the form of a violent arraignment of the general conduct of George III's Ministers and called for their removal; but, this time, the grievances were limited to half the number. Though nominally a petition, it bore only one signature; it was handed to the King by the Lord Mayor and the four London M.P.s in the course of a distinctly chilly ceremony on 5 July.[2]

Before the London petition had been agreed, Horne and Bellas had been busy in Surrey, where Horne himself had a small freehold farm and the Society enjoyed the particular support of Sir Joseph Mawbey, Bart., M.P. for Southwark and Vauxhall malt-distiller. A preliminary meeting was held on 16 June at the St. Alban's Tavern, St. Alban Street, where a drafting committee of a dozen justices was appointed; on it Rockingham supporters far outnumbered those of the Bill of Rights Society.[3] Ten days later, a county meeting was held at Epsom and attended by nearly two thousand freeholders. Considerable efforts were exerted to ensure its success and we read that Sir Joseph Mawbey on his way from Botleys was met at Morden by freeholders from Wandsworth, Putney and Wimbledon, and, at Ewell, by others from Chertsey, Kingston, Croydon and adjacent villages who, 'to the number of 400, fell into the cavalcade according to a previous agreement for that purpose'. 'After which,' the report continued, 'the whole body that attended him was near 1,000, and they proceeded in great order with French horns into the town of Epsom.'[4] The meeting was presided over by the Hon. Peter King of Dorking, son

[1] R. Burke to E. Burke, 24 June 1769, *Burke Correspondence*, ii. 32–34. 'It was wonderful,' wrote Richard, 'it was as peaceable an assembly, and as free from tumult, except their applauses and censures may be called tumult, as you can well conceive. If the Ministry can stand this, the people certainly have no kind of influence.'

[2] H.O. 55/6; *Pol. Reg.*, v. 49–50; Maccoby, *English Radicalism 1762–1785*, p. 120. The King's lack of courtesy prompted Beckford to remark to his colleagues: 'If we have only this treatment, we have no business here' (J. R. Owen Cambridge to Hardwicke, 6 July 1769, Add. MSS. 35609, ff. 8–9).

[3] Those appointed were Hon. Thomas Howard, son of the Earl of Suffolk and Berkshire and M.P. for Malmesbury; Hon. Peter King, J.P., of Dorking, son of Thomas, Baron King of Ockam; Hon. C. Howard; Sir Anthony Abdy, Bart., of Chobham, M.P. for Knaresborough; Sir George Colebrooke, Bart., of Gatton, M.P. for Arundel (see p. 88 above); Sir Joseph Mawbey, Bart., of Botleys; Robert Scawen, J.P.; Joseph Martin, of Eastwick, M.P. for Gatton; Anthony Chapman, J.P., of Norbury; William Gill, J.P.; William Ellis, J.P., and P. C. Webb junior, J.P., son of the former Solicitor to the Treasury.

[4] *Read. Merc.*, 3 July 1769.

of Lord King, and addressed by Sir George Colebrooke, Bart., Sir Robert Clayton, Bart., P. C. Webb junior, and three Supporters of the Bill of Rights — Mawbey, Horne and Dr. Joseph Allen, Master of Dulwich College.[1] It was decided to send the petition to all market towns in the county[2] and ten gentlemen were appointed to present it to the King.[3] The petition was moderate enough, Horne's original draft having been rejected: it confined itself to the single grievance of 'the right of election in the people . . . violated in the late instance of the Middlesex election' and called on the King, by the exercise of his prerogative powers, 'to give us such relief as to your royal wisdom shall seem meet'.[4] Nevertheless, Rockingham had been considerably alarmed by the activites of John Horne and, before hearing the final outcome, he wrote to Burke:

> I wish the zeal of the Revd. Mr. Horne may not have gone too far and that the petition that will be presented will be too much in the general vague and wild manner of the other two.[5]

Though these particular fears proved to be ill-founded, Sir Anthony Abdy, who could speak for that 'grave, sober and firm part of the considerable gentlemen of the County' to whom Lord Rockingham looked for support, drew back in alarm at the zeal displayed by the Society's spokesmen and, pleading gout, took no further part in the promotion of the petition. Writing to Sir George Colebrooke in early July, he protested at 'the wild and warm proceedings of Messrs. Horne, Bellas etc., and others of the London Tavern, the generality of whose opinions and ideas I cannot agree or subscribe to'.[6] And when the petition, signed by 1,494 freeholders (representing, it was said, 'a great majority

[1] Other speakers were Claude Crespigny, LL.D., and James Evelyn, J.P. (*Read. Merc.*, 19 June 1769). Sir Robert Clayton was M.P. for Bletchingley.

[2] Different skins were left for this purpose at Kingston, Dorking, Chertsey and Guildford, and at places nearer town for residents of Southwark, London and Westminster (*Worcs. J.*, 27 July 1769). Even so, the petition was not seen in several parts of the county, owing to lack of time, and there was even talk of holding a second freeholders' meeting at Runnymede (*Read. Merc.*, 3 July, 28 Aug. 1769).

[3] They were Abdy, Chapman, Clayton, Thos. Howard, P. King, Colebrooke, Mawbey, Martin (see p. 110, n. 3, and n. 1 above); Joseph Clarke, J.P., of Moulsey; and Sir Francis Vincent, Bart., M.P. for Surrey (*Pol. Reg.*, v. 50–2).

[4] H.O. 55/1; *Pol. Reg.*, v. 182.

[5] Rockingham to Burke, 29 June 1769, *Burke Correspondence*, ii. 36. In a scribbled note to 'Lord —' (undated) Rockingham wrote that he had not yet seen the Surrey petition, but 'thought chance of it being good as petn drawn up by Revd — had not been adopted' (W.W. MSS., R 1/1206).

[6] Cit. Sutherland, op. cit., p. 29.

of the freeholders resident in the county'),[1] was presented to the King on 24 August, Abdy once more pleaded gout as his reason for not accompanying his fellow-sponsors to St. James's Palace.[2]

Meanwhile, the London petition had roused a sympathetic response in the fellow-trading city of Bristol. Bristol merchants, alarmed at the decision to tax British manufactures imported into America, had already 'instructed' their M.P.s in March.[3] As a counter-blast, its strictly loyalist Corporation had sent a 'humble address' to the King,[4] and both its Members, Matthew Brickdale and Lord Clare, were, though in varying degrees, supporters of Administration. But Henry Cruger, to become Burke's fellow-M.P. and rival and to be known as 'a hot Wilkite', was already a rising force in city politics and, with the backing of the newly-formed Independent Society, was able to convene and preside over a large meeting on 18 July, summoned to consider a petition to the King.[5] Letters of support had previously appeared in the *Bristol Journal*. One, signed 'Atticus', urged 'the worthy freemen of the City of Bristol' to follow London's example:

The triumph of our brethren in London over an abandoned A—n is an event unspeakably joyous. I hope the rotten foundations of Bribery and Corruption have received a shock by the spirited conduct of the patriotic Livery, which will at length terminate in their total destruction . . . The Iron Hand of Arbitrary Power has been stretched out to crush you . . . Rouse, my countrymen! rouse! lay your grievances at the foot of the Throne. You have a King who is the Father of his People, who only wants to *know* in order to *redress* your complaints.

In a second, 'John Hampden' enthusiastically welcomed the decision to petition:

It is high time to take the alarm. There is no denying that the present times are more peculiarly critical than most of the past . . . Venality and corruption were never so barefaced; nor was public spirit at so low an

[1] *Read. Merc.*, 28 Aug. 1769. According to another report, it was signed by nine-tenths of the county's freeholders (*Worcs., J.*, 27 July 1769).

[2] *Worcs. J.*, 31 Aug. 1769. Later, however, Abdy strongly favoured a petition in Yorkshire and took steps to promote one in Essex (Burke to Rockingham, 9 Sept. 1769, *Burke Correspondence*, ii. 75–76).

[3] *Lond. Chron.*, 11–14 March 1769.

[4] *Brist. J.*, 25 March 1769.

[5] P. T. Underdown, 'Henry Cruger and Edmund Burke: Colleagues and Rivals at the Bristol Election of 1774', *The William and Mary Quarterly*, xv (1958), 14–34.

ebb . . . It is from the *Throne* alone you are to expect redress of those intolerable grievances under which the whole Nation groans.[1]

Assured of success, Cruger addressed his audience at the Guildhall on 'the present lamentable state' of the American colonies and on 'the numberless persecutions and cruelties exercised against the person of Mr. Wilkes'. With one dissentient voice, it was agreed to draw up a petition, which was 'universally approved of' two days later and displayed to attract initial signatures at the Fountain Tavern in the High Street; subsequently, it was promised, it would 'be offered to the citizens of Bristol for signing at their respective houses with all convenient speed'.[2] Following the example of London, the petition listed some ten grievances calling for immediate redress, but, in response to local discontents, it particularly castigated the action of 'obnoxious' Ministers in 'ruining our manufactories by invidiously imposing and establishing the most impolitic and unconstitutional taxations and regulations on your Majesty's colonies', and called for their summary dismissal. The petition was signed by 2,445 of the city's 5,000 electors and presented to the King by Henry Cruger, Samuel Span, a Bristol merchant, and two M.P.s on 5 January 1770.[3]

Up to this point, the running had been made by the Supporters of the Bill of Rights and their London associates, but now Burke and his friends were beginning to show results for their own vigorous campaigning. Their first success was scored in Worcestershire, where Dowdeswell was one of the County Members. It does not seem to have been handled with any great skill. According to a hostile critic, a petitioning meeting 'was first proposed by a shatter-brained fellow, Holland Cooksey (who is Chairman, to the disgrace of the County) at the sessions. A meeting was afterwards advertised at the Assizes which, nothing being then done, was adjourned to the Race Week.'[4] In mid-July, 'a Freeholder of

[1] *Brist. J.*, 8, 15 July 1769. The opposing view was also expressed: 'Civis' warned his readers, 'inclined to imitate the Livery of London', to consider carefully before '*swimming in a troubled sea*'; while, after the event, 'Truman' denounced 'the emissaries of a turbulent faction [who] have prevailed on a part of you to determine upon troubling the Throne with a petition for redress from pretended grievances' (ibid., 15, 22 July 1769).

[2] Ibid., 22 July 1769.

[3] H.O. 55/6 (the petition is dated 25 July 1769); *Pol. Reg.*, vi. 115–16; *Lond. Chron.*, 23–25 Nov. 1769; *General Evening Post*, 4–6 Jan. 1770. The M.P.s were Sir William Codrington, Bart. (Tewkesbury), and Richard Hippisley Coxe (Somerset). Neither Cruger's nor Span's signature appears on the petition.

[4] Chas. Cocks to Hardwicke, 17 Sept. 1769, Add. MSS. 35609, ff. 43–44.

Forty Shillings a Year', in a letter to the *Worcester Journal*, showed that he, at least, was fully prepared to widen the field of agitation far beyond the limits prescribed by Burke and Dowdeswell:

A day is at last appointed [he wrote] when we shall come prepared to enquire whether, notwithstanding the proud connexions of families, the weight of overgrown estates and the wretched dependence of our Boroughs, sneers upon the very existence of patriotism, and the opprobrious epithet of Faction; whether, notwithstanding the intrigues of Great Men in Parliament, their influence in some of the Courts of Law, the Massacre in St. George's Fields, and the many other breaches of the Constitution; whether, notwithstanding even that last breach of the Right of Election, which cuts off LIBERTY from the land, we have not still the POWER in our hands to do ourselves justice if we can but use it.[1]

Yet the freeholders' meeting, held at the Worcester Guildhall on 9 August, resolved 'to present a petition to the Throne . . . and that the charge in the said petition should be confined to a certain vote in the House of Commons by which Mr. Luttrell was declared duly elected for Middlesex against the sense of a very large and determined majority of voters in that election'.[2] All M.P.s within the county were to be invited to present the petition when completed and a committee was appointed to distribute it round the county for the benefit of those who had not attended the meeting.[3] Dowdeswell was well satisfied with the day's work and wrote to Burke:

Yesterday we agreed to petitioning, confining our complaint to the injury done to the rights of the electors. We have kept in the distinction between the virtues of the King and the vices of the Administration and imputed the ill conduct of the House of Commons to the bad practices of the latter. The meeting was not numerous but the subscription will be large.[4]

But, a month later, he wrote complaining that the petition

[1] *Worcs. J.*, 20 July 1769.

[2] As adopted, the petition introduced new arguments: (*a*) In persecuting Wilkes, Ministers were accused of being prompted in fact 'by designs of a more dangerous nature'; (*b*) Luttrell is described as 'a candidate avowedly set up . . . and rendered capable of becoming a candidate by the grant of an office under your Majesty for that purpose only'; and (*c*) the issue is termed 'the common cause of all the electors of Great Britain' (H.O. 55/2; *Pol. Reg.*, vi. 119–20).

[3] *Worcs. J.*, 27 July, 10 Aug. 1769. Chas. Cocks wrote that the petition was only signed by 'a few gentlemen' present 'after being corrected by Mr. Dowdeswell' (see p. 113, n. 4, above).

[4] Dowdeswell to Burke, 10 Aug. 1769, *Burke Correspondence*, ii. 53.

> goes *slowly*. There is wanting a management in circulating the petition through the different parts of the county. However, some of the duplicates are now going. Wilkes's character, of which men are inclined to think much worse than it really deserves, and the advantage that he necessarily must receive from the restitution to the public of its rights at present lost, have check'd this proceeding in most places.

He added pertinently: 'It is amazing how in most places people of rank and fortune shrink from this measure, and with what deference all others below them wait for their leaders.'[1] His hopes, however, that, in spite of all, 'the subscription to it will fill sufficiently well' were to be reasonably justified: when presented, the petition bore some 1,475 signatures.[2]

The Wiltshire petition, which followed soon after, once more bore the mark of the City of London and the Bill of Rights Society. The moving spirits appear to have been William Beckford who, as the proprietor of Fonthill, was a freeholder and justice of the county, and Edward Popham, M.P. for Wiltshire.[3] The freeholders' meeting, after due notice had appeared in the press,[4] took place at Devizes on 16 August. Beckford attended with Lord Temple, who was his guest at Fonthill.[5] John Talbot, a local justice, proposed a petition in two parts — the first protesting against Luttrell's adoption in the place of Wilkes, the second against the reprieve of McQuirk, the Irish chairman found guilty at the Old Bailey of the Brentford election murder. According to James Harris, M.P. for Christchurch and a hostile observer, 'a petition of a much greater variety of complaints was proposed, but rejected'; others wished to delete the reference to McQuirk, but Talbot's compromise was carried — with two dissentient voices: those of 'Mr. Fox and the parson of his parish'.[6] The speakers (ran a press report) were, in addition to Beckford, Talbot and the 'Hon. Mr. Fox', Charles Penruddock, future County Member, William Hussey, M.P. for Hindon (Wilts), and two local justices — Ambrose Audrey and William Temple.[7] The petition got off to a

[1] Ibid., ii. 70.

[2] H.O. 55/2. A petition in similar terms was adopted by the City of Worcester and bears the signatures of some 650 of its citizens (H.O. 55/4).

[3] Sutherland, op. cit. p. 27 n. 3.

[4] Burke to Rockingham, 30 July 1769, *Burke Correspondence*, ii. 50.

[5] *Worcs. J.*, 17 Aug. 1769; Sutherland, loc. cit.

[6] Jas. Harris, M.P., to Hardwicke, 7 Sept. 1769, Add. MSS. 35609, ff. 34–35. 'Mr. Fox' was Stephen Fox, M.P. for Salisbury, son of Lord Holland and elder brother of C. J. Fox.

[7] *Worcs. J.*, 24 Aug. 1769.

good start and, three weeks later, it was reported that 'the signing of the Wiltshire petition in the City of Salisbury goes with great spirit; one large skin of parchment is already filled with names, and another preparing'. Some 1,200 signatures were eventually collected.[1]

So far, the petitions, whether inspired by the Rockingham Whigs or by the Supporters of the Bill of Rights, had, in varying terms, called on the King to exercise his prerogative according to his own discretion: at most, he had been urged to dismiss his Ministers. But, at the end of August, a new stage was reached in the campaign when the inhabitants of Westminster, though concentrating on the single grievance of Luttrell's adoption, directed their main fire against the House of Commons itself by calling for the dissolution of Parliament and for the convening of another 'as speedily as may be'.[2] This became a model that the majority of subsequent petitioning counties and boroughs were quick to follow. Once more, it was the Supporters of the Bill of Rights that set the pace. After preliminary meetings held at the Globe Tavern in the Strand and the Standard Tavern in Leicester Fields, citizens were summoned to the Westminster Hall on the 29th, where Sir Robert Bernard, Bart., of Huntingdon, took the chair, supported by Robert Jones, chairman of the organizing committee, Dr. Thomas Wilson, Prebendary of Westminster, and Humphrey Cotes, wine-merchant of St. Martin's Lane and a close friend of Wilkes.[3] Edward Langton, a hostile eyewitness, reported to Hardwicke that 'they were received in the Hall with the shouts of between 2 & 3,000 people to say the most (though those who were fond of the meeting estimated them above double that number)';[4] and he added that the petition having been proposed by Jones and seconded by either Mr. Martin, Serjeant Glynn's attorney, or John Lycett, upholsterer of Golden Square, was 'received with violent shouts of applause, both of huzzas &

[1] *Exeter Flying Post*, 5–11 Sept. 1769; H.O. 55/2.

[2] H.O. 55/1. A precedent for directly petitioning the King had been provided as recently as 1764 in the City's petition against the Cider Act (Sutherland, op. cit., p. 25 n. 1); but precedents for praying the Crown to dissolve Parliament had to be sought in Charles II's reign (*Mid. J.*, 25–28 Nov., 5-7 Dec. 1769; *Glos. J.*, 6 Nov. 1769).

[3] *Worcs. J.*, 17, 24 Aug. 1769. Sir Robert Bernard was former M.P. for Huntingdonshire. All four were prominent Supporters of the Bill of Rights.

[4] The press gave the number as 7,000 (ibid., 31 Aug. 1769; *Read. Merc.*, 4 Sept. 1769).

clapping of hands'.[1] Signatures were invited forthwith and it was reported that, by early afternoon, 2,000 names had been signed.[2] According to Langton's account, 'the majority of the assembly were rather well dressed creditable looking people'; though he added that 'that part of the company who seemed eager for signing were of the shabby sort.' By early November, 4,000 had signed, and these had grown to 5,137 ('which is a respectable majority') by the time the petition was carried in mid-December to St. James's to the accompaniment of a salvo of gun-fire from Standgate, by Lambeth.[3]

The first county to follow Westminster's example in demanding a dissolution of Parliament was Buckinghamshire, whose petition eventually emerged, after much delay, in early September. As a freeholder of the county and M.P. for the borough of Wendover, Burke took more than a casual interest in what would be undertaken in this stronghold of the Temple-Grenville connexion. In July, Rockingham had been thoroughly pessimistic about the outcome,[4] but Burke persisted and, writing on 21 August, to Thomas Whately, M.P. for Castle Rising and an intimate of Grenville, he asked what was intended and urged that any action should take the form of a petition to the King.[5] Whately's reply was reassuring: 'The sentiments of my friends on the subject of a petition I know to be exactly agreeable to yours: to keep to the principal point and to express themselves upon that with vigour and decency.' A week later, he wrote further to inform Burke that Lord Temple had drafted a petition along these lines and would submit it to him for his approval.[6] The freeholders were canvassed for their opinion at Race Week on 7 September; however, the weather was bad and the company 'thin' and Lord Temple 'said he found the freeholders in general totally ignorant of the question, and but very little affected with it'. But the gentry seemed to favour a petition and Burke considered it probable that on the day

[1] E. Langton to Hardwicke, 29 Aug. 1769, Add. MSS. 35609. ff. 32–33.
[2] *Read. Merc.*, 4 Sept. 1769.
[3] *Worcs. J.*, 9 Nov. 1769; *Mid. J.*, 15–17 Dec. 1769; H.O. 55/1. Westminster had an electorate of a little over 9,000 (see p. 75, n. 2, above).
[4] Rockingham to Burke, 17 July 1769, *Burke Correspondence*, ii. 48. The meeting of freeholders, called for 12 September, had been advertised as early as 4 July. The delay Burke attributed both to 'the politics of Stowe' and to a desire to see what would happen in Yorkshire (Burke to Rockingham, 9 July, 6 Sept. 1769, ibid., ii. 45, 71–2).
[5] Burke to Thos. Whately, 21 Aug. 1769, ibid., ii. 56.
[6] Whately to Burke, 23, 30 Aug. 1769, ibid, ii., 56, 59.

of business our appearance will be decent at least'.[1] In fact, the outcome 'proved beyond expectation'. On the appointed day, John Aubrey, M.P. for Wallingford, rode into Aylesbury 'at the head of sixty-five freeholders'; 400 or more turned up in the Town Hall, 'many of them substantial people, who came forward to the work with a great countenance and an *alacrity* equal to that of the Third Regiment of Guards'.[2] George Grenville stayed away, but Lord Temple assured his supper audience later in the day that both Grenville and Chatham 'would support this and every constitutional measure for the general good'. Speakers at the meeting noted by the press were Earl Verney, County Member; John Calcraft, M.P. for Rochester; Murrough O'Brien, J.P.; John Aubrey and Edmund Burke.[3] 'I can take it,' wrote Burke, 'the signatures will be general. Above three hundred signed upon the spot. We have not, I believe, two thousand in the county.'[4] The signatories rose eventually to a little over 1,800, which John Aubrey claimed to represent four-fifths of all the county's freeholders.[5]

A few days after the Aylesbury meeting, the Gloucestershire freeholders were summoned by their High Sheriff, William Singleton of Norton, to assemble at the Bell Inn in Gloucester. Here, as in certain other western counties, the impetus to petition seems to have come more from the local gentry and freeholders themselves than from any outside group. Yet the gentry was divided and no help came from the two County Members, Thomas Tracy and Edward Southwell, who remained either indifferent or hostile to the movement.[6] Dowdeswell noted in early September that 'the disposition is good in general, but leaders are wanting'.[7] The meeting on 16 September was well supported by the gentry: according to a press report, 'a very considerable number of gentlemen of the greatest property of this

[1] Burke to Rockingham, 9 Sept. 1769, *Burke Correspondence*, ii. 76.

[2] Burke to Rockingham, 13 Sept. 1769, ibid. ii. 78–79. It was the Third Regiment of Guards that had fired on demonstrators in St. George's Fields.

[3] *Brist. J.*, 16 Sept. 1769; *Worcs. J.*, 21 Sept. 1769.

[4] Burke to Rockingham, 13 Sept. 1769, *Burke Correspondence*, ii. 79. See also *Read. Merc.*, 18 Sept. 1769.

[5] H.O. 55/6; *Lond. Chron.*, 28-30 Nov. 1769; Eg. 3711, p. 50. In reply to suggestions made in the Commons that there were 4,500 freeholders in Buckinghamshire, G. Grenville stated categorically that 'there are not above 26 or 2700 voters' (ibid., pp. 50–51, 53).

[6] W. R. Williams, *The Parliamentary History of Gloucestershire* (Hereford, 1898), pp. 66–67.

[7] Dowdeswell to Burke, 5 Sept. 1769, *Burke Correspondence*, ii. 71.

county assembled'; but it added that a proposal to petition the King 'was received with general disapprobation'. Nevertheless, it was agreed to leave the petition at the King's Head Inn where, 'within two hours afterwards, [it] was signed by a great number of gentlemen and freeholders'.[1] A month later, the same journal gave a precise account of the methods used to obtain signatures within the county:

> The Gloucestershire freeholders' petition to his Majesty, having been already signed by a great number of gentlemen and freeholders . . . the same is now left at the King's Head Inn in Gloucester, to be perused and signed by those of the neighbourhood thereof who have not yet had an opportunity of doing it; and for the conveniency of other gentlemen and freeholders who live in different parts of the County, duplicates of the petition are now in the following market towns:—viz. Tewkesbury, Cirencester, Stroud, Hampston, Painswick, Stonehouse, Cheltenham, Newent, Newnham and Chipping Sodbury; and on the 24th day of October inst. (being Fair-Day at Stow) and on the 4th day of November next (being Fair-day at Chipping Campden) a person will attend at those respective places, to the intent that the same may be perused and signed by the gentlemen and freeholders of the upper part of the County.[2]

Though opponents of the petition had argued 'how easily signing addresses as well as petitions could be procured', some freeholders do not appear to have been so readily persuaded. One, at least, refused to sign 'the present circulating petition' until he received satisfactory answers to three pertinent questions that he published in the press: Had the Commons 'an acknowledged right' to expel their own Members? If they had, did such an expulsion create 'an absolute incapacity' to sit again in that House? If so, could Wilkes have been admitted to sit again for Middlesex, even had the Commons wished it, 'without a violation of the usage of that House'?[3] Administration itself would have been at pains to find a clear and truthful answer — and there was none forthcoming. But,

[1] *Glos. J.*, 18 Sept. 1769. See also *Worcs. J.*, 21 Sept. 1769, and, in the same, a report that the Ministry were trying to promote a loyal address and to scotch the petition (28 Sept. 1769).

[2] *Glos. J.*, 23 Oct. 1769.

[3] Ibid., 6 Nov. 1769. This was the crux of the question debated in the Commons on 31 Jan. 1770 on Dowdeswell's motion 'that no person eligible by law can be incapitated from election by a vote of the House, but by Act of Parliament alone'. Lord North, in moving the previous question, argued ambiguously that 'a vote of the House cannot create an incapacity, but there is one case in which a vote doth incapacitate, and that is a sentence of expulsion'. The House was clearly not impressed and only accepted the previous question by a majority of 40 (Eg. 3711, pp. 173–246).

despite such misgivings and the obvious hostility of a part of the gentry, the petition, which was moderate in tone and made no extravagant demands, was supported by nearly 2,000 freeholders.[1]

Later in September, the most important of the county petitions, and that most eagerly awaited, was adopted in York and began to circulate among the Yorkshire gentry and freeholders. Some action in Yorkshire had been mooted as early as June but, at this stage, Rockingham favoured an address to the County Members.[2] Burke, however, declared himself to be 'rather more fond of the method of petition, because it carries more the air of uniformity and concurrence; and, being more out of the common road . . . it will be more striking and more suitable to the magnitude of the occasion'.[3] A month later, encouraged by developments in other counties, he had become more pressing. He insisted that, 'if we want to get *redress*, we must strengthen the hands of the minority within doors by the accession of the publick opinion', and he added:

> I assure your Lordship, by every thing that I can find, that both friends and foes look with very anxious eyes towards Yorkshire, the one very eagerly expecting, the other heartily dreading some motion of yours. I hear the language of the Courtiers is that your Lordship has put a stop to the design of petitioning in your county, and they have commended you for it; but I trust you will not long suffer the disgrace of their praises.[4]

A fortnight later, he insisted further;

> We are come to a great crisis, and much of the future of all public affairs will depend upon your Lordship's conduct at this time.[5]

In early September, Rockingham was still expressing doubts as to the proper procedure and wrote to explain why he had discouraged the calling of a county meeting by public advertisement a week before: such precipitate action, he felt, 'would scarce be fully approved to be the cool, prudent, firm and dignified sense of the county'; but following a deputation of county gentry attending

[1] H.O. 55/6; *Lond. Chron.*, 25–28 Nov. 1769; *Glos. J.*, 27 Nov. 1769.
[2] Rockingham to Burke, 29 June 1769, *Burke Correspondence*, ii. 38.
[3] Burke to Rockingham, 2 July 1769, ibid., ii. 41.
[4] Burke to Rockingham, 30 July 1769, ibid., ii. 51–52.
[5] Burke to Rockingham, 13 Aug. 1769, ibid., ii. 54. He added loyally: 'Be that conduct what it may. I shall easily persuade myself that it is right.'

the races,[1] the High Sheriff had agreed to call a meeting for 27 September.[2] In welcoming the news, Burke replied:

I do assure your Lordship that the supposed inaction of Yorkshire was a matter of greater pleasure to enemies, and of despair to friends of every sort, than can well be expressed. The well-wishers of the cause now begin to brighten up and to entertain livelier hopes.

And he wrote to David Garrick: 'Yorkshire has begun to move and its progress will be, I trust, great and powerful like a giant refresh'd with wine.'[3]

Burke was not to be disappointed. The meeting, held in York on 24 September, drew about 800 persons — an imposing array of nobility, gentry, clergy and prosperous freeholders. Among them a 'letter from York' to the *Reading Mercury* noted Lord Downe, Viscount Belasyse, Lord John Cavendish, Sir James Ibbetson, Sir Digby Legard, Sir William Anderson, Sir James Norcliffe, Sir George Savile, Sir George Armytage, Sir Cecil Wray, Sir Marmaduke Wyvill, Sir George Metham; half a dozen other M.P.s: Alexander Wedderburn, Edwin and Daniel Lascelles, Beilby Thompson, Charles Allanson, Nathaniel Cholmondeley, Charles Turner and William Weddell; and a score of other worthies — 'all gentlemen of great property'.[4]

A considerable number of the clergy were there [wrote Burke], men of weight and character; and I am glad of it, because some people were

[1] The deputation included a number of M.P.s: Nathaniel Cholmondeley (Boroughbridge), Viscount Belasyse (Peterborough), Sir Cecil Wray (E. Retford), Edwin Lascelles (Yorks.) (Rockingham to Burke, 1, 3 Sept. 1769, ibid. ii. 63). Sir George Savile had declined to join them (ibid.; Eg. 3711, p. 33; Savile to Rockingham, 24 Sept. 1769, *Rockingham Memoirs*, ii. 132–6).

[2] Rockingham to Burke, 1, 3 Sept. 1769, *Burke Correspondence*, ii. 61–65. In reporting the decision to Chatham, John Calcraft enclosed an extract from a 'letter from York', according to which 'Lord Rockingham has brought it all about and has been indefatigable' (Calcraft to Chatham, — Aug. 1769, Chatham Correspondence, P.R.O., 30/8/25, f. 28). For Rockingham's ambiguous attitude, see J. Robinson to Chas. Jenkinson: 'It is said Ld Rockingham at his own table publicly talks of the petition & condemns it, & yet it is certain he was privy & in consultation when it was settled. He affects even to write agt the measure to some, while underneath every engine is at work to spread the contagion & to get it supported and signed' (J. Robinson to Chas. Jenkinson, 3 Nov. 1769, Add. MSS. 38206, ff. 149–50).

[3] Burke to Rockingham, 6 Sept. 1769; Burke to Garrick, 18 Sept. 1769; *Burke Correspondence*, ii. 71, 84.

[4] *Read. Merc.*, 9 Oct. 1769. The others mentioned were William Blomberg, Stephen Cross, William Danby, J.P., Francis Edmunds, E. M. Ellerker, J.P., John Grimston, J.P., Robert Grimston, J.P., Stanhope Harvey, Salward Hewitt, Mann Horsfield, J.P., William Sothern, J. Hail Stevenson, Richard Thompson, J.P., William Jolliffe, J.P., Childers Welbank, Peter Wentworth, Henry Willoughby, J.P., and Richard Wilson. Twenty-seven of these thirty-nine 'gentlemen of great property' signed the petition (see p. 138 and ns. 3–4 below).

willing to cast a stain of profaneness upon our conduct from our supposed patronage of Wilkes.

Among the latter was Dr. John Fountayne, Dean of York, who had risen from his sick-bed to attend the meeting, and lent to the occasion both the dignity of his office and the weight of his considerable landed property — estimated (it was said) at £4,000 or £5,000 a year.[1] The petition was moved from the chair by Sir George Armytage and seconded by Sir Cecil Wray, and was adopted after speeches by Alexander Wedderburn and Sir George Savile: the latter thought it 'in every respect by a great deal the best of any yet produced in any county; indeed I think the only one that is correct and constitutionally to the point'.[2] Later, there were rumours, said to have been fostered by the Court party, that the petition would not be presented, and Burke wrote anxiously to Rockingham: 'I hope the Yorkshire petition is in forwardness and will now be presented.'[3] Wedderburn reported on 9 December that the petition 'has had a very sensible effect upon the country in general', that the Ministry had been 'exceedingly alarmed by it', and that their supporters were attempting to belittle its significance by exaggerating the number of freeholders in the county.[4] They had, perhaps, cause for alarm: when presented a month later, the petition bore the remarkable total of nearly 11,000 signatures.[5]

The Yorkshire petition was to have considerable influence on the campaign in the north; but, meanwhile, a number of meetings were held in the west country, which adopted petitions that were either (like that of Gloucestershire) remarkably free of the influence of any particular opposition group or leaned towards the Supporters of the Bill of Rights rather than towards the Rockingham Whigs. The first of these was held in Herefordshire on 4 October and was preceded by some discussion in the public press. When it became known that, following the refusal of the High Sheriff to act, a meeting had been called by some of the local gentry, 'A. B.' of Hereford sent the following questions to the *Gloucester Journal*:

[1] Burke to Chas. O'Hara, 24 Oct. 1769, *Burke Correspondence*, ii. 96–97. He added that no old Tories attended; 'but most of the young ones were there, and very sanguine and earnest for the petition'.

[2] Savile to Serjeant Hewitt, 2 Oct. 1769, *Rockingham Memoirs*, ii. 136–7.

[3] Burke to Rockingham, 5 Dec. 1769, *Burke Correspondence*, ii. 115.

[4] Wedderburn to Rockingham, 9 Dec. 1769, W.W.MSS., R 1/1251.

[5] H.O. 55/2.

Do I understand what I am going to petition against? Is it not the measure that the greatest and ablest lawyers of the Kingdom have decided perfectly legal, and no infringement of the Constitution? Do I feel any real grievance? *Are my apprehensions of Tyranny of Government equal to those I have from the Licentiousness of the People?* May not the petition I am going to sign be an encouragement to the latter instead of a security against the former?[1]

The last two questions were, of course, very much to the point and elicited a number of replies. One of these, from 'A Freeholder', warned his readers that 'those who have at any time planned the establishment of Arbitrary Power have always covered the first strokes they gave to the Rights and Liberties of the People with the specious pretence of curbing their Licentiousness'. Another, from 'C. D.', less subtly, ended with the question: 'Are [you not], Mr. A. B. . . . under the influence of any great man, which great man may also be under the influence of some still greater person or persons?'[2] Meanwhile, preparations for the meeting went ahead with the full blessing of the county's two M.P.s.;[3] it was held at the Swan and Falcon in Hereford on 4 October; and a report sent to the *Gloucester Journal* reads:

A meeting of freeholders of this county . . . was held here this day and was attended by a greater appearance of gentlemen of quality and fortune than perhaps ever were assembled on this or any other occasion in this county.

The freeholders, it went on, 'were unanimous in favour of a petition to the Throne, except a few, very few individuals, whose motives to opposition were very apparent'.[4] The petition was short and moderate in tone: it concentrated mainly on the Middlesex election issue, though brief reference was made to the squandering of public monies; the King was urged to exercise his prerogative powers but no call was made for the dissolution of Parliament.[5] After the petition had been signed (ran a report) 'by a great number of the principal gentlemen of the county', 'proper persons' were instructed to display it at the several market towns at the times and places following:

[1] *Glos. J.*, 25 Sept. 1769 (my italics). *Pugh's Hereford Journal*, the local equivalent of the *Gloucester* and *Worcester Journals*, only began publication on 9 Aug. 1770.
[2] *Glos. J.*, 2 Oct. 1769.
[3] Thos. Foley senior and Thos. Foley junior. The latter alone signed the petition (see p. 142 below).
[4] Ibid., 9 Oct. 1769.
[5] H.O. 55/1; *Pol. Reg.*, vi. 119.

At the Falcon in Bromyard, Monday the 16th instant;
The King's Arms in Ledbury, Tuesday the 17th;
The King's Head in Ross, Thursday the 19th;
The Swan and Falcon in Hereford, Friday and Saturday the 20th and 21st;
The King's Head in Kingston, Wednesday the 25th;
The Crown in Leominster, Friday the 27th;
And, in the meantime, at Mr. Arnold Russell's in Hereford, where the petition will remain until signed.[1]

Villages, too, were canvassed, as we learn from the following news item:

They write from Winsorton, a small parish in Herefordshire, about three miles in circumference, that a gentleman, on Tuesday last, in his road to Kingston with the petition of grievances, stopped there; and in that little place no less than 45 signed the said petition, upon which occasion [says our correspondent] all the bells were set a-ringing, and several hogheads of cider were given to the populace.[2]

When presented by Thomas Foley junior, M.P., on 5 January, the petition contained some 1,800 signatures.[3]

The City of Hereford had its own petition, composed in similar terms and signed by no less than 475 of its 600 resident freemen.[4] In October, it was reported in the *Worcester Journal* that 'most of the inhabitants of that City are determined to petition the Throne for a redress of grievances, but that their intention meets with great opposition from a dignitary in the Church'.[5] However, they found support in John Scudamore, one of their M.P.s, who addressed their meeting at the Black Swan in Hereford on 5 December. The petition was moved from the chair 'in a very warm and pathetic speech' by John Caldecott, a local justice, and supported by the Hon. Captain Savage and William Parry, an eminent attorney. 'The whole affair was carried on with the greatest unanimity and decorum, and near two hundred signed it that night.'[6]

The Devonshire freeholders had a recent history of disturbance and agitation. Devon had been the main centre of the opposition to the Cider Act in 1763, and, at this time, the Earl of Hardwicke had written to the Duke of Newcastle:

1 *Glos. J.*, 23 Oct. 1769.
2 Ibid., 30 Oct. 1769.
3 H.O. 55/1.
4 H.O. 55/4; *Mid. J.*, 14–16 Dec. 1769.
5 *Worcs. J.*, 26 Oct. 1769.
6 *Glos. J.*, 11 Dec. 1769. 400 were reported to have signed by 10 December (*Mid. J.*, 14–16 Dec. 1769).

The riots in Devonshire about the tax upon cider makes a great deal of noise . . . My Lord B.[1] has been hung up in effigy upon a gallows this fortnight at one of ye principal gates of Exeter; nor has any body, in all this time, dar'd to cut the figure down.[2]

The dispute was not without its echo in the meeting held on 5 October in the grounds of Exeter Castle and presided over by the High Sheriff. The Plymouth Corporation had, it was said, declined to attend 'in obedience to the particular directions of a noble person' (named elsewhere as 'L–B–n'); yet Sir John Roger, the city's Recorder, 'distinguished himself in an animated speech'.[3] Serjeant Glynn, M.P. for Middlesex and a leading Supporter of the Bill of Rights, was the chief speaker, yet the petition adopted was the most moderate — and the least precise — of all the petitions of that year: it forbore even to mention the Middlesex election and, in terms that would have delighted Montesquieu, expressed the conviction 'that the stability of government and of that happy Constitution' must 'depend upon the maintenance of the rights, privileges and prerogatives of the three Estates of the Realm distinct from and not to be impaired by each other'.[4] This, no doubt, was the price its organizers had to pay for being able to boast of an unusually high number of clergy and gentry among its 2,800 supporters.[5]

John Glynn's personal impact was more evident in the petitions adopted, the same month, by the City of Exeter and the freeholders of Cornwall. There had been a minor riot in Exeter on 24 July, when the Duke of Bedford paid a visit and was believed to have come to promote a 'humble address'. There were shouts of 'Wilkes and Liberty!', 'Sir R . . . B . . . ' was reputed to have lost a joint in one of his fingers, and 'a well-dressed man' observed amiably to the Duke: 'The red in your G—'s face is dyed with the

[1] Lord Barrington. M.P. for Plymouth and Secretary at War.

[2] Hardwicke to Newcastle, 1 Aug. 1763, Add. MSS. 32950, f. 1.

[3] *Exeter Flying Post*, 29 Sept.–6 Oct. 1769. The same issue gave notice of the publication on 29 September of *The Freeholder's Magazine*, or *Monthly Chronicle of Liberty*, price 6d. and 'embellished with a Head of John Wilkes Esq. finely engraved'.

[4] H.O. 55/1. The *Worcester Journal* wrongly reported that it 'called for a dissolution of Parliament' (12 Oct. 1769); and *Jackson's Oxford Journal* reported, equally wrongly, that the petition was signed by over 5,000 freeholders (13 Jan. 1770). At the Exeter meeting, the two County Members were instructed 'to move for an enquiry into the several grievances complained of' (*Exeter Flying Post*, loc. cit.).

[5] H.O. 55/1; Eg. 3711, p. 51.

ruin of your country.'[1] The petition-meeting, held in the Guildhall on 24 October, was opened by the Mayor and addressed by John Glynn, the city's Recorder, and John Buller, one of its M.P.s.[2] The petition adopted was distinctly 'popular' in tone: it spoke of the 'wishes of millions' for a redress of grievances, and it was signed by 860 freemen out of a little over 1,000.[3] The Cornish freeholders met at Bodmin on 6 October; the meeting was described as 'the largest and most respectable ever known in the county'. John Blewett, the High Sheriff, took the chair; the petition was proposed by Thomas Pitt, M.P. for Oakhampton, who spoke so well that Glynn said there was no need to add anything — and spoke for half an hour. Sir John Molesworth, County Member, also made 'a bold and spirited speech', in the course of which he claimed 'that he already had signed the Middlesex petition, intended to sign the Devonshire petition, and was ready to present the Cornish one when called on'.[4] Being 'universally approved of', it was supposed that the petition would be signed 'by 19 out of 20 of the freeholders of the county';[5] in fact, it was signed by no more than 1,500. Yet the petition is of special interest: more than any other, it bears the mark of a lawyer's hand and sets out in the greatest detail the opposition's answer to the legal niceties by which Administration justified its conduct in the case of the Middlesex election.[6]

The last of the western counties' petitioning meetings was held at the Town Hall, Wells, in Somerset, on 18 October. Wilkes had a following in the county; and the news of his electoral victory over Luttrell in April had been greeted at Somerton by the ringing of bells, illuminations, and a solemn procession, headed by '2 ushers of the grammar school representing Liberty' and '45 gentlemen scholars with blue favours'.[7] This time, the initiative was taken by a County Member, Richard Hippisley Coxe, who, having first tested the feelings of the gentry attending the Bridgewater Races, found little difficulty in persuading William Rodbart, the High Sheriff, to call a meeting.[8] Two thousand freeholders attended and

[1] *Ann. Reg.*, 1769, pp. 117–18; *Brist. J.*, 29 July 1769.

[2] His colleague, John Rolle Walter, was detained on other business in Oxfordshire, but had promised his support (*Exeter Flying Post*, 20–27 Oct. 1769).

[3] H.O. 55/2; Namier, op. cit., p. 80.

[4] His name appears on the Cornish petition but not on those for Devonshire and Middlesex (see p. 139 below).

[5] *Exeter Flying Post*, 13–20 Oct. 1769.

[6] Like the Devon and Herefordshire petitions, it did not follow Westminster's lead in calling for a dissolution of Parliament.

[7] *Mid. J.*, 20–22 April 1769.

[8] *Worcs. J.*, 24 Aug. 1769.

it was reported that the gentlemen present owned land in Somerset alone to the value of £100,000 per annum.[1] Among them were several M.P.s: Richard H. Coxe (Somerset), his brother John (sometime M.P. for Wells), Benjamin Allen (Bridgewater), Henry Seymour (Huntingdon) and John Smith (Bath); also present were Lord Cork, Sir Thomas and William Acland and a number of local justices.[2] William Beckford, a freeholder of some influence, was unable to attend but sent a letter, 'enclosing my sentiments freely and a copy of the principal grievance'.[3] John Coxe's draft petition was accepted: it concentrated on the single issue of Middlesex and called for the dismissal of Ministers and the dissolution of Parliament; it was signed by 2,800 freeholders.[4]

By this time, the northern counties were beginning to react to the stimulus given by the Yorkshire petition. Even before the York meeting, Burke had written to Rockingham:

> I find that the people here expect that the other counties in which your Lordship's friends have a powerful interest should follow your pattern with speed and vigour. Lancashire is by no means wholly in the hands of Lord Strange so as to prevent the exertion of a strong spirit there, as well as in Liverpool and Lancaster; to say nothing of what may be done in the City of York, Nottinghamshire, Derbyshire, Cumberland, Westmorland, etc. etc. . . .[5]

The first to move was Liverpool; but far from the Rockinghamite M.P.s for the town, Sir William Meredith and Richard Pennant, giving the movement a lead or accepting it with enthusiasm, they were taken entirely by surprise and gave the petition but grudging support. This was perhaps all the more remarkable as, in the preceding General Election, these Members had owed their seats to the common freemen and Tradesmen's Companies, who had helped them defeat the violent opposition, supported by bludgeon-armed 'mobs', of the dominant group on the Corporation.[6] On

[1] *Read. Merc.*, 23 Oct. 1769.

[2] Those mentioned by the press were Robert Balch (Bridgewater), Edward Clarke, John Collins (Ilminster), Thomas Horner, William Sandford and Philip Stevens. Clement Tudway, M.P. for Wells, and Sir Charles Tynte, the other County Member, stayed away—presumably because, as Administration supporters, they were out of sympathy with the purposes of the meeting (ibid.).

[3] Cit. Sutherland, op. cit., p. 127 n. 3. See also *Exeter Flying Post*, 20–27 Oct. 1769.

[4] H.O. 55/5.

[5] Burke to Rockingham, 6 Sept. 1769, *Burke Correspondence*, ii. 73–74.

[6] *Liverpool Chronicle*, 24 March 1768; *Williamson's Liverpool Advertiser*, 25 March 1768.

27 March, true to its anti-Whig tradition, the Corporation had sent a loyal address to the King.[1] In October, the 'lower freemen' riposted with a petition. Sir William Meredith's own account of what happened is instructive:

> On the 8th was an appointed meeting of Mr. Pennant's friends and mine, which is confined to the higher ranks of people, & the expense therefore *contrived* to be pretty large for a common dinner. At this meeting we had 107 gentlemen. About six o'clock, there came a smart letter from some of the lower freemen, desiring the persons assembled would draw up a petition to the King. As soon as it was read, they all cried out for a *Petition*. Pennant was gone. I spoke rather against it, thinking I ought to tell them they were continually asking for assistance of Ministers & should therefore be cautious of offending them. But what I said made them more eager; & there was a Scotch gentleman present whose opposition had the effect of stirring up. Accordingly, they ordered a petition to be prepared, in order to be signed at a further meeting, the Thursday following – to which Pennant and I were sent for. The meeting was ordered at noon, which is the worst time to collect the poeple, & I think there were above 300. But I believe the petition will be generally signed.[2]

Though promoted by the 'lower freemen', the petition was drawn up in true Burkeian style: it called for redress on the single issue of the Middlesex election and for the dissolution of Parliament. It was signed by 1,100 freemen, said to be 'an undoubted majority'; yet it was condemned in a subsequent counter-address of 450 supporters of the Corporation as the product of 'a small, partial and inconsiderable meeting of the inhabitants of this town' and promoted 'to serve the sinister views of factious and designing men'.[3]

In Derbyshire, stronghold of the Cavendish family, there were no such divided counsels. In August, Burke had told Whately that the Cavendish brothers were only hesitating to petition in order not to embarrass the Duke of Devonshire, their nephew, who would shortly be of age, 'and they make it almost a principle to deliver up the county to him quite clear'.[4] But, by October, these scruples had been overcome[5] and a petition must have been adopted by late November, for a letter sent to the *Middlesex*

[1] *Ann. Reg.*, 1769, p. 86.
[2] Meredith to Rockingham, 18 Oct. 1769, W.W.MSS., R 1/1237.
[3] H.O. 55/4; *Pol. Reg.*, vi. 120; *General Evening Post*, 4–6 Jan. 1770.
[4] Whately to Grenville, 7 Sept. 1769, *Grenville Papers*, iv. 445.
[5] Rockingham to Burke, 15 Oct. 1769, *Burke Correspondence*, ii. 90.

Journal in December ran: 'Our petition was at Derby the 7th inst. and was signed by at least four-fifths of the freeholders in the neighbourhood and it has met with like success in every place in the Peak.'[1] The petition was admirably concise: in terms which suggest the authorship of Burke or Dowdeswell it concentrated on the single issue of 'a late determination of the House of Commons', and requested the King to dissolve Parliament. When presented by Lord George Cavendish in January 1770, it bore some 2,850 signatures.[2]

Other petitioning counties in the north were Durham and Northumberland. The Durham petition was a late starter and was only presented in April. It contained 1,375 signatures and was couched, once more, in Rockinghamite terms.[3] In Northumberland, the decision to petition must, as in Derbyshire, have been taken in the late autumn, for, in December, we learn that five hundred 'substantial freeholders' had signed it and it was hoped to gain the support of the majority of the county's 2,000 voters.[4] The towns of Berwick and Newcastle-upon-Tyne submitted separate petitions. The freemen of Newcastle, who, in April, had already 'instructed' their M.P.s, were said, in early October, to be 'warm for a petition', and leaflets were distributed with the caption: 'No Petition, no Mayor and Sheriff.'[5] 900 burgesses eventually signed their demand for a redress of grievances.[6] In Berwick, the petitioning burgesses were supported by John Burn, the Mayor, who, in November, called a special meeting of the Guild at which, in spite of strenuous efforts by one of the town's M.P.s to discredit the affair, a motion was carried in favour of a petition by 135 to 58 votes:[7] it was presented by Sir Joseph Mawbey a month later.[8] In Cumberland

[1] *Mid. J.*, 23–25 Dec. 1769. The next number (28–30 Dec. 1769) reported that 'the petition is countenanced by two very eminent noblemen' — presumably, the Duke of Devonshire and the Marquess of Rockingham.

[2] H.O. 55/3; *Ann. Reg.*, 1770, p. 66.

[3] H.O. 55/3. I have found no mention in the press of this petition.

[4] *Mid. J.*, 26–28 Dec. 1769. In fact, some 750 freeholders signed (H.O. 55/4). The petition claimed that the dissolution of Parliament would respond to 'the request of millions of your Majesty's subjects'.

[5] *Worcs. J.*, 12 Oct. 1769.

[6] H.O. 55/5. This represented nearly half the electorate (Namier, op. cit., p. 80 n. 3).

[7] *Mid. J.*, 23–25 Nov. 1769. See also *Ann. Reg.*, 1769, p. 153.

[8] It is not among the petitions in the H.O. papers in the P.R.O., though it is *listed* at the end of these petitions and described as having been presented by Sir Joseph Mawbey, Bart., on 20 Dec. 1769 (H.O. 55/6). A petition from the borough of Morpeth in Northumberland is also listed and alleged to have been presented in Jan. 1770 by Mr. Delaval.

and Westmorland, Burke's hopes of a petition seem, as in the case of Lancashire,[1] to have come to nothing. From his remote fastness of Appleby, John Robinson, Secretary to the Treasury, had, in November, anxiously watched the progress of the Yorkshire petition and expressed alarm at the possibility of its 'baneful influence' and 'infectious poison' spreading into his own county of Westmorland. He was particularly concerned 'that the Quakers and Dissenters are so infatuated, I will call it, as to sign and support it'. He was afraid, too, that the quarter sessions in January might prove a dangerous moment for similar proposals in Westmorland and Cumberland, but, on the 14th, he wrote with relief to Jenkinson:

> I have but just to say that no steps hath been taken either at Kendall or in Cumberland relative to a petition; we shall therefore, I hope, be perfectly quiet in these counties.[2]

In the meantime, there had been other movements farther south. Some of these had, either from the timidity of their promoters or the energetic counter-measures of Administration, proved still-born or been thwarted before fulfilment. Sir Cecil Wray had to give way before powerful opposition at Lincoln;[3] Richard Rigby, M.P. for Tavistock and one of the government's most zealous watch-dogs, had successfully defeated petitioning attempts in Norfolk and at Northampton.[4] In Hampshire, despite a good 'disposition', 'leaders' were wanting.[5] In Nottinghamshire, proposals for a petition, aired in exchanges between Rockingham and the Duke of Portland, came to nothing — possibly owing to the lukewarmness and hesitations of Sir George Savile, who 'entered very little into these kinds of schemes'.[6] His personal authority and private sympathies notwithstanding, the Duke of Richmond

[1] For expectations regarding Lancashire, see Burke to Rockingham, 6 Sept. 1769; Rockingham to Burke, 15 Oct. 1769; *Burke Correspondence*, ii. 73–74, 90; and Meredith to Rockingham, 18 Oct. 1769, W.W.MSS. R 1/1237.

[2] J. Robinson to Chas. Jenkinson, 3 Nov. 1769; 5, 10, 14 Jan. 1770; Add. MSS. 38206, ff. 149–50, 175–6, 190–1. Dr. Sutherland, however, includes Cumberland among petitioning counties (op. cit., p. 29). The *Annual Register*, it is true, reports the presentation of such a petition on 6 April 1770; but its evidence on such matters is sometimes contradictory and not confirmed elsewhere.

[3] Rockingham to Burke, 17 July 1769, *Burke Correspondence*, ii. 48; Whately to Burke, 30 Aug. 1769, ibid., ii. 60.

[4] Burke to Rockingham, 30 July 1769, ibid., ii. 50–51.

[5] Dowdeswell to Burke, 5 Sept. 1769, ibid., ii. 71. In Wickham, Hants, Wilkes's birthday was publicly celebrated on 17 October—the 'Old Style' date of that event (*Read. Merc.*, 23 Oct. 1769).

[6] Savile to Serjeant Hewitt, 24 Sept. 1769, *Rockingham Memoirs*, ii. 137–8.

declined to promote a petition in Sussex: 'In so doing [he wrote], I should have appeared factious; besides it must have created divisions in the county, which I think is always an evil.'[1] There was talk of a petition in Glamorgan – the only county outside England where it appears to have been entertained – but it remained talk.[2] In Oxford and Canterbury, a start, at least, was made: according to a press report of 13 October,

> The independent freemen of the City of Oxford met at the Mitre Tavern and chose Sir James Cotter their chairman, when a motion was made to implore the intervention of the royal prerogative by a speedy dissolution of P—t, which was carried unanimously;

but no more was heard of it.[3] At Canterbury, when the Mayor elect was sworn in before the Corporation on 29 September, there was an unexpected shout for a petition. This was agreed and a petition was read out, calling for a dissolution of Parliament; it was approved and signed by most of those present, and left for further signatures at the Guildhall.[4] In Essex, the petitioners' plans appear to have reached an even more advanced stage. After being thwarted by Rigby in July, they roused Burke's hopes again in September.[5] A meeting was eventually called at Chelmsford on 15 December, and (it was reported)

> the zeal of the independent gentry and yeomanry was such that many rode on horseback upwards of 20 miles from all different parts of the county in a day of almost continuous rain.

The moving spirits were Sir Joseph Mawbey, who seconded the motion for a petition, and Sir Robert Bernard, who took the chair.[6] The petition, restricted to the single issue of the Middlesex election, was unanimously approved and signed before evening by 'upwards of 500 freeholders'.[7] Mawbey was also successful in promoting a petition along similar lines in his own borough of Southwark: it was adopted on 17 October and signed eventually

[1] Richmond to Burke, 2 Sept. 1769, *Burke Correspondence*, ii. 67.

[2] *Mid. J.*, 5–7 Dec. 1769.

[3] *Gent's Mag.*, 1769, p. 508. I have seen no other report of activity at Oxford.

[4] *Worcs. J.*, 12 Oct. 1769; *Glos. J.*, 9 Oct. 1769. It does not appear to have been presented (but see Sutherland, op. cit., p. 30 n. 1.).

[5] Burke to Rockingham, 30 July 1769, *Burke Correspondence*, ii. 50; the same to the same, 9 Sept. 1769, ibid., ii. 76.

[6] John Calcraft was also active in Essex, according to Horace Walpole (cit. Sutherland, op. cit., p. 27 n. 5).

[7] *Mid. J.*, 5–7, 17–19 Dec. 1769. I have no evidence that the petition was ever presented.

by 1,200 of its 1,500 enfranchised inhabitants.[1] In Coventry, of 1,500 electors, 900 petitioned.[2] Finally, in Kent, John Calcraft and William Gordon, M.P.s for Rochester, aided by John Sawbridge, M.P. for Hythe, and spurred on by the Earl of Chatham, managed to wrest a petition from the freeholders in face of determined opposition from the gentry. At the meeting in Maidstone Town Hall on 27 November, 700 freeholders attended, but both County Members – Sir Brook Bridges and Sir Charles Farnaby – and other resident M.P.s were conspicuous by their absence.[3] Sir John Filmer, M.P. for Steyning, and members of the Maidstone Corporation attended, but in order to obstruct the proceedings: they called out (ran a news report), 'No meeting – no petition!', and Sir John Filmer, 'true to his name and descent', objected 'because he did not see at that meeting several gentlemen of the oldest families in the county'. It was, however, agreed by 700 to 7 votes to proceed with a petition, deploring the attack made 'upon the fundamental rights of election' and calling on 'the Royal Father of his people' to dissolve Parliament.[4] Four hundred signed the same afternoon, and Calcraft wrote Chatham a letter of qualified enthusiasm:

> In spite of every desertion of gentn except Mr. Sawbridge, Mr. Gordon and myself, we have carried our petition with great spirit . . . The spirit of the freeholders is equal to your Lordship's expectation. There were at least 400 freeholders & they are signing away; hitherto every gentleman has kept back. But those who profess themselves friends to the Constitution must stir to get it sign'd.[5]

When presented by John Calcraft six weeks later, it bore the names of over 2,800 freeholders.[6]

The bulk of these petitions were presented at St. James's Palace between May 1769 and January 1770. When Parliament assembled on 9 January and the Commons began to debate the Address to the King's speech, a dozen county petitions and eleven borough petitions had been presented; two more counties and one city followed the day after, and, finally, the county of Durham closed

[1] *Worcs. J.*, 19 Oct. 1769; *Read. Merc.*, 23 Oct. 1769; *Ann Reg.*, 1769, pp. 142, 206; H.O. 55/5; Namier, op. cit., p. 80.

[2] H.O. 55/3; Namier, loc. cit.

[3] For example. William Evelyn (Helston) and Chas. Masham (Maidstone) (Calcraft to Chatham, ?27 Nov. 1769, Chatham Correspondence, P.R.O., 30/8/25, f. 76). Masham had voted with the minority on 15 April; Evelyn had voted with the majority; the County Members had been absent or had abstained.

[4] *Lond. Chron.*, 23–25 Nov., 30 Nov.–2 Dec. 1769; *Mid. J.*, 28–30 Nov. 1769.

[5] Calcraft to Chatham, loc. cit.

[6] H.O. 55/3.

the lists on 6 April 1770. The petitions, it was repeatedly claimed in the debates, represented no less than 60,000 freeholders, freemen and citizens of England.[1] There were others, no doubt, that might have been added had the King or the Commons given a more encouraging response to the petitions already presented. But when the first few days' debates showed that the government could, in spite of the opposition's attacks from within and the weight of 'the publick opinion' from without, still command tolerable majorities for its stubborn resistance to redress,[2] they may have become discouraged. This, at least, is suggested in the following news report:

As a dissolution of P—t is no longer expected, even by the opposition, and as all the petitions that have hitherto been presented will plainly have no effect, it is generally believed such counties and corporations as had intended to add to the numbers will now save themselves the unnecessary trouble.[3]

By the end of January, at any rate, it had become clear that the King would not intervene and that, even on the knotty question of Luttrell's right to sit in Parliament for Middlesex, the government could still rely on majorities of 40 or more in the Commons and on a considerably greater degree of support in the Lords.[4]

[1] The fifteen counties actually presenting petitions to the King appear to have been the following: Bucks, Cornwall, Derbyshire, Devon, Durham, Gloucestershire, Herefordshire, Kent, Middlesex, Northumberland, Somerset, Surrey, Wiltshire, Worcestershire and Yorkshire. In addition, Essex (and possibly others) had begun to circulate a petition.

The twelve cities, boroughs and corporations presenting petitions were: Berwick, Bristol, Coventry, Exeter, Hereford, Liverpool, London, Morpeth(?), Newcastle, Southwark, Westminster and Worcester. In addition, Canterbury appears to have begun to collect signatures, and the *Ann. Reg.* (1769, p. 206) reported that petitions were presented by Durham and Wells (though there appears to be no other evidence on this). The total number of signatures to the fifteen county and ten borough petitions found among the H.O. papers do not exceed 51,000 (approx. 38,000 freeholders and 13,000 burgesses); but some allowance has to be made for London (5,000?) which did not invite signatures, and for Canterbury, Essex and others. See also Appendix VII.

[2] Eg. 3711, pp. 1–66.

[3] *Ox. J.*, 20 Jan. 1770. It is no doubt indicative of further petitioning activities in other counties that the editors of the *Independent Chronicle*, in publicly advertising their thanks to the gentlemen, clergy, freeholders and principal inhabitants of ten counties, include with the petitioning counties of Bucks, Gloucester, Hereford, Wilts and Worcester those of Berks, Hertford, Northants, Oxford and Warwick (ibid., 13 Jan. 1770).

[4] The two main votes in the Commons were taken on 26 Jan. and 1 Feb. 1770: on the first occasion, it was agreed by 224 to 180 votes that the Commons resolution of 17 Feb. 1769 declaring Wilkes's 'incapacity' was 'agreeable to the law of the land'; on the second, North's previous question to a motion by Dowdeswell was carried by 226 to 186 votes (Eg. 3711, pp. 106–246; E. Langton to Hardwicke, Add. MSS, 35609, ff. 139–44). In the Lords debate on 2 February, the opposition peers were defeated by 96 to 47 votes (ibid., f. 144).

On 19 February, it was finally decided by a majority of 69 that in excluding Wilkes and declaring his future 'incapacity' the Commons had acted 'in conformity with the laws of the land'.[1]

In the course of all this, the name of John Wilkes, though it was rarely uttered by the opposition's spokesmen in Parliament, was not forgotten in the streets of London, and when the King returned from opening Parliament on 9 January,

> he was followed by a Mob who kept shouting 'Wilkes for ever!'; which his Majesty was so far from resenting that he was observed to smile.[2]

No doubt, he had cause for satisfaction, yet, as it turned out, it was not he or the Commons' majority, but Wilkes and the petitioners, that had the final word.

[1] J. Harris, M.P., to Hardwicke, Add. MSS. 35609, ff. 149–50.
[2] *Ox. J.*, 13 Jan. 1770.

VIII

THE PETITIONERS OF 1769

WRITING to Charles Jenkinson in November 1769, when the effects of the Yorkshire petition were beginning to be felt in the north of England, John Robinson observed:

> I think not ye number of petitions is of very great consequence because the soberest & most weighty part of the nation don't join, & it is well known that nothing is so easy as to get a petition from ye lowest of ye people in any country; but yet nos. affect the vulgar & may rouse a spirit which wd better be quieted.[1]

The numbers of both petitions and of petitioners were indeed impressive and, at the time John Robinson was writing, they looked like becoming even more impressive than they eventually turned out to be. Even so, the 38,000 petitioning freeholders accounted for something between one-third and a quarter of all the county voters of England and Wales and the 17,000 petitioning in the towns and cities represented no less than one in five of the enfranchised burgesses and citizens.[2] In the petitioning centres themselves the weight of numbers was, of course, more impressive still: thus Yorkshire's 11,000, Westminster's 5,000, Surrey's 1,500, Buckinghamshire's 1,800, Derbyshire's 2,850, Southwark's 1,200, Liverpool's 1,100, Coventry's 900, and even Hereford's 450, were clear majorities — or were reputed to be such — of the voters resident in those areas.[3] These numbers were remarkably evenly distributed between the main areas of petitioning in north, south and west; and, as might be expected, the Rockinghamite influence was predominant in the counties (notably so in the north) and the influence of the Supporters of the Bill of Rights

[1] J. Robinson to Chas. Jenkinson, 3 Nov. 1769, Add. MSS. 38206, ff. 149–50.

[2] In 1780, it was reported to the Westminster Association that, of 214,000 voters in England, there were 130,000 in the counties and 84,000 in the towns and cities (G. S. Veitch, *Genesis of Parliamentary Reform* (1913), p. 2). Sir Lewis Namier, on the other hand, estimates the total number of county voters in 1761 as being 160,000 (*The Structure of Politics*, p. 65). I have allowed 5,000 petitioners for the City of London (see p. 133, n. 1, above). Inevitably, government spokesmen claimed that there were non-voters among the petitioners (Eg. 3711, pp. 46, 50). This was probably true; but, in the case of Middlesex, at least, they do not appear to have been numerous (see pp. 145–46 below).

[3] See pp. 117, 122, 124, 126, 129, 131–32 above.

was more strongly felt in the cities — particularly in the great commercial cities of Bristol, Westminster and London.[1]

But to the Commons majority as to John Robinson, the weight of absolute numbers — even of lawful voters — was not the ultimate criterion as to the political importance of these county and borough petitions. For them, the simple freemen's and freeholders' signatures must be supported by those of, at least, a substantial portion of 'the soberest & most weighty part of the nation' in order to command respect and to merit serious consideration. This point was emphasized, with varying degrees of insistence, by government spokesmen and supporters in the Commons debates in January. Some, like Lord North, merely expressed mild contempt for such a petition as that of Westminster, as it was 'a difficult thing to find a justice of the peace there'. Others were more violent or explicit in their denunciations of 'riff-raff' and 'scum of the earth'. William de Grey, Member for Newport, considered that 'there is a distinction between the genuine son of Liberty and the base-born son of Licentiousness', and he was shocked to find 'such base-born people as these [he was referring to the 'mechanics and booksellers' of Westminster] to address the Throne, whose gates they ought not to enter'. Luttrell, he insisted, in a later debate, should have special consideration as his supporters were 'men of property, of moderation, of candour, who have a great stake to lose', whereas the 1,100 and more that had voted for Wilkes 'have some certain rights but little or nothing to lose'.[2] Opposition speakers reacted strongly to these attempts to belittle the voting rights of the smaller property-owners. George Grenville deplored the separation of nobility and gentry 'from the riff-raff freeholders of the Kingdom, the rabble of the Kingdom'. Burke warned the gentry of what happened when they 'deserted the freeholders' under Charles I: 'The body of freeholders got up; the gentlemen were trampled down: they were made slaves to draymen & brewers.' Colonel Barré, given to more violent expression, considered that 'a House that can bear to hear the words of freeholders and base-born put together ought not to be suffered to sit an hour longer'; whereas William Beckford, with characteristic vigour, observed:

The 40s. freeholder has as good a right as a large property-owner to send a man to Parliament. I never measure the patriotism of a man by the

[1] See Appendix VII.
[2] Eg. 3711, pp. 27, 47, 213.

number of his acres. I have known the greatest rascals in the Kingdom in laced coats.[1]

In these particular exchanges there is, of course, the underlying assumption that the simple freeholders and freemen were the solid backbone of the petitions and that 'the most weighty part of the nation' or 'the gentlemen of known property' played little part in them. Some opposition speakers, Sir Anthony Adby and Serjeant Glynn among them, were at pains to show that, in some counties at least, this was not the case; yet they would probably have accepted as reasonably accurate the moderate assertion of the *Annual Register*

> that the majority of gentlemen of large fortunes, of justices of the peace, and of the clergy, in some of the counties had not signed the petitions.[2]

Even so, it would not be without interest to discover in which counties such elements gave more support than in others, how the petitioners were composed, and how far considerations other than the mere weight of numbers may have entered into the calculations of the promoters. The petitions themselves, with their long lists of appended signatures, must be the main basis from which any such inquiry, however rudimentary, must begin; but Lord North himself, on 9 January, in the course of the debate on the Address, made a suggestion that can certainly not be ignored:

> One test [he said] is to look upon the gentlemen of known property from the Commission of the Peace: the modern Commission of the Peace comprehends most of the gentlemen of property.[3]

With records such as these, imperfect as they are,[4] we can, at least, begin to get nearer to the root of the problem.

The degree of support given to the petitions by men of property and country gentlemen naturally varied from one county to another. This would depend on a variety of factors. The crucial question

[1] Ibid., pp. 40, 56–57, 144, 213.

[2] *Ann. Reg.*, 1770, p. 60; cit. Postgate, *That Devil Wilkes*, p. 154.

[3] Eg. 3711, pp. 46–47.

[4] I have not been able to see or to obtain copies of Commissions of the Peace for Derbyshire or the West Riding of Yorkshire; in the case of Durham and Worcester, it has only been possible to obtain lists of justices attending quarter sessions in 1769. The Commission is by no means an infallible source for the resident 'gentlemen of known property'. Apart from the omission of many, there are on the Commissions numerous justices (even among the non-'official' justices) who were not resident freeholders — e.g., in Middlesex, only about *one-third* voted in the elections of 1768–69. As for the petitions, signatures are often illegible and some names (e.g. Smith, Jones, Hill) are too frequent to make for precise identification.

might be the personal sympathy or influence exerted by the local territorial magnate or reigning county family — such influence, for example, as Rockingham had at his command in Yorkshire, the Grenvilles in Buckinghamshire, Richmond in Sussex, or the Cavendish family in the county of Derby. Again, the determining factor might be, as in the more 'independent' of the western counties, the dissatisfaction with government policy of 'the warm spirits' or more active elements among the county gentry itself; or the outcome might, as in Middlesex and Surrey, where the landed interest counted for less, be determined by the particular sympathies and energies of the 'middling' freeholders in urban and commercial districts. Such support would be particularly strong where more than one of these factors operated in unison — in Yorkshire, for example, where the Marquess of Rockingham, sympathetic though hesitant, could be prodded into taking decisive action by the enthusiasm of the county gentry. The York meeting of 27 September, Burke had written, 'must be very great in point of number, and still more considerable from the opulence both landed and commercial of those who compose it;'[1] and Sir George Savile told the Commons that the petition 'has been presented by a property which wd make a figure in some counties'.[2] Heading the lists of signatures, we find those of Lords Downe and D'Erlanger; of both County Members of Parliament — Sir George Savile and Edwin Lascelles; of nine other M.P.s, including the ubiquitous Sir Joseph Mawbey (Southwark), Sir Cecil Wray (E. Retford), and Sir Thomas Frankland (Thirsk) who had voted for Proctor in Middlesex.[3] Among other signatories of note were Sir George Armytage, former Member for York and chairman of the county meeting on 27 September; Sir James Ibbetson; Sir George Strickland; Sir Digby Legard; Sir James Norcliffe; Sir Marmaduke Asty Wyvill; Sir George Montgomery Metham; George Lascelles; Dr. John Fountayne, Dean of York; and several others described as 'gentlemen of great property'.[4] There were

[1] Burke to Chas. O'Hara, 24 Oct. 1769, *Burke Correspondence,* ii.6.

[2] Eg. 3711, p. 33.

[3] The others were Lord John Cavendish (York), Nathaniel Cholmondeley (Boroughbridge), Beilby Thompson (Hedon), Chas. Turner (York), Alexander Wedderburn (till recently, M.P. for Richmond); and William Weddell Kingston-upon-Hull).

[4] The following are also described as such: William Danby, J.P.; Francis Edmunds; E. M. Ellerker, J.P.; John Grimston, J.P.; Stanhope Harvey; Salward Hewitt; Mann Horsfield, J.P.; William Tuffnell Jolliffe, J.P.; J. Hail Stevenson; and Childers Welbank (*Read. Merc.*, 9 Oct. 1769).

professional men of substance among them, too: we note the names of John Dealtry, doctor of physic, of Dr. Thomas Franks, M.D., and of one who signs himself 'nephew of Sir Isaac Newton'. Wedderburn wrote to Rockingham that a 'Mr. Berwick tells me those who have signed at his Chambers are in general very respectable'.[1] Of the 400 local justices appearing on the Commissions of the Peace for the North and East Riding, some seventy-five signed their names.[2]

In the case of Derbyshire, where support by the Cavendishes was a matter of paramount importance, we find the petition headed by a galaxy of members of that family. Among the first eight signatures are those of Lord George Cavendish, County Member and second son of the third Duke of Devonshire; Lord Frederick, third son and M.P. for Derby; Lord John, fourth son and M.P. for York; and of Sir Henry Cavendish, a cousin, M.P. for Lostwithiel. In close and, possibly dutiful, attendance appears that of the other County Member, Geoffrey Bagnall Clarke.[3] In Cornwall, Glynn claimed that 'no undue influence' had been exerted and that the petition was supported by 'a fair majority in both property and numbers'.[4] Here, too, we find the signatories headed by the two County Members, Sir John St. Aubin and Sir John Molesworth. Supporting them are Sir Richard Vyvian, Bart., and two members of his family — Thomas Vyvian and Thomas Vyvian junior, both justices; and the High Sheriff of the county, John Blewett. The justices themselves, described by Glynn as 'men of family and fortune', gave good support: no less than forty of them, or one-third of all the non-official justices enrolled on the Commission, are among the signatories.[5]

More surprisingly, Glynn claimed in the Commons debate that nine out of ten justices 'have subscribed to the petition of Devonshire'.[6] This is certainly an exaggeration: many signatures are illegible, it is true, but only forty-five or fifty appear to have signed of the 300 whose names are on the Commission. Yet, in other respects, the Devon petition was well supported: one County Member, John Parker, signed his name; as did Henry Fownes

[1] Wedderburn to Rockingham, 9 Dec. 1769, W.W.MSS., R1/1251.
[2] H.O. 55/2; Commission of the Peace, E. Riding, 3 Jan. 1771; ditto for N. Riding. 5 June 1769.
[3] H.O. 55/3.
[4] Eg. 3711, p. 51.
[5] H.O. 55/4; Commission of the Peace, Cornwall, 9 June 1769.
[6] Eg. 3711, p. 51.

Luttrell, M.P. for Minehead, and John Buller, M.P. for Exeter; also Lord Courtenay and two baronets: Sir John Carew and Sir Bourchier Wrey of Tavistock. Other local notables who gave support were Samuel Cholwick, doctor of laws; Dr. R. Veale, M.D.; Dr. J. Robinson, M.D.; John Fortescue, doctor of physic; William Molesworth; Richard Strode; John and Henry Fownes Luttrell; and several of the Acland family.[1]

Other counties in which the petitions were well supported by the gentry were Buckingham, Surrey, Somerset and Wiltshire. In Buckinghamshire, it was observed a few days after the petition was launched

> that there are more respectable names already to the Aylesbury petition than to all those which have hitherto been presented. The list of names undoubtedly is a plain contradiction to the assertion of a certain Nobleman's Cub that there are none inclined to petition but the SCUM OF THE EARTH.[2]

Among these 'respectable names' was that of a County Member, Earl Verney; a former County Member (and Medmenham Monk), Sir William Stanhope; and those of four other M.P.s: John Aubrey (Wallingford), Edmund Burke (Wendover), John Calcraft (Rochester) and Thomas Hampden (Lewes). Other notables included Sir John Vanhatten and Murrough O'Brien, the future Marquess of Thomond. One of the Grenvilles signed,[3] but not George Grenville: 'I did not sign,' he was to explain, 'because whenever Mr. Wilkes is mentioned, I wish not to be a party.'[4] The names of some forty local justices appear.[5] In Surrey, in spite of differences between the promoters, there were among the petitioners, Sir Anthony Abdy told the Commons, 'gentlemen of the first property, of the gravest, of the best characters in the county'.[6] They included a County Member, Sir Francis Vincent; Sir Robert Clayton, M.P. for Bletchingly; Joseph Martin (Gatton); Sir George Colebrooke (Arundel); Sir Joseph Mawbey (Southwark); Henry Crabb Boulton (Worcester), who — like Colebrooke

[1] H.O. 55/1; Commission of the Peace, Devonshire, 4 July 1769.

[2] *Worcs. J.*, 21 Sept. 1769. The 'Nobleman's Cub' was the Hon. Stephen Fox, M.P. for Salisbury.

[3] The initial is not clear: it can hardly be Henry Grenville, M.P. for Buckingham. as he was found not be a freeholder (Burke to Rockingham, 13 Sept, 1769, *Burke Correspondence*, ii. 78); but it might be William or Thomas Grenville, both of whom were justices.

[4] Eg. 3711, p. 53.

[5] H.O. 55/6; Commission of the Peace, Buckinghamshire, 24 June 1765.

[6] Eg. 3711, p. 25.

— had voted for Proctor in Middlesex; and Thomas Howard (Malmesbury), who boasted in the Commons of having been the first to sign the petition.[1] Among other supporters were Claude Crespigny, doctor of laws and later secretary of the South Sea Company; Hon. Peter King; Francis Vincent of Stoke d'Abernon; Philip Carteret Webb junior; and two 'hot Wilkites', George Bellas and William Ellis; while even such a disgruntled opponent of petitioning as George Onslow, the second County Member, believed that sixty or seventy justices had signed the petition.[2] The Somerset petitioners could, on the other hand, boast of no County Member among their number: Richard Hippisley Coxe, although he played a leading part in promoting the petition, does not appear to have signed it; but four other M.P.s are among its signatories: John Smith (Bath), Benjamin Allen (Bridgewater), Henry Seymour (Huntingdon) and Alexander Popham (Taunton). Here, too, we find the signature of the High Sheriff, William Rodbart of Norton; together with the names of Sir Thomas Grimston, Bart.; John Dyke Acland, son of Sir Thomas Dyke Acland; H. Hippisley Coxe; John Strode; and fifty-two justices of the peace.[3] In Wiltshire, one County Member, Thomas Goddard, signed, as did also his successor Charles Penruddock; they are supported by William Hussey, M.P. for Hindon, and an 'outsider', William Beckford, lord of Fonthill and M.P. for the City of London. Two other members of the influential Goddard family signed: Edward Goddard of Hartham and Richard Goddard of Marlborough, both J.P.s; also John Pitt of Stratford, William Bythesea of Workhouse, Henry Penruddock Wyndham, John Talbot of Lacock, Peter Bathurst of Clarendon Park, and William Temple of Bishopstrow. In all, some thirty-five justices are among the signatories.[4]

In some western counties, opinion appears to have been more divided. In Gloucestershire, where the preliminary meeting, attended largely by the nobility and gentry, had voted against the adoption of a petition, there was, nevertheless, fair support from justices and men of property. Among those signing the petition are Sir William Guise, Bart., future County Member; Charles

[1] Ibid., p. 30.
[2] Ibid., p. 25. I have not been able to find more than forty-five of these (H.O. 55/1; Commission of the Peace, Surrey, March 1769).
[3] H.O. 55/5; Commission of the Peace, Somerset, 27 June 1766.
[4] H.O. 55/2; Commission of the Peace, Wiltshire, 30 Nov. 1767.

Barrow, M.P. for Gloucester; William Dowdeswell, M.P. for Worcestershire; and his brother-in-law, Sir William Codrington, M.P. for Tewkesbury. Charles Dowdeswell was also a petitioner, as were Sir John Guise, Bart., Sir George Onesiphorus Paul; James and Richard Clutterbuck; and some thirty justices of the peace.[1] In Herefordshire, among some thirty petitioning justices we find the names of Thomas Foley junior, County Member, Dr. Robert Foley, D.D., and Sir James Hereford of Sutton.[2]

In other counties, the gentry's response was noticeably lukewarm or chilly. Dowdeswell had written to Burke of the difficulties encountered in Worcestershire, where the 'people of rank and fortune' were hesitant to sign a petition that they associated with John Wilkes or with 'the injudicious list of grievances' of the Middlesex freeholders.[3] It is, therefore, not altogether surprising that we find among the signatories the names of remarkably few gentlemen and justices. Among them was 'G. Dowdeswell, M.D.'; but neither William Dowdeswell himself (who signed in Wiltshire) nor Holland Cooksey, the chairman of the freeholders' meeting in August, appear to have signed the petition; and of fourteen justices attending the county quarter sessions in 1769, only one — William Bund junior — appears among the signatories.[4] In Durham, two justices only of sixteen attending quarter sessions signed their names — Francis Jenison and John Tempest junior, also M.P. for Durham City;[5] Sir Thomas Clavering, County Member, although voting with the minority against Luttrell's adoption in April, did not sign the petition. In Northumberland, a mere dozen justices gave support — among them a baronet, Sir Francis Blake.[6] In Kent, it was notorious that the gentry and Members of Parliament had either boycotted the meeting of 27 November or attended in order to obstruct its purposes. Calcraft had warned Chatham at the time that 'hitherto every gentleman has kept back';[7] and Wedderburn wrote to Rockingham a fortnight later: 'The Kent petition takes very much amongst the freeholders but not amongst the gentlemen.'[8] In fact, among the county's

[1] H.O. 55/6; Commission of the Peace, Gloucestershire, 1762.
[2] H.O. 55/1; Commission of the Peace, Herefordshire, 22 March 1771.
[3] Dowdeswell to Burke, 5 Sept. 1769, *Burke Correspondence*, ii. 70.
[4] H.O. 55/2; Worcs. R.O., Q.S. Order Book, 1769.
[5] H.O. 55/4; Shire Hall, Durham, Q.S. Order Book, 1769.
[6] H.O. 55/4; Commission of the Peace, Northumberland, 26 July 1775.
[7] See p. 132 above.
[8] Wedderburn to Rockingham, 9 Dec. 1769, W.W.MSS., R 1/1251.

2,800 petitioners we find the name of no single Member of Parliament, knight or baronet, and ten at most of the 300 or more non-official justices enrolled on the Commission of the Peace.[1] In Middlesex, too, the cleavage between gentry and common freeholders was, as it had been in the elections of 1769, almost complete. Of over 550 non-official justices, a mere dozen signed the petition: of these, James Townsend, M.P. for West Looe, was the only person of note. Other signatories included John Sawbridge, M.P. for Hythe, James Adair, George Bellas, Rev. John Horne, Samuel Vaughan, and William Bridgen, alderman of Farringdon Within.[2]

In some counties, the clergy gave good support to the petitions: this was more likely to be the case where the territorial magnate, a respectable portion of the gentry, or even a high Church dignitary, had already given the movement their blessing. Among the Yorkshire petitioners we find, in addition to Dr. John Fountayne, Dean of York, the Rev. Theophilus Lindsay, J.P., of Catterick; P. Bateman, D.D.; James Godmond, vicar of Howden; and four other clerks — Robert Bitchard, Thomas Savage, H. Crooke and Benjamin Smith.[3] In Devonshire, nearly thirty clergymen signed the petition. They included three justices: John Lee of Exminster, John Cruys and Peter Beavis, vicar of Chiddlehampton; three other vicars: George Rhodes, Charles Steer and John Thorpe of Seaton and Beer; four rectors: John Burford Copleston of Ottwell, Richard Blake of Fairway, Richard Priest of Lout, and Thomas Hugo of Welborough; one curate, Thomas How; and eighteen other clerks.[4] In the county of Buckingham, a score of clergy signed: Purchase Denchfield, a justice and rector of

[1] H.O. 55/3; Commission of the Peace, Kent, 16 Dec. 1769. John Calcraft (Rochester) signed in Bucks and John Sawbridge (Hythe) in Middlesex. E. Sawbridge and Rev. Wanley Sawbridge are among the signatories.

[2] H.O. 55/4; Commission of the Peace, Middlesex, 24 Jan. 1769. Several of the gentry, of course, signed borough petitions: John Scudamore, M.P. for Hereford, Jas. Walwyn, J.P., Harcourt Aubrey, J.P., and William Hoskyns, J.P., signed at Hereford; Sir Robert Bernard, Bart., and Robert Jones, of Fonmon Castle, Glam., signed at Westminster; and Thomas Dodge, the Mayor, signed at Worcester (H.O. 55/4, 1, 2).

[3] There may of course, have been many more. It is only when the petitioner firmly adds 'vicar', 'Rector', 'curate', 'D.D.', or (more commonly) 'clerk' or 'cl.' to his name that we can be certain.

[4] They were W. Anstey, John Blake, Thomas Bliss, — Borsther (?), Joseph Bassett (or Brissett), Chas. Buckland, William Carter, William Eastern, Philip Elston, William Hole, Henry Land, Hoper Morrison, Fred. Parmeinter of Stone Ainey, John Rouse, William Smith, Robert Taylor, John and W. Walter, and William Wood.

Amersham; John Lockman, J.P., of Drayton Beauchamp; Thomas Willis, J.P.; Edmund Millward, J.P.; Moses Browne, vicar of Olney; Robert Pomfrey, rector of Emberton; and ten other clerks.[1] In Cornwall, of eighteen clerical justices eight signed the petition: John Collins, Thomas Carlyon, Joshua Howell, John Snow, Henry Hawkins Tremayne, Mydhope Wallis and Francis Webber, D.D. In Gloucestershire, too, we find half a dozen clerical petitioners, one of whom was a justice.[2] In other counties, the clergy appear to have been more hesitant — or, possibly, as petitioners, they were more discreet in revealing their calling. In the county of Hereford, three clerical justices signed: Dr. Robert Foley, Rev. Thomas Griffith and Rev. William Hopton; in Kent, Rev. Wanley Sawbridge, J.P.; in Northumberland, Rev. James Forster, J.P., of Brantingham, Yorks; in Somerset, Rev. Henry Harris, J.P.; in Surrey, Rev. William Stead and Rev. John Tattersall, both justices; in Worcestershire, Rev. T. J. Read, vicar of Tenbury; and, finally, in Middlesex, we find the signatures of Rev. Anthony Hinton, vicar of Hayes, who had voted for Proctor in both elections of 1768; Joshua Fleetwood, clerk of St. John the Evangelist, Westminster; and, of course, of John Horne, parson of New Brentford vicarage. In brief, some eighty clergymen are known to have petitioned in a dozen counties. This is not impressive as a total; but the support given by the clergy to the petitions of the counties of Buckingham and Devon is, none the less, remarkable.

It would be, of course, of the greatest interest to discover the degree of support that the petitions found among the freeholders of the 'middling sort' — those engaged in trade or manufacture or those, in country districts, who, while not qualifying for the title of 'gentlemen', yet owned or occupied substantial freeholds and properties. In the case of great commercial centres like Liverpool, Westminster and Bristol, where a high proportion of the enfranchised citizens are known to have signed, we may assume that this was considerable; but for the great majority of petitioning counties we have to rely, where we have any information whatever, mainly on hearsay or on evidence of the most general kind. We know, for example, that John Robinson expressed particular

[1] L. Butler, Jas. Eyre, Francis Gresley, William Hutton, Samuel Long, John Lovell, Robert Pargeter, Salisbury Price, Robert Twycross, and John Warren.

[2] Rev. John Rogers, J.P.; Rev. Chas. Hawkins; Rev. Richard Lockey; and Geo. Gwinnett and Rice Jones, clerks.

concern at the spread of the 'infectious poison' of the Yorkshire petition among the Quakers and Dissenters:[1] these were undoubtedly, for the most part, engaged in trade or manufacture; and Burke referred to the commercial as well as the landed 'opulence' of the supporters of the Yorkshire freeholders' meeting.[2] Among the Devon signatures we find that of Richard Rose, 'shopkeeper'. Again, in asserting the claims of the Cornish petitioners in the House of Commons, Serjeant Glynn stressed that 'the middling people in the county felt their liberties invaded'.[3] On the Buckinghamshire petition, too, we find the names of several of Wilkes's old friends and supporters of the 'middling sort' from his Aylesbury days: among them, John Dell, his former election agent; Francis Neale, writing master at the Aylesbury Free School; Edward and Richard Terry, brewers; and Henry Sheriff, publican of the George Inn.[4] These are, of course, only casual indications and we can only surmise that in other counties, too, the petitions met with a fair measure of support among manufacturers and tradesmen in market towns and centres of rural industry.

In the case of Middlesex we are on more certain ground, and the picture turns out to be substantially the same as for the elections of 1768–69.[5] When discussing the Middlesex petitioners in the Commons, Lord North asked: 'How can it be proved that they are freeholders?'[6] The answer is perhaps simpler than he imagined: by comparing them with the voters in the three preceding elections. The concordance of petitioners and previous Wilkite supporters is remarkably close: of the 1,553 petitioners 1,259 had voted in one or more of these elections; four in five of them had voted predominantly for Wilkes or Glynn; the remainder, though previously Proctorite in sympathy, had been won over to support the petition of May 1769. Thus, broadly speaking, the complexion of the petitioners is similar to that of the Wilkite voters whom we studied in an earlier chapter. We noted then the disproportionately high vote that Wilkes attracted among the residents of the commercial

[1] Robinson to Jenkinson, 3 Nov. 1769, Add. MSS. 38206, f. 150.
[2] Burke to Chas. O'Hara, 27 Sept. 1769, *Burke Correspondence*, ii. 86.
[3] Eg. 3711, p. 51.
[4] See pp. 17–18 above. Some fourteen of the thirty-three Aylesbury citizens who wrote in support of Wilkes to their M.P.s on 30 April 1768 (see p. 67 above) signed the petition.
[5] See chapter v above.
[6] Eg. 3711, p. 46.

'out'-parishes lying to the east and north of the City of London.[1] The proportion is even higher among the petitioners: no less than 54.6 per cent of all those signatories who had voted in the preceding elections held freeholds in land, messuages, tenements or warehouses in these parishes. There are other indications, besides, of support among these freeholders of the 'middling sort' – as the adherence to Wilkes's cause against Luttrell of a number of voters of this kind who had previously voted Proctor: such men as William Chancellor of Enfield, whose freehold was assessed for the Land Tax at £94 p.a.; Richard Fletcher, also of Enfield, owning and occupying property assessed at £156; George Jennings of Staines, with properties at £74; William Wilson, brewer, of St. George's Middlesex, with land and messuages at £80; and George Prescot, again of Enfield, with land assessed at £58 and himself converted from a Proctorite supporter to one instructed, with nine others, to present the Middlesex petition to the King.[2]

No doubt, a close study of the Land Tax registers would yield similar results in other counties; yet, for all their importance and the influence they may have exerted on others, it is not these 'middling' freeholders, any more than the county gentry or clergy, that are the typical signatories of the county petitions of 1769. Overwhelmingly, these were the petty freeholders of the market towns and villages – such as those forty petitioners of Padbury in Buckinghamshire, who signed their names, somewhat unsteadily for the most part, alongside those of their parson and curate. Sometimes comments are added, such as 'John Hampden and King George for ever!' on the Bucks petition, or the following on the petition for Kent: '12 Janny W. McEwin after having attended the House of Commons on Thursday the 9th Instant'. Often, on west country petitions, we find names that have the authentic flavour of the 'Puritan Revolution' of the seventeenth century: in Somerset, in sequence we read: Caleb Edwards, Zephaniah Modcaley and Isaac Edwards; in Gloucestershire, we find in close proximity Baptist Smart, Obadiah Paul, Caleb Dudley and Shadrach Charleter. On several, the initial neatly grouped names of Members of Parliament, gentry and justices are succeeded by the signatures of the mass of petitioners, some

[1] See p. 81 above.

[2] Middlesex R.O., L.T. assessments, 1767, nos. 68 (Enfield), 6631 (Staines); Guild. Lib., L.T. duplicates, 1768, St. George Middlesex, MS. 16016/57–8; Middlesex Poll Books, 1768–69.

carefully written, others sprawling untidily over the sheets that follow. Illiteracy or unsteady handwriting is obviously no certain indication of a lesser freeman or freeholder; but such factors as these may serve as a rough and ready guide. The proportion of those 'signing' with a 'mark' or a cross certainly varied widely from county to county and from one borough to the next; nor can this be explained purely in terms of a higher rate of literacy in urban than in rural areas. On the Westminster petition we find 12 'marks' among the 5,137 signatures — remarkably few considering the unflattering reputation of these 'mechanics and booksellers'! But there are no such 'marks' whatever on the petitions presented by Bristol, Hereford, Exeter, Worcester, and Liverpool; whereas among the more widely enfranchised inhabitants of Newcastle we find 36 'marks' and no less than 109 among Coventry's 900 petitioners. In the counties, as might be expected, the 'marks' tend to be more numerous; but, here again, there are startling divergencies: 297 'marks' in the case of Yorkshire (but among 11,000 signatures), 168 for Kent, 130 for Buckinghamshire, 105 for Derby, 104 for Worcestershire; fewer, as might be supposed for Middlesex (36) and Surrey (28); but, surprisingly, only 16 for Wiltshire, 12 for Cornwall, 10 for Gloucestershire, 9 for Durham, and 2 each in the case of Devon, Hereford and Somerset. Evidently, we are not likely to believe that the rate of literacy was markedly higher among the inhabitants of Liverpool than among those of Coventry, or among the freeholders of the western counties than in those of Kent or Buckingham. In the case of the cities, the explanation presumably lies in the differing property qualifications attaching to the franchise; in that of the counties, an explanation must be sought elsewhere, and it would seem to lie in the differing policies pursued by the local (or even national?) promoters. Where these were confident of a reasonable response from the gentry and 'middling' freeholders, did they hesitate to 'scrape the barrel' by enlisting the 'marks' or crosses of those who could not sign their names?[1] Where, on the other hand, as in Kent and Worcestershire, they met with the

[1] According to E. Langton's eyewitness account of the Westminster meeting on 29 August, copies of the petition were carried to different parts of Westminster Hall 'for all those to sign who could write their names & chose to do so' (E. Langton to Hardwicke, 29 Aug. 1769, Add. MSS. 35609, ff. 32–33). The suggestion that there were illiterates present may, of course, have been purely spiteful.

indifference or hostility of men of 'property and fortune', may they not have looked on every freeholder, whether literate or not, as an ally whose support could not lightly be rejected?[1] If some such explanation as this is valid, it is perhaps ironical that the Rockinghamite promoters and their allies in Derbyshire, Buckingham and Kent should have been more ready to receive the support of the most unlettered of the freeholders than Serjeant Glynn and the Supporters of the Bill of Rights!

However this may be, it does little to substantiate the charge made by the Attorney-General in the Commons debate on 9 January that 'certain demagogues have used undue influence to obtain subscriptions to the petitions'.[2] Inevitably, it was the gentry and men of substance in both cities and counties that were called upon to promote and organize them; but they were drawn up in such a manner as to appeal directly to the smallest of the 40s. freeholders and borough voters, who valued their traditional franchise and felt it threatened by Parliament's decisions in the case of the Middlesex electors. No doubt, the government and its majority in Parliament would have had greater cause for alarm had more 'people of family and fortune' in a number of counties given the petitions their support. But in some this, too, was forthcoming; and even where it was lacking, the mere weight of numbers was a factor that, as John Robinson had noted, 'would better be quieted'; and, sooner or later, it would be a force to be reckoned with, as well.

[1] It may be significant of local variations that, on the Derbyshire petition, 84 of the 105 'marks' are concentrated on 4 out of 13 skins of parchment; on the Kent petition, 144 of the 168 'marks' are concentrated on 9 out of 23 skins; while, in Wiltshire, all 16 'marks' appear on one skin.

[2] Eg. 3711, p. 20. Note also Mr. Brooke's comment: 'The petitioning movement was artificially, stirred up by the politicians for their own ends' (*The Chatham Administration 1766–1768*, p. 231). For hostile contemporary comment, see Samuel Johnson, *The False Alarm* (1770).

IX

THE CITY OF LONDON

HAVING served his full term, John Wilkes was released from the King's Bench prison on 17 April 1770. It was another occasion for celebration by his many friends and supporters in England and America. In Bristol, there were illuminations and banquets; in Boston, Massachusetts, the health of 'the illustrious martyr to Liberty' was drunk at a public dinner; Colonel Luttrell was hanged in effigy in a west country market place; and, in London, Alderman Beckford's mansion in Soho Square was festooned with the word *Liberty* in letters three feet high.[1] But, the *Annual Register* demurely added, 'to the praise of the lower order of patriots, no disorders have been complained of anywhere'.[2]

Soon after his release, Wilkes came to live at 7 Prince's Court, Great George Street, a house within a stone's throw of Parliament that he rented for fifty guineas a year.[3] Yet his immediate prospects of assuming his seat in the Commons were very slender indeed: the petitions of the preceding year had been followed by attempts to promote a similar round of Remonstrances to the Crown;[4] these, however, held fire and aroused little response outside the capital,[5] and he soon turned his energies towards capturing a strong position in the City of London.

The City was, by long tradition, governed by a Common Council

[1] *Brist. J.*, 21 April 1770; Walpole, *Memoirs*, iv. 78; Bleackley, p. 249.

[2] *Ann. Reg.*, 1770, p. 94.

[3] Wilkes to Polly, 11 May 1770, *The Correspondence of the late John Wilkes with his Friends* (5 vols., 1805), iv. 31. Yet the house was assessed for the Poor Rate at only £30 p.a. (Poor Rate, 1771, St. Margaret (Abbey Division), West. Lib., F 457, p. 7).

[4] The City of London sent Remonstrances in March, May, July and November 1770 (H.O. 55/6; Sharpe, *London and the Kingdom*, iii. 91–103, 106–7; W. P. Treloar, *Wilkes and the City* (1917), pp. 86–100; Maccoby, op. cit., pp. 139–47); Middlesex adopted a Remonstrance in March (*Ann. Reg.*, 1770, p. 87) and Surrey in June 1770 (H.O. 55/6). For attempts by the Rockingham and Chatham groups to promote Remonstrances in Yorks, Bucks and Kent in June–Sept. 1770, see *Burke Correspondence*, ii. 142, 152, 156–7, 162; and Chatham-Calcraft correspondence, P.R.O., 30/8/25, ff. 49, 53, 57, 60.

[5] For Burke's disenchantment, see his letter to Chas. O'Hara on 9 Aug. 1770: 'As to politics we have none. Everything is sullen and quiet' (*Burke Correspondence*, ii. 148).

of something under 240 members, elected within the wards by nomination of the livery companies, and a Court of Aldermen representing each one of the twenty-six wards. The power of election rested firmly with the freemen of the livery companies, who collectively formed a Common Hall, and the initiative in City political action generally sprang from the Common Hall, from the various wards or within the Common Council. Yet the Court of Aldermen was often able to determine the outcome — both because it met more frequently, was a smaller and more malleable body, and because it had what amounted to a casting vote in such matters as the election of the Lord Mayor.[1] In addition, the aldermen were more liable to penetration by the influence of the Court or by competing groups of aristocratic managers, both by reason of their smaller numbers and of their closer identification with the 'monied interest' that gravitated towards national, rather than towards purely City, politics.[2] This division between aldermen and 'commoners' on social and economic lines was clearly marked during the years that Wilkes rose to the highest office in the City. Of the 416 Common Council men who, at various times, held office between 1768 and 1774, the great majority followed the usual occupations of the City as merchants, wholesalers, brokers, retail tradesmen, craftsmen, manufacturers and professional men; an insignificant minority only held directorships in banking or insurance companies.[3] Among the forty-three aldermen, however, who held office during this period, no less than a dozen were or became bankers (two of them as directors or Governor of the Bank of England), one was a director of London Assurance, one Governor of the Hudson's Bay Company, two were West India merchants, several were gentlemen of apparent leisure, and only a handful followed the usual City crafts or trades.[4]

[1] See Treloar, *Wilkes and the City*, pp. 126–36; also pp. 167–70 below.

[2] See p. 5 above.

[3] Of 311 whose occupations and addresses appear in the *London Directory*, 1774, 124 were merchants, wholesalers and brokers; 89 were apparently engaged in the retail trade (27 as linen-drapers, 39 others in textiles, 15 booksellers and stationers); 83 were craftsmen and manufacturers (38 in sundry metal trades); 13 were professional men (11 lawyers); 1 was a director of the Sun Fire Office; and another combined the occupation of bank director with that of drugs and wine-merchant (*Royal Calendar*, 1768–74; *London Directory*, 1774). See also Appendix IX.

[4] Bankers or bankers-to-be were Sir Chas. Asgill, Bart. (Candlewick, 1749–77); Sir James Esdaile (Cripplegate, 1767–93); Sir Samuel Fludyer, Bart., (Cheap, 1751–68. Deputy-Governor, Bank of England); Sir Richard Glyn, Bart., (Dowgate, 1750–73); Sir Francis Gosling (Farringdon Without, 1756–68); Sir Thomas

Political divisions corresponded by no means exactly to these distinctions in wealth and social status; but even at the height of Beckford's and Wilkes's ascendancy in City politics, the Court was able to exercise a preponderant influence within the Court of Aldermen, in which Thomas Harley of the Portsoken Ward acted for long as its chief spokesman and correspondent.[1] Before Wilkes's arrival on the scene this influence was already being challenged — both among the aldermen and in the Common Council — by rival factions directed by the leaders of parliamentary groups. Of these, by far the most important was the growing faction of 'patriots' dominated by William Beckford, who, as Chatham's mouthpiece in City politics, won the mayoralty in 1763 and 1770 and was elected Member for London in 1768; he was supported by John Sawbridge and James Townsend who, with Richard Oliver, became, after Beckford's death in June 1770, the leaders of the new Shelburne (ex-Chatham) group in the City that gradually broke with Wilkes.[2] The third group, directed by the Marquess of Rockingham, had little effective influence and found its solitary aldermanic spokesman in Barlow Trecothick, America merchant of Vintry ward, who, as Beckford's ally in 1768, was elected to Parliament that year. The Rockinghamites' hopes of extending their influence in the City rose high in the summer of 1770, when Trecothick was elected Lord Mayor for the completion of Beck-

Hallifax (Aldersgate, 1766–89); Sir Joseph Hankey (Langbourn, 1737–69); Rt. Hon. Thos. Harley (Portsoken, 1761–85); Benjamin Hopkins (Broad Street, 1773–76. Director of Bank of England); Sir Robert Ladbroke (Bridge Without, 1741–73); Joseph Martin (elected Lime Street, Sept. 1772, but never served) and Sir Walter Rawlinson (Dowgate, 1773–77). Samuel Turner (Tower, 1762–75) was Governor of London Assurance and Sir William Baker (Bassishaw, 1759–70) was Governor of the Hudson's Bay Co. (*London Directory*, 1774; A. B. Beaven, *The Aldermen of the City of London*, ii. 127–35, 197–201). See also Appendix x.

[1] The following fifteen may, during this period, be accounted steady supporters of Administration and opponents of the 'patriot' groups: Sir Thos. Hallifax (Aldersgate), John Shakespear (Aldgate, 1767–75); John Bird (Bassishaw, 1770–72), Sir Robert Ladbroke (Bridge Without), Samuel Plumbe (Castle Baynard, 1767–82), James Rosseter (Broad Street, 1769–73), Robert Alsop (Coleman Street, 1745–73; Bridge Without, 1773–85), Benjamin Hopkins (Broad Street), Sir Henry Bankes (Cordwainer, 1762–74), Brackley Kennet (Cornhill, 1767–82), Sir Jas. Esdaile (Cripplegate), Sir Richard Glyn (Dowgate), Thos. Harley (Portsoken), Samuel Turner (Tower), and William Nash (Walbrook, 1766–72). See also Appendix x. Thomas Harley corresponded with John Robinson at the Treasury (see, e.g., Fortescue, ii. no. 773; iii. no. 1324).

[2] See, e.g., Calcraft to Chatham, 12 March 1770; to Lady Chatham, 12 Aug. 1770; and to Chatham, 18 and 30 Sept. 1770; Chatham Correspondence, P.R.O., 30/8/25, ff. 40–42, 51, 57–59, 61.

ford's second term of office and two members of their parliamentary group, William Baker and Joseph Martin, were elected sheriffs for 1771.[1] But Trecothick failed at the next contest and drifted further away from his former 'patriot' allies, and Baker and Martin lost all popularity in their year of office and, in spite of Burke's efforts to sustain them, retired in disgust from active City politics.[2]

When Wilkes stood for election in the City in March 1768, he had already roused widespread sympathy among both livery and smaller tradesmen for his courageous stand over general warrants and for his continued challenge to Administration during his years of exile. Yet he had taken no steps to build up a separate party for himself, had come to no electoral agreement with Beckford's group of 'patriots', and had to take his chance as another contender for the 'patriot' vote. Even so, he would have carried the election with a large majority had it depended on the smaller craftsmen and journeymen who hailed him in the streets and on the hustings; among the livery, too, he attracted considerable support (though not enough to secure election); but he made little impression as yet on the Common Council or Court of Aldermen. Of the liverymen, two voters in every nine cast their votes for him — a proportion that rose to one in three and more in the case of his own company (the Joiners) and some of the other smaller companies, and to one in four even in the case of some of the largest and wealthiest among them.[3] Two aldermen, William Bridgen of Farringdon Within and Sir William Baker of Bassishaw, voted for Wilkes, and a mere thirteen of the 236 members of the Common Council.[4] But his support began to grow soon after. Two Common Council men who had voted against him in the City voted for him, a few days later, in Middlesex, and three more voted for him in April 1769 against Luttrell.[5] More signifi-

[1] See Rockingham to Burke, 15 Oct. 1769; Burke to Rockingham, 7, 8 and 23 Sept. 1770; Burke to William Baker, 26 Sept. 1771; *Burke Correspondence*, ii. 90, 157–8, 159–60, 241–2. See also editorial notes by Dr. Sutherland, ibid., pp. 240–1.

[2] See Burke to William Baker, 1 October 1771, ibid., ii. 242–3.

[3] Of 5,694 voters 1,247 voted for Wilkes. Among these were 92 of 282 voting Joiners, 36 Bakers (118), 7 Brewers (23), 42 Butchers (121), 13 Embroiderers (38), 18 Plasterers (57), 15 Scriveners (38) and 25 Upholders (82). Of the 'Big Twelve', 31 Drapers (126), 35 Fishmongers (125) and 36 Vintners (150) voted for Wilkes (*The Poll of the Livery of London*, 1768). See also Appendix VIII

[4] Ibid.; *Royal Calendar*, 1768–69.

[5] Ibid.; Middlesex Poll Books, 1768–69. See also p. 83 and n. 1 above.

cant perhaps was the election to the Common Council in the years that followed of a far higher proportion of Wilkes supporters from among the livery; whereas only one in every sixteen voting Common Council men of 1768 had cast his vote for him, his supporters of this time included no less than one in three of those among the voting liverymen who were promoted to the Common Council between 1769 and 1774.[1]

Meanwhile, in January 1769, one of the two largest of the City wards, that of Farringdon Without, had unanimously elected him to be their alderman in succession to Sir Francis Gosling, former bookseller and Fleet Street banker; but the election was challenged by the Court of Aldermen on transparently political grounds and its validity remained in doubt until Wilkes's release from prison.[2] In the following months, as we have seen, two of Chatham's lieutenants in the City, John Sawbridge and James Townsend, had joined with Richard Oliver, Sir Joseph Mawbey and others to form the Society of Supporters of the Bill of Rights which, for some time to come, provided a common platform for the metropolitan radicals and, in particular, for Chatham's and Wilkes's supporters in the City. The strength that the united 'patriots' could command among the more active of the liverymen at this time was reflected in the great meeting of 24 June 1769 which, by an overwhelming majority, promoted the London petition to the King,[3] but it was far less evident in the Common Council which, seven weeks earlier, had, by 92 votes to 72, endorsed the Lord Mayor's action in refusing to summon a Common Hall for this very purpose.[4] The 'patriots', however, used the elections of the following December to strengthen their position on the Council, lampooned their opponents in the press, and succeeded in re-

[1] Of 236 Common Council men of 1768, 33 voted for Wilkes, 190 voted for other candidates only, and 33 abstained or were not eligible to vote; of 143 new entrants to the Common Council in 1769–74, 27 had voted for Wilkes in 1768, 56 had voted for other candidates only, and 59 had abstained or had not been qualified to vote (*The Poll of the Livery of London*, 1768; *Royal Calendar*, 1768–76).

[2] See p. 61 above; and Treloar, op. cit., pp. 70–76, 94–95. To celebrate his initial victory, some of his supporters in that ward — Messrs. J. Brome, W. Chamberlayne, J. Hitchcock, W. Richardson, Thos. Sainsbury and Geo. Wyatt — dined with him in the King's Bench prison on 10 Jan. 1769 (ibid., p. 71).

[3] See p. 108 above.

[4] *Mid. J.*, 4–6, 9–11 May 1769 (with division lists). The aldermanic minority on this occasion were Beckford (Billingsgate), Trecothick (Vintry) and Sir William Stephenson (Bridge).

moving a number of 'anti-petitioners' from office. Of the Bridge ward, for example, we read that, at a general meeting of the inhabitants,

four of the present Council of that ward, who had declared against a petition to his Majesty . . . were put in nomination for the year ensuing, but universally rejected, some of them not having a single hand in their favour.[1]

Similar steps were taken in Farringdon Without, Castle Baynard, Tower and Walbrook, in some of which, too, 'patriot' candidates emerged at the top of the poll.[2] This change in the balance of forces was reflected in the subsequent vote of March 1770, when the Common Council carried by a majority of 112 to 76 a proposal to summon a further Common Hall in order to follow up the petition with a Remonstrance — a decision that led in turn to counter-protests by sixteen aldermen of the Court party and by the officers of the Goldsmiths', Weavers' and Grocers' companies.[3]

So, when Wilkes returned to the City to assume his aldermanic seat in April 1770, he was assured of a considerable following both among the livery and within the Common Council. His diary for the following months shows that he became quickly involved in an exacting round of social and political engagements;[4] his company was widely sought in the City and elsewhere, and we find John Calcraft writing to Lady Chatham on 12 August:

I hope Mr. Wilkes will not lead us wrong. He is at Mr. Sawbridge's where a great party assemble tomorrow. I am much press'd to make one & see good reason for so doing.[5]

Soon after, he appears to have played an important part, together with Richard Oliver, in assuring the election of Brass Crosby as

[1] *Mid. J.*, 25–28 Nov. 1769.

[2] Ibid., 21–23, 23–26, 26–28 Dec. 1769 (with lists of candidates and votes for Billingsgate, Broad Street, Castle Baynard, Cordwainer, Cornhill, Dowgate, Farringdon Within, Farringdon Without, Tower and Walbrook). George Bellas, for example, headed the poll in Castle Baynard; and Chamberlayne, Hitchcock, Richardson and Sainsbury (all Wilkes supporters) were among the first elected in Farringdon Without.

[3] Treloar, op. cit., pp. 86–87, Sharpe, op. cit. iii. 93–4. No less than 153 Common Council men accompanied the Lord Mayor, sheriffs and 4 aldermen to St. James's to present the Remonstrance (Treloar, op. cit., p. 91).

[4] Add. MSS. 30866; cit. Treloar, op. cit., pp. 259 ff.

[5] Calcraft to Lady Chatham, 12 Aug. 1770, P.R.O., Chatham Correspondence, 30/8/25, f. 51.

Lord Mayor to succeed Trecothick.[1] At this time, too, he led a movement of protest against the issue of warrants by City magistrates to authorize the impressment of men for the Navy. He had some success: not only did other magistrates, in defiance of Lord Mayor Trecothick's wishes, follow his example, but the Common Council called, on 22 January 1771, for the prosecution of 'magistrates backing press warrants and constables executing the same'.[2] But this issue was soon overshadowed by another in which Wilkes was intimately involved — the great battle that broke out a few weeks later between City and Commons over the reporting of parliamentary debates in the press. 'The printers' case' was to be one of the great episodes in Wilkes's tumultuous career.

The publication of parliamentary debates in the newspapers had long been forbidden — most recently by Commons resolutions of 26 February 1728. It was a time-honoured and cherished privilege of Parliament that only such reports of its proceedings should percolate to the public as had been authorized by its own officers; for, in the words of Speaker Norton in one of the numerous debates to which 'the printers' case' gave rise:

> Modest timid Members would never give us their sentiments if they were liable to be misrepresented and made the subject of ridicule and contempt thereby. The public have the notes and journals which is enough.[3]

Occasional breaches of the regulation occurred throughout the eighteenth century, but it was only since 1768 that, led by John

[1] See Calcraft to Chatham, 18 Sept. 1770 (with enclosure from a City correspondent, dated 13 Sept. 1770), ff. 57–59. Calcraft's correspondent wrote: 'I am sorry to tell you that all measures to set Alderman Crosby aside in the City are in vain. A plan has been formed some time to return him and Mr. Sheriff Townsend, and the persons who have now got possession of the City will not recede . . . A little Junto of Mr. Oliver's friends now manage everything . . . *It has been resolved at a private meeting of Mr. Oliver's friends to return Mr. Crosby and Mr. Townsend. Both Mr. Wilkes and Mr. Beardmore concur in the resolution;* Mr. Freeman is also for it; Mr. Bellas is out of town. I had a great deal of talk with Mr. Beardmore this morning upon the subject. He is determined to support the return of Messrs Crosby and Townsend. Mr. Wilkes gave me his sentiments some days ago'. [My italics]

Arthur Beardmore, Lord Temple's solicitor, was a Wilkes supporter and Common Council man for Walbrook; he had been arrested with Rev. John Entick in 1763 for publishing the *Monitor* (see p. 29 above). Samuel Freeman of Tower Ward was one of thirteen Common Council men voting for Wilkes in March 1768.

[2] An attempt to rescind this resolution was defeated by 95 votes (2 aldermen and 93 commoners) to 69 (14 aldermen and 55 commoners) on 15 March 1771 (*Mid. J.*, 14–16 March 1771 (with division lists)).

[3] The Parliamentary Diary of Matthew Brickdale (11 vols. in manuscript, 1770–74, Univ. of Bristol Library), iv. 31–32.

Almon in the *London Evening Post*, editors had begun to make it a regular practice to instruct and entertain their readers with detailed accounts of parliamentary proceedings: by the spring of 1771, over a dozen daily and weekly papers were regularly reporting debates.[1] On 5 February of that year, Colonel George Onslow, a government supporter and cousin of the Member for Surrey, raised the matter in the Commons with a view to enforcing the provisions of the resolutions of 1728. Not only did the bulk of reporting newspapers take no notice of the warning, but two of them, the *Middlesex Journal* and the *Gazetteer*, accompanied their defiance with insulting references to 'little cocking George Onslow' himself. The result was a stiffer attitude by the Commons which, on 8 February, by a vote of 90 to 55, called for the attendance of the offending printers, John Wheble of the *Middlesex Journal* and R. Thompson of the *Gazetteer*. Thompson attended, as ordered, on 11 February but, after that, both printers were openly defiant, and when the House ordered their arrest by the serjeant-at-arms, they went into hiding and obstinately refused to attend or to surrender to justice. 'The City patriots', wrote Mrs. Harris to her son at this time,

> will not give up the printers and threaten if the serjeant-at-arms should attempt to seize them he shall be sent to Newgate; if that should be the case, it would be a most disagreeable affair . . . If they commit the serjeant-at-arms to Newgate, they talk of the Speaker and all the House marching to demand him back; that event, I hope, may never happen. 'Tis said the printers are gone off, and that will put an end to further trouble.[2]

The hope proved over-sanguine. The Commons had at first proceeded cautiously, and even George III had shown commendable restraint,[3] but when the serjeant-at-arms reported on 4 March that neither Wheble nor Thompson could be found, the King was requested to issue a proclamation, offering a £50 reward for the arrest of each of the printers; this duly appeared in the *London Gazette* on 9 March.[4]

[1] Peter D. G. Thomas, 'The Beginning of Parliamentary Reporting in Newspapers, 1768–1774,' *E.H.R.*, lxxiv (1959), 623–36.

[2] Mrs. Harris to Jas. Harris junr., 1 March 1771, *Letters of the First Earl of Malmesbury*, i. 217.

[3] See the King to North, 20 Feb. 1771, Fortescue, ii. no. 913.

[4] For most of the above and for much that follows, see Peter D. G. Thomas, 'John Wilkes and the Freedom of the Press (1771)', *Bulletin of the I.H.R.*, May 1960, pp. 86–98. This is the most recent, the best and the most complete account of the affair that has appeared. The only other reasonably adequate account is by Sharpe, op. cit. iii. 107–19.

By this time, it was widely known that the printers were being encouraged in their defiance to Parliament by 'City patriots' and that it was even planned to broaden the whole attack by involving more newpapers and by pitting the privileges of the City against the power and privileges of the House of Commons. Colonel Barré, a Chathamite M.P., having wind of the project through his City connexions, warned his leader of what was afoot on 18 February; and, while unable or unwilling to arrest the course of events, they succeeded in dissuading their City followers, Sawbridge and Townsend, from taking any active part in them.[1] Horne later claimed credit for the initial obduracy of Wheble and Thompson but the wider plan of action appears to have been hatched by John Wilkes himself, in association with John Almon, the printer and bookseller, and Robert Morris, a lawyer and former secretary of the Supporters of the Bill of Rights.[2]

But, though forewarned of the dangers that lay ahead, the Commons majority pressed their attack. On 12 March, Colonel Onslow moved that six further printers be ordered to attend: Woodfall of the *Morning Chronicle*, Baldwin of the *St. James's Chronicle*, Evans of the *London Packet*, Bladen of the *General Evening Post*, Miller of the *London Evening Post*, and Wright of the *Whitehall Evening Post*. James Townsend objected on the grounds that the order of February 1728 was obsolete and out of date; Thomas Pownall considered that the printers' offence was great, 'but they have offended no law'; Sawbridge warned that the proclamation was 'waste paper' and could not be acted upon without offending the law, and the opposition as a whole resorted

[1] Thomas, op. cit., p. 88. See also Chatham's letter to Barré of 17 March 1771: 'I am not a little happy that Mr. T. and Mr. S. are upon clear ground, and would fain hope that they may venture to continue in the right, without losing all their weight with the livery. I am, however, aware that their situation is delicate and demands a line somewhat nice' (*Correspondence of William Pitt, Earl of Chatham*, iv. 118).

[2] For the evidence on this point see Thomas, op. cit., pp. 88–89. Dr. Thomas bases his case largely on Walpole's *Memoirs of the Reign of King George the Third* and on an important letter sent by Robert Morris to Wilkes on 13 March 1771, in the course of which he writes: 'I have been all this day upon the wing about the business of the printers and hitherto unable to call upon you, agreeable to my inclinations. I would not have the affair sleep for the universe. The Ministry take care it shall not on their side; we must therefore be staunch on ours . . . Some of the six newly ordered to attend, I believe make their appearance tomorrow at the House — those are Bladon (Gen. Evg.), Wright (Whitehall) and possibly Evans (L. Pack.). There will be business new for all of us. Different games must be played. But if we can, we must take into our assistance some more of the Aldermen; and I hope also we shall have the Sheriffs. Messengers may yet be sent to Newgate, and printers lodged there be let out . . .'

to obstructive tactics that divided the House twenty-three times before it broke up, having adopted Onslow's motion, at 4.45 the next morning.[1] On the 14th, four of the printers duly obeyed the summons, the absentees being Woodfall who (it turned out) had been detained by the Lords and John Miller who refused to appear. The occasion was marked by an interesting question from Sir Joseph Mawbey:

> If the Lord Mayor of London shd do his duty & commit any man who executed the order of this House of the proclamation wd you commit him to Newgate?

Charles Cornewall also struck a warning note:

> Harsh measures are not proper to be used at this time, & in the temper the people are in, the best way to cure the evil wd be to take no notice of it.

But the majority's blood was up and, after the Speaker had reprimanded and discharged the attendant printers, it was ordered that Miller be taken into custody by the serjeant-at-arms.[2]

It was this decision that gave Wilkes and his associates their awaited opportunity. But even before Miller's case came to their notice, John Wheble of the *Middlesex Journal*, who had been evading the attentions of the serjeant-at-arms for the past two weeks, was apprehended on 15 March by one of his own servants, Edward Carpenter, under the terms of the recent proclamation. Brought before Wilkes at the Guildhall, he was released on the grounds that he was a London freeman and that his captor was neither a constable nor a peace officer of the City. Carpenter, for his part, was handed a certificate, proving his capture of Wheble, so that he might claim his £50 reward! The same afternoon, William Whittam, a Commons messenger, attempted to arrest John Miller at his house. Miller resisted and a constable, standing conveniently at hand, charged the messenger with assault and brought both men to the Mansion House, where Wilkes was in attendance on Brass Crosby, the Lord Mayor, who was bedridden with gout. At Whittam's request, the hearing was adjourned until the evening, by which time the Speaker had been apprised of his messenger's fate and Crosby and Wilkes had been joined by Alderman Richard Oliver, a fellow-conspirator, and Robert

[1] Brickdale Diary, iv. 1–12; *Malmesbury Letters*, ii. 220–1.
[2] Brickdale Diary, iv. 13–37.

Morris as counsel for Miller. The Speaker's request for Whittam's release was refused, and Crosby, having ascertained that the messenger was not a constable of London and that the Speaker's warrant had not been backed by a City magistrate, ruled that Miller's arrest was illegal and ordered Whittam to appear at the next quarter sessions to answer the charge.[1]

Administration was in a quandary. Some, including Lord North himself, still favoured moderation; Sir Gilbert Elliot and others of the 'King's Friends' urged that strong and exemplary action be taken: in this they were supported by George III, who wrote to North on 17 March:

> The authority of the House of Commons is totally annihilated if it is not in an exemplary manner supported tomorrow, by instantly committing the Lord Mayor and Alderman Oliver to the Tower.

'As to Wilkes', he added wisely, 'he is below the notice of the House.'[2] Accordingly, on the 18th, Welbore Ellis, for the government, moved that Crosby should attend in his place the next day. This was agreed, but only after opposition speakers had voiced further warnings. 'This is a matter', proclaimed Sir William Meredith, 'that may involve the House, this Kingdom, the King on the Throne and his posterity into distress and difficulties.' Henry Herbert warned that the House was standing 'on the slippery verge of another contest with the people more complicated, more difficult and more dangerous than the former one'. Burke argued that 'this fresh turn with Wilkes is a fresh disgrace to us, but a fresh service to him'. Sawbridge went so far as to commend the Lord Mayor's action 'as worthy of the thanks of every Englishman'. Meanwhile, motions to extend the order of attendance to Oliver and Wilkes were deferred; but, the next day, Wilkes's attendance was again urged by Mawbey who, in this, was evidently working in alliance with Wilkes himself, whose insistence that he should be heard 'in his place' was but another assertion of his right to sit in the House as Member for Middlesex.[3] For a time, to the King's dismay, it seemed indeed that Wilkes

[1] Thomas, op. cit., pp. 90–91; Brickdale Diary, iv. 37–39; *Gent's Mag.*, 1771, p. 139.

[2] Fortescue, ii. nos. 933–4; cit. Thomas, op. cit., p. 92. The King further suggested that Crosby should be escorted to the Tower by water — 'that no rescue may ensue'.

[3] See his letter to the Speaker of 20 March 1771, *Gent's Mag.*, 1771, p. 140.

would be summoned to the bar, but, after various adjournments and subterfuges, the order was allowed to lapse.[1]

Considerable pains were taken to ensure that Lord Mayor Crosby should have a suitable escort to the Commons on 19 March. Handbills had been distributed in the City, inviting 'Liverymen, Freemen and Citizens' to assemble at the Mansion House and give him a good send-off. In fact, it was reported,

> a prodigious crowd of the better sort were at the Mansion House and in the streets near it, who testified their approbation by repeated huzzas, which were continued quite from the Mansion House to the House of Commons. On his arrival there, one universal shout was heard for near three minutes; and the people, during the whole passage to the House, called out to the Lord Mayor as the *People's Friend*, the *Guardian of the City's rights and the Nation's Liberties*.

Wilkes followed in John Reynolds' coach as far as Palace Yard.[2] In the House, Crosby defended his conduct on the grounds that he would have betrayed his trust and broken his oath to uphold the City's charters had he acted otherwise. He was then allowed to retire in order to nurse his gout and to instruct counsel and returned home, 'attended by a great number of people', while others unharnessed his horses at St. Paul's and drew his carriage in triumph to the Mansion House.[3] Meanwhile, the Commons decided to call Oliver on the next day and the debate was enlivened by a violent outburst from Charles James Fox, who called for immediate measures against Wilkes and Oliver,

> for our existence is at stake, and we should do no private business while it is doubted whether we are alive or not. If an assassin comes to murder me, I must struggle as long as I can.

However, what with the Lord Mayor's ill-health and the briefing of counsel, the whole case was further postponed until 25 March.[4]

In the meantime, the City had temporarily closed its ranks and, by an unwonted display of unanimity, the Common Council had, on 21 March, passed a vote of thanks to the Lord Mayor and

[1] Brickdale Diary, iv. 39–56, 62, 87; v. 1–6, 15. See also Thomas, op. cit., pp. 92–93. The King expressed considerable alarm at the prospect of Wilkes being summoned to attend (see letter to North, 20 March 1771, Fortescue, ii. no. 938). North did not favour the idea and blamed Mawbey for the suggestion (Brickdale Diary, v. 2). Burke appears to have taken the order for Wilkes to attend seriously — even after various adjournments (see draft speech of (?) 28 March 1771, W.W.MSS., Bk papers ('Wilkes')).

[2] *Gent's Mag.*, 1771, pp. 139–40; *Mid. J.*, 19–21 March 1771.

[3] Brickdale Diary, iv. 57–61; *Gent's Mag.*, loc. cit.

[4] Brickdale Diary, iv. 62–91; v. 1–12.

Aldermen Oliver and Wilkes 'for having on a late important occasion supported the privileges and franchises of this City and defended our excellent Constitution'; and a committee was set up, empowered to employ counsel and to spend up to £500.[1] On the 25th, there was a further 'prodigious concourse of people about the Mansion House' to see the magistrates off and great crowds, who had gathered volume and momentum from the City to Westminster, surged round the Houses of Parliament, many among them wearing labels inscribed 'Crosby, Wilkes, Oliver, and the Liberty of the Press'.[2] Members had difficulty in entering St. Stephen's Chapel and were subjected to insults (wrote Mrs. Harris) 'by a most blackguard set of shabby fellows', who were eventually dispersed by the High Constable and the Westminster justices.[3] In view of the restrictions imposed by the House on the use of counsel, Crosby declared his intention of conducting his own case and refused to make concessions: 'I glory in what I did . . . in protecting the liberty of the subject.' In moving that the discharge of Miller was a breach of privilege, Welbore Ellis insisted:

> It is unfit the people should be misled by printers and it is for their good that they should know nothing but came from the authority of this House;

and he demagogically asked: 'How can anyone think themselves engaged in the cause of Liberty when they are about to take away the power from this House which is the check to the executive power of this country?' James Townsend retorted: 'When the House of Commons exceed their authority, their orders may be resisted . . . the people see with jealousy the attempts on the liberty of the press.' The Rockingham group were content to move the previous question and, when Ellis's motion was carried, several of them left the Chamber. Meanwhile, Crosby had once more been allowed to retire and was drawn in his carriage by waiting crowds 'all the way from St. Stephen's Chapel to the Mansion House'.[4] In spite of the lateness of the hour, it was decided to proceed with Oliver's case. Asked to state his defence he replied curtly:

[1] *Ann. Reg.*, 1771, p. 189.

[2] *Gent's Mag.*, 1771, p. 140; *London Evening Post*, 26 March 1771 (cit. Thomas, op. cit., p. 94); *Ox. J.*, 30 March 1771 (1¾ columns).

[3] Mrs. Harris to Jas. Harris junr., 26 March 1771, *Malmesbury Letters*, i. 221–3. See also Brickdale Diary, v. 27–30.

[4] *Hereford J.*, 28 March 1771.

I shall make no defence. I shall say nothing. You may do as you please. I defy you.

Though Grenville warned that 'if we sent him to the Tower, we shall send him among the acclamations of the enraged citizens', the decision was taken none the less, and, in the early morning, shortly after the House rose, he was escorted to the Tower by the Serjeant-at-arms.[1]

The final act of the drama was played on Wednesday, 27 March, when Crosby, still swathed in bandages, was escorted once more by vast crowds to Westminster. 'When the carriage reached St. Martin's Lane, the populace took off the horses and drew it to the King's Arms Tavern, Palace Yard.' 50,000 people, 'most of whom appeared to be respectable tradesmen' (ran one report), were assembled at the approaches to the House and Members, particularly those of the Court party, had the greatest difficulty in getting through to the Commons. According to the same account,

Lord North's chariot glasses were broken to pieces, as was the carriage soon afterwards, by which he received a wound, and was exceedingly terrified. The populace also took off his hat and cut it to into pieces, and he narrowly escaped with his life.[2] The two Cubs[3] and Mr. Hans Stanley were greatly insulted and pelted with mud.[4]

The King himself was insulted the next day as the State coach passed down Parliament Street, and Gregory Brown, a hosier of Coleman Street, is reputed to have shouted, 'No Lord Mayor, no King!'[5] Pandemonium reigned within and without the House as the Westminster magistrates struggled unsuccessfully to control the crowds and Members on both sides taunted each other with having organized 'mobs'. Alexander Wedderburn, now back in

[1] Brickdale Diary, v. 15–44. *The General Evening Post* of 26–28 March added the caustic comment: 'Mr. Alderman Oliver was greatly caressed by the mob upon the day of his commitment to the Tower; and had the honour done him to have three handkerchiefs picked out of his pocket, being supposed to have been taken as relics.'

[2] He was rescued by Sir William Meredith (Brickdale Diary, v. 45, 52).

[3] Charles James and Stephen Fox, who (according to another account) also had their carriages broken, 'their clothes torn, and [were] greatly spattered with mud, by the incensed populace' (*Gent's Mag.*, 1771, p. 141).

[4] *Mid. J.*, 26–28, 28–30 March 1771. See also *Ann. Reg.*, 1771, p. 85.

[5] Brown was arrested but released by a Westminster Grand Jury a few days later (Middlesex R.O., Sessions Rolls (Westminster), no. 3240, 2 April 1771). Keys, another rioter, was arrested for assaulting a constable at the House of Commons and sent to Bridewell to await trial at quarter sessions (*Ann. Reg.*, 1771, p. 92). Three other arrested rioters were said to have been released by the crowd (*Mid. J.*, 28–30 March 1771).

the government fold as Solicitor-General, charged the London magistrates with 'coming down at the head of a mob', and demanded an inquiry. 'Handbills may be put out by any man,' riposted Townsend and asked, 'where did the Brentford Riot proceed from? When I see a mob, I always conclude where they come from.' North commented sadly, and no doubt with justice: 'No one can suppose I hired this mob. I never had a hand in any.' Burke observed that there were 'two ways of hiring mobs: one by hiring, another by provoking'; and wrote frantic notes to Rockingham, demanding political reinforcements:

'We are in our usual disarray . . . People are crowding down pretty fast. When I said people come down fast, I don't mean ours, for very few are here. We shall bungle it worse than before . . . Nothing is concerted or disposed. I am totally at a loss what to do.

And again:

The Mob is grown very riotous. Very few friends of ours here. It is impossible to know what to do. For God's sake let Dowdeswell and Lord J. Cavendish come down. I am monstrously vexed.[1]

Eventually, after five hours of disturbance, as the result of the combined efforts of Alderman Trecothick, the two sheriffs and opposition Members (including both Burkes), a large part of the crowds was dispersed and the business of the day proceeded. Crosby was found guilty of a breach of privilege and, having refused the more lenient treatment of being 'committed to the custody of the serjeant-at-arms', was sent to join Oliver in the Tower.[2]

Parliament, though it might pride itself on having acted vigorously in defence of its privileges, was able to draw little comfort from the consequences of these actions. Chatham, while critical of the City for its 'absurdity' in challenging Parliament's right to defend its 'most tenable privilege', was even more incensed by

[1] Burke to Rockingham, 27 March 1771, *Burke Correspondence*, ii. 203–4. There were evidently differences between the Rockinghamites as to tactics. Savile, Dowdeswell and Lord J. Cavendish had walked out before sentence was passed on Oliver on 25 March, and Rockingham approved Dowdeswell's action in staying away from the House on the 27th (Dowdeswell and Rockingham to Burke, 27, 28 March 1771, ibid., ii. 204–5).

[2] Brickdale Diary, v. 44–67.

the wrong-headedness and folly of the Court, ignorant how to be four-and-twenty hours in good ground; for they have most ingeniously contrived to be guilty of the rankest *tyranny* in every step taken to assert the right.[1]

Even an ardent supporter of Administration, in a letter to Charles Jenkinson, expressed alarm at the dangers that might arise from such violent measures:

The ferment now raised is certainly symptomatic of a disease much more dangerous, which must be subdued or we shall live to see this country without a King or Parliament.[2]

The imprisoned magistrates were certainly not forgotten. The Common Council voted them 'tables' at the City's expense.[3] Lord Temple visited them in the Tower, as did the Dukes of Manchester and Portland, the Marquess of Rockingham, Earl Fitzwilliam, Sir Charles Saunders, Admiral Keppel, Dowdeswell and Edmund Burke.[4] Popular demonstrations followed: on 1 April, a hearse and two carts appeared on Tower Hill, and figures representing the Princess Dowager, Lord Bute, the Speaker and the two Foxes were beheaded by a chimney-sweep in clerical garb, and burnt. A few days later, a similar fate befell the stuffed dummies of Lord Halifax, Lord Barrington, Alderman Harley, Colonel Luttrell ('the usurper'), Lord Sandwich ('Jemmy Twitcher'), Colonel Onslow ('cocking George') and William de Grey, the Attorney-General.[5] On 8 May, when Parliament was prorogued, the two magistrates were released from the Tower to a salute of twenty-one guns of the Hon. Artillery Company and escorted in a triumphal procession of fifty-three carriages by almost the entire Common Council, 'and saluted with loud and universal huzzas'. At night, the City was illuminated in their honour and angry crowds smashed Speaker Norton's windows.[6] Meanwhile, congratulatory messages flowed in to the Lord Mayor from the Welsh counties, the towns of Newcastle, Stratford and Honiton, and most of the City's wards, and the cities of Bedford and Worcester conferred their Freedom on him.[7] The

[1] Chatham to Temple, 17 April 1771, *Grenville Papers*, iv. 533.

[2] Craggs Clare to Chas. Jenkinson, 8 April 1771, Add. MSS. 38206, f. 370.

[3] Sharpe, op. cit. iii. 116–17. The Lord Mayor, however, declined the offer.

[4] *Gent's Mag.*, 1771, p. 141; *Rockingham Memoirs*, ii. 208–9. In a letter to Dowdeswell of 28 March, Rockingham argued the justice of visiting the prisoners in the Tower against objections raised by Burke and Savile (ibid. ii. 207–8).

[5] *Mid. J.*, 2 April 1771; *Gent's Mag.*, 1771, p. 188.

[6] *Ann. Reg.*, 1771, pp. 104–5.

[7] *Gent's Mag.*, 1771, p. 191.

only genuine 'martyr' in the cause was the unfortunate Edward Carpenter who, found guilty at the Guildhall of having unlawfully arrested Wheble, was fined one shilling for his pains and imprisoned for two months — and never received his £50 reward. The Commons, in spite of their display of authority, suffered a total loss: not only did the defiant printers go unpunished, but the newspapers went on or resumed printing debates, and the House, fearful of stirring up another hornet's nest, had to accept the accomplished fact.[1]

But the unanimity of the City was soon shown to have been only a temporary patching-up of differences in the face of common danger. 'Courtiers' and 'patriots' resumed hostilities, and the 'patriots' themselves divided into mutually antagonistic groups. Already in September 1770, the Bill of Rights Society was beginning to break up: the resignation of its Secretary, Robert Morris, a Wilkes supporter, was followed, some weeks later, by a public clash between Sawbridge and Wilkes at a meeting of Westminster electors.[2] 'Parson' Horne, for many years Wilkes's most devoted ally, took Sawbridge's part and, from November onwards, struck the first blows in a prolonged verbal duel from which Wilkes eventually emerged the victor.[3] Soon after, James Townsend, leader of what soon became known as the 'Shelburne' or 'Malagrida' faction in the City,[4] joined with Horne, and, in early February, we find Rockingham, while mainly concerned to promote his own political advantage from these new alignments, inclined to favour Wilkes rather than his opponents:

> In regard to the great quarrel now subsisting between Mr. Wilkes and Mr. Horne and Js. Townsend & c., I own my partiality is towards Mr. Wilkes . . . If in the end Wilkes gets the better, he will be a great power but perhaps not so dangerous as the others would be if they get the rule, and probably too *Wilkes single* in the end would be easier to manage than a whole pandaemonium.[5]

[1] Thomas, op. cit., p. 98.

[2] *Lond. Chron.*, 4–6 Sept., 1–3 Nov. 1770. See also Burke to Rockingham, 23 Sept.; and Rockingham to Burke, 26 Sept. 1770; *Burke Correspondence*, ii. 157, 163.

[3] Walpole, *Memoirs*, iv. 204, 216; Postgate, pp. 207–8; Bleackley, pp. 258–9.

[4] See Burke to Rockingham, 29 Dec. 1770, *Burke Correspondence*, ii. 175: 'The Corporation of London [whatever it may be] possessed more entirely than ever by the Shelburne faction.'

[5] Rockingham to Burke, 3 Feb. 1771, *Burke Correspondence*, ii, 192. He went on hopefully: 'I should think that it is probable the end will be that the contention between Wilkes and Horne &c. will weaken and destroy both those parties, and may afford a good opportunity for Trecothick and our other friends in the City to take the good men there may be in either party.'

In April, fresh from his triumphs in 'the printers' case', Wilkes was nominated sheriff for the following year by the Common Council members of his ward. He hoped to persuade Richard Oliver to run in harness with him, but from the Tower Oliver sent him a curt refusal and insulting reply that made it evident that he had decided to throw in his lot with his opponents. In the election that followed, however, Wilkes not only defeated the Court party but more than got his own back on the dissident 'patriots': he topped the poll with 2,315 votes, while Oliver, though fresh from 'martyrdom', scored a mere 245. The same night the effigy of Horne,

> in a canonical habit, with a pen in one hand and in the other a salt-box . . . was consumed in a bonfire, which the populace made for that purpose before the Mansion House.[1]

Burke was delighted at the outcome:

> What say you [he wrote to O'Hara] to Wilkes's triumph over the Court and his own revolted officers in conjunction? . . . The treacherous patriots of the Malagrida faction . . . thought that they had some popularity of their own; and having fought successfully for Wilkes, they flatter'd themselves that they could defeat the general under whose auspices they had conquer'd heretofore.[2]

Yet, in the next round, the dissensions among the 'patriots' assured the Court of an otherwise undeserved success: William Nash, Cannon Street grocer and alderman of Walbrook, was elected Lord Mayor for 1772 in opposition to Sawbridge and Crosby, who stood for a second term of office. A confused situation had arisen from which each group and faction sought to derive some political advantage. The Court unequivocally supported Nash. Wilkes promoted Crosby and, in order to secure his re-election, entered into complicated manœuvres to have him returned to the Court of Aldermen for final selection with a former mayor, William Bridgen.[3] The elusive Junius even took a hand and tried to persuade Wilkes to abandon Crosby and throw his

[1] *Gent's Mag.*, 1771, pp. 189, 230. The other votes polled were as follows: Frederick Bull (Wilkite), 2,194; Ald. John Kirkman (occasional 'Courtier'), 1,949; Ald. Samuel Plumbe (Court), 1,875.

[2] Burke to Chas. O'Hara, *post* 14 July 1771, *Burke Correspondence*, ii. 221–2.

[3] Alderman of Farringdon Within and Lord Mayor in 1764, Bridgen had voted for Wilkes in the City in 1768 and for Glynn against Proctor in Middlesex, and was later to vote for Wilkes as Lord Mayor in 1772 and for Glynn as City Recorder the same year. But he rarely attended meetings of ward or Council, was not popular, and was only intended by Wilkes as a foil to draw votes from Sawbridge, Townsend and the Court candidates.

influence behind Sawbridge.[1] Townsend, for fear of letting in Wilkes's ally Crosby, refused to withdraw his own nomination in favour of Sawbridge, while the followers of Rockingham deserted all the 'popular' candidates and voted for Nash.[2] Something of this confusion and intrigue is reflected in the following letter addressed on the eve of the election to Earl Temple by one of his City correspondents:

> Mr. Ald. Bridgen's refusal brought on great confusion, as your Lordship will observe, and, I firmly believe, will lose the present Lord Mayor his re-election. The Shelburne party will be totally ruined in less than forty-five hours.
>
> The friends of the Lord Mayor, who support Sawbridge, sent to Mr. Townsend to desire he would decline the poll, as he had no chance of succeeding, and, by that means he would secure the return of Mr. Sawbridge and the present Mayor. He listened awhile the overture of strengthening Mr. Sawbridge's interest, but wanted terms for himself to succeed another year; *that* was absolutely denied him; upon which he took time to consider of it till six this evening, when he returned a very insolent answer in the negative. The application and answer I have drawn up and sent, by the desire of the Committee, to the papers. It will most effectually do his business with the Livery, and what was only suspicion before, of his dividing the popular interest to serve the Court, will now be conviction to the citizens at large.
>
> Nash is most likely to be Mayor, which we do not secretly dislike, as he is more likely to be with us than any of the Shelburnes can be.[3]

Nash and Sawbridge were returned at the head of the poll, with Crosby in close attendance but Townsend nowhere in the running;[4] and the Court of Aldermen, exercising its right to choose from the two leading candidates, as expected, chose Nash — much to the delight of George III, who had written to North a week before the final selection:

[1] For the correspondence of Junius and Wilkes on this point, see Sharpe, op. cit., iii. 124–7.

[2] See Barlow Trecothick to Burke, 8 Oct. 1771, *Burke Correspondence*, ii. 245: 'My vote in the Court has been in favour of Mr. Nash — differing as I do from his political principles, I still consider him as having done nothing worthy of degradation from his turn.'

[3] E. Dayrell to Temple, 27 Sept. 1771, *Grenville Papers*, iv. 535–7. He added: 'If that should be the case, a certain person whom your Lordship knows [presumably Wilkes. G. R.] has a trap for *him* which he begs to communicate to your Lordship with many other important things now in plan, particularly an attack upon the privilege of commitment the House of Lords has lately exercised upon the printers, and Mr. Bull has agreed to act with him in everything.'

[4] The votes were: Nash, 2,199; Sawbridge, 1,879; Crosby, 1,795; Hallifax, 846; Townsend, 151; Bankes, 36 (*Ann. Reg.*, 1771, p. 147).

I sincerely rejoice at the prospect of Mr. Nash's success; if the same zeal is shown in the rest of the poll [it] will greatly tend to restore the tranquillity of this greatest Trading City in the world.[1]

The 'popular' party's supporters, however, were outraged and, on his return from the hustings on 2 October, Nash was 'grossly ill-treated . . . by the populace; and had not Mr. Wilkes taken him away in his chariot, the consequences might have been fatal'.[2]

A year later, Wilkes made his first bid for the mayoralty, and while Trecothick once more (to Burke's annoyance) cast his vote for the Court candidates,[3] the Court party among the aldermen, when faced with the choice, preferred Townsend to Wilkes and secured his election. Wilkes had decided to team up with Townsend in order to form a common front against Aldermen Hallifax, Bankes and Shakespear, the Court candidates. Bankes made little impression, but Hallifax and Shakespear got off to a good start and the King, kept posted by North, followed the results of each day's polling excitedly. 'I trust by your account of this day's poll,' he wrote on 3 October, 'that there can be no doubt that it will end favourably; the mob being less quiet this day is a proof that to (*sic*) *riot*, not numbers, the *patriots* alone can draw advantage.' Two days later, when the 'Courtiers' appeared to be losing ground, he commented:

The unpromising appearance of this day's poll does not in the least surprise me, knowing that Wilkes is not bound by any ties, therefore would poll non-freemen rather than lose the election.

The King's hopes were somewhat damped by North's enclosure of the final state of the poll on 6 October; but North added the comforting observation:

There is the greatest reason to believe that many of his [Wilkes's] votes are illegal. The strange ragged figures whom he brought up today were such as were never seen at any poll before, except at his own when he stood for sheriff.[4]

Accordingly, a scrutiny was demanded; it dragged on for over a

[1] The King to North, 30 Sept. 1771, Fortescue, ii. 284–5.

[2] *Ann. Reg.*, 1771, p. 146.

[3] Burke to Rockingham, 29 Oct. 1772, *Burke Correspondence*, ii. 356: 'I am vexed that Trecothick voted for these shabby fellows. His known and well grounded aversion to Wilkes and Townsend might prevent his voting for either of them; but there was no necessity of voting for the Courtiers.'

[4] The King to North, 3 Oct.; King to North, 5 Oct.; North to King, 8 Oct. 1772; Fortescue, ii. 1137, 1141, 1143.

fortnight, was eventually boycotted by the very candidates in whose interest it had been called for, and it did not alter the previous result by a single vote.[1] The Court of Aldermen, now called upon to choose between Wilkes and Townsend, departed from traditional practice by 'scratching' for the one of the two candidates who had the lower poll, and returned Townsend as Lord Mayor.[2]

Wilkes's supporters were enraged and (it was reported) 'the scene of confusion that ensued [was] inconceivable';[3] but it was as nothing compared with the popular outburst that broke out on Lord Mayor's Day (9 November). That evening, when the new Lord Mayor returned to the Guildhall after his inaugural procession, a crowd of 3,000, 'headed by some sailors', filled the yard. The constables were forced to beat a hasty retreat, while the crowd proceeded to attack the iron gates at the entrance to the Hall 'and pulled down and burnt the different temporary erections for the day'. Ladies arriving for the Lord Mayor's party were asked for money 'to drink Mr. Wilkes's health' and there were angry shouts of 'It is Wilkes's turn' and 'Da—n my Lord Mayor for a scoundrel, he has got Wilkes's right, and we will have him out.' Distinguished guests were molested by the rioters: 'One gentleman I saw,' stated a witness, 'had a part of his head of hair cut off.' Bonfires were lit and the riots continued until two in the morning. The Hon. Artillery Company, whom the crowd (after first mistaking them for the Guards) treated with scant respect, took seven prisoners; of these, three appeared for trial at the Old Bailey, where two were acquitted and a third sentenced to five weeks in prison.[4]

Two years passed before Wilkes realized his ambition. In 1773, he ran in harness with Frederick Bull, a loyal supporter, recently elected alderman of Queenhithe and shortly to succeed Sir Robert

[1] The voting was: Wilkes, 2,301; Townsend, 2,278; Hallifax, 2,126; Shakespear, 1,912; Bankes, 3 (*Gent's Mag.*, 1772, p. 490).

[2] Treloar, op. cit., pp. 126–8. Bleackley, like Treloar, accepts H. Walpole's account according to which Oliver brought about Wilkes's defeat by deliberately convening a Court of Aldermen before the Wilkite aldermen could be mustered (pp. 275–6). Sharpe, on the strength of City records, considers it 'scarcely probable' (op. cit., p. 134).

[3] *Gent's Mag.*, 1772, p. 493.

[4] O.B. *Proceedings*, 1773, pp. 46–59, 68, 114–15; Corp. London R.O., Sessions Minute Bks., vol. xxi (Oct. 1772–Oct. 1773); *Gent's Mag.*, 1772, pp. 595–6; *London Evening Post*, 7–10 Nov. 1772. According to the latter account, there were 'several wounded' and sixteen arrested persons were lodged in two compters, there being an epidemic of jail fever in Newgate.

Ladbroke as M.P. for London.[1] The Shelburne faction put up Sawbridge and Oliver, and when Wilkes and Bull headed the poll (Wilkes leading Bull by 35 votes), 'Courtiers' and Wilkites were evenly matched in the Court of Aldermen, and it needed Townsend's casting vote to secure Bull's election.[2] But, this time, there were no recriminations:[3] Bull was a useful ally, Townsend's authority was in decline, and Wilkes's own stock – even in the Court of Aldermen[4] – was rising with every contest. Finally, in October 1774, Wilkes was, for the third time in succession, returned by the livery at the head of the mayoral poll. Sawbridge had been conciliated and withdrew his nomination; the Court candidates, Esdaile and Kennet, disappointed North's hopes and were hardly in the running;[5] and Wilkes's partner was once more Frederick Bull, the retiring mayor. Consequently, the Court of Aldermen had neither the pretext nor the inclination to repeat its discrimination of the two preceding years, and Wilkes was returned Lord Mayor with only two aldermen – the implacable Townsend and Oliver – voting against.[6] The news was received

[1] On the occasion of Ladbroke's death in October, North wrote to George III that it would be difficult to prevent Bull's election in his place; for he feared 'that every attempt to overturn Wilkes in Guildhall will, at present, be fruitless, as the liverymen who are not his friends, though they are a majority, have not zeal enough to hustle through a tumultuous election in order to disappoint him' (Fortescue, iii. no. 1308). At that stage, too, the King thought it 'best not to interfere' (ibid., no. 1319).

[2] Treloar, op. cit., p. 128. The voting was: Wilkes, 1,683; Bull, 1,649; Sawbridge, 1,177; Oliver, 1,093. The Court party did not contest. The aldermanic vote went as follows: for Wilkes – Bull, Crosby, Watkin Lewes, Plomer, Sawbridge, Stephenson, Thomas, *Hopkins*, *Turner*; for Bull – *Alsop*, *Bankes*, *Esdaile*, *Kennet*, *Plumbe*, Oliver, Townsend, Trecothick, Wilkes and Lord Mayor's casting vote ['Courtiers' in italics] (*Gent's Mag.*, 1773, pp. 517, 519).

[3] There was, however, another demonstration against Townsend on Lord Mayor's Day: stones were thrown and the glass of his coach broken (for the case of John Smith, found guilty of the offence, see Lond. Corp. R.O., Sessions Minute Bks, vol. XXII (Dec. 1773–Dec. 1774)).

[4] The new aldermen of 1773–74 tended to be sympathetic to Wilkes rather than to the Court, and Townsend received no reinforcements. By October 1774, there were only nine seasoned 'Courtiers' left on the Court of Aldermen: Alsop, Esdaile, Hallifax, Hopkins (a newcomer), Harley, Kennet, Plumbe, Shakespear and Turner. These were exactly balanced by the Wilkites, both old and new: Bull, Crosby, Bridgen, Hayley (Wilkes's brother-in-law), Plomer, Stephenson, Nathaniel Thomas, Watkin Lewes and Wilkes himself. See also Appendix X.

[5] See North to the King, 30 Sept., 1, 4 Oct. 1774; Fortescue, iii. nos. 1519–21, 1524.

[6] Sharpe, op. cit. iii. 144. According to Bleackley, there was a third aldermanic opponent, but he gives no name or evidence (p. 283). The voting was: Wilkes, 1,957; Bull, 1,923; Esdaile, 1,474; Kennet, 1,410 (*Gent's Mag.*, 1774, p. 491).

in the City with tumultuous acclaim. 'On this occasion,' wrote the *Gentleman's Magazine*,

> the joy of the populace was so great that they took the horses from the coach, and, in the struggle for the honour of drawing it to the Mansion House, one man lost his life and another was much hurt.

The unpopular Alderman Harley once more had his windows broken; and, two days later, the Lord Mayor elect had the duty — and, no doubt, the grim satisfaction — of committing the culprit for trial at the Old Bailey.[1]

It was the last of the Wilkes riots, and the crowning of his City ambitions marked the beginning of the end of 'Wilkes and Liberty'.

[1] Ibid.

X

WILKES AND HIS SUPPORTERS

IN the case of so colourful and arresting a phenomenon as John Wilkes it is easy to be misled both as to the measure of his historical importance and to the scope of the social and political movements that sprang up in his wake. His exploits, successes and misfortunes were so widely and continuously recounted in the press and the writings of memorialists, and 'Wilkes and Liberty' aroused such passions and left so many memories, that the historian (and still more the biographer) may be tempted to present a false and exaggerated picture. Before attempting in a final chapter to present Wilkes in his historical perspective, it is, therefore, here proposed to define the geographical and social boundaries of 'Wilkism' and of the 'Wilkes and Liberty' movement which, for all its astonishing vigour and resilience, did not long outlast Wilkes's election as Lord Mayor of London.

Wilkes's early support and following clearly sprang from London and the Home Counties. We have seen how, after his release from the Tower and his first triumph over Administration in the affair of *The North Briton* and general warrants, he was hailed with enthusiasm in the streets of the capital and the cry of 'Wilkes and Liberty' echoed from Aylesbury to Canterbury and Dover.[1] But while his encounters with authority had already been sympathetically broadcast by the opposition and radical press all over the country, it is doubtful if anything like a Wilkite movement may be said to have, at this time, spread beyond these limits, and William Mackenzie, Privy Seal of Scotland, had probably ample justification for writing, in July 1763, to Charles Jenkinson at the Treasury of

> that cursed spirit of faction which prevails so much at present in the southern part of the Kingdom. I say the southern part, because I would fain hope that it is confin'd to London, its environs and the Cider Counties. As to this part of the U.K., I am happy to find the greatest unanimity among all descriptions of men here; all express the strongest

[1] See pp. 30–31 above.

sense of duty and affection to the King's person . . . they feel with indignation the insults offer'd to their sovereign.[1]

It is perhaps hardly likely that the author of *The North Briton* would arouse much enthusiasm among any 'descriptions of men' north of the Border; but the north country as a whole remained largely untouched by the agitation associated with Wilkes or with the City radicals. Even after Wilkes had returned from exile and won his first election in Middlesex, Alexander Wedderburn could write with some justice — though with exaggerated venom — to George Grenville that, whereas the north of England was

a country of plenty, frugality and sobriety . . . where the name of *Wilkes* is never profanely joined with Liberty, nor mentioned but with detestation;

the south was

a great Bedlam under the dominion of a beggarly, idle and intoxicated mob without keepers, actuated solely by the word *Wilkes*, which they use as better savages do a walrus to incite them in their attempts to insult Government and trample upon law.[2]

But the north was soon — if not already — beginning to be invaded by the same 'cursed spirit'; and though Wilkes might (exceptionally) be burned in effigy by Edinburgh apprentices,[3] the Newcastle sailors, according to a press report of the same month, had begun to espouse his cause:

At Newcastle, the cry for Wilkes and Liberty is said to be as loud among the sailors as at London, and attended with the same violence. The women interest themselves in his favour, and are as zealous as the men, but not so *outrageous*.[4]

Sympathy for Wilkes in the north country appears to have spread during his confinement in the King's Bench prison; and we read of two casks of hams and tongues being sent to him by the inhabitants

[1] W. Mackenzie to Chas. Jenkinson, 16 July 1763, Add. MSS. 38201, ff. 27–8 (my italics).

[2] Alex. Wedderburn to G. Grenville, 3 April 1768, *Grenville Papers*, iv. 264–5.

[3] See letter from Edinburgh of 25 April in *Annual Register*, 1768, p. 99: 'A number of apprentice boys, amounting to several hundreds, assembled here, and carried on their shoulders a figure which they called Mr. Wilkes. After parading the street and shouting *Wilkes and Liberty*, they carried him to the Grass-Market, where they chained the mock hero on the stone where the common gallows is usually fixed at execution. After making a fire they committed the effigy to the flames, and scattered the ashes in the air, & then quickly dispersed to their respective homes.'

[4] *Gent's Mag.*, 1768, p. 241. The London sailors' demonstrations, however, were not pro-Wilkite (see pp. 103–4 above).

of Stockton in the county of Durham — delivered, it was reported, by the same person who lately brought him 'a present of the same kind' from the magistrates of Richmond in Yorkshire.[1] Liverpool may have been influenced by the Wilkite or radical agitation of the south when the Trading Companies of the town ensured the return, in the General Election of 1768, of the 'popular' candidates, Sir William Meredith and Richard Pennant; yet this is admittedly conjectural.[2] But a Liverpool paper certainly put before its readers the aims of the Supporters of the Bill of Rights in June 1769,[3] and a Liverpool potter presumably thought it profitable a year later to manufacture a tea-pot adorned with the portrait of 'John Wilkes Esq., the Patriot'.[4] Newcastle, alone of northern towns and cities, 'instructed' its M.P.s to protest against Wilkes's exclusion by Luttrell in April 1769.[5] While Newcastle and Liverpool joined other northern boroughs and counties in petitioning the King in the following autumn, we have no evidence that it was the result of any specifically Wilkite influence: in the counties, at least, it is certain that the paramount influence was that of the Rockinghams and Cavendishes rather than of the Supporters of the Bill of Rights. In brief, it would appear that the Wilkite movement in the north was largely confined to such commercial centres as Newcastle and Liverpool.

In the west country and eastern counties 'Wilkes and Liberty' appear to have aroused a more lasting response. Admittedly, Essex failed to present a petition, but several hundred signatures were collected and the movement was solidly in the hands of Sir Joseph Mawbey and other Supporters of the Bill of Rights,[6] and both Essex and Norwich were on the point of 'instructing' — if they did not actually 'instruct' — their M.P.s in the spring of 1769.[7] Furthermore, among boroughs celebrating Wilkes's release from prison in April 1770, Horace Walpole makes specific mention of Lynn, Norwich and Swaffham,[8] and King's Lynn

[1] *Mid. J.*, 20–22 April 1769.
[2] See p. 127 above.
[3] *Williamson's Liverpool Advertiser*, 2 June 1769.
[4] E. S. Price, *John Sadler, a Liverpool Pottery Printer* (West Kirby, 1948), Plate XI. I am indebted to Mr. R. B. Rose, of the University of Sydney, for sending me these items concerning Wilkes and Liverpool.
[5] *Mid. J.*, 2–4 May 1769. See p. 105, n. 1, above.
[6] See p. 131 above.
[7] L. S. Sutherland, *The City of London and the Opposition to Government, 1768–1774*, p. 24 n. 1.
[8] *Memoirs*, iv. 79; cit. Sherrard, *A Life of John Wilkes*, p. 230.

actually conferred its Freedom on Wilkes in October 'for his constitutional, spirited and uniform conduct in support of the Liberties of this country'.[1] But the response went deeper in the west country and 'Cider Counties' — partly, no doubt, because of the personal influence of Londoners such as Beckford and Glynn, but also because the Wilkite movement of the metropolis appeared to give new and pointed expression to their own accumulated grievances. We have seen that a Somerset township welcomed Wilkes's election victory over Luttrell with processions and illuminations; that Exeter rang with the cry of 'Wilkes and Liberty' on the occasion of a memorable visit by the Duke of Bedford; that several of the western counties' petitions reflected the views of Wilkes and the Supporters of the Bill of Rights rather than those of the Chathamites and Rockingham Whigs; and that Bristol both 'instructed' its M.P.s in March 1769 and celebrated Wilkes's release from prison with illuminations and public banquets.[2] In Bristol, in particular, Wilkes had a substantial following, centred in the Independent Society formed by Henry Cruger and his father-in-law, Samuel Peach, banker and director of the East India Company.[3] John Wilkes's various trips to Bath were prominently featured in the Bristol press,[4] and on a ceremonial visit that he paid to Bristol with Frederick Bull and Watkin Lewes in the New Year of 1772, he was rapturously received by some of its leading citizens and a large banquet was held in his honour.[5] In Hereford, too, his support was by no means limited to the petitioning of 1769. In October 1773, when the news arrived from London that Wilkes, with Bull, was leading in the contest for the mayoralty, the *Hereford Journal* commented:

> Nothing can be more favourable to the cause of Liberty than the certainty of having a patriotic Lord Mayor for the year ensuing, as it not only shows the strength of popularity by so large a majority of uninfluenced liverymen, but it gives the friends of freedom a promising appearance . . . of their having the next City Members of Parliament of the same independent stamp as the Lord Mayor.[6]

[1] *Gent's Mag.*, 1770, p. 482.

[2] See pp. 112–26, 149 above.

[3] P. T. Underdown, 'Henry Cruger and Edmund Burke: Colleagues and Rivals at the Bristol Election of 1774', *The William and Mary Quarterly*, xv (1958), 14–34; *London Directory*, 1774.

[4] *Brist. J.*, 9 April 1768, 28 Dec. 1771. (In the former report, the names of 'John Wilkes Esq. and Miss Wilkes' head the list of visitors, taking precedence over those of the Earl and Countess of Blessington and Lord and Lady Napier.)

[5] Ibid., 4, 11, 18 Jan. 1772.

[6] *Hereford Journal*, 14 Oct. 1773.

And when Thomas Harley, leader of London's Court party, stood for election to Parliament in Hereford in 1774, a correspondent of the same paper considered that no self-respecting 'patriot' of the borough could vote for him in view of his sustained record of hostility to Wilkes:

You have been long accustomed to hear of Alderman Harley and Mr. Wilkes. Mr. Harley, who now so strongly solicits your votes, is that same alderman. If you approve of Mr. Wilkes for standing for the support of your rights, you must of course dislike Alderman Harley, for he has been the Minister's champion to oppose Mr. Wilkes, and so support every measure of the Ministry.[1]

But, with all this, as the preceding chapters have amply demonstrated, it was London and Westminster and the adjoining counties of Middlesex and Surrey that were both the starting-point and the permanent core of the Wilkite movement, which (it has been claimed) was 'essentially . . . a product of the metropolis'.[2] And it was because of his remarkably loyal and lasting following in the metropolis that Wilkes's earliest biographer could assert, with reasonable accuracy as early as 1769:

History can furnish no one instance of any private man being so long and so extensively the subject of public attention and discourse as Mr. Wilkes has been for now seven years.[3]

So much for the geographical distribution of Wilkes's support.[4] The distribution of his opponents and supporters along social lines may be harder to define, but in some respects, at least, we are on more certain ground. His active opponents, though fewer in number, were as dedicated in their hatred as his followers in their devotion. George III, for one, gave 'that devil Wilkes' no quarter and, having vigorously intervened in order to secure his conviction, outlawry, imprisonment, expulsion, exclusion and declaration of 'incapacity', intervened with equal vigour to prevent his election as Lord Mayor of London and his re-election, for the fourth time, as M.P. for Middlesex in September 1774.[5] It was a forlorn and ill-starred venture, in which the King was loyally supported—

[1] *Hereford Journal*, 6 Oct. 1774.
[2] Sutherland, op. cit., pp. 15–16.
[3] *The Life and Political Writings of John Wilkes Esq.* (J. Sketchley & Co., Birmingham, 1769).
[4] Further local research and study of the provincial press may, of course, considerably modify this picture.
[5] See pp. 66–70, 167–8 above, and Fortescue, iii. nos. 513–28.

though with varying degrees of zeal — by a succession of Chief Ministers from George Grenville to Lord North. With few exceptions, the Lords and others of 'the sober, large-acred part of the nation' were equally persistent in their detestation of Wilkes and their support of the numerous measures undertaken by the government to restrain him. This was not true, of course, of the patriarchal brotherhood of peers who, at one stage or another of Wilkes's career, led the opposition groups in Parliament. Their attitude towards Wilkes ranged between genuine or grudging affection, fascinated horror and a sort of malevolent neutrality. Temple alone was a loyal friend — at least until the scandal aroused over the *Essay on Woman* — and his 'warmth' and 'forwardness' in espousing Wilkes's cause that year not only lost him the Lord Lieutenancy of Buckinghamshire but earned him the disapproval of the Duke of Newcastle and the Earl of Hardwicke.[1] But Temple never entirely deserted Wilkes and we find him corresponding with him affectionately after his return from exile, offering to visit him in the King's Bench prison, and he appears to have been associated with him in City politics, if only through a third party, as late as the autumn of 1771.[2] Chatham, on the other hand, broke off all personal associations with Wilkes after the publication of No. 45 of *The North Briton*, became one of his most virulent detractors over the affair of the *Essay on Woman*, and refused to intercede on his behalf during his own administration and the latter part of Wilkes's exile. Yet he stoutly defended his right to parliamentary privilege, vigorously opposed and countered the legal arguments used by Administration to justify his exclusion and 'incapacity', and, being as willing as any, when the occasion appeared suitable, to 'play the popular engines', joined with Temple and Rockingham in promoting the petitions of 1769.

The Duke of Grafton, though less given to personal rancour, was far more guarded in his personal associations with Wilkes. After visiting him in the Tower, he rejected a request to stand bail for him. Later, as a Minister and supporter of Administration, he played a rather half-hearted role in the further prosecution and expulsion of Wilkes; but he had doubts about the justice of the decision to recognize Luttrell as Member for Middlesex, though he

[1] See Hardwicke to Newcastle, 30 April 1763; Newcastle to Devonshire, 2 May 1763; Add. MSS. 32948, ff. 189, 204.

[2] See Temple to Wilkes, 28 April 1768, *Grenville Papers*, iv. 280; and p. 167 and n. 3 above.

condoned it on the grounds of political expediency and added lamely: 'How this decision could have been avoided, or better substituted, I cannot well pronounce.'[1] Richmond, like Newcastle, was prepared to recognize Wilkes as a 'Friend (or would-be friend) to Liberty' and a victim of Ministerial persecution,[2] yet he took no initiative in promoting his cause or that of the electors of Middlesex.[3] The Marquess of Rockingham, who succeeded Newcastle as the leader of the main opposition group in Parliament, followed a policy in regard to Wilkes that, for being ambivalent, was none the less consistent. The Marquess refused all personal contacts with him, though he maintained a line of communication open through Burke;[4] he ignored his requests for a free pardon and an early return from exile, yet he contributed materially to his upkeep — a subsidy that must have been continued at intervals since, as we find evidence of Wilkes receiving 'gratuities' from Rockingham, as from the Dukes of Portland and Devonshire, in both 1772 and 1773.[5] Rockingham, like his fellow-peers of the opposition, was willing enough to use 'Wilkes's affair' as a stick with which to beat the government, but he was as scared as they were of getting his fingers burned by appearing in any way to further the personal cause of the man rather than the wider political issues with which his name was associated. Burke, who had some regard and affection for Wilkes and understood him better, neatly summed up this distinction in a letter to Charles O'Hara:

> We had not the least desire of taking up that gentleman's cause as personally favourably to him; he is not ours. . . . Had they attempted to attack him . . . we must have defended him, and were resolved to do it; but still as the Cause and not the Person.[6]

Among the gentry, as among the clergy, Wilkes found only occasional and exceptional support. We have noted the zeal displayed for his cause in Middlesex and during his stay in the King's Bench prison by John Sawbridge and James Townsend, who later became two of his bitterest enemies in the politics of the City. There was also Robert Jones, owner of Fonmon Castle in Glamor-

[1] Grafton, *Autobiography*, pp. 195–6, 229.

[2] See p. 46 above.

[3] See pp. 130–31 above.

[4] See p. 37 above.

[5] J. Wilkes to Chase Price, M.P., 6 Nov. 1773; C. Price, M.P., to Rockingham, 16 Nov. 1773; *Rockingham Memoirs*, ii. 235–7.

[6] Burke to O'Hara, 9 June 1768, *Burke Correspondence*, i. 352–3.

gan and a devoted Supporter of the Bill of Rights; and we counted among voters of Wilkes and Glynn in Middlesex the Hon. John Scott of Ealing and Sir John Danvers of Hanover Square.[1] Among other early Supporters of the Bill of Rights were Sir Francis Blake Delaval, Bart., of Seaton Delaval, Northumberland, former Member for Andover; and Sir Robert Bernard, Bart., of Brampton, Huntingdonshire, who became M.P. for Westminster in 1770.[2] Yet these were notable exceptions; and among the sixty-five or more M.P.s who promoted, signed, or presented petitions in 1769–70, a mere handful could with any accuracy be termed Wilkites. We have seen the case of such men as Henry Crabb Boulton (Worcester), Sir George Colebrooke (Arundel) and Sir Thomas Frankland (Thirsk), who, while they signed petitions against the declaration of Wilkes's 'incapacity', had previously voted for Proctor or Cooke against Wilkes or Glynn.[3] The same sort of distinction must be made in the case of the great majority of petitioning justices, gentry and clergy, whose signatures in support of the rights of the Middlesex electors cannot be taken as support for the personal cause of John Wilkes.[4]

Far more solid was the body of support that Wilkes was able to command among merchants — particularly those of the 'middling' and lesser sort — in both London and other commercial cities. In July 1763, he had written to Temple that 'the merchants . . .are firm in the cause of liberty' and that it was in them that 'the strength of our cause really lies'.[5] There were always a number of wealthy merchants among his adherents: Richard Oliver and Samuel Vaughan in London; Sir Joseph Mawbey in Southwark; Samuel Peach, banker and East India merchant in Bristol; Sir Ben Trueman, brewer of Brick Lane, Spitalfields, who voted for Wilkes and Glynn in Middlesex; not to mention such City leaders as Sir William Stephenson, hop-merchant and distiller of Bridge Within; William Bridgen of Farringdon Within and Forty Hill, Enfield; and Sir William Baker, Governor of the Hudson's Bay

[1] See pp. 82, 116 above.
[2] Sutherland, op. cit., p. 20 n. See also pp. 116 and n. 3 above.
[3] See pp. 77 n. 4, 88 above.
[4] For clerical voters for Wilkes and Glynn, see p. 82; for clerical petitioners of 1769, see pp. 143–44; for Dr. Thomas Wilson, Prebendary of Westminster and Supporter of the Bill of Rights, see p. 116; and for prayers read on Wilkes's behalf in City and Westminster churches, see p. 40 above and *Read. Merc.*, 30 May 1768.
[5] Wilkes to Temple, 9 July 1763, *Grenville Papers*, ii. 71–72.

Company and alderman of Bassishaw.[1] And yet, as we have seen, the hard core of the Court of Aldermen and the City's 'monied interest' — large merchants, government contractors, bankers and directors of trading and insurance companies — were, on the whole, hostile to Wilkes and the 'patriot' groups. It was not from them but from the smaller and 'middling' merchants and tradesmen that he drew his main support. We saw that, in Liverpool, it was the 'lower freemen' that prodded Sir William Meredith's and Richard Pennant's friends among 'the higher rank of people' into drawing up a petition on the Middlesex election issue in October 1769.[2] In the Middlesex elections of 1768–69, we noted the solid weight of support for the Wilkite candidates that came from the commercial parishes lying to the east and north of the City — and from coal-merchants, brewers, warehousemen, shipbuilders and timber-merchants such as Thomas Allen and John Curteis of Wapping, James Minestone and David Trinder of Shadwell, and Allen Spenceley of Aldermanbury and Islington.[3] Again, in Westminster, among a score of Wilkes's most active associates of 1770 were three apothecaries, two carpenters, a prosperous poulterer, a stable-keeper, an engraver, a bookseller, an upholsterer, a coach-maker and a working jeweller.[4] On the Common Council of the City of London during the years 1768–74, he found his most stalwart supporters among men of the typical City crafts and trades — men like Joseph Partridge, packer, of 112 Fenchurch Street; John Webb, upholder, of Gracechurch Street; Henry George, haberdasher, of Bishopsgate; James Cotterell, chinaman, of Mansion House Street; Samuel Baughan, hatter, of Fish Street Hill; Stephen Camm, linen-draper, of Cheapside; William Bishop, saddler, of 27 Coleman Street; Joseph Stevenson, cooper, of Upper Thames Street; Stanley Crowder, bookseller, of Paternoster Row; Ingham Foster, ironmonger, of Lombard Street; Samuel Freeman, lead-merchant, of Mark Lane; James Stracey, cider-merchant, of Dowgate Hill; and Thomas Axford, broker, of Walbrook.[5] Yet the main bulwark of Wilkes's electoral strength and political authority in the City remained the Common Hall, composed of the 8,000 liveried freemen of the Companies; and it was from them, as we have seen, that he was able to draw a considerable vote even in his

[1] See pp. 61, 83, 175 above and Appendix x below.
[2] See p. 128 above.
[3] See p. 88 above.
[4] Sutherland, op. cit., p. 18.
[5] See Appendix IX.

first City contest, before he had had time to build up a position within the Courts of Aldermen and Common Council.[1]

And, outside the City, there were the freeholders of Middlesex, whose obstinate and continuous support in the face of every obstacle and discouragement sustained Wilkes in his political battles of this period and, eventually, in the General Election of 1774, assured him of a secure and uncontested seat in Parliament. Some of these freeholders belonged to social groups that have already been mentioned: a handful of gentry and considerable numbers of tradesmen and manufacturers. But the great bulk of Wilkite voters and supporters in Middlesex were formed, as we saw in an earlier chapter, by the lesser freeholders of both urban and rural districts, who owned or occupied freeholds of a value ranging from 40s. to £10 a year.[2] These, then, form a distinctive social category, and one as essential to the strength of the 'Wilkes and Liberty' movement in the metropolis as they were to the success (in point of numbers, at least) of the county petitions of 1769.[3]

Yet these by no means exhaust the number of social ingredients of which the Wilkite movement was compounded. Most active and vociferous of all Wilkes's supporters were those who demonstrated in St. George's Fields, at Hyde Park Corner, at the Mansion House, in Parliament Square and at St. James's Palace; who shouted, or chalked up, 'Wilkes and Liberty' in the streets of the City, Westminster and Southwark; who pelted Sheriff Harley and the common hangman at the Royal Exchange when they attempted to burn No. 45 of *The North Briton*; who smashed the windows of Lords Bute and Egmont and daubed the boots of the Austrian Ambassador; who paraded the Boot and Petticoat in the City streets, and burned Colonel Luttrell and Lords Sandwich and Barrington in effigy outside the Tower of London. These are the elements whom contemporaries and later historians have — either from indolence, prejudice or lack of more certain knowledge — called 'the mob', and, though the evidence on this point is slight,

[1] See p. 152 above. Dr. Sutherland believes that Wilkes's voting strength in the Common Hall 'depended largely on the liverymen of the numerous lesser companies, for which the fines were low' (op. cit., p. 17). But the available evidence — the Poll Book of 1768 (the only record of the livery's vote for this period) and the returns of fines paid for admission to the freedom and livery of the companies — do not bear out this contention (see Appendix VIII).

[2] See pp. 86–87 above.

[3] See pp. 146–8 above.

they are not likely to have been composed to any considerable degree of City merchants or of freeholders or manufacturers of the 'middling sort'. Yet there were exceptions: the judicial records tell us that, in the riots of March 1768, Robert Chandler, a City tea-broker, was believed to have 'headed a Mob in Westminster';[1] that, on the same occasion, one Matthew Christian, 'a gentleman of character and fortune', filled demonstrators with beer and drank with them to 'Wilkes and Liberty'; and that, in Southwark in the following May, Justice Capel was 'insulted' by Richard Gilbert, who stood in a group with 'several well-dressed persons'.[2] Again, eyewitnesses tell us that those who, on an historic occasion, noisily escorted the triumphant Wilkes from Westminster Hall to his house in Great George Street were 'of a higher rank than Common Mob';[3] that the 'people who gave Lord Mayor Crosby a rousing send-off from the Mansion House on 19 March 1771 were 'of the better sort'; and that crowds demonstrating in Parliament Square a week later appeared to be composed largely of 'respectable tradesmen'.[4] But, even if we take all these reports at their face value, they do not amount to very much. More typical, perhaps, were the Spitalfields weavers who (so Horace Walpole assures us) pelted Proctor and his supporters in Piccadilly in March 1768; or the coal-heavers of East London who, a few weeks later, were drawn, if only briefly, into the Wilkite movement.[5] In the following year, it was observed that,

> at the last two Middlesex elections, that part of the mob who behaved most riotously have been chiefly composed of gentlemen's servants, especially at Hyde Park Corner.[6]

Again, to Mrs. Harris (possibly not a reliable witness in such matters) the rioters who blocked the entrance to St. Stephen's Chapel to Members of Parliament on the day that Oliver was committed to the Tower appeared to be 'a most blackguard set of shabby fellows'—a term not dissimilar to that used by her husband, James Harris, M.P., in describing to the Earl of Hardwicke the 'dirty people' that crowded the Lobby in protest against Luttrell's adoption on 15 April 1769.[7] Yet all such descriptions

[1] S.P. Dom., Entry Bks., 44/142, p. 157.
[2] See pp. 44, 52–3 above.
[3] G. Onslow to Newcastle, 6 May 1763, Add. MSS. 32948, ff. 234–5.
[4] See pp. 160, 162 above.
[5] See pp. 42, 47 above.
[6] *Mid. J.*, 15–18 April 1769.
[7] See pp. 70, 161 above.

tend to be coloured by the prejudices of their authors. To obtain a more objective, though more limited, picture of these rioters we have to rely on the meagre sample afforded by those who were arrested, committed, brought to trial, released on bail, or against whom 'informations' were preferred in London, Westminster, Southwark and Middlesex, for being implicated in Wilkite riots and demonstrations. Of a total of sixty-four such persons, the occupation or social status[1] of forty-four appears in the records. These include two gentlemen, three merchants or dealers,[2] thirteen tradesmen (who may have been small masters, journeymen or independent craftsmen),[3] four vaguely classified as 'labourers', and twenty-two who were probably wage-earners.[4] The great majority were, in fact, labourers, servants, journeymen, small craftsmen, or petty traders, and we must assume that nearly all lived in lodgings, as not one of those whose addresses appear in the records — not even the two 'gentlemen' — are to be found in the Poor Rate books of Land Tax registers of their parishes. So, in spite of the occasional report of 'well-dressed persons' or 'tradesmen of the better sort' among the rioters, we must conclude, for lack of further evidence, that these formed but a small minority and that the most active elements in Wilkite street-demonstrations and riots, while by no means drawn exclusively from the wage-earners, were overwhelmingly composed of 'the lower orders of the people'.

Yet these, it must be insisted, formed but one of the social elements — however important in point of numbers — of which Wilkes's following was composed. It is misleading to contend, as one of his biographers has done, that, in London, 'Wilkes's supporters were notoriously overwhelmingly of the working class'.[5] It was, in fact, one of the most significant of Wilkes's achievements

[1] By 'social status' I mean such broad classifications as 'gentleman', 'yeoman' or 'labourer'. The latter is commonly used in indictments to include urban workers, small traders and craftsmen; in recognisances the precise occupation is more frequently given, and the term 'labourer' is generally reserved for wage-earners.

[2] These were: a tea-broker, a bottle merchant, and the wife of a dealer in clothes.

[3] They were: 3 shoe-makers, 2 weavers, a peruke-maker, a sail-maker, a carver, a sawyer, a cooper, a blacksmith, a pewterer, and a hosier.

[4] They were: 10 labourers (or 'poor'), 2 lightermen, a mariner, a soldier, a 'servant', a ship's steward, a porter, a warehouseman, a coachman, a waggoner, a paper-hanger, and a watch-finisher. For details relating to all 64 arrested persons, see Appendix XI.

[5] Postgate, op. cit., p. 177.

that he was able to tap the loyalties and political energies of such varying and distinctive social groups as City merchants, the 'middling' and lesser freeholders of Middlesex, and the small craftsmen, petty traders and wage-earners of the capital.

This phenomenon does require some explanation. What prompted so many people, drawn from so wide a range of social classes, to centre their political hopes, loyalties and aspirations over so long a period on a man whose reputation was consistently blackened by those in authority, who was no orator, who offered no social panacea, whose political ideas were without originality, who never attained public office outside the City of London, and whose career within Parliament had, up to 1774, been brief, undistinguished and uneventful? Wilkes's biographers have not failed to stress his charm, his wit, his ready pen and colourful personality, the consistency of his political principles and of the 'image' that he presented to his public, his brazen defiance of authority and considerable courage in the face of adversity, qualities that could not but win him a martyr's crown whether deserved or not. He knew, too, on occasion, how to address himself to, or to solicit the support of, those 'middling and inferior set of people who stand most in need of protection', and whom he declared to be his particular concern;[1] and he understood better than most that Liberty and freedom from subservience to foreigners — even those from north of the Border — were catch-words that, if manipulated with skill and persistence, could yield political dividends both among Londoners and among the county gentry and freeholders.[2] Such qualities must certainly have played their part in evoking a more than ephemeral response from the merchants, craftsmen, freeholders and propertyless classes of the capital, of whom many had already, on more than one occasion, in the name of 'Revolution principles', championed the cause of the City magistrates and of the Earl of Chatham — and, as Burke understood, their 'adoption' of Wilkes was, in a sense, but a logical sequel to the former popularity of Chatham.[3] But Wilkes's support in the metropolis was considerably more wide-

[1] See his speech at Westminster Hall on 6 May 1763, pp. 26–7 above.

[2] For Londoners' concern for 'liberty' and distaste for 'Popery and wooden shoes', see p. 13 above and my article, 'The London "Mob" of the Eighteenth Century', *The Historical Journal*, II, i (1959), 1–18.

[3] Burke to O'Hara, 11 April 1768: 'Since the fall of Chatham, there has been no hero of the Mob but Wilkes' (*Burke Correspondence*, i. 348).

spread than that of either Chatham or his lieutenants, or their predecessors, in the City of London: it extended, as we have seen, into Westminster, Southwark and the rural and 'out-parishes' of Middlesex; and here, for the first time, we have a London movement that is metropolitan in scope rather than limited, as hitherto, to the confines of the City, though occasionally 'spilling over' into Westminster and the urban parishes of Surrey and Middlesex.[1] This has, of course, a great deal more to do with the development of London at this time into a unified capital city, the growth and spread of its population, and the stirring of the social aspirations of its citizens than it has with the personal attributes or qualities of John Wilkes.

There were other factors besides, which, while lying outside Wilkes's own control, must have contributed not a little to the impact that he was able to make on the society of his day. The accession of George III, the dismissal of the old Whig 'undertakers', the resignation of Pitt, the promotion of Lord Bute and his friends, and peace preliminaries with France and Spain had caused a ferment not only among Whig peers but among a substantial part of the country gentry and the citizens of London, Bristol and Liverpool.[2] Temple, who had resigned office with Pitt, wrote to Wilkes in September 1762,

> that there never was at any period of time so ardent a zeal in the whole body of the country gentlemen, a very few placemen excepted, as at present against the Ministry.[3]

Even allowing for the wishful-thinking natural in a disgruntled ex-Minister, the discontent was genuine enough; and it was further exacerbated, and spread among the larger body of freeholders, by such measures as the application of the Cider Acts to the west country and the attempts by the Ministry in the General Election of 1768 to impose Sir James Lowther, Bute's son-in-law, on the electors of Cumberland in spite of the higher vote won by Henry Curwen contesting in the Duke of Portland's interest.[4] The unrest among freeholders and gentry was matched by that in the great trading cities, where the government's failure to retain

[1] Sutherland, op. cit., pp. 18–19.

[2] For a brief summary, see p. 20 above.

[3] Temple to Wilkes, 14 Sept. 1762, *Grenville Papers*, i. 470.

[4] For a protracted correspondence on this issue in April-May 1768, see Add. MSS. 32989 (Newcastle Papers), ff. 371–96.

intact the conquests in the Carribean and the imposition of new restrictions on the American trade excited alarm and protracted resentment[1] — often among men who combined a passionate concern for the Englishman's liberties with a vigorous prosecution of the slave-trade with America and the West Indies.[2] Nor was this all. It was widely believed — and it needed no invention by Burke and the Rockingham Whigs — that corruption was more rampant than ever it had been, and that the influence of the Crown was being used to staff the administration with new Favourites and 'King's Friends', who formed a secret Closet party, beyond the control of Parliament and guided behind the scenes by the sinister combination of the Earl of Bute (who had resigned office in 1763) and the Princess Dowager of Wales. Opponents of the new system talked darkly of a repetition of 'the end of King Charles II's reign' — and such talk was not confined to the circles of the Duke of Newcastle and others, who might be inclined to identify the eclipse of their own public authority with that of the national interest.[3] Merchants and tradesmen, too, might suffer the arrogance and resent the slights of courtiers like Lord Pomfret who, in the House of Lords, commented on the City's Remonstrance to the King in May 1770 in the following inelegant and contemptuous terms:

[1] See pp. 16, 20, 112 above.

[2] For Liverpool's petition demanding the retention of Guadaloupe, in the interests of the slave trade, see p. 20, n. 5, above. Cruger's father-in-law, Samuel Peach, the Bristol radical, was a slave-trader. Note also the following advertisement in the *Bristol Journal* of 30 Jan. 1768: 'To be sold. A healthy NEGRO SLAVE named Prince, 17 years of age, measuring Five Feet and Ten inches, and extremely well grown. Enquiries of Joshua Springes, in St. Stephen's Lane.'

[3] Such expressions were common currency and abound throughout this period both in the press, in Burke's *Thoughts on the present Discontents* (1770), in personal correspondence, pamphlet literature and speeches in Parliament. For a City spokesman, see Captain Allen's speech to the London livery in support of Wilkes's candidature for Lord Mayor in October 1772: 'The times, gentlemen, are so corrupt, the age is so abandoned, that instead of an House of Commons favourable to the rights of their countrymen, you have an Assembly filled with Pensioners and Placemen, and Peerage. Title, or Place is all the majority of the Members seek for . . . ' (*Gent's Mag.*, 1772, p. 91). For a Chathamite view, see Col. Barré's speech to the Commons on the motion to send Oliver to the Tower on 25 March 1771: 'The Treasury is directed by the junto of Carlton House. Carlton House sets all the Administration in motion; and the Administration issued their mandates to the machines that compose the majority' (*Mid. J.*, 26–28 March 1771). In the same debate, James Townsend called for an inquiry into 'what influence the Princess Dowager of Wales has on the Councils of this Kingdom' (Brickdale Diary, v. 20). The point here argued is not so much that these views were justified as that they were widely believed to be true and aroused widespread 'discontents'.

However swaggering and impudent the behaviour of the low Citizens in their own dunghill, when they came into the Royal Presence, their heads hung down like bulrushes and they blinked with their eyes like owls at the rays of the sun.[1]

Small wonder, then, that among such citizens and gentry, alarmed at the whole trend of events since the accession of George III, there should be many to whom Wilkes, who had been persecuted more relentlessly than any other by the new administration and returned blow for blow and insolence for insolence, might appear as an object of sympathy, respect, or even of veneration.

While small freeholders, City craftsmen and wage-earners were touched by similar considerations, they had grievances of their own, besides, that may have inclined them to espouse the cause of Wilkes. Enclosing landlords and turnpike trusts had long since set their stamp on the countryside. In Herefordshire, memories were still fresh of the turnpike riots that had inflamed the west country thirty years before when, owing to strong local feelings of sympathy, rioters arrested at Hereford had been brought to Worcester for trial.[2] Enclosure had aroused resentment among the smaller freeholders and cottagers even in rural parishes adjoining London. In 1767, the villagers of Stanwell in Middlesex had marched to Westminster to protest against an Enclosure Bill;[3] while it did not appear overtly as an issue in the county elections that followed, who can tell how far it stimulated the lesser freeholders to seek the support of new men in Parliament?[4] The payment of tithe in kind was another grievance of the countryside. In December 1766, a west country farmer, in a letter to the *Gloucester Journal*, contrasts the happy condition of one village with the prevailing misery of its neighbour. In the one (he writes), 'all are happy, and no murmurs or discontents, much less mobs and riots are heard of amongst them even in these times. 'But [he continues] cross the rivulet and the scene is changing; poverty and distress stare you in the face at once . . . for tithe is there taken up in kind.'[5] The same year, owing to the shortage and high price of wheat and flour, there had

[1] Cit. Treloar, *Wilkes and the City*, p. 99. [2] S.P. Dom., 36/38, ff. 3, 17, 47.
[3] M. Robbins, *Middlesex*, p. 126.
[4] It is no doubt significant that two prominent signatories of a petition against the Stanwell Enclosure Bill of 1767 were Wilkite supporters in the Middlesex elections of 1768–69: John Bullock Esq. and George Richard Carter Esq., both substantial property-owners in the parish (J. L. & B. Hammond, *The Village Labourer* (2 vols. 1948): i. 153; Mid. R.O. Land Tax (1767) for Stanwell, no. 6681; Middlesex Poll Books, 1768–69, pp. 1–3). [5] *Glos. J.*, 1 Dec. 1766.

been unprecedentedly widespread riots all over the country: market towns had been invaded by hungry villagers, miners and weavers, who had compelled bakers to sell their bread at a reduced price.[1] At Gloucester alone, ninety-six men and women were brought to trial at the winter Assizes, and nine men were sentenced to death and seven to transportation.[2]

Whether such factors as these played any part in determining small freeholders to ventilate their grievances by signing the county petitions of 1769 it is impossible to say; yet they may be worthy of attention. Far more tangible is the evidence of a concordance between the movement of food-prices and of certain phases of the 'Wilkes and Liberty' movement in the metropolis. The years 1763–64 were years of low and stable prices, the quarter of wheat, quoted monthly at the London Corn Exchange, ranging between a 'mean' of 32s. and 32s. 6d. It rose sharply in the autumn of 1766, reached a peak of 50s. in July and October 1767, fell to 44s. 9d. in December, and rose by stages to a higher peak of 50s. 6d. in May 1768; the price of bread followed a similar, though less erratic course.[3] Not surprisingly, we find the discontent that this aroused reflected in the agitation of the period. In mid-April, for instance, the *Annual Register* reported that

> a ½-penny loaf, adorned with mourning crepe, was hung up at several parts of the Royal Exchange, with an inscription thereon, containing some reflections touching the high price of bread and other provisions;[4]

and — even more significantly — demonstrators at the House of Lords on 10 May accompanied their chanting of the slogan 'Wilkes and Liberty!' with shouts of: 'It was as well to be hanged as starved!'[5] And it is surely no coincidence that the numerous industrial disputes of that year, prompted by a similar concern at the rising cost of living, should have come to a head at the same time — and thus appearing to be related to the Wilkite political movement.[6] After that, there was a sharp drop in wheat-prices to 31s. 9d. in January 1769, followed by slight rises in July-August and December, yet, generally, the price of wheat and bread in London remained low throughout 1769 and continued to be so in the

[1] See R. W. Wearmouth, *Methodism and the Common People of the Eighteenth Century* (1945), chaps. I–III, who, from press-reports, records such incidents from no less than 24 towns in different parts of the country.

[2] *Glos. J.*, 8, 16, 22 Dec. 1766.

[3] For sources and fuller details, see my article, 'Wilkes and Liberty, 1768–69', *The Guildhall Miscellany*, no. 8, July 1957, p. 23.

[4] *Ann. Reg.*, 1768, p. 96. [5] See p. 53 above. [6] See chapter VI above.

early months of 1770. In fact, for some time after the early summer of 1768, rising food-prices cease to be a factor for consideration, and the next phases of the Wilkite movement — including the excitement over the Middlesex election of December 1768, the new outbreak of political rioting in London in March 1769, and the petition-campaign that followed — cannot be explained in such terms.

The years 1771–73 were once more years of steeply rising and fluctuating food-prices; they were marked by renewed demands for higher wages, and the movement of prices may have contributed (though not so evidently as in 1768) to the vigour of the Wilkite movement in the City of London. After rising to 46s. in July 1771, the price of the quarter of wheat fell sharply in the autumn and then rose again to new and higher peaks of 52s. in April 1772, of 56s. in November, and of 58s. in July-August 1773, before falling to 42s. 9d. (still a high price) in the autumn of that year. Already in March 1771, the Mayor and principal inhabitants of Norwich, 'being greatly alarmed at the increasing prices of corn and grain in general', petitioned Parliament to import wheat duty-free from the American colonies.[1] London does not appear to have felt these effects so sharply, for it was not until April 1772 that the *Gentleman's Magazine* reported that

> great numbers of inflammatory hand-bills were dispersed in Spitalfields & the parts adjacent, with a view to excite the populace to rise on account of the high price of provisions.[2]

The same months, angry crowds in Chelmsford and Sudbury besieged flour-mills and food-convoys; while, in London, Lord Mayor William Nash, returning from Church, 'was roughly used by the populace for not lowering the price of bread'; and the press reported that 'letters from almost every part of the Kingdom bring melancholy accounts of the distress of the poor and of their readiness to rise and to do mischief'.[3] At this time, too, the journeymen tailors were petitioning the London magistrates for an increase in wages 'on account of the dearness of provisions';[4] and, in October of the same year, while the City echoed with the 'tumults' attending Wilkes's first bid for the mayoralty of London, 'a great number' of sailors assembled at Tower Hill to demand a

[1] *Mid. J.*, 9–12 March 1771.

[2] *Gent's Mag.*, 1772, pp. 194–5.

[3] Ibid., 1772, p. 196.

[4] Ibid., 1772, p. 241. They won an increase of 6d. a day 'at ordinary times' and of 1s. a day 'in times of general mourning'.

restoration of wage-cuts imposed by their employers.[1] A few weeks later, shortly after the great riot in Guildhall Yard provoked by Townsend's election in preference to Wilkes, Sheriff Watkin Lewes presented a petition to the Commons on behalf of the City 'relative to the high price of provisions'.[2] Shortly after, ten journeymen curriers were tried (and acquitted) at the Old Bailey for conspiring to raise their wages.[3] A lull followed until March 1773, when the Commons rejected a request by the Lord Mayor and sheriffs of London to impose a bounty of 4s. a quarter on imported wheat; the same day, it was reported that the artificers and labourers in H.M. dockyards had petitioned Parliament for 'a trifling increase of wages'.[4] And, a month later, we find Wilkes, in the course of a perennial letter to the Speaker demanding his right to be seated in the Commons, taxing Parliament with 'indulging in supine ease and luxury amidst the cries of the starving poor'.[5]

While, then, rising food-prices can be seen as the immediate cause of the wages demands and industrial disputes of the period they can only serve as a partial explanation of certain phases of the 'Wilkes and Liberty' movement. Besides contributing substantially to 'a general dissatisfaction [that] unhappily prevailed among several of the lower orders of the people',[6] they no doubt had the effect of adding something to the volume and the vigour of the riots and disturbances of 1768 and 1771–73. Beyond that, we must look to a complex of political, social and economic factors, in which the underlying social changes of the age, the political crisis of 1761, the traditional devotion to 'Revolution principles', and Wilkes's own astuteness, experiences and personality all played their part.

[1] *Gent's Mag.*, 1772, p. 492.
[2] Ibid., 1772, p. 541.
[3] Ibid., 1772, p. 596; Lond. Corp. R.O., Sessions Minute Bks, vol xxi (Oct. 1772–Oct. 1773).
[4] *Gent's Mag.*, 1773, p. 148.
[5] Ibid., 1773, pp. 200–1.
[6] *Ann. Reg.*, 1768, p. 243.

EPILOGUE

THOUGH 'Wilkes and Liberty' began to lose its vigour after the autumn of 1774, John Wilkes himself lived on for another twenty-three years of political life. His mayoralty was a great success: it was as brilliant, as popular and as lavish as that of any of his immediate predecessors in the office, he entertained the Archbishop of Canterbury and five other prelates to dinner at the Mansion House, and the whole experience left him more heavily indebted and more financially dependent on his wealthy supporters than ever before.[1] By a happy chance (or so it seemed), the Chamberlainship of the City of London, a lucrative sinecure, fell vacant three months after his retirement from office; Wilkes contested but was narrowly defeated by an old enemy, Benjamin Hopkins, alderman of Broad Street Ward. But, after further defeats, Hopkins died in December 1779 and Wilkes, with little opposition, stepped into his shoes. The post carried emoluments of some £1,500 a year and duties that were anything but arduous: it enabled him to pay off his debts and engaged him in such eventful ceremonies as conferring the Freedom of the City on William Pitt and Lord Nelson.[2] Meanwhile, the year 1774 had also brought to an end his long exclusion from Parliament; and, in December, in spite of George III's persistent attempts to find suitable candidates to oppose him,[3] he took his seat for Middlesex, having been returned uncontested. But all fears and expectations that he might become the centre of a new party, or at least of an active group of radical opponents of Administration, proved ill-founded. For the first half-dozen years, he spoke regularly and persuasively in a number of great debates — on parliamentary reform, on the rights of the American colonists, on religious toleration — but he made little mark as a Parliamentarian; he rarely addressed the House after 1780, and when he retired from Parliament in 1790, he probably well deserved his own epithet of having become 'an extinct volcano'.

[1] Treloar, *Wilkes and the City*, pp. 140 ff.; Bleackley, pp. 288–92.
[2] Treloar, op. cit., pp. 193–205; Bleackley, pp. 371–3.
[3] Fortescue, iii. nos. 1513, 1518, 1528.

His re-entry into Parliament had been marked, too, by a gradual change of political allegiance and a cooling of his relations with the most loyal and vociferous of his old supporters of the days of 'Wilkes and Liberty' — the London craftsmen, journeymen and labourers. Having realized his civic and parliamentary ambitions, it seemed that he no longer sought or depended on the acclaim of the 'lower orders' of citizens. His appearance in public continued, for some years, to arouse the old enthusiastic response, but such occasions became rare, and, for all his championship 'within doors' of the American colonists and of an extension of the franchise, neither he nor any other of the old 'patriot' leaders of the City made any attempt to elicit the sympathies of 'the inferior set of people' for these causes. His links with them were finally broken in June 1780 when, at the height of the Gordon Riots, Wilkes shouldered a musket in defence of the Bank of England and shot down rioters — composed, in the main, of the same social elements who, a mere half-dozen years before, had shouted for 'Wilkes and Liberty'.[1] After 1783, he attached himself to the younger Pitt and gradually abandoned reform. A few years later, he greeted the outbreak of the French Revolution with suitable expressions of horror and a complete lack of comprehension of the issues at stake. He had become reconciled to his old enemies, George III and Samuel Johnson, and when he died in 1797, he had long lived in the odour and sanctity of the new Toryism.

The historian may, of course, be tempted, depending on his sympathies, either to explain away such vagaries or to attribute them wholly to the fickleness of character of a shallow demagogue and political adventurer, who had only become (to quote Wilkes's own phrase) 'a patriot by accident' or in pursuit of his own personal ambitions. But neither course would be particularly helpful or realistic. Wilkes's repeated professions of devotion to the cause of liberty may, or may not, have been entirely sincere; but such a rigid test of devotion to principle would have found nearly all of his eminent contemporaries sadly wanting — with the possible exception of the stolidly stubborn George III himself. Edmund Burke and William Pitt can certainly not lay claim to any such consistency of conduct; still less, of course, Charles James Fox, soon to succeed Wilkes as the King's most consistent object of

[1] See my article, 'The Gordon Riots: a Study of the Rioters and their Victims', *Trans. Royal Hist. Soc.*, 5th series, vi (1956), 93–114.

hatred; not to mention such lesser luminaries that have appeared in these pages as George Onslow or Alexander Wedderburn. What such facile charges of inconstancy leave out of reckoning are, of course, the changing historical circumstances in the course of which a man of principle (even one as highly principled as Edmund Burke) may undergo a subtle or sudden change of political attitude or affiliation. The England of the 1780s and 1790s was no longer the England of the 1760s and early 'seventies, the still Augustan England of Wilkes's heyday and whose political life he helped to mould. He was not the only one among the former 'patriots' for whom the social changes being slowly wrought by the Industrial Revolution remained a closed book and whom the challenge and impact of the French Revolution reduced to a state of impotent rage or confusion. And yet, in his own age, which lay at the threshold of these events, Wilkes's contribution was solid enough. It did not lie in the originality of his ideas, which were part and parcel of the traditional stock-in-trade of Whigs and other upholders of the Good Old Cause. He was certainly no revolutionary, either in purpose or in practice. His whole argument, presented in a series of brilliantly polemical speeches, letters and addresses, lay in the constantly repeated refrain that the Englishman's liberties were, in his person, being invaded and violated by a tyrannical executive and, equally in his person, required to be defended. It was an argument that harked back to the body of fundamental freedoms elaborated from myth and precedent by parliamentary lawyers, crowned in the 'glorious Constitution' that emerged from 1689, and nourished since by 'country party', Chathamites and City radicals. His success was partly due to chance and to the deep emotions already stirred by the 'palace revolution' of 1761; but it was also in large part due to his own courage, persistence, vigour and political sensibilities that he became the central figure in a number of constitutional disputes, the outcome of which was permanently to extend the Englishman's liberties and to enrich his political experience. The issue of general warrants by the Secretaries of State in the case of persons suspected of treasonable or seditious libel had become a common practice in the course of the century, yet it had gone virtually unchallenged until Wilkes, with the aid of Temple and the powerful legal backing of Pratt, questioned their validity in the affair of *The North Briton* – a challenge that led rapidly to the declaration of their invalidity in the case of *Entick* v. *Carrington*.[1] It did more: it created further constitutional precedents besides, because, from now on, Ministers could no longer so easily shelter behind the dignity and authority of the Sovereign in order to protect the King's Speech from censure and criticism in the public press. Again, the long-protracted dispute over Wilkes's right to sit in Parliament ended to Wilkes's complete satisfaction and to that of the electors of Middlesex, but, once more, it was far more than a merely personal victory or one limited to the electors of any one county. When, after suffering annual defeats in the years 1775 to 1781, Wilkes eventually carried his motion on 3 May 1782 that the resolution of 17 February 1769, declaring his 'incapacity', be expunged from the Journals of the House 'as being subversive of the Rights of the whole body of Electors of this Kingdom', it meant that henceforth Parliament no longer claimed, and was no longer able to claim, the right to declare the ineligibility of a Member eligible by law and lawfully elected to sit in the House of Commons.[2] Wilkes, too, played his part — and recent research strengthens the view that it was a predominant part — in helping to break down the wall of secrecy that separated the proceedings of Parliament from an increasingly literate and politically curious reading public. After 'the printers' case' of 1771, the printing of parliamentary debates by the newspapers became a regular and unchallenged practice, and it no longer needed the authority of Parliament's own officers to enable such proceedings to be freely circulated and discussed 'without doors', although the free admission of reporters and the daily publication of Hansard were still matters of the distant future.[3] Again, it was 'Wilkes's affair' that prompted the launching of another brand-new political enterprise in the form of the Society of Supporters of the Bill of Rights. While the first of its original aims was merely to raise money to pay off Wilkes's debts and current expenses, it rapidly engaged in activities that became models for later Radical politicians and political associations to follow. We have seen the part the Society played in drafting and promoting petitions in 1769; even more important

[1] See pp. 29–30 above.

[2] Treloar, op. cit., pp. 170–2; Erskine May, *Treatise on the Law, Privileges, Proceedings and Usage of Parliament* (1950), pp. 106–7; F. W. Maitland, *The Constitutional History of England* (1946), p. 372. Parliament, of course, still retained the right to suspend or to expel Members; but that is another matter.

[3] A. Aspinall, 'The Reporting and Publishing of the House of Commons' Debates', in *Essays presented to Sir Lewis Namier* (1956), pp. 227–57.

for the future was its novel device of 'instructing' M.P.s on their conduct in Parliament and, after that, of eliciting pledges from parliamentary candidates to support a listed number of popular causes at Westminster. Frederick Bull, when elected in London in November 1773, was the first Member to enter Parliament after giving such pledges to his electors,[1] and, in September 1774, prior to his taking his seat for Middlesex, we find Wilkes at the county freeholders' meeting pledging himself to support shorter Parliaments, more equal representation, the exclusion of placemen, and the repeal of the Quebec Act, said to be 'establishing Popery and French laws' in Canada.[2] Such election pledges were eagerly revived by parliamentary reformers and nineteenth-century Radicals, and were a feature of the election that preceded the passage through Parliament of the great Reform Bill of 1832.[3] It was a device, however, that was looked on with the greatest suspicion by Edmund Burke and prompted his famous Speech to the Electors of Bristol in November 1774, in which he argued against Henry Cruger the right of the Member to speak and vote in Parliament according to his personal judgment, untrammelled by 'the coercive authority' of the mandate or 'instructions' of his constituents.[4]

It was in pursuit of this same objective of opening wider the channels of communication between Parliament and the 'political nation' outside that Wilkes supported proposals, already voiced in the City of London, for annual or triennial Parliaments and a more equal representation – measures that, it was argued, would weaken the power of 'corruption' and bring the Member more frequently and closely under the control of his constituents. Here again he was no innovator: he merely followed in the path already trodden by William Beckford,[5] and, after Beckford's death, it was Sawbridge, another follower of Chatham, rather than Wilkes that kept the issue of shorter Parliaments alive at Westminster and in the City. Wilkes added his voice to theirs, but far more important for the future of reform than his parliamentary speeches was the stirring of the combative spirit of the county freeholders in defence of their rights, that flowed from the Middlesex election issue.

[1] *Gent's Mag.*, 1773, p. 579. [2] Ibid., 1774, p. 444.
[3] Norman Gash, *Politics in the Age of Peel* (1953), p. 29.
[4] Edmund Burke, *Speeches and Letters on American Affairs* (Everyman, 1945), pp. 68–75.
[5] L. S. Sutherland, *The City and the Opposition to Government, 1768–1774*, pp. 10–11.

Such a record alone[1] entitles Wilkes, whatever his personal follies and indiscretions, his political vagaries and eventual apostasy, to the proud but simple device that he had inscribed on his coffin — 'A Friend of Liberty'. But he has as great a title to fame, though one often ignored by historians, as one of the principal founders of a mass radical movement in Britain. It is true that the germs of radicalism, emanating from the City of London, can already be traced to the speeches and activities of William Beckford and others in the late 'fifties, several years before Wilkes's own appearance on the metropolitan scene, and that, in this as in other matters, he merely followed and ploughed more deeply where others had sown the seeds.[2] But Beckford's voice, though prompted by the great William Pitt himself, barely reached beyond the City or the confines of Westminster and St. James's — though it found echoes in other quarters in the General Election of 1768.[3] It was one of Wilkes's great achievements not only to win to his cause many freeholders and freemen who had been stirred by the earlier agitation, but to harness the political energies and support of many thousands more — extending beyond London and its adjoining counties — who had previously been considered outside the 'political nation' and had remained untouched by parliamentary or municipal elections. This was, of course, quite a different matter from the old time-honoured device of 'raising a Mob': to quote Burke in 1768, 'Many in the House find an use in Mobs';[4] and we have seen what use was made of this device by Sir William Beauchamp Proctor and the Court party at the Brentford election in December of that year.[5] Wilkes only once put himself at the head of a London crowd — on 26 April 1773, when he marched with them to Westminster to make his annual claim to his seat in Parliament;[6] on other occasions, he was conspicuously careful to avoid such contacts and to call on his followers to vote or demonstrate without disorders or violence.[7] Yet, in such cases, crowds were not rioting or demonstra-

[1] Part of this record, too, were his determined opposition to the operations of press-gangs and his insistence (with his fellow-sheriff Frederick Bull) that 'no man in England ought to be compelled to plead while in chains' (Treloar, op. cit., pp. 124–5).

[2] Sutherland, op. cit., pp. 7–9.

[3] S. Maccoby, *English Radicalism 1762–1782*, pp. 79–88.

[4] Draft of speech relating to the St. George's Fields 'massacre' of 10 May 1768, W.W.MSS., Bk 8b.

[5] See pp. 59–61 above.

[6] Sherrard, *A Life of John Wilkes*, pp. 258–9.

[7] See pp. 42–43, 48 above; and Walpole, *Memoirs*, iii. 194, 211; iv. 78, 103.

ting to promote a purely outside interest, but in a cause which they believed, however vaguely and incoherently, to be their own. For all its immaturity and lack of definition, the cry of 'Wilkes and Liberty' was a political slogan and stirred the political passions of not only freeholders and freemen but of the unenfranchised craftsmen and journeymen, who were its most vocal and enthusiastic promoters. This was something new in the nation's political life and raises the popular movement associated with Wilkes above the level of the mere food-riot or such blind outbursts as those provoked by the employment of Irish labour and the passage of the Gin Act of 1736 — still more above the activities of 'mobs' hired to promote the interests of contending political factions.[1]

It took time, of course, before such movements of 'the inferior set of people' became impregnated with a more solid body of political ideas and principles and before the notion of 'liberty', after being precariously attached to the cause of a single leader or hero, began to clothe itself in the more tangible garb of demands for annual Parliaments or an extension of the franchise — demands already voiced by tradesmen and freeholders but not as yet by the smaller craftsmen, journeymen and urban wage-earners. Nor was the path of progress steady and unchequered. After 'Wilkes and Liberty' came the wilder orgy of the Gordon Riots, when the political lessons of the 1760s and 1770s seemed to have been largely forgotten and middle-class radicals were discouraged from making further appeals to 'the inferior set' for a decade to come.[2] But with the French Revolution and the writings of the English democrats the movement gained more solid substance among the petty craftsmen of Thomas Hardy's London Corresponding Society. From then on, the mass radical movement, stemming from 'Wilkes and Liberty', had acquired a more stable base and gained further depths and experience from its migrations northwards, where early nineteenth-century Radicalism found new support among the factory towns emerging from the Industrial Revolution.

Meanwhile, the freeholders' petitioning movement of 1769 had also borne fruit — and not only in the Commons' resolution to

[1] For a fuller discussion, see my article, 'The London "Mob" of the Eighteenth Century', *The Historical Journal*, II, i (1959), 1–18.

[2] Dr. Sutherland quotes a City worthy, Joseph Brasbridge, as saying of this episode: 'From that moment . . . I shut my ears against the voices of popular clamour' ('The City in Eighteenth-Century Politics', in *Essays presented to Sir Lewis Namier*, p. 73).

expunge the record of Wilkes's 'incapacity' from their Journals. On 8 February 1780, another massive petition was presented to Parliament by Sir George Savile in the name of several thousand Yorkshire gentry, clergy and freeholders demanding 'economical' reform and launched, it was claimed, by an assembly representing 'more landed property than was possessed by all the Members in the House.'[1] It was the first step in a great movement for the reform of Parliament conducted by the Yorkshire Association,[2] recently founded by Christopher Wyvill, kinsman of that Sir Marmaduke Asty Wyvill who had signed the freeholders' petition of 1769.[3] As its activity developed, it was joined by others besides who had played a part in the earlier movement.[4] In Gloucestershire, too, there was a similar continuity of tradition. Among those attending meetings in Gloucester in January 1780 in order to promote a county petition in the image of that already drafted in Yorkshire were Sir William Guise, Bart., County Member; Sir William Codrington, Bart., M.P. for Tewkesbury; Charles Barrow, M.P. for Gloucester; and Sir George Onesiphorus Paul, chairman of the freeholders' meeting — all signatories of the earlier petition that had protested at the adoption of Luttrell in the place of Wilkes as the Member for Middlesex.[5]

Thus did the various currents of the Wilkite movement revive in new forms, bear richer fruit, and, by devious routes, flow into the main stream of British Radicalism and nineteenth-century movements for parliamentary reform.

[1] *Gent's Mag.*, 1780, pp. 96–97.

[2] Ian R. Christie, 'The Yorkshire Association, 1780–4: a Study in Political Organization', *The Historical Journal*, II, iii (1960), 144–61.

[3] Wyvill actually printed the Yorkshire proceedings of 1769–70 as an introduction to his political papers (Sutherland, *The City of London* . . . , p. 33).

[4] Among signatories of the earlier petition who were active in the Association I note the names of Sir James Ibbetson, Thomas Weddell and Stephen Croft of Stillington (Christie, op. cit., pp. 147, 153). There were, no doubt, many more.

[5] Glos. R.O., Proceedings of the Gloucestershire Committee in the Years 1780, 1781 and 1782.

APPENDIX I

Eyewitnesses' Accounts of the Attack on Edward Russell's House in Southwark on the Night of 10-11 May 1768 (T.S.11/443/1408)

1. *The examination on 3 June 1768 of William Hipgrave,* charged with 'burglariously' entering the house of Wm. Russell, distiller, and subsequently fined 13s. 4d. and sent to prison for 15 months.

About 6 to 7 p.m. on Tuesday 10th May, 'he was at the Baptist Head in the Old Bailey with Jas. Winchelow & hearing that there was firing in St. George's Fields they agreed to a walk there. Set forward to Blackfriars Bridge, took a boat there to the Falcon where they went into a house and had some [beer]. Set forward to St. George's Fields where they found a great Mob near the King's Bench Prison, went up to the Mob and were told that the *Justices had been reading something* & stayed there about one Hour. In that time were frequently drove with the Mob up Horsemongers Lane by the soldiers, often lost his Companion Whichelow but afterwards finding him about 9 they set forward from that Place to return Home and when they came to the Distiller's at the Bridge Foot [meaning Mr. Russell's] found the Mob breaking the windows. He . . . again lost Whichelow, staid and saw them break Mr. Russell's House by the help of an Iron Crane at the Door. Saw Thomas Greenwood about a quarter of an hour after 9 at night in the Mob who shewed him a Bayonet or some such Yard or Instrum^{t} wh^{ch} he had concealed under his Coat . . . That the Mob after they broke into the House of Mr Russell drank spirituous liquors out of their Hats and they made use of his hat among others for that purpose; and then he went homewards, called in at the Baptist's Head in the Old Bailey on his way but did not stay & so went home.'

2. *The information of Samuel Wood, clerk to Edward Russell Esq.,* regarding the attack made on Russell's house on the night of 10 May (heard 3 June 1768).

'This informant . . . saith that between hours of 9 and 10 p.m. Tuesday 10th May . . . the family was alarmed with a sudden breaking of the windows and, supposing it to be the Mob to require them to put out lights as had been practised for some nights before, this Deponent with other assistants hastened to the Dining windows for that purpose, and saw a great Crowd of Riotous persons who still continued throwing of stones insomuch they were obliged to shut the window shutters. However, that proved ineffectual, for these were soon broke to pieces and numbers of great stones thrown into the Room. And having entirely demolished the windows, sashes, frames and shutters, the Mob began to force the Door open and by the help of a Crane there, which they rested their hands upon, broke the pannels of the Door with their feet, huzzaing and exciting one another to such violence. When some of the Rioters got into the shop, rolled away a pipe of spirits which was placed to prevent the Door being forced open and then opened the street Door and let in their companions, who immediately ran the cocks of spirituous liquors, then set the cocks a-running and soon they pulled out, catching the liquor in buckets, hats, caps or any thing that came in their way, insomuch that they drank and wasted great quantities of spirituous liquors in the said shop; besides which, a twenty-gallon cask was by them rolled away from the Premises. That this deponent [and others] . . . were put in great fear and manifest danger of their lives . . . That he believes such Mob consisted of *some hundred persons*, many of whom, not content with these Acts of violence, said *they would set the house on fire*, and he has reason to think that they would have affected that or suchlike evil design if the report of the soldiers coming had not *prevented and drove them away* . . .'

APPENDIX II

The Marquess of Rockingham and the Middlesex Petition of 29 April 1769

At the end of chapter IV (p. 71–72 above) I dealt briefly with the part played by the Rockingham Whigs in the re-drafting and submission of the first Middlesex petition protesting against the Commons' adoption of Luttrell in the place of Wilkes, presented by Sir George Savile on 29 April 1769. In Albemarle's *Memoirs of the Marquis of Rockingham*, the incident is thus briefly related:

On the 29th of April, Sir George Savile presented a petition from some of the electors of Middlesex against the return of Colonel Luttrell, and a hearing was allotted on the 6th of May (vol. ii, p. 110).

In fact, it was then referred to 8 May, when the Commons decided by 221 to 152 votes 'that Henry Lawes Luttrell is duly elected a Knight of the Shire to serve in the present Parliament for the County of Middlesex' (*Journals*, xxxii (1769), 451).

But the problem remains, how was it that a petition adopted by a meeting of Middlesex freeholders, held under largely Wilkite auspices at the Mile End Assembly Room on 27 April, should, two days later, have been presented, in a form and style agreeable to the Rockingham Whigs, by one of their leading spokesmen in the Commons? Or were there, in fact, two petitions drafted and presented at this time, as might possibly be inferred from Albemarle's phrase, 'a petition from some of the electors of Middlesex'? Yet there is no record of any other petition being drafted and presented in April, and the following notes from the Rockingham papers among the Wentworth Woodhouse MSS. (R 87 1 (1–2)) in the Sheffield Central Library, while not telling the whole story, do something to clear up the mystery. It would appear from them that Rockingham, having been approached by persons unknown, drafted or re-drafted a form of petition, submitted it to Burke and Dowdeswell for their approval or amendment, and passed the finally agreed text to Savile for presentation in the Commons. It appears also that all this was done in a hurry on the afternoon of 29 April and that Burke's addition was preferred to Dowdeswell's.

Here I have attempted to clarify the procedure by arranging the documents in the following order:

(*a*) Rockingham's draft (indicating where Burke's and Dowdeswell's additions would fit in);
(*b*) Burke's addition;
(*c*) Dowdeswell's addition and amendment to Burke's; and
(*d*) Dowdeswell's note to Rockingham at 5 p.m. on 29 April, enclosing (presumably) the original draft and Burke's and his own additions.

1. *Rockingham's draft petition*

To . . . The Humble petition &c. &c. sheweth

That your Petitioners being informed by the Votes of this honourable House that the Return for the said County of Middlesex has been *amended* by razing out the name of John Wilkes Esq & inserting the name of Henry Lawes Lutterel Esq instead thereof & that leave was given to petition this House touching the Election of Henry Lawes Lutterel Esq.

Your Petitioners in consequence thereof beg leave to represent to this honourable House that the said H. L. Lutterel Esq. had not the Majority of *Legal Votes* at the said Election, nor did the majority of the H'seholders when they voted for John Wilkes Esq. mean thereby to throw away their Votes or to waive their Right of representation, nor would they by any means have chosen to be represented by the said H. L. Lutterel Esq. [*Burke's and Dowdeswell's proposed additions would fit in here*].

Your Petitioners therefore apprehend that he can not sit as the representative of the said County without manifest infringement of the Rights & and Priviledges of the Freeholders thereof.

Your Petitioners humbly hope that the honourable House will give leave that they may be heard by their counsel agt the said Election & Return, & grant them such further Relief as they in their wisdom and justice shall think meet.

2. *Burke's proposed addition to the 2nd paragraph*
. . . nor did they know it to be understood in any legal construction that they shd throw away their Votes by giving them for the said John Wilkes, he being as they apprehended under no legal incapacity.

3. *Dowdeswell's proposed addition*
. . . nor do they apprehend in any legal construction they can be understood to have thrown away their votes by giving them to the sd J. W. he being as they apprehend under no legal incapacity.

Your Pet[rs] therefore humbly represent that the said H. L. L. is not duly elected a Member to serve in this present Parliament for the county of Middlesex, & that he cannot sit . . .

(These three documents are in R87 1(2)).

4. *Dowdeswell's accompanying note to Rockingham*
My dear Lord,

I approve the idea of petitioning the H. of C. very much & have suggested an alteration in the draft which I think will be very right. Part of my addition is in correcting what I see in Burke's hand, the rest is new. I very much wish it may be presented by one of our Friends.

I am – ever yours

Wm Dowdeswell (R 87 1(1)).

A study of the petition as printed in the *Commons Journals* (xxxii. 447) will show that the final version presented by Sir George Savile was, to all intents and purposes, Rockingham's draft supplemented by Burke's (but not Dowdeswell's) addition.

One further question remains: who made the approaches to Rockingham on behalf of the Middlesex petitioners? It may have been Serjeant Glynn, who was originally intended to present the petition (see pp. 71–72 above). But it seems more probable that it was James Adair, who had presided over the freeholders' meeting and who, although a Wilkes supporter in Middlesex, remained on close and cordial terms with Rockingham: there is, in fact, among these papers, a note dated 17 May 1769, in which the Marquess invites Adair to write a pamphlet on the Middlesex election issue (R 1 — 1184), a task which, as we saw, was eventually undertaken by Sir William Meredith instead.

APPENDIX III

*Industrial Unrest, 1768–69: persons arrested and convicted**

Name	Occupation	Date of Incident	Charge	Sentence (if any)
Daniel Clare	Coal-heaver	20–21 April 1768	Shooting at John Green, publican, in his house in Shadwell	Sentenced to death at O.B., July 1768, and hanged at Sun Tavern Fields, Stepney
Rich. Cornwall	,,	,,	,,	,,
Peter Flaherty	,,	,,	,,	,,
John Grainger	,,	,,	,,	,,
Patrick Lynch	,,	,,	,,	,,
Nicholas McCabe	,,	,,	,,	,,
Thomas Murray	,,	,,	,,	,,
Peter Berkley	,,	,,	Rioting in Shadwell and going armed	?
Matthew Byrne	,,	,,	,,	3 years' prison (Hicks Hall, Jan. 1769)
Philip Conolly	,,	,,	,,	,,
David Creamer	,,	,,	,,	7 years' prison (Hicks Hall, Oct. 1768)
James Dignam	,,	,,	,,	?
Thomas Kelly	Publican	,,	,,	?
John Mahoney	Coal-heaver	,,	,,	7 years' prison (Hicks Hall, Jan. 1769)
Dennis Toners	,,	,,	,,	7 years' prison (Hicks Hall, Oct. 1768)
As a result of these incidents, 9 publicans of Shadwell and Wapping lost their licences				
James Duggan / James Murphy	Coal-heaver	24 May 1768	Murder of John Beatty, sailor, at Shadwell	Sent. to death at O.B., July 1768, and hanged at Tyburn
Thos. Carnan	,,	,,	,,	Acquitted at O.B., July 1768
John Costello	,,	,,	,,	,,
Thomas Davis	,,	,,	,,	,,
Malachi Doyle	,,	,,	,,	,,
Thomas Farmer	,,	,,	,,	,,
James Hammond	,,	,,	,,	,,
Hugh Henley	,,	,,	,,	,,
Edward Castle	—	10 May 1768	Attack on Chas. Dingley's saw-mill in Limehouse	Acquitted at O.B., July 1768
John Smith	'Labourer'	,,		Sent. at Hicks Hall, Jan. 1769, to 7 years' jail
Thos. Fitzhugh	Hatter	16 June 1768	Threatening John Dyer, hat-maker of St. Olave, Southwark	To attend Guildford Q.S. on 12 July 1768 — then 'disappears'

* For sources, see p. 204.

Name	Occupation	Date of Incident	Charge	Sentence (if any)
Peter Perryn	Weaver	4 Jan. 1768	Intent to destroy 4 looms in John Clare's house in Stepney	Sent. to death at O.B. Oct. 1769
Cornelius Cavalier	,,	,,		Acquitted at O.B. Oct. 1769
John Read	,,	,,	,,	,,
William Evans	,,	Jan. 1768	'Cutting' work in loom	Committed to Newgate by Sir John Fielding
William Tilley	,,	10 April 1769	'Cutting' work of Lydia Fowler	12d. fine at Mid'x Q.S., 9 May 1769
John Doyle }	,,	7 Aug. 1769	'Cutting' silk in looms of Thos. Poor in Shoreditch	Sent. to death at O.B., Oct. 1769, and hanged Bethnal Grn, 6 Dec. 1769
John Valline }		,,		
William Horsford	,,	9 Aug. 1769	,,	Sent. death O.B., Oct. 1769
William Eastman	,,	11 Sept. 1769	'Cutting' silk in loom of Daniel Clark, Bishopsgate	Sent. death O.B., Dec. 1769
Thomas Hadden	,,	,,	,,	Acquitted Lond. Q.S., Dec. 1769
John Fessey	,,	22 Sept. 1769	'Cutting' silk of John Dupree, B.Gn.	Sent. to death at O.B., Oct. 1769
John Carmichael	,,	Sept. 1769	,, c/o Rich. Cromwell, Moorfields	Sent. to death at O.B., Dec. 1769
Nathaniel Norris	,,	,,	Riot at Lewis Chauvet's house, Spitalfields Market	Sent. 1 year's prison at Mid'x Q.S., Dec. 1769
Daniel Murphy	,,	30 Sept. 1769	Murder of Adam McCoy, soldier	Sent. to death at O.B., Oct. 1769
Robert Campbell	,,	Sept.–Oct. 1769	Parading with weapons in Vine Court, Christ Church, Mid'x	Discharged
John Chapman	,,	,,		,,
Joseph Coleman	,,	,,	,,	,,
David Collings	,,	,,	,,	,,
William Duff	,,	,,	,,	,,
John Horsford	,,	,,	,,	,,
William Jacks	,,	,,	,,	,,
Andrew Mahoney	,,	,,	,,	,,
Cornelius Mahoney	,,	,,	,,	,,
Michael Moore	,,	,,	,,	,,
Daniel Murphy	,,	,,	,,	,,
Joseph Palmer	,,	,,	,,	,,
Patrick Pickle	,,	,,	,,	,,
William Ran	,,	,,	,,	,,
Michael Duff	,,	4 Oct. 1769	Extracting money for weavers' fund with threats	Acquitted at Mid'x Q.S., Dec. 1769
Simon Rawlings	—	6 Dec. 1769	Breaking windows of L. Chauvet's house	?
Thomas Clements	Weaver	?	'Cutting' silk in loom	Case dismissed, Mid'x. Q.S., April 1771

* *Sources*: O.B. *Proceedings*, 1768–70; Middlesex R.O., Sessions Rolls (Mid'x. & West.) and Process Reg. Bks. of Indictments, 1761– [illegible]

APPENDIX IV

Industrial Unrest, 17–6869: journeymen weavers' letters to Peter Auber, weaver of Spital Square, August 1769 (T.S. 11/818/2696)

Peter Auber's house was attacked by a band of 'cutters' during the night of Friday, 11 August 1769. Previously, his assailants had left him the following notes:

1. Mr. Obey, we are inform'd that your Character is but very indiferent in regard to the welfare of Trade. Without any Hesitation we demand you to order your Men to embody next Saturday Night when your Man is demanded to pay 6d per Man donation for the good of the Cause & those that refuses to comply will be treated with contempt as likewise yourself if you take or call the Mens Works in or stop them from Labour. We have many Masters agreed to prove themselves Honest Men – but your the least and on your Neglect of Duty to shake of your bad Name you may perhaps lose by itt.

An answer to this imediately,
From your,
Defiance Sloop.

2. Mr Obey, As you are to give an Answer now to enform a Select Body of your Ententions it is hoped that you will give a satisfactory one for the good of Trade and before any of your Works shall suffer. An imense grate Body of Men will opose all Enemies to the Welfare of Trade, from your Friend,

Unknown at present.

3. Mr. Obey, we give you now an Egg Shell of Honey, but if you refuse to comply with the demands of yesterday, we'll give you a Gallon of Thorns to your final Life's End.

APPENDIX V

*Middlesex Electors, 1768–69: voting and value of properties**

Parish	Voters		Ann. values of predom. 'Proctorite' voters					Ann. values of predom. 'Wilkite' voters				
	Proctor/ Lut.	Wilkes/ Glynn	No. found	Total value	Av. value	£50 and over	£100 and over	No. found	Total value	Av. value	£50 and over	£100 and over
I. WESTMINSTER												
St. John Evangelist	6	8	6	£55	£9	—	—	8	£97	£12	—	—
St. Margaret	51	53	18	£539	£30	5	—	17	£452	£26½	3	—
St. Martin-in-Fields	21	42	14	£341	£24⅓	—	—	23	£445	£19⅔	3	—
St. Paul Cov. Garden	14	19	10	£536	£53½	5	2	17	£537	£31½	2	—
St. George Hanover Sq.	17	16	11	£789	£71½	7	4	12	£393	£33	4	—
Total (5)	109	138	59	£2,260	£38⅓	17	6	77	£1,924	£25	12	—
II. MIDDLESEX 'OUT'-PARISHES												
1. *Finsbury Div.*												
St. James Clerk'll	30	70	11	£353	£32	2	—	26	£461	£18	—	—
St. Luke Old St.	43	105	19	£434	£23	2	1	44	£655	£15	2	—
St. Mary Islington	10	22	4	£365	£91	1	1	14	£351	£25	1	1
Wellclose and Old Artillery Ground	5	2	3	£36	£12	—	—	1	£12	£12	—	—
2. *Holborn Div.*												
St. Andrew, Holborn and St. George Martyr	41	54	18	£580	£32	3	—	23	£631	£27½	3	—
St. Giles-in-Fields	28	41	13	£228	£17½	—	—	12	£286	£24	—	—
3. *Tower Div.*												
Tower and Minories	10	20	2	£45	£22½	—	—	6	£266	£44½	2	—
St. Anne Limehouse	24	67	14	£1,017½	£73	5	4	45	£868	£19	3	—
St. Botolph Aldgate	3	10	—	—	—	—	—	2	£36	£18	—	—
St. Dunstan Stepney	6	5	3	£93	£31	1	1	1	£7½	£7½	—	—
Christchurch Spital'ds	13	21	10	£212	£21	—	—	10	£490	£49	1	1
St. George Mid'x and St. Paul Shadwell	27	65	20	£446½	£22	3	—	48	£909½	£18½	2	2
St. John Hackney	17	8	13	£444	£34	3	1	7	£135	£19⅓	1	—
St. John Wapping	20	87	10	£517	£51½	5	1	41	£1,390	£34	7	4
Mile End	5	8	2	£51	£25½	—	—	5	£101	£20	—	—
St. Mary Whitech'l	15	33	8	£306	£38¼	2	1	14	£453	£32⅓	4	—
East Smithfield	[illegible]	[illegible]	[illegible]	[illegible]	[illegible]			[illegible]	[illegible]	[illegible]		

III. RURAL PARISHES												
1. *Edmonton Hundred*												
Edmonton	11	26	8	£796	£99½	3	3	16	£668	£42	3	2
Enfield	41	50	27	£969	£36	6	3	28	£748	£27	5	2
S. Mimms	13	5	12	£886	£72	4	1	3	£125	£41⅓	1	1
Tottenham	14	24	7	£567	£80½	2	2	15	£1,631	£109	3	2
2. *Elthorne H.*												
Harefield	10	3	7	£1,431	£204½	4	3	2	£35	£17½	—	—
Harlington	9	7	6	£204½	£34	2	1	5	£70	£14	—	—
Hayes	13	8	7	£841	£120	4	4	5	£34½	£7	—	—
Hillingdon	28	6	20	£1,085	£54¼	4	2	3	£91	£30⅓	—	—
Norwood	6	1	6	£121	£20	1	—	1	£126	£126	1	1
Ruislip	7	3	3	£38¾	£13	—	—	3	£173¾	£54½	1	1
Southall	3	9	2	£146	£73	1	1	6	£95	£16	—	—
Uxbridge	35	20	25	£474⅓	£19	1	1	11	£185	£17	—	—
3. *Isleworth H.*												
Heston	8	12	7	£1,061½	£151½	5	3	8	£601	£75	4	4
Isleworth	24	19	16	£498	£31	2	2	10	£129	£13	—	—
Twickenham	16	7	12	£398½	£33	2	1	6	£126½	£21	1	—
4. *Ossulston H.*												
Brentford	35	38	19	£365	£19	2	1	13	£280	£21½	1	—
Finchley	15	12	12	£1,133	£98½	6	5	7	£500	£71	3	2
5. *Spelthorne H.*												
Shepperton	4	19	2	£149	£74½	1	1	12	£215½	£18	1	—
Staines	20	37	14	£489	£35	3	2	16	£381½	£24	2	1
Stanwell	5	28	5	£113	£22½	1	—	16	£504	£31½	3	2
Sunbury	10	30	7	£301	£43	1	1	13	£176	£13½	1	—
Teddington	2	5	2	£56	£28	1	—	2	£5	£2½	—	—
Total (22)	329	369	226	£12,123	£53½	56	37	201	£7,199	£36	30	18
Totals												
1. Westminster (5)	109	138	59	£2,260	£38⅓	17	6	77	£1,924	£25	12	—
2. 'Out'-parishes (17)	296	664	151	£5,167	£34	27	10	307	£7,196	£23½	28	8
3. Rural parishes (22)	329	369	226	£12,123	£53½	56	37	201	£7,199	£36	30	18
Grand total (44 parishes)	734	1,171	436	£19,550	£45	100	53	585	£16,319	£28	70	26

**Sources*: Middlesex Poll Books, 1768–69; Land Tax assessments and/or Poor Rate Books for 44 parishes.

APPENDIX VI

Middlesex Electors, 1768–69: voting record of M.P.s and clergy

*A. M.P.s**

M.P.	Constituency	Middlesex Freehold	March 1768			Dec. 1768		April 1769	
			PROCTOR	COOKE	WILKES	PROCTOR	GLYNN	LUTTRELL	WILKES
(?) Edward Bacon	Norwich	Grays Inn	—	—	—	P		—	—
Viscount Bateman	Leominster	Buckingham St.	—	—	—	—	—	L	
Thomas Brand	Oakhampton	St. James's Sq.	—	—	—	P		—	—
Charles Brett	Lostwithiel	Willesden	—	—	—	P		—	—
Sir Chas. Bunbury, Bart.	Suffolk	St. James's St.	—	—	—	P		—	—
Henry C. Boulton	Worcester	Blackhall	—	—	—	P		—	—
George Byng	Wigan	Wrotham Pk. S. Mimms	—	—	—	P			W
Sir G. Colebrooke, Bart.	Arundel	Manor in Stepney	P	C		—	—	—	—
John Dodd	Reading	Hillingdon	—	—		—	—	L	
Sir John H. Cotton	Cambridgeshire	East Smithfield	—	—	—	P		—	—
Sir William Dolben	Northants	Hoton Court	—	—	—	P		—	—
J. St. Leger Douglas	Hindon	Willesden	—	—	—	P		L	
John Eames	Newport, Hants	Master in Chancery	—	—	—	P		—	—
(?) Wm. Fitzherbert	Derby	Dean's Yard, West.	P	C		—	—	—	—
Hon. Chas. Fitzroy	Edmondsbury	Tottenham Court	—	—	—	—	—	L	
Stephen Fox	Sarum	Kensington (?)	—	—	—	—	—	L	
Sir Thos. Frankland	Thirsk	Old Bond St.	P	C		P		—	—
Viscount Gage	Seaford	Arlington St.	—	—	—	P		—	—
Philip Jennings	Totnes	Hendon		C		P		—	—
Sir. Rob. Ladbroke	London	Spitalfields	—	—	—	P		—	—
Benjamin Lethuillier	Andover	Huckton	—	—	—	P		—	—
Sir James Lowther	Cumberland	Laleham Manor Hse.	—	—	—	—	—	L	—
Sir Roger Newdigate	Oxford Univ.	Harefield	—	—	—	P		L	
Henry Visc. Palmerston	Southampton	St. James's Sq.	—	—	—	—	—	L	
(?)William Plumer	Hertfordshire	Holborn	—	—	—	P		—	—

Harcourt Powell	Newton, Hants	Lincoln's Inn	—	—	—	—	—	L	
Isaac M. Rebow	Colchester	Limehouse	—	—	—	P		—	
John Sawbridge	Hythe	Tottenham	—	—	—		G		W
Hans Sloane	Newport, Hants	Chelsea	—	—	—	P		L	
John Stephenson	St. Michael	Brentford Butts	—	—	—	P		L	
William Strode	Yarmouth, Hants	Finchley	—	—	—	P		—	—
Sir Simeon Stuart	Hampshire	Buckingham St.	—	—	—	P		L	
James Townsend	West Looe	Tottenham.	—	—	—	—	G		W
Richard Vernon	Bedford	George St., West.	—	—	—	P		—	—
(?) Nathaniel Webb	Taunton	St. Giles-in-the-Fields	—	—	—	P		L	
Samuel Whitbread	Bedford	Chiswell St.	P	C		P		—	—
Robert Wood	Brackley	St. George, Han. Sq.	—	—	—	P		L	
Hon. Chas. Yorke	Cambridge Univ.	Lincoln's Inn	P	C		P		—	—
Hon. John Yorke	Reigate	Lincoln's Inn	—	—	—	P		—	—

*Sources: Middlesex Poll Books, 1768–69; Court and City Register, 1769.
(?) Denotes uncertainty of identification.

*B. Clergy**

Parish	Name	Address or living							
Brentford	Rev. Wm. Baker	—	P	C		P		—	—
Brentford	Rev. J. Horne	The Parsonage, New B.			W		G		W
Chelsea	Rev. Thos. Martin	Church Lane	P	C		P		—	—
Chiswick	Arthur Cohan	The Vicarage	P	C		P		—	—
Ealing	John Botham	The Vicarage	P	C		P		L	
Edmonton	Wm. Pinkney	The Vicarage	P	C		P		—	—
Enfield	Rich. Newbon	The Vicarage	—	—	—	(?)P	(?)G	—	—
Finchley	Jas. Waller	The Rectory	P	C		—	—	L	
Fulham	Ant. Hamilton	The Vicarage	P	C		P		L	
Hackney	R. T. Cornthwaite	The Vicarage	P			P		—	—
Hammersmith	Thos. Sampson	(curate)	P			P		L	
Harefield	Wm. Williams	The Rectory		C		P		—	—
Harlington	John Williams	The Rectory	—	—	—	P		—	—
Hayes	Anthony Hinton	The Vicarage	P	C		P		—	—
Heston	John Gibson	The Vicarage	P	C		?P		?L	
Hillingdon	Richard Mills	The Vicarage	P	C		P		—	—
Ickenham	Thos. Clarke	—	—	—	—	P		—	—
Islington	R. Smith	Vicar, St. Mary's	—	—	—	P		—	—

Parish	Name	Address or living	March 1768			Dec. 1768		April 1769	
			PROCTOR	COOKE	WILKES	PROCTOR	GLYNN	LUTTRELL	WILKES
Kensington	T. Russell, D.D.	—	P	C		—	—	—	—
Lib. of Rolls	Jos. Williamson	The Vicarage	—	—	—	—	G	—	—
Littleton	Henry Allen	The Rectory	P	C		P		—	—
Norwood	G. Chas. Black	(minister)	P	C		P		—	—
Pinner	Walter Williams	(curate)	P	C		P		—	—
Ruislip	Henry Duckworth	The Vicarage	—	—	—	P		—	—
St. Anne, West.	R. Hinde, D.D.	The Rectory	P		W	P		L	
St. George, Han. Sq.	Martin Justice	—	—	—	—		G		W
St. George the Martyr, Holb.	Stephen Eaton, D.D.	—	P	C		P		—	—
St. James, Picc.	Wm. Parker, D.D.	The Rectory	P	C		P		—	—
St. James, Picc.	Capel Barrow	Wych St. St. James	P	C		—	—	—	—
St. Martin-in-the-Fields	Erasmus Saunders	The Vicarage	P	C		—	—	—	—
St. Paul, Cov. Gdn.	Jas. Tattershall	The Rectory	P	C		—	—	—	—
Shadwell	Joseph Butler	The Rectory	—	—	—	P		L	
Shepperton	Thos. Harwood	The Rectory	P	C		P		—	—
Stratford	Thos. Foxley	Rectory, Bow St.	—	—	—	P		—	—
Tottenham	William Dowding	The Vicarage	—	—	—	P		—	—
Twickenham	Samuel Hemming	—	P	C		—	—	—	—
Twickenham	George Costard	The Vicarage	P	C		P		L	
Uxbridge	James Price	—	P	C		—	—	—	—
Wapping	Dr. Francis Wallis	The Rectory	—	—	—	P		—	—
Wapping	William Prior	(curate)	—	—	—	—	—	—	W
Willesden	C. Sturges	—	—	—	—	P		—	—
Willesden	Moses Wight	—	—	—	—	P		L	

*Sources: Middlesex Poll Books, 1768–69; Episcopal Visitation Books, 1769.

APPENDIX VII

*Petitions of 1769: signatures and signatories**

(see chaps. VII and VIII)

A. Counties	Signatures	'Marks'	M.P.s	J.P.s	Clergy	Political Influence
Buckinghamshire	1,845	130	5	40	16	Temple/Rockingham
Cornwall	1,510	12	2	40	8	Bill of Rights Soc.
Derbyshire	2,850	105	5	—	—	Rockingham/Cavend.
Devon	2,800	2	3	50	29	Bill of Rights (?)
Durham	1,370	9	1	—	—	Rockingham
Gloucestershire	1,960	10	3	30	6	Mixed
Herefordshire	1,800	2	1	30	3	Rockingham (?)
Kent	2,825	168	0	10	—	Chathamite
Middlesex	1,565	36	1	12	3	Bill of Rights
Northumberland	750	32	0	12	1	Rockingham (?)
Somerset	2,800	2	4	52	1	Mixed
Surrey	1,494	28	7	65	2	Bill of Rights
Wiltshire	1,180	16	3	35	1	Bill of Rights
Worcestershire	1,475	104	0	—	1	Rockingham
Yorkshire	11,000	297	11	75	8	Rockingham
B. Boroughs, etc.						
Berwick-on-Tweed	?	—	—	—	—	Bill of Rights (?)
Bristol	2,245	0	—	—	—	Bill of Rights
Coventry	900	109	—	—	—	?
Exeter	860	0	—	—	—	Bill of Rights
Hereford	475	0	1	1	1	Rockingham (?)
Liverpool	1,100	0	—	—	—	Mixed
London	(5,000)	—	—	—	—	Bill of Rights
Morpeth (?)	?	—	—	—	—	?
Newcastle-on-Tyne	900	36	—	—	—	?
Southwark	1,200	0	—	—	—	Bill of Rights
Westminster	5,137	12	1	—	—	Bill of Rights
Worcester	640	0	—	—	—	Rockingham

**Sources*: H.O. 55/1–6 (petitions); London and provincial press; Commissions of the Peace for 1769, etc.

APPENDIX VIII

London Livery Companies: membership, livery fines, support for Wilkes in 1768

Company[1]	Membership[2] (1756)	Livery Fine[3]	Voting in City Election, March 1768[4]: Votes cast	Votes for Wilkes	Prop. of vote
Apothecaries	145	£20 + fees (1779)	92	17	2 in 11
Armourers and Brasiers	74	£25 (craft) or £30	60	12	1 in 5
Bakers	139	£10–£20	118	36	1 in 3
Barbers	295	£10 + 10s. fees	239	50	1 in 5
Blacksmiths	169	£8 15s.	122	25	1 in 5
Bowyers	36	£25 or £50 + fees	19	4	1 in 5
Brewers	115	£21 (1812)	23	7	1 in 3
Bricklayers and Tylers	92	£12	81	18	2 in 9
Butchers	173	£28 10s. (incl. fine re steward)	121	42	1 in 3
Carpenters	100	£9	86	17	1 in 5
Clockmakers	60 (1766)	£10	56	11	1 in 5
CLOTHWORKERS	138	£20 + 9s. fees	132	28	1 in 5
Coachmakers	92	?	81	16	1 in 5
Cooks	54	£10 + 7s. 6d. fees	37	7	2 in 11
Coopers	248	£21 + 23s. 6d. fees	222	59	1 in 4
Cordwainers	79	£20 (1834)	63	8	1 in 8
Curriers	87	£15 (1818)	62	11	1 in 6
Cutlers	62	£31 + 2½ gns fees	54	16	2 in 7
Distillers	103	£13 6s. 8d. + 31s. 6d. fees	43	6	1 in 7
DRAPERS	156	£25	126	31	1 in 4
Dyers	96	£29 13s. or £34 18s.	82	17	1 in 5
Embroiderers	74	?	38	13	1 in 3
Farriers	66	£5 + 15s. fees	57	12	1 in 5
Feltmakers	100	£15 (1787)	68	8	2 in 17
FISHMONGERS	159	£13 6s. 8d. + fees	125	35	2 in 7
Fletchers	31	£21 or £26 (1835)	25	4	1 in 6
Founders	100	£8 + 7s. 6d. fees	73	16	2 in 9
Framework-knitters	51	?	49	10	1 in 5
Fruiterers	41	£15 + 20s. 6d. fees: (1835)	24	6	1 in 4

Glovers	200	£10 10s. (1797)	170	47	1 in 4
GOLDSMITHS	162	?	133	18	1 in 7
GROCERS	125	?	97	10	2 in 19
HABERDASHERS	312	£25 (1815)	167	22	1 in 8
Innholders	111	£10+10s. fees	114	28	1 in 4
Joiners	370	£10+£10+31s. fees	282	92	1 in 3
IRONMONGERS	88	?	85	15	1 in 6
Leathersellers	118	£20–£25	86	22	1 in 4
Loriners	97	£12+7s. 6d. fees	59	13	2 in 9
Masons	78	£15 15s. (inc.)	59	7	2 in 17
MERCERS	146	£2 13s. 4d.+fees	83	14	1 in 6
MERCHANT TAYLORS	275	£30+£5 fees	170	34	1 in 5
Musicians	100	?	110	32	2 in 7
Needlemakers	46	£5 13s. 4d.	34	10	2 in 7
Painter-stainers	99	£14	59	13	2 in 9
Pattenmakers	54	£12+20s. fees	30	6	1 in 5
Pewterers	96	£20+fees	72	12	1 in 6
Plaisterers	74	£13 17s. 6d. (inc.) (1835)	57	18	1 in 3
Plumbers	55	£10+£5 fees	45	7	2 in 13
Poulterers	91	£20 10s. 6d. (incl.)	54	14	1 in 4
Sadlers	65	£15 15s. (1815)	59	9	2 in 13
SALTERS	125	£20 (1833)	78	11	1 in 7
Scriveners	52	£5	38	15	2 in 5
SKINNERS	117	£20+26s. 8d. fees	103	9	1 in 11
Stationers	199	£50+31s. fees (1835)	205	46	2 in 9
Surgeons	89	?	19	4	1 in 5
Tallow Chandlers	159	£31 (inc. steward fine)	93	15	1 in 6
Tinplate-workers	60 (1766)	£10	51	10	1 in 5
Turners	133	?	117	22	1 in 5
VINTNERS	186	?	150	36	1 in 4
Upholders	95	?	82	25	1 in 3
Wax Chandlers	104	£10 or £15	66	10	2 in 13
Weavers	203	£10+12s. fees	146	22	2 in 13
65 Companies	7,503		5,694	1,247	2 in 9

[1] The 'Big Twelve' companies are in capital letters.

[2] *A List of the Liverymen of the several Companies of the City of London* (1756).

[3] *Second Report of the Commissioners appointed to enquire into the Municipal Corporations in England and Wales* (H. of Commons, 1837), pp. 1–346.

[4] *The Poll of the Livery of London* (1768).

APPENDIX IX

*Wilkes Supporters on the Court of Common Council, 1768–71**

Ward and Name	City Company	Trade and address	City Election March 1768[1]	Middlesex Elections, 1768–69[2]	C.C. vote, 5.5.1769[3]	C.C. vote, 15.3.1771[4]
Aldersgate						
Geo. Lewis Carr	Weavers	Mercer, 9 Ludgate Hill	X	W/G/W	—	—
Aldgate						
Thos. Cocksedge	Stationers	Mercer, 1 Crescent Minories	X	—	P	P
Jos. Partridge	Clothworkers	Packer, 112 Fenchurch St.	—	—	P	P
Wm. Plomer	Bricklayers and Tylers	Oilman, 13 Aldgate St.	X	—	P	P
Bassishaw						
John Webb	?	Upholder, 22 Gracechurch St.	—	—	P	P
Billingsgate						
Chas. Motley	?	Orange merchant, 7 Lower Thames St.	—	—	P	P
Bishopsgate						
John Austin	Skinners	Corn-factor, Red Lion Wharf	W	—	—	—
Samuel Crosley	Fishmongers	Linen-draper, 39 Bishopsgate, W't.	W	—	—	—
John Fasson	Pewterers	Pewterer, 48 Bishopsgate W'n.	W	—	—	—
Henry George	Merch. Taylors	Haberdasher, 96 Bishopsgate St.	W	—	—	P
George Paillet	Upholders	Glover, 55 Bishopsgate W'n.	—	W/G/—	—	P
Richard Townsend	Goldsmiths	Ironmonger, 3 Gracechurch St.	—	—	P	P
Bread Street						
John Partridge	Innholders	?	W	—	P	P
Broad Street						
Jas. Cotterell	Glass-sellers	Chinaman, 9 Mansion House St.	X	—	P	P
Chas. Wenman	Haberdashers	Lottery office, 11, Poultry	X	W/—/W	—	—
Bridge						
Samuel Baughan	Dyers	Hatmakers, 21 Bell Yd., Fish St. Hill	W	—	P	P
Geo. Cooper	Goldsmiths	Tobacconist and teaman, 7 Old Swan Stairs	W	—	P	P
Edward Cowell	Turners	?	W	—	—	—
Wm. Jebson	Framework-knitters	Mercer, 58 Gracechurch St.	W	—	—	P

* For sources see p. 216.

Castle Baynard						
Geo. Bellas	Carpenters	Attorney, Doctor's Commons	W	W/G/W	P	P
Wm. Hurford	Barbers	Coal-merchant, 3 Coal Exchange	W	—	—	P
R. Manning	Drapers	?	W	—	—	P
John Wilson	Bowyers	(?) Grocer, 77 St. Paul's Church Yard	—	W/P/—	—	—
Cheap						
Rich. Bristow	Goldsmiths	Attorney, 16 Bucklesbury	W	—	—	P
Stephen Camm	Musicians	Linen-draper, 32 King St. Cheapside	X	—	P	P
Coleman St.						
Wm. Bishop	Saddlers	Saddler, 27 Coleman St.	X	—	P	P
Robt. Wimbolt	Goldsmiths	?	—	—	P	P
Cordwainer						
Thos. Board	Tallow Chandlers	Chemist, 89 Gracechurch St.	W	—	—	P
Wm. Poole	?	Weaver and haberdasher, 53 Cheapside	—	—	P	P
Cornhill						
Wm. Dawson	Merch. Taylors	Hop-merchant, 140 Upper Thames St.	X	—	P	P
Cripplegate Within						
John Anderson	Drapers	Haberdasher, 4 Cateaton St.	X	—	P	P
Stephen Unwin	Grocers	Hardwareman, 121 Cheapside	X	—	P	P
Dowgate						
Francis Hamilton	Dyers	Dyer, Montague Close, Southwark	X	—	P	P?
Jos. Stevenson	Coopers	Cooper, 5 Coal Harbour, Upper Thames St.	W		P	P
Farringdon Within						
Thos. Caston	Stationers	Bookseller, 4 Stationers Court, Ludgate St.	W	—	—	X
Stanley Crowder	Stationers	Bookseller, 12 Paternoster Row	W	—	—	P
Thos. Hyde	Fishmongers	Goldsmith, 33 Gutter Lane	W	—	—	P
John Lokes	Wax Chandlers	Wax-chandler, 39 Newgate St.	W	—	—	P
Farringdon Without						
John Mansfield	Joiners	?	W	—	—	P
Thos. Salter	Turners	?	W	—	—	—
Langbourn						
Ingham Foster	Ironmongers	Ironmonger, 29 Clement's Lane, Lombard St.	X	—	P	P
John Reynolds	Upholders	Mercer, The Cloisters, W. Smithfield	W	—	—	P
Lime Street						
Humphrey Jones	Glovers	Merchant, 137 Leadenhall St.	X	—	P	P
James Sharp	Needlemakers	Ironmonger, 15 Leadenhall St.	X	—	P	P
Portsoken						
John Brazier	Clockmakers	Gunmaker, 122 Minories	W	—	—	—
Geo. Holgate	Salters	?	W	—	—	X

Ward and Name	City Company	Trade and Address	City Election, March 1768[1]	Middlesex Elections 1768–69[2]	C.C. vote 5.5.1769[3]	C.C. vote, 15.3.1771[4]
Tower						
James Ansell	Coopers	Cooper, 17 Water Lane, Tower St.	W	—	—	P
Samuel Freeman	Wax-chandlers	(?)Lead-merch., 48 Mark La.	W	—	P	P
Joseph Speck	Coopers	Wine-cooper, 90 Lower Thames St.	X	—	P	P
Vintry						
Joseph Downes	Haberdasher	Oilman, 13 Holborn Ct.	X	—	P	P
Higgins Eden	Dyers	Silkman, 1 King St. Cheapside	X	—	P	P
Priest Shrubb	Plumbers	?	X	—	P	P
James Stracey	Coopers	Cider-merch., Elbow La. Dowgate Hill	W	—	P	P
Godfrey Wilson	Farriers	Coal-merch., 51 Queen St.	W	—	P	X
Walbrook						
Thos. Axford	Musicians	Brokers, 27 Walbrook	W	—	—	P
Arthur Beardmore	Glovers	Solicitor	X	—	P	—

* *Sources: Royal Calendar*, 1768–71; *London Directory*, 1774; Baldwin's *Guide to the City of London*, 1770; *The Poll of the Livery of London*, 1768; Middlesex Poll Books, 1768–69; *Mid. J.*, 6.5.69 and 16.3.71.

1 Wilkes voters are marked 'W'; those voting, but not for Wilkes, are marked 'X'.

2 'W' = Wilkes, 'C' = Cooke, 'P' = Proctor.

3 This was the Common Council vote on a proposal to summon a Common Hall to consider a petition on the Middlesex election issue (see p. 153 above). Supporters of the proposal (the minority) are here marked 'P' (= 'Patriots'); opponents are marked 'X'.

4 This was the Common Council vote on a proposal to rescind a previous decision to prosecute magistrates backing press warrants (see p. 155 and 2 above). Opponents (the majority) are here marked 'P' (= 'Patriots') and supporters are marked 'X'.

APPENDIX X

*City of London Aldermen, 1768–74**

	Ward and Aldermen[1]	City Company	Trade and Address	City Election, 1768	Middlesex elections, 1768–69	Common Council Vote, 5 May 1769	Common Council Vote, 15 March 1771[2]	Election of Glynn as City Recorder 14 Nov. 1772[3]
	1. *Aldersgate*							
C	Sir Thos. Hallifax (1766)	Goldsmiths	Banker, 18 Birchin Lane	—	—	X	X	X
	2. *Aldgate*							
C	John Shakespear (1767)	Embroiderers	Merchant, 10 Billiter Sq.	X	—	X	X	X
	3. *Bassishaw*							
W/I	Sir Wm. Baker (1739)	Weavers	Governor, Hudson's Bay Co., Winchester St.	W	—	—		
C	John Bird (1770)	Goldsmiths	Jeweller, 19 Cornhill	X	—	—	X	—
W	William Plomer (1772)	Bricklayers	Oilman, 13 Aldgate St.	—	—	(P)	(P)	P
	4. *Billingsgate*							
Ch	Wm. Beckford (1752)	Ironmongers	W. India merch., Soho Square	X	-/G/-	P		
Ch	Rich. Oliver (1770)	Drapers	W. India merch., 107 Fenchurch Street	—	—	—	—	P
	5. *Bishopsgate*							
I	Sir Mat. Blakiston (1750)	Grocers	Grocer, Strand	—	—			
Ch	Jas. Townsend (1769)	Mercers	Merchant, 6 Austin Friars	—	-/G/W	—	—	P
	6. *Bread Street*							
W	Brass Crosby (1765)	Musicians	Attorney, 9 Cecil St. Strand	X	—	—	—	P
	7. *Bridge Within*							
W	Sir Wm. Stephenson (1754)	Grocers	Hop-merchant, 12 Old Swan Lane, Thames St.	X	—	P	P	P
I	John Hart (1774)	Skinners	Drysalter, 149 Up. Thames St.	—	—			

	Ward and Alderman[1]	City Company	Trade and Address	City Election, 1768	Middlesex elections 1768–69	Common Council Vote, 5 May 1769	Common Council Vote, 15 March 1771[2]	Election of Glynn as City Recorder 14 Nov. 1772[3]
	8. *Bridge Without*							
C	Sir Rob. Ladbroke (1749)	Grocers	Banker, 10 Lombard Street	X	-/P/-	—	X	X
C	Robert Alsop (1773)	Ironmongers	Merchant, Gt. Marlborough St.	X	—	(X)	(X)	(X)
	9. *Broad Street*							
I	Sir T. Rawlinson Bt. (1746)	Grocers	Merchant, Fenchurch Street	X	—			
C	Jas. Rosseter (1769)	Feltmakers	Hatmaker, Pudding Lane	—	—	—	X	X
C	Benj. Hopkins (1773)	Drapers	Dir. Bank of Eng. and merchant, 58 Old Broad St.	—	-/P/-			
	10. *Candlewick*							
I	Sir Chas. Asgill Bt. (1749)	Skinners	Banker, Lombard Street; St. James's Sq.	X	—	—	—	P
	11. *Castle Baynard*							
C	Samuel Plumbe (1767)	Wiredrawers	Refiner, 23 Foster Lane	—	—	—	X	X
	12. *Cheap*							
I	Sir Sam. Fludyear Bt. (1751)	Bricklayers	Deputy Governor, Bank of Eng.; ex-warehouseman, Basinghall St.	—	—			
I	John Kirkman (1768)	Fishmongers	Silkman, 21 College Hill	—	—	X	X	P
	13. *Coleman Street*							
C	Robert Alsop (1745)	Ironmongers	Merchant, Gt. Marlborough St.	X	—	X	X	X
I	Robert Peckham (1773)	Wheelwrights	Merchant, 8 Austin Friars	—	—			
	14. *Cordwainer*							
C	Sir Henry Bankes (1762)	Grocers	Sugar merchant, St. Mary-at-Hill	X	—	—	—	X
W	George Hayley (1774)	Armourers	Merchant, 18 Gt. Ayliff St.	—	—			
	15. *Cornhill*							
C	Brackley Kennet (1767)	Vintners	Wine merchant, Pall Mall	X	—	X	X	X
	16. *Cripplegate*							
C	Sir Jas. Esdaile (1767)	Coopers	Banker, Bunhill Row, Moorfields	—	-/P/-	—	X	X

	17. *Dowgate*							
C	Sir Rich. Glyn Bt. (1750)	Salters	Banker, Lombard Street	X	PC/-/L	—	—	X
I	Sir Walt. Rawlinson (1773)	Grocers	Banker, 10 Lombard Street	X	—			
	18. *Farringdon Within*							
W	William Bridgen (1754)	Cutlers	Merchant, 34 Cornhill	W	-/G/-	—	—	P
	19. *Farringdon Without*							
I	Sir Franc. Gosling (1756)	Stationers	Bankers, 19 Fleet Street	—	—	—		
W	John Wilkes (1769)	Joiners	7 Princes Ct., George St.	—	—	—	P	P
	20. *Langbourn*							
I	Sir Jos. Hankey (1737)	Haberdashers	Bankers, 7 Fenchurch Street	—	—	—		
Ch	John Sawbridge (1769)	Framework Knitters	New Burlington Street	—	-/G/W	—	—	P
	21. *Lime Street*							
I	Sir Robert Kite (1756)	Skinners	Skinner, 40 Cannon Street	X	—	—	—	—
R	Joseph Martin (Sept. 1772)	Goldsmiths	Banker, Lombard Street	—	—			
W	Sir Watkin Lewes (1772)	Joiners	Attorney, Cecil St., Strand	—	—			P
	22. *Portsoken*							
C	Rt. Hon. Thos. Harley (1761)	Goldsmiths	Merchant, 152 Aldersgate St.; later, Banker, George St., Mansion House	X	—	X	X	X
	23. *Queenhithe*							
I	Richard Peers (1765)	Clothworkers	Grocers and Warehousemen, 9 Queenhithe	—	—	—	X	—
W	Frederick Bull (1772)	Salters	Tea dealer, 7 King Street, Cheapside	W	—			P
	24. *Tower*							
C	Samuel Turner (1762)	Clothworkers	Governor, London Assurance and merchant, 11 Mincing Lane	X	—	—	X	X
	25. *Vintry*							
R	Barlow Trecothick (1764)	Clothworkers	America merchant, John St., Bedford Row	X	—	P	—	P
L	Nath. Newnham junr. (1774)	Mercers	Grocer, Lower Thames St.; later, Banker of Lombard St.	—	—			
	26. *Walbrook*							
C	William Nash (1766)	Salters	Grocer, Cannon Street	X	—	—	X	X
W/I	Nath. Thomas (1773)	Wax Chandlers	Merchant, 2 George Street, Mansion House	—		(P)		

* *Sources: London Directory*, 1768–74; A. B. Beaven, *The Aldermen of the City of London*, vol. ii; London *Poll*, 1768; Mid. Poll Bks, 1768–69; *Mid. J.*, 6.5.69 and 16.3.71; *Lond. Evening Post*, 14–17 Nov. 1772.

[1] The prefix 'C' = Courtier, 'Ch' = Chatham/Shelburne faction, 'R' = Rockinghamite, 'W' = Wilkite, 'I' = Independent, and 'W/I' = Wilkite-cum-Independent. The date in brackets is the date of election to the Court of Aldermen.

[2] For explanatory notes to these four columns see Appendix IX, ns. 1–4.

[3] Serjeant Glynn was elected Recorder in preference to a Mr. Hyde on 14 Nov. 1772. Here supporters of Glynn, the 'Patriot' candidate, are marked 'P'; Hyde's supporters are marked 'X'.

APPENDIX XI

*Persons suspected, arrested and convicted in Wilkite disturbances in London, 1763–74**

Name	Occupation	Address	Occasion	Date	Charge	Sentence (if any)
John Franklin	Ship's steward	Cannon Street	Burning of *The North Briton* at Royal Exchange	3 Dec. 1763	Riot and wounding Ld. Mayor Harley	Sent. at O.B. to 6s. 8d. fine and 3 months' jail
Matthew Christian	Gentleman	St. Paul's Church Yard	Wilkes election celebrations	29.3.1768	Rioting	—
Robert Chandler	Tea-broker	City	,,	,,	'Heading a mob'	—
—	Soldier in the Guards	—	,,	,,	Breaking windows	—
Thomas Brady	—	—	,,	,,	Riotous assembly	12d. fine and 3 months' jail at London Q.S.
Richard Dakin	—	—	,,	28.3.1768	Breaking windows at Mansion House	—
John Philip Pennie	Paper-hanger	Haymarket	,,	29.3.1768	Breaking windows of John Walker	12d. fine at London Q.S.
Alex. Thompson	'Labourer'	Haymarket	,,	,,	,,	,,
Daniel Saxton	Watch-finisher	Jewin St., City	,,	,,	Breaking windows at Mansion House	Acquitted at O.B.
Henry Jefferson	Lighterman	St. John, Southwark	Rioting at K.B. Prison	30.4.1768	Tumultuous assembly	—
John Robinson	Labourer	St. Mary Magdalene, Bermondsey	,,	,,	Destroying wooden posts	Acquitted at Surrey Q.S.
Edward Tobias	Labourer	Christ Church, Surrey	,,	,,	,,	13s. 4d. fine and 1 month's jail at Surrey Q.S.
Robert Hall	—	—	,,	9.5.1768	Demolishing lobby of prison	—
Jane Murray	—	—	,,	,,	Aiding and abetting	Discharged

William Hawkins	Lighterman	Old Street	Mansion House riots	9.5.1768	Breaking windows	Sent. at O.B. to 12d. fine and 12 months in Newgate
Joseph Wild	—	—	,,	,,	,,	Acquitted at O.B.
Thomas Woodcock	—	—	,,	10.5.1768	Rioting	Sent. at O.B. to 12d. fine and 12 months in Newgate
Henry Davis	—	—	,,	,,	,,	—
John Williams	—	—	,,	,,	Breaking windows	Discharged
John Biggs	'A low creature'	—	Riot at H. of Lords	,,	Riotous assembly	Acquitted after reprimand
Samuel Bennett	Labourer	St. Saviour, Southwark	'Massacre' of St. George's Fields	,,	Divers misdemeanours at King's Bench prison	Discharged after detention
Jacob Tarr	,,	,,	,,	,,	,,	,,
Richard Johnson	Shoe-maker	St. James, West'r	,,	,,	,,	,,
Michael Harrison	Labourer	St. Olave, Southwark	,,	,,	,,	,,
Samuel Wanhagen	Carver	St. Clement Dane's	,,	,,	,,	,,
Charles Musto	Peruke-maker	St. John, South'k	,,	,,	,,	,,
William Bailey	Labourer	Christchurch, Surrey	,,	,,	,,	,,
Francis Morgan	,,	Suffolk St., West'r	,,	,,	,,	,,
Benjamin Ruffey	,,	Bell Yd., Gracechurch St., City	,,	,,	,,	,,
David Venner	Blacksmith	Christchurch, Surrey	,,	,,	,,	,,
Thomas French	Mariner	St. Saviour's, South'k	,,	,,	Unlawful assembly	,,
John Rouden	Cooper	Kent St., Newington	,,	,,	,,	,,
Peter Jones	Porter	John St., Clerken'l	,,	,,	,,	,,
William Tear	Shoe-maker	White St., South'k	,,	,,	,,	,,
Joseph Rivington	—	St. Leonard, Shoreditch	,,	,,	Riotous assembly	,,
James Lovet	Weaver	Golden Lane, St. Luke's	,,	,,	,,	,,
Michael Budd	Sawyer	Ewers St., St. Saviour, South'k	,,	,,	,,	,,
			,,	,,	,,	,,

Name	Occupation	Address	Occasion	Date	Charge	Sentence (if any)
Elizabeth Munday	Wife of a clothes dealer	Nightingale Lane	'Massacre' of St. George's Fields	10.5.1768	Riotous assembly	Discharged after detention
George Minor	Labourer	Woolpack Yd., South'k.	,,	,,	Tumultuous assembly	,,
Ann Nicholas	(Widow)	St. James St., Grosvernor Sq.	,,	,,	,,	,,
David Pritchard	—	—	,,	,,	No particular charge	Released
Thomas Greenwood	—	—	Southwark riots	10–11.5. 1768	Naked bayonet under coat	13s. 4d. fine and 15 months' jail at Surrey Assizes
William Hipgrave	—	City	,,	,,	Entering Russell's house	?
John Percival	Pewterer	St. Saviour, South'k.	,,	,,	Obstructing Justice Capel	2 years' prison at Surrey Assizes
Richard Gilbert	'Well-dressed'	—	,,	,,	,,	—
James Truckle	Sailmaker	City	,,	,,	Obstructing Constable Nath. Skinner	9 months' jail at Surrey Q.S.
James Jacob	Servant	c/o John Mills, City	Wilkes's birthday celebrations	28.10.1768	Attacking James Pearson's house	£5 fine at London Q.S.
Joseph Rawlinson	'Labourer'	St. James's, West'r.	Riot in St. James's Palace	22.3.1769	Riotous assembly	Discharged at West'r Guildhall
Robert Spencer	,,	,,	,,	,,	,,	,,
Thomas Hughes	,,	,,	,,	,,	,,	,,
Samuel Westguard	Bottle merchant	City	,,	,,	,,	,,
Thomas Rose	Shoe maker	St. James's St.	,,	,,	,,	,,
Stephen Parrant	Coachman	c/o Rich. Davenport, St. James's	,,	,,	,,	,,
Gregory Brown	Hosier	St. Stephens', Coleman St.	'Printers' Case' riots	28.3.1771	Shouting 'No Lord Mayor, no King!'	Discharged at West'r Guildhall
— Keyes	—	—	,,	,,	—	—

James Heyborne	Warehouseman	10 Garlick Hill	Riots in Guildhall Yd.	2.10.1771	'Ill-treating' Wm. Nash Esq. Lord Mayor elect	12d. fine at London Guildhall Q.S.
Daniel Fann	Weaver	Wheeler St., Spitalfields	,,	,,	,,	Acquitted
Edward Daniel	—	—	,,	,,	Assaulting City Marshal	12d. fine at London Q.S.
James Rose	—	—	,,	,,	,,	£10 fine at London Q.S.
Edward Brockett	Waggoner	Austin Fryars, City	Riot in Guildhall Yd., Ld. Mayor's Day	9.11.1772	Riotous assembly	Acquitted at O.B.
James Harrison	—	—	,,	,,	Assaulting Capt. Crocker	5 weeks' prison at O.B.
William Fowler	—	—	,,	,,	—	Acquitted at O.B.
John Smith	'Poor'	—	Lord Mayor's Day Riot 1773	9.11.1773	Assaulting Ald. Jas. Townsend	Found guilty at London Q.S., but not fined, as 'poor'
—	—	—	Wilkes's election as Ld. Mayor	Oct. 1774	Breaking Ald. Harley's windows	?

*_Sources_: O.B. _Proceedings_, 1763–74; London, Westminster, Middlesex and Surrey Sessions Papers and Process Register Bks.; S.P. Dom., Entry Bks; T.S. 11/818/2696; _Gent's Mag._, 1763–74.

BIBLIOGRAPHY AND ABBREVIATIONS

A complete record of source-materials consulted appears in the footnotes. What follows is a full summary of *primary* sources only – both manuscript and printed. Only those *secondary* works to which more than merely casual reference has been made are listed below.

I. Manuscript Sources

British Museum — Cited as B.M.

Hardwicke MSS. Additional MSS. 35607–9.

Liverpool MSS. Add. MSS. 38200–06.

Newcastle MSS. Add. MSS. 32948–51, 32989–991A.

Journal of Debates in the House of Commons, 9–31 January 1770, by Sir Henry Cavendish, Bart. Egerton MS. 3711. — Cit. Eg. 3711

Place MSS. Add. MSS. 27825–30.

Wilkes MSS. Add. MSS. 30865–96 (casually consulted except 30884–5).

Public Record Office — Cit. P.R.O.

Assizes 35/208. Surrey Summer Assizes, 1768.

Chatham MSS. Correspondence with John Calcraft, M.P., 3 April 1769–5 July 1772. 30/8/25.

Home Office Papers: Redress of grievances, 1769–70. H.O. 55/1–6 (petitions).

State Papers Domestic, 37/6. — Cit. S.P. Dom.

S.P. Dom., Entry Books, 44/142.

Treasury Minutes. T 29/39.

Treasury Solicitors' Papers. T.S. 11/443/1408; 11/818/2696; 11/946/3467; 11/1027/4317.

Sheffield Central Library

Wentworth Woodhouse MSS. R I, 87 (Rockingham Papers); Bk 8b (Burke Papers). [By permission of Earl Fitzwilliam and the Trustees of the Wentworth Woodhouse Settled Estates.] — Cit. W. W. MSS.

Guildhall Library Muniment Room — Cit. Guild. Lib.

Correspondence and Papers of John Wilkes. MSS. 2739, 2892, 3332, 3724.

'The King *v.* Wilkes. Original Papers and Correspondence connected with the Prosecution of John Wilkes Esq., M.P.' 3 vols, 1761–5. MSS. 214/1–3. — Cit. Guild. MSS.

Land Tax duplicates (1768–69) and Poor Rate Books (1767–69) of a dozen Middlesex parishes and liberties.
London Diocese. Episcopal Visitation Books, 3 May 1769. MSS. 9537/42–3.
Wardmote Inquest and Vestry Minutes (occasional).

Middlesex Record Office — Cit. Mid. R.O.
Commission of the Peace, no. 133, 24 Jan. 1769.
Freeholders' Book, no 12, 1767–71.
Land Tax assessments (1767) for 30 Middlesex parishes (for details see my article, 'The Middlesex Electors of 1768–1769', *E.H.R.*, Oct. 1960, p. 603 n.).
Middlesex Poll Books, 1768–69 (undated transcript in 1 vol.).
Sessions Books, 1768–74; Sessions Papers (Middlesex), Sept. 1768; Sessions Rolls (Westminster and Middlesex), 1768–71; Process Register Books of Indictments, vols. xvii (1761–69) and xviii (1769–75).

Corporation of London Record Office — Cit. Corp. Lond. R.O.

Journals of the Court of Common Council, vol. lxiv (1765–69).
Mansion House Committee Papers, 1768.
Sessions Files, 1763, 1768; Sessions Minute Books, vols. xii (1763–64), xvii–xxii (1768–74).
Surrey Record Office
Commission of the Peace, March 1769.
Freeholders' Book, 1762–71.
Sessions Bundles, 1768; Sessions Rolls, 1768; Process Register Book of Indictments, 1767–86; Q.S. Minute Book, 1767–69; Q.S. Order Book, 1767–71.

Other local Collections
Aylesbury Museum. Wilkes-Dell Correspondence (transcripts).
Bristol University Library. The Parliamentary Diary of Matthew Brickdale (11 vols. in manuscript, 1770–74). — Cit. Brickdale Diary
Bucks R.O. Commission of the Peace, 24 June 1765; Jury Book, 1769 (JB/1); Sir William Lee Correspondence.
Cornwall R.O. Commission of the Peace, 9 June 1769.
Devon R.O. Commission of the Peace, 4 July 1769.
Durham, Shire Hall. Q.S. Order Book, 1769.
East Riding R.O. Commission of the Peace, 3 Jan 1771.
Glos. R.O. Commission of the Peace, 1762.

Herefords. R.O. Commission of the Peace, 22 March 1769.

Kent R.O. Commission of the Peace, 16 Dec. 1769.

North Riding R.O. Commission of the Peace, 5 June 1769.

Northumberland R. O. Commission of the Peace, 26 July 1769.

Somerset R.O. Commission of the Peace, 27 June 1766.

Wilts. R.O. Commission of the Peace, 30 Nov. 1767.

Worcs. R.O. Q.S. Order Book, 1769.

Also sundry Rate Books in *Holborn* and *Westminster* Libraries.

II. Printed Correspondence, Memoirs, Reports, Poll Books, etc.

Autobiography and Political Correspondence of Augustus Henry Fitzroy, Third Duke of Grafton. Ed. Sir William Anson. London, 1893. — Cit. Grafton, *Autobiography*.

Boswell's London Journal 1762–1763. Ed. F. A. Potter. London, 1950.

Correspondence of the Rt. Hon. Edmund Burke. Ed. Earl Fitzwilliam and Sir R. Bourke. 4 vols. London, 1844.

The Correspondence of Edmund Burke. Gen. ed. Thos. W. Copeland. 9 vols. Cambridge, 1958–70; particularly vols. I (April 1744–June 1768) and II (July 1768–June 1774). — Cit. *Burke Correspondence*

Correspondence of King George the Third from 1760 to December 1783. Ed. Sir John Fortescue. 6 vols. London, 1927–28. — Cit. Fortescue

Correspondence of William Pitt, Earl of Chatham. Ed. W. S. Taylor and J. H. Pringle. 4 vols. London, 1838–40. — Cit. *Chatham Correspondence*

The Grenville Papers. Ed. W. J. Smith. 4 vols. London, 1852–53. — Cit. *Grenville Papers*

Letters of the First Earl of Malmesbury from 1745 to 1820. Ed. J. H. Harris. 2 vols. London, 1870. — Cit. *Malmesbury Letters*

The Letters of Horace Walpole, Fourth Earl of Orford. Ed. P. Cunningham. 9 vols. London, 1906. — Cit. Walpole, *Letters*

George Thomas, Earl of Albemarle. *Memoirs of the Marquis of Rockingham*. 2 vols. London, 1852. — Cit. *Rockingham Memoirs*

Horace Walpole. *Memoirs of the Reign of King George III*. Ed. G. F. Russell Barker. 4 vols. London, 1894. — Cit. Walpole, *Memoirs*

Calendar of Home Office Papers, George III. vols. i (1760–1765) and ii (1766–1769). Ed. J. Redington. London, 1878–79. — Cit. *Cal. H.O. Papers*

English Liberty: being a collection of Interesting Tracts from the Year 1762 to 1769, containing the Private

Correspondence, Public Letters, Speeches and Addresses of John Wilkes Esq. 2 vols. bound in one. London, 1770.

The Journals of the House of Commons — Cit. *Commons Journals*

The whole Proceedings on the King's Commission of the Peace, Oyer and Terminer, and Gaol Delivery for the City of London and . . . for the County of Middlesex. Ed. J. Gurney. London, 1763–76. — Cit. O.B. *Proceedings*

A List of the Liverymen of the several Companies of the City of London, London. 1756.

The Poll of the Livery of London. London, 1768.

Baldwin's *Guide to London*, 1770; *Royal Calendar*, 1768–74; *Court and City Register*, 1769; *London Directory*, 1768–74.

III. Periodicals

Annual Register	*Ann. Reg.*
Barrow's Worcester Journal	*Worcs. J.*
Felix Farley's Bristol Journal	*Brist. J.*
The General Evening Post	
The Gentleman's Magazine	*Gent's Mag.*
Gloucester Journal	*Glos. J.*
Jackson's Oxford Journal	*Ox. J.*
The Liverpool Chronicle	
Lloyd's Evening Post	
The London Chronicle	*Lond. Chron.*
The London Evening Post	
The Middlesex Journal	*Mid. J.*
The North Briton	
John Almon's *Political Register*	*Pol. Reg.*
The Reading Mercury and Oxford Gazette	*Read. Merc.*
The Oxford Magazine	*Ox. Mag.*
The Public Advertiser	
Pugh's Hereford Journal	
St. James's Chronicle	
Trewman's Exeter Flying Post	
Williamson's Liverpool Advertiser	

IV. A Select List of Secondary Works

A. Beaven. *The Aldermen of the City of London.* 2 vols. London, 1908.

H. Bleackley. *Life of John Wilkes.* London. 1917.

John Brewer. *Party Ideology and Popular Politics at the Accession of George III.* Cambridge, 1976.

J. Brooke. *The Chatham Administration 1766–1768.* London, 1956.

John R. Christie. *Wilkes, Wyvill and Reform.* London, 1962.

M. Dorothy George. *London Life in the Eighteenth Century*. London, 1925. Reprint, 1951.

M. Dorothy George. *English Political Caricature. A Study of Opinion and Propaganda to 1792*. Oxford, 1959.

J. Grego. *A History of Parliamentary Elections and Electioneering from the Stuarts to Queen Victoria*. London, 1892.

Jack Lindsay. *1764*. London, 1959.

S. Maccoby. *English Radicalism 1762–1785*. London, 1955.

Sir Lewis Namier. *The Structure of Politics at the Succession of George III*. 2nd edition, London, 1957.

Raymond Postgate. *That Devil Wilkes*. London, 1930. Second edition, 1956.

Peter Quennell. *Four Portraits: Studies of the Eighteenth Century*. London, 1945.

M. Robbins. *Middlesex*. A new Survey of England. London, 1953.

R. R. Sharpe. *London and the Kingdom*. 3 vols. London, 1895.

Walter, J. Shelton. *English Hunger and Industrial Disorders*. London, 1973.

O. A. Sherrard. *A Life of John Wilkes*. London, 1930.

Lucy S. Sutherland. 'The City in Eighteenth-Century Politics', in *Essays presented to Sir Lewis Namier*, Ed. R. Pares and A. J. P. Taylor. London, 1956.

Lucy S. Sutherland. *The City and the Opposition to Government, 1768–1774*. London, 1959.

Peter D. G. Thomas. 'John Wilkes and the Freedom of the Press (1771)', *Bulletin of the Institute of Historical Research*, May 1960, pp. 86–98.

Peter D. G. Thomas. *Sources for Debates of the House of Commons 1768–1774*. *Bull. Inst. Hist. Res.* Special Supplement No. 4, Nov. 1959.

W. P. Treloar. *Wilkes and the City*. London, 1917.

G. S. Veitch. *The Genesis of Parliamentary Reform*. London, 1913.

H. B. Wheatley and P. Cunningham. *London Past and Present*, 3 vols. London, 1891.

Note

Spelling and *Punctuation* have been modernized except in cases where it was considered preferable to maintain the flavour and atmosphere of the original documents.

INDEX

Abdy, Sir Anthony, Bart., 110 n., 111 and n., 112 and n., 137, 140
Acland, Sir Thomas Dyke, 127, 141
Adair, James, 3, 71, 72 and n., 143, 202
addresses, 'loyal' or 'humble', 62-65, 66, 105, 112, 125, 127-8
Allanson, Charles, M.P., 121
Allen, Benjamin, M.P., 127, 141
Allen, Capt., 186 n.
Allen, Dr. Joseph, 111
Allen, Thomas, brewer, 84 n., 88, 180
Allen, William, publican's son, 51, 54, 64
Almon, John, bookseller and printer, 155-6, 157
American colonies, America, 16, 20, 103 n., 109, 112-13, 149, 151, 186, 189, 191, 192
Anderson, Sir William, 121
aristocracy, nobility, peers, 1-3; and the petitions of 1769, 121, 136, 138; 150, 185; and Wilkes, 82, 177-8
Armytage, Sir George, M.P., 121, 122, 138
arrests, 34, 45, 48-49, 50 n., 53 n., 54, 58, 65, 162 n., 169 and n., 183, 203-4, 220-3
Asgill, Sir Charles, Alderman, 2, 3-4, 150 n., 218
Auber, Peter, master weaver, 101, 205
Aylesbury, 17-18, 19, 30, 67, 118, 140, 145, 172
Ayscough, Francis, gentleman, 72 n.

Bacon, Anthony, M.P., 67
Bacon, Edward, M.P., 77 n., 208
Baker, Sir William, Alderman, 41 n., 150 n., 152, 179-80, 217
Baker, William, Sheriff, 152
Balfe, Lawrence, Irish chairman, 61, 109
Balfe, Richard, printer, 23-24
bankers, 1, 2, 5, 83, 88, 150 and n., 180
Bankes, Sir Henry, Alderman, 151 n., 167 n., 168, 169 n., 218
Bank of England, 5, 63 and n., 83, 150 n.
Barré, Isaac, M.P., 136, 157, 186 n.
Barrington, Viscount, M.P., 44, 55, 67, 125 n., 164, 181
Barrow, Charles, M.P., 141-2, 198
Beardmore, Arthur, solicitor, 29 n., 30, 155 n., 216
Beckford, William, M.P., 3-4, 5 n., 16, 40, 41 n., 70, 79 n., 96-97, 110 n., 115, 127, 136-7, 141, 149, 151, 153 n., 175, 195, 196, 217
Bedford, 4th Duke of, 20, 55, 67, 98, 125, 175
Belasyse, Viscount, M.P., 121 and n.
Bellas, George, attorney, 71 and n., 72 n., 83 n., 109, 110, 141, 143, 154 n., 155 n.
Bernard, Sir Robert, Bart., M.P., 116 and n., 131, 143 n., 179
Berwick-on-Tweed, 18; and the petitions of 1769, 129, 211
Blake, Sir Francis, Bart., J.P., 142
Blewett, John, High Sheriff, 126, 139
Bolton, 6th Duke of, 25
Boswell, James, 2, 4, 12-13, 19
Boulton, Henry Crabb, M.P., 63 n., 77 n., 83 n., 140-1, 179
Brand, Thomas, M.P., 77 n.
Brentford, 41-43, 59-61, 64, 68-70, 79 and n., 87, 104, 163, 196
Brett, Charles, M.P., 77 n., 208
Brickdale, Matthew, M.P., 112

Bridgen, William, Alderman, 41 n., 83 n., 143, 152, 166 and n., 167, 170 n., 179, 219
Bridges, Sir Brook, M.P., 132 and n.
Bristol, 105, 106, 112; and the petitions of 1769, 112-13, 136, 144, 147, 211; 149, 175, 179, 185, 195
Briton, The, 20-21
Brown, Gregory, hosier, 162 and n.
Buckinghamshire, 18, 19, 107, 118 n., 138, 149; and the petitions of 1769, 108, 117-18, 135, 140, 145, 146, 147, 148
Bull, Frederick, M.P., 5 n., 41 n., 166 n., 167 n., 169, 170 and nn., 175, 195, 219
Buller, John, M.P., 126, 140
Bunbury, Sir Charles, Bart., M.P., 77 n.
Burke, Edmund, M.P., 21, 35-36, 37, 46, 51, 72 n.; and the petitions of 1769, 107-9, 114, 117 and n., 120 and n., 121-2, 127-8, 131, 136, 138, 146; 149 n., 159, 160 n., 163, 164 and n., 168; and Wilkes, 178; 184, 192-3, 195, 196, 201-2
Burke, Richard, M.P., 37, 109, 110 n., 163
Bute, Earl of, 2, 3, 16, 19, 20, 21, 22, 31, 43, 47, 53, 55, 164, 181, 185, 186
Byng, George, M.P., 82, 88

Calcraft, John, M.P., 118, 121 n., 131 n., 132, 140, 142, 143 n., 154
Camden, Lord, *see* Pratt, Charles
Canterbury, 30; and the petitions of 1769, 131; 172
Capel, Richard, J.P., 52, 54, 182
Carew, Sir John, Bart., 140
Carpenter, Edward, printer's servant, 158, 165
Cavendish, Lord Frederick, M.P., 139
Cavendish, Lord George, M.P., 128-9, 139
Cavendish, Sir Henry, M.P., 139
Cavendish, Lord John, M.P., 121, 139, 163 and n.
Chandler, Robert, tea-broker, 44 n., 182
Chapman, Anthony, J.P., 110 n., 111 n.
Chatham, Earl of, *see* Pitt, William
Chathamites, 41, 107 n., 149 n., 151, 153, 157, 175, 193, 219
Chauvet, Lewis, merchant, 63, 101-2, 102 n.
Cholmondeley, Nathaniel, M.P., 121 and n., 138 n.
Christian, Matthew, gentleman, 44, 182
Churchill, Charles, 4, 20
Clare, Lord, M.P., 112
Clarke, Geoffrey Bagnall, M.P., 139
Clarke, George, lawyer, 61, 64
Clavering, Sir Thomas, M.P., 142
clergy, 75, 198; and the Middlesex elections, 75, 77, 78, 82, 83, 89, 209-10; and the petitions of 1769, 121-2, 133 n., 137, 143-4, 144 n., 211; and Wilkes, 40, 178, 179 n.
coal-heavers, *see* wage-earners
cock-fighting, 11, 12-13
Codrington, Sir William, Bart., M.P., 113 n., 142, 198
Colebrooke, Sir George, Bart., M.P., 77 n., 79 n., 83 n., 88, 110 n., 111 and n., 140, 179, 208
Common Hall, *see* London
Common Council, Court of, *see* London
Common Pleas, Court of, 25, 26
Cooke, George, M.P., 41 and n., 42, 58, 75 and n.; and the Middlesex electors, 75 ff.
Cooksey, Holland, J.P., 113, 142
Cornewall, Charles Wolfran, M.P., 158
Cornwall, 18, 68, 106; and the petitions of 1769, 125-6, 139, 147, 211

Cotes, Humphrey, wine-merchant, 116 and n.
Cotton, Sir John Hynde, M.P., 77 n., 208
Court, 'Courtiers', Court party, 1-3, 15, 20, 35, 41, 58-59, 64, 68, 78, 81, 85 n., 89, 120, 122, 186; and the City of London, 150, 151 and n., 154, 219; 162, 164, 165-8, 170 and n., 176, 196
Courtenay, Lord, 140
Coventry, 51, 66; and the petitions of 1769, 132, 135, 147, 211
Coxe, John Hippisley, M.P., 127
Coxe, Richard Hippisley, M.P., 113 n., 126-7, 141
Crespigny, Claude, doctor of laws, 111 n., 141
crime, criminals, 9, 10-11, 11 n., 15, 34
Croft, Stephen, J.P., 198 n.
Crosby, Brass, Alderman, 5 n., 154, 155 n.; and 'the printers' case', 158-64; 166-7, 167 n., 182, 217
Cruger, Henry, M.P., 112, 113 and n., 175, 186 n., 195
Cumberland, 106; and the petitions of 1769, 127, 129-30, 130 n.; 185
Curry, Michael, foreman printer, 31-33, 36
Curteis, John, brewer, 84 n., 88, 180

Danvers, Sir John, 82, 179
Dashwood, Sir Francis, Lord le Despenser, 19, 64
De Grey, William, M.P., 136, 164
Delaval, Sir Francis Blake, Bart., M.P., 79 n., 179
Dell, John, surveyor, 17, 18, 67, 145
Derbyshire, 106, 138; and the petitions of 1769, 127, 128-9, 135, 139, 147, 148 and n., 211
D'Erlanger, Lord, 138
Devonshire, 106, 124; and the petitions of 1769, 125 and n., 126, 139-40, 145, 147, 211
Devonshire, 4th Duke of, 21, 23 n., 25
Devonshire, 5th Duke of, 128, 129 n.
Dingley, Charles, merchant, 53, 62-63, 68, 69, 93
Dodington, George Bubb, M.P., 19
Dolben, Sir William, M.P., 77 n., 208
Douglas, John St. Leger, M.P., 77 n., 208
Dowdeswell, Charles, 142
Dowdeswell, William, M.P., 8, 17; and the petitions of 1769, 106-8, 113-15, 118, 119 n., 129, 133 n., 142, 201-2; and Wilkes, 115; 163 n., 164 and n.
Downe, Lord, 121, 138.
Doyle, John, weaver, 101-2, 204
Durand, John, M.P., 67
Durham, 106, 174; and the petitions of 1769, 129, 132, 142, 147, 211
Dyer, John, hatter, 93

Eames, John, M.P., 77 n., 83 n., 208
East India Company, 5, 63 and n., 83 and n., 88, 175
Egmont, Lord, 43, 181
Egremont, Earl of, 23, 28, 32-33
Elliot, Sir Gilbert, M.P., 67, 159
Ellis, Welbore, M.P., 159, 161
Ellis, William, J.P., 110 n., 141
enclosure, 5, 187 and n.
Entick, Rev. John, 29 and n., 30, 155 n.
Entick v. *Carrington*, 29 n., 30, 194
Esdaile, Sir James, Alderman, 83 n., 151 n., 170 n., 218
Essay on Woman, An, 31-33, 35, 36, 177
Essex, 106; and the petitions of 1769, 112 n., 131, 174
Evelyn, James, J.P., 111 n.
Evelyn, William, M.P., 132 n.

Exeter, 106, 125 and n.; and the petitions of 1769, 125-6, 146, 211
Eyre, Walpole, 71 and n., 72

Faden, William, printer, 32, 36
Farnaby, Sir Charles, M.P., 132 and n.
Fielding, Sir John, 6, 10, 44, 45, 47, 48, 68, 94, 102, 103
Filmer, Sir John, M.P., 132
Fitzherbert, William, M.P., 77 n., 208
Fitzhugh, Thomas, hatter, 93 and n.
Fitzroy, Hon. Charles, M.P., 77 n., 208
Fitzwilliam, Earl, 164
Foley, Robert, D.D., 142, 144
Foley, Thomas, junior, M.P., 123 n., 124, 142
Foley, Thomas, senior, M.P., 123 n.,
Fountayne, Rev. John, D.D., 122, 138, 143
Fox, Henry, Lord Holland, 34
Fox, Charles James, M.P., 160, 162 and n., 164, 192-3
Fox, Stephen, M.P., 77 n., 115 and n., 140 and n., 162 and n., 164, 208
Frankland, Sir Thomas, M.P., 77 n., 138, 179, 208
Franklin, Benjamin, 41 n.
Franklin, John, ship's steward, 34
freeholders, *see* Middlesex
Freeman, Samuel, lead-merchant, 155 n., 180, 216

Gage, Viscount, M.P., 77 n., 208
Garrick, David, 4, 121
General Warrants, 22 n., 23, 24, 26, 27, 28-30, 39, 109, 152, 172, 193-4
gentry, gentlemen, 1, 12, 43, 150, 181, 184, 185, 187, 198; and the Middlesex elections, 82, 83, 87-89; and the petitions of 1769, 106, 111, 115, 117, 118-19, 120, 121, 122-3, 126-7, 128, 131, 132, 133 n., 136, 137, 138-43, 146-8; and Wilkes, 88, 115, 178-9
George III, 1, 16, 20, 22-23, 28, 33, 36, 37, 39, 46; and Wilkes's expulsion from Parliament, 65-67; and the Middlesex elections, 70, 71; and the City, 160 n., 162, 167-8, 170 n., 173; and Wilkes, 176-7; 185, 187, 192
Gillam, Samuel, J.P., 50-51, 55
gin, 9-10, 11, 14, 197
Gloucestershire, and the petitions of 1769, 118-20, 122, 141-2, 146, 147, 198, 211; 188
Glyn, Sir Richard, Bart., Alderman, 41 n., 79 n., 83 and n., 150 n., 219
Glynn, Serjeant John, M.P., 5 n., 26, 27, 29, 41, 57, 59-60, 71 n., 72 n.; and the Middlesex electors, 75 ff.; 125-6, 137, 139, 145, 148, 175, 202, 217-19
Goddard, Thomas, M.P., 141
Gordon Riots, 3, 4, 8, 10, 14, 192, 197
Gordon, William, M.P., 132
Gosling, Sir Francis, Alderman, 150 n., 153, 219
Grafton, 3rd Duke of, 25, 37, 39, 46, 53, 66, 90, 92, 104; and Wilkes, 177-8
Green, John, publican, 47, 96, 97 and n.
Grenville, George, M.P., 18, 22, 23, 39; and the petitions of 1769, 106-7, 117, 118 and n., 136, 138; and Wilkes, 140; 162, 173, 177
Grenville, Henry, M.P., 140
Grimston, Sir Thomas, Bart., 141
Guise, Sir John, Bart., 142
Guise, Sir William, Bart., M.P., 141, 198

Hake, Abraham, South Sea Co. director, 83
Halifax, Earl of, 23-24, 28, 29, 33-34, 39, 59, 164
Hallifax, Sir Thomas, Alderman, 151 n., 167 n., 169 n., 170 n., 217

Hampden, Thomas, M.P., 140
Hardwicke, Earl of, 2, 23, 25, 29, 57 n., 116, 124, 177, 182
Harley, Rt. Hon. Thomas, Alderman, 5 n., 33, 34 and n., 41 and n., 49-50, 53-54, 90, 92, 98, 150 n., 164, 170 n., 176, 181, 219
Harris, James, M.P., 65, 115, 182
Harris, Mrs. James, 12, 33, 64-65, 156, 161, 182
Hassall, Lionel, printer, 32, 36
hatters, *see* wage-earners
Hell-Fire Club, *see* Medmenham Monks
Herbert, Henry, M.P., 159
Hereford, 106, 175-6, 187; and the petitions of 1769, 124, 135, 147, 211
Herefordshire, 187; and the petitions of 1769, 122-4, 147, 211
Hertford, Earl of, 67
Hinton, Rev. Anthony, 144, 209
Hodgson, Ralph, J.P., 96-97
Hogarth, William, 4 n., 10, 31
Hopkins, Benjamin, Alderman, 63 n., 83, 150 n., 151 n., 170 n., 191, 218
Horne, Rev. John, 41 and n., 48, 57, 61, 70, 71, 82, 103; and the petitions of 1769, 109-11; 143, 144, 157, 165 and n., 166, 209
Howard, Hon. Thomas, M.P., 110 n., 111 n., 141
Huckle, William, printer, 28, 29, 30
Hudson's Bay Company, 92, 150 and n., 179-80
Hussey, William, M.P., 115, 141

Ibbetson, Sir James, 121, 138, 198 n.
industrial disputes, *see* wages movements
'inferior set of people', 'lower orders', 'the Mob', 6-7, 9, 13, 15, 26, 27, 33, 34 n., 43, 44 n., 46, 49, 52-53, 55, 56, 57, 58, 64-65, 136, 161, 163; and Wilkes, 181-3, 184; 190, 192, 197
Insurance Companies, Offices, 5, 63 and n., 150 and n., 180
'instructions' to M.P.s, 105 and n., 107, 112, 129, 174, 175, 195
Irish, 11 and n., 13 and n., 14, 47, 59 and n., 60-61, 95, 97, 197

Jacob, James, servant, 58, 222
Jenkinson, Charles, M.P., 2 n., 20 n., 23, 32, 34, 99, 130, 135, 172
Jennings, Philip, M.P., 77 n., 208
Jennings, Samuel, printer, 32-33
Johnson, Dr. Samuel, 4, 9 n., 12, 148 n., 192
Jones, Robert, J.P., 59 n., 116 and n., 143, 178-9
Junius, 166-7, 167 n.
Justice, Rev. Martin, 82, 210
Justices of the Peace, 5 n., 27, 39, 46, 50, 52, 96, 137 n.; and the Middlesex elections, 77-78, 82, 89; and the petitions of 1769, 110 n., 111 n., 115, 121 n., 124, 127, 136, 137, 138-43, 146, 211

Kearsley, George, printer and publisher, 23-24
Kennet, Brackley, Alderman, 5 n., 150 n., 170 nn., 218
Kent, 107, 149 n.; and the petitions of 1769, 132, 142-3, 146, 147, 148 and n., 211
Keppel, Admiral Augustus, M.P., 13, 164
Kidgell, Rev. John, 32, 36
King, Hon. Peter, 110 and n., 111 n., 141
King's Bench, Court of, 28, 35, 46, 49, 57
King's Bench Prison, 48-50, 57, 149, 153, 173, 177
'King's Friends', 159, 186
King's Lynn, 174-5
Kingston, 2nd Duke of, 64 n.
Kirkman, John, Alderman, 109 n., 166 n., 218

Ladbroke, Sir Robert, M.P., 41 and n., 77 n., 83 n., 150 n., 151 n., 169-70, 170 n., 218
Lancashire, 106; and the petitions of 1769, 127, 129-30
Lascelles, Daniel, M.P., 121
Lascelles, Edwin, M.P., 121 and n., 138
Lascelles, George, M.P., 138
Leach, Dryden, printer, 23-24, 28
Legard, Sir Digby, 121, 138
Lethuillier, Benjamin, M.P., 77 n., 208
Lewes, Sir Watkin, Alderman, 170 n., 175, 190, 219
Leyden, 17, 38
Liverpool, 20 and n., 106, 109 n., 127, 174, 180, 185, 186 n.; and the petitions of 1769, 127-8, 135, 144, 147, 170, 211
Livery, Livery Companies, *see* London
London, City of, 1, 4, 5, 6 and n., 9 n., 10, 14, 15-16, 20 and n., 26, 30, 38, 39, 43, 48, 50 n., 61, 62, 63, 67, 78, 79, 105, 106, 107, 108 and n., 116 n., 144, 149 and n., 150-4, 176, 177, 181, 184-5, 195-6
—— *Aldermen, Court of Aldermen*, 5, 15, 45, 61, 150-4, 154 n., 155 n., 157 n., 166, 167, 169 and n., 170 and n., 181, 217-19; and the Middlesex elections, 83 and n.; and Wilkes, 169 and n., 170 and n., 180, 217-19
—— *Common Council, Court of*, 5, 6, 15-16, 34, 38, 45, 108, 149-54, 154 n., 160-1, 164, 181; and the Middlesex elections, 78, 83 and n.; and Wilkes, 152-3, 153 n., 180, 214-16
—— *Common Hall*, 5, 6, 15, 108, 150, 153, 180
—— *Livery, Livery Companies*, 5, 6, 39, 42, 79, 107, 108 n., 109-10, 112, 113 n., 150, 153-4, 157 n., 167, 180 and n., 186 n., 212-13
—— *petition of 1769*, 109-10, 110 n., 112-13, 115, 135 n., 136, 153, 211
—— *trades, tradesmen*, 4, 6, 15, 40, 43, 62-63, 84, 150 and n., 180, 183
—— *Wards*, 217-19; Bassishaw, 180; Billingsgate, 96, 154 n.; Bridge, 154, 179; Broad Street, 63 n., 154 n., 191; Castle Baynard, 154; Cordwainer, 154 n.; Cornhill, 154 n.; Dowgate, 154 n.; Farringdon Within, 154 n., 166 n., 179; Farringdon Without, 61, 153, 154 and n., 166; Queenhithe, 169; Tower, 154 and n., 155 n.; Walbrook, 154 and n., 155 n.
Lowther, Sir James, M.P., 185, 208
Luttrell, Henry Fownes, M.P., 139-40
Luttrell, Henry Lawes, M.P., and his contest with Wilkes, 68-71; 72 and n., 74 n.; and the Middlesex electors, 75 ff.; 104, 106, 108, 114 and n., 126, 133, 136, 149, 164, 174, 177, 181, 182, 198
Lycett, John, upholsterer, 116

Mackenzie, William, M.P., 172-3
'Malagrida' faction, *see* Shelburne, Earl of
Manchester, 4th Duke of, 164
Mansfield, Earl of, 3, 28, 47-48, 57, 71
manufacturers, 4, 5, 182; and the Middlesex elections, 84, 89; and the petitions of 1769, 144-6; and the Common Council, 150 and n.; and Wilkes, 179-80
March, Earl of, 32
Martin, Joseph, M.P., 110 n., 111 n., 140, 150 n., 152, 219
Martin, Samuel, M.P., 34
Masham, Charles, M.P., 132 n.
Mawbey, Sir Joseph, Bart., M.P., 4, 61, 110 and n., 111 and n., 129, 130 n., 131, 138, 153, 158, 159, 174, 179

McLane, Donald, grenadier, 55
McQuirk, Edward, Irish chairman, 59 and n., 61, 109, 115
Meade, Mary, Mrs John Wilkes, 17
Medmenham Monks, 19, 31, 33
merchants, 4-5, 5 n., 6, 15, 20, 30, 53, 61, 79, 84, 91, 181, 182, 183, 184, 186; and a 'loyal' address to the King, 62-65; and the Middlesex elections, 84, 88, 89, 145-6; and the petitions of 1769, 112-13, 138, 144-6; and the Common Council, 150 and n.; and Wilkes, 179-80
Meredith, Sir William, M.P., 105, 127-8, 159, 162 n., 174, 180, 202
Metham, Sir George Montgomery, 121, 138
Middlesex, 1, 9, 35, 41, 44, 46, 50 n., 55, 61, 68, 78-79, 80 n., 105, 106, 107, 149 n., 176, 185; its 'out'-parishes, 1 and n., 4-5, 15, 79, 80 and n., 81, 84, 85-86, 89, 180, 185; its rural parishes, 75, 79, 81 and n., 85-86, 184; its electors and freeholders, 6 and n., 41 and n., 60, 61, 67-73, 74-89, 138, 142, 145-6, 178, 181, 194, 206-7; and the elections of 1768-69, 41-43, 59-60, 62, 68-70, 74-89, 123, 125-7, 128, 131, 133, 137, 173, 180, 182, 194, 195, 198; and the petitions of 1769, 71-73, 107 n., 108 and n., 109, 126, 135 n., 138, 145-6, 147, 211
Middleton, Lord, 25
Miller, John, printer, 157-9, 161
Minestone, James, ship-builder, 88, 180
Molesworth, Sir John, M.P., 126 and n., 139
Monitor, The, 21, 29, 155 n.
Morpeth, and the petitions of 1769, 130 n., 211
Morris, Robert, lawyer, 157 and n., 158-9, 165
Murphy, Daniel, weaver, 102, 204
Murray, Captain Alexander, grenadier, 51, 55

Nash, William, Alderman, 5 n., 151 n., 166, 167 and nn., 168, 189, 219
Neale, Francis, writing master, 145
Neale, Robert, churchwarden, 17, 67
Nelson, Lord, 191
Newcastle, 1st Duke of, 3, 7, 18, 20, 23 and n., 25, 26, 27, 44, 47, 55, 57, 58, 75, 78, 90, 95, 106, 124, 177; and Wilkes, 46, 178, 186
Newcastle-on-Tyne, 91, 103-4, 105 n., 173, 174; and the petitions of 1769, 129, 147, 174, 211
Newdigate, Sir Roger, M.P., 77 n., 208
Norcliffe, Sir James, 121, 138
North, Lord, M.P., 2, 65, 66; and the petitions of 1769, 119 n., 133 n., 136-7, 145; 160 n., 162, 167, 170 and n., 177
North Briton, The, 19, 20-22, 22 n., 23, 25, 28, 30, 31, 34, 35, 172, 177, 181, 193
Northumberland, and the petitions of 1769, 129, 142, 211
Northumberland, 1st Duke of, 3, 43, 44, 59 n., 64, 67 n.
Norton, Sir Fletcher, M.P., 23, 155, 164
Norwich, 66, 108 n., 174, 189

O'Brien, Murrough, J.P., 118, 140
Oliver, Richard, M.P., 5 n., 57, 61, 151, 153, 154-5, 155 n.; and 'the printers' case', 158-63, 163 n.; 166, 169 n., 170 and nn., 179
Onslow, George, M.P., 25, 27, 70, 141, 193
Onslow, Colonel George, M.P., 156-8, 164
Oxford, and the petitions of 1769, 131 and n.

Palmerston, Viscount, M.P., 77 n., 208

Pardoe, John, E. India Co. director, 63 n., 83 n.
Parker, John, M.P., 139
Parliament, Members of, and the Middlesex elections, 77 and n., 78, 82, 208-9; and the petitions of 1769, 110 and n., 111 n., 112, 114-18, 120-1, 124-7, 129-30, 132, 136-7, 138-43, 146, 179, 211
Parliamentary Opposition, 21, 25, 35, 45-46, 55, 59, 133, 134, 157-8, 177-8
Parliamentary Reform, 16, 191-2, 195, 197, 198
'patriots', 37, 40, 41, 42, 102, 103, 109, 114, 151 and n., 152-4, 156, 157, 165-8, 174, 176, 180, 193, 216, 219; *see also* radicals
Patten, Robert, innholder, 17
Paul, Sir George Onesiphorus, 142, 198
Peach, Samuel, banker, 175, 179, 186 n.
Pennant, Richard, M.P., 127-8, 174, 180
Penruddock, Charles, M.P., 115, 141
Perkins, John, merchant, 17-18
petitioners of 1769, 135 ff.; *see also* Bristol, London, Middlesex, etc.
petitions of 1769, 105 ff.; *see also* Bristol, London, Middlesex, etc.
Pitt, Thomas, M.P., 126
Pitt, William, Earl of Chatham, 2, 13, 16, 18, 20, 22, 25, 33, 37, 46, 57 n., 76; and the petitions of 1769, 106-8, 118, 132 and n.; 149, 153, 163-4; and Wilkes, 177; 184 and n., 185, 192, 195, 196
Pitt, William, the Younger, 191, 192
Place, Francis, 8, 9, 11-12, 15
Plumbe, Samuel, Alderman, 109 n., 166 n., 170 nn., 218
Plumer, William, M.P., 77 n., 208
police, troops, peace officers, law and order, 14, 43, 44-45, 46-47, 48, 49-52, 53 n., 55-56, 57, 65, 67, 68-69, 90, 91, 97, 102, 118 n., 161, 163
Pomfret, Lord, 186-7
Popham, Alexander, M.P., 141
Popham, Edward, M.P., 115
population, 1, 5
Portland, 3rd Duke of, 3, 27 and n., 130, 164, 185
Potter, Thomas, M.P., 18, 30
Pownall, Thomas, M.P., 157
Pratt, Charles, Lord Camden, 24, 27, 28-29, 30; and Wilkes, 45-46, 46 n.; 193
Prescot, George, gentleman, 72, 146
Press Warrants, 196 n., 214-16
prices of bread, food, 8-9, 9 n., 13, 38, 90, 188-9, 190
Princess Dowager of Wales, 21, 53, 164, 186 and n.
printers, 7, 31-32, 36; and *The North Briton*, 23, 24, 28, 29 n., 30, 31; and 'the printers' case', 155-9, 161, 165, 166, 194
Prior, Rev. Williams, 82, 210
Proctor, Sir William Beauchamp, 41 and n., 42, 58-60; and the Middlesex electors, 74 ff.; 182, 196
'Proctorites', 85-87, 145-6

radicals, radicalism, 63, 68, 78, 81, 84, 89, 103 n., 106, 107 and n., 108, 153, 173, 174, 191, 193, 194, 195, 196-8; *see also* 'patriots'
Rebow, Isaac, M.P., 77 n., 209
Redburn, William, weaver, 51, 55
Remonstrances, 149 and n., 154 and n., 183, 186
rents, 8
Reynolds, Francis, attorney, 96
Reynolds, John, attorney, 62, 160
Richmond, 3rd Duke of, 130-1, 138; and Wilkes, 40, 178
Rigby, Richard, M.P., 130-1
riots, demonstrations, popular celebrations, 3, 9, 13-15, 39, 125, 126, 168, 181-3, 187-8, 189, 190; of May-December 1763,

27, 30, 33-34; of March 1768, 42, 43-45; of April 1768, 47-48, 97; of May 1768, 44 n., 45 n., 49-54, 67, 93, 98, 188; of October 1768, 58; of December 1768, 59-60, 64; of February 1769, 67; of March 1769, 63-66; of April 1769, 69-70, 70 n., 71; of April 1770, 149; of March-July 1771, 160-61, 162-3, 164, 166; of November 1772, 169, 190; of October 1774, 170-1; *see also* Gordon Riots, wages movements and wage-earners

Roach, Captain David, 68-70

Robinson, John, M.P., 130, 135-6, 144-5, 148, 151

Rockingham, Marquess of, 2, 3, 37, 57; and the petitions of 1769, 111 and n., 120, 121 n., 129 n., 130, 138, 142, 200-2; 149 n., 151, 163 and n., 164 and n., 165, 167, 174, 177; and Wilkes, 165 and n., 178

Rockingham Whigs, Rockinghamites, 68, 72, 106, 107 and n., 109, 110, 113, 116, 122, 148, 149 n., 151-2, 161, 163 n., 165 n., 175, 186, 200-2, 219

Rodbart, William, High Sheriff, 126, 141

Roger, Sir John, Recorder, 125

Russell, Edward, J.P., 52, 54, 182, 199-200

St. Aubin, Sir John, M.P., 139

St. George's Fields, 49-52, 55, 57, 64, 67, 92, 93, 104, 114, 117, 118 n., 181

St. James's, St. James's Palace, 1, 2, 4, 11, 15, 39, 50, 63-65, 66, 68, 71, 92, 98, 112, 117, 132, 154 n., 181, 196

Sandwich, Earl of, 4, 19, 33-34, 36, 164, 181

Saunders, Sir Charles, M.P., 164

Savile, Sir George, Bart., M.P., 72, 108, 121 and n., 122, 130, 138, 163 n., 164 n., 198, 200

Sawbridge, John, M.P., 2, 3-4, 57, 61, 71, 72, 82, 87, 102, 103, 109, 132, 143 and n., 151, 153, 154, 157, 159; breaks with Wilkes, 165; 166, 167 and n.; reconciled to Wilkes, 170; 170 n., 178, 195, 209

Sawbridge, Rev. Wanley, 143 n., 144

Scots, 13, 14, 21, 49, 54, 128, 184

Scott, Hon. John, 82, 179

Scudamore, John, M.P., 124, 143 n.

Sewell, Sir Henry, Master of the Rolls, 83

Seymour, Henry, M.P., 127, 141

Shakespear, John, Alderman, 79 n., 151 n., 168, 169 n., 170 n., 217

Shelburne, Earl of, Shelburne faction, 39, 99, 151, 165 and n., 166, 167, 170

Sheriff, Henry, publican, 17, 67, 145

sickness and mortality, 7

Singleton, William, High Sheriff, 118

Sloane, Hans, M.P., 77 n., 209

Smith, John, M.P., 127, 141

Smollett, Tobias, 20

Somerset, 126, 175; and the petitions of 1769, 126-7, 141, 146, 147, 211

South Sea Company, 5, 63 and n., 83

Southwark, 1, 4, 6 n., 15, 50 and n., 52, 54, 61, 67, 93, 106, 179, 181, 185; and the petitions of 1769, 131-2, 135, 211

Southwell, Edward, M.P., 118

Span, Samuel, merchant, 113 and n.

Spenceley, Allen, warehouseman, 88, 180

Spitalfields, 4, 6, 7, 14, 15, 38-39, 42, 48, 88, 98, 100-3, 179, 182, 189

Stanhope, Sir William, M.P., 140

Stanley, Hans, M.P., 162

Stephens, Rev. John, 17, 67

Stephenson, John, M.P., 63 n., 77 n., 83 n., 209

Stephenson, Sir William, Alderman, 153 n., 170 nn., 179, 217
Stowe House, 18-19, 20, 117 n.
Strickland, Sir George, 138
strikes, *see* wages movements
Strode, William, M.P., 77 n., 209
Stuart, Sir Simeon, M.P., 77 n., 209
Supporters of the Bill of Rights, Society of, 61-62, 66, 82, 106, 107 and n., 108-9, 110-11, 113, 115, 116, 122, 125, 135-6, 148, 153, 157, 165, 174, 175, 179 n., 194-5
Surrey, 15, 30, 47, 49, 55, 88, 93 n., 106; and the petitions of 1769, 110-12, 135, 138, 140-1, 147, 211; 149 n., 176, 185

tailors, *see* wage-earners
Talbot, Earl, 21, 64
Talbot, John, J.P., 115, 141
Tempest, John, junior, M.P., 142
Temple, Earl, 16, 18, 19, 20, 21-22, 24-26, 29-31, 33, 35, 37-38, 46, 48; and the petitions of 1769, 106-8, 115, 117; 164, 167; and Wilkes, 177, 185, 193
Temple, William, J.P., 115, 141
Terry, Edward, brewer, 17, 145
Terry, Richard, brewer, 17, 145
Thompson, Beilby, M.P., 121, 138 n.
Thompson, Richard, printer, 156
Townsend, Chauncy, M.P., 63
Townsend, James, M.P., 5 n., 57, 61, 63, 70, 71, 72, 82, 87 n., 102, 103, 104 n.; and the petitions of 1769, 108-9, 143; 151, 153, 155 n., 157, 161, 163; breaks with Wilkes, 165; 167 and n., 168 and n.; elected Lord Mayor, 168-9, 169 n.; 170 and nn., 178, 190, 209, 217
Townshend, Charles, M.P., 17
Tracy, Thomas, M.P., 118
Trecothick, Barlow, M.P., 5 n., 40, 41 and n., 110, 151-2, 153 n., 155, 163, 168, 170 n., 219
Trinder, David, timber-merchant, 88, 180
Trueman, Sir Ben, brewer, 84 n., 88, 179
Tudway, Clement, M.P., 127 n.
Turner, Charles, M.P., 121, 138 n.
Turner, Samuel, Alderman, 109, 150 n., 151 n., 170 nn., 219
Tyburn, 11-12, 15, 103
Tynte, Sir Charles, M.P., 127 n.

unemployed, 93-94

Valline, John, weaver, 101-2, 204
Vaughan, Samuel, merchant, 43, 61, 62, 179
Verney, Earl, M.P., 118, 140
Vernon, Richard, M.P., 77 n., 209
Vincent, Sir Francis, Bart., M.P., 111 n., 140
Vyvian, Sir Richard, Bart., 139

wage-earners, journeymen, labourers, 6-8, 9, 15, 49-50, 65, 90, 183, 184, 192, 197; *coal-heavers*, 6, 7, 38, 47, 90, 95-98, 182; *coopers*, 94, 104; *glass-grinders*, 94, 104; *hatters*, 6, 93 and n., 104; *sailors*, 6, 30, 90, 91-92, 98, 103-4, 169, 173, 189-90; *sawyers*, 53, 93-94, 104; *tailors*, 6, 7, 8, 94-95, 104, 189-90; *watermen*, 6, 92, 104; *weavers*, 6, 38-39, 90, 98-103, 104; among Wilkite rioters, 104, 183 and n., 197, 220-3
wages, 7, 8, 59, 91, 92, 95, 96, 100
wages movements, 9, 38-39, 90-103, 188, 189-90; *see also* wage-earners
Wallinger, Arnold, gentleman, 72 n.
Walpole, Horace, M.P., 2, 10, 59, 103, 104, 174, 182
Walter, John Rolfe, M.P., 126 n.
Warburton, Dr. William, Bishop of Gloucester, 31
watermen, *see* wage-earners
Way, Benjamin, South Sea Co. director, 83
weavers, 42, 98-99, 103 and n., 182; *see also* wage-earners

Webb, Nathaniel, M.P., 77 n., 209
Webb, Philip Carteret, M.P., 23, 24 n., 28-29, 31-33, 36
Webb, Philip Carteret, junior, 110 n., 141
Weddell, Thomas, 198 n.
Weddell, William, M.P., 121, 138 n.
Wedderburn, Alexander, M.P., 121, 122, 138 n., 139, 142, 162-3, 173, 193
Welch, Saunders, J.P., 9 n., 64 and n.
West, James, M.P., 47, 55 and n., 90, 95
Westminster, City of, 1 and n., 4, 6, 10, 14, 15, 43, 46, 50 n., 53, 61, 63, 65, 67, 68, 78, 79 n., 80; and the Middlesex elections, 75, 79, 80-81, 85-86; and the petitions of 1769, 116-17, 135, 136, 145, 147, 211; 162, 176, 180, 181, 185, 196
Westmorland, and the petitions of 1769, 127, 129-30
Weymouth, Viscount, 44, 46, 48, 56, 68, 92, 94, 101, 104
Whately, Thomas, M.P., 117
Wheble, John, printer, 156, 158
Whitaker, Serjeant William, 68-70
Whitbread, Samuel, M.P., 4, 77, 84 n., 209
Wilkes, Heaton, 38
Wilkes, Isaac, 17
Wilkes, John, M.P., 1, 4, 5, 6, 13, 14, 16; early years, 17-20; and *The North Briton*, 20-31, 34; and *An Essay on Woman*, 31-33, 35; in France and Italy, 36; returns to England, 37-38; stands for election in the City, 39-41; elected in Middlesex, 41-42; 43; and the opposition leaders, 45-46; surrenders to his outlawry, 46-47; and the East London coal-heavers, 47; committed to King's Bench prison, 47-48; and the St. George's Fields 'Massacre', 49-50, 55-56; in King's Bench prison, 57-58; birthday celebrations, 58; alderman of Farringdon Without, 61; and the Supporters of the Bill of Rights, 61-62; expelled a second time from Parliament, 66-67; re-elected in Middlesex and disqualified, 67-68; his contest with Luttrell, 68-70; 71; declaration of his 'incapacity', 72-73; and the Middlesex electors, 74-89; and industrial unrest, 90-91, 97, 103-4; and the petitioners of 1769, 105-9, 113, 114 n., 115, 119, 122, 125 n., 126, 130 n., 133 n., 134 n., 140, 145-6; released from prison, 149; toasted in America, 149; his support in the City, 149-54, 214-19; and press warrants, 155, 196 n.; and 'the printers' case', 155, 157-61; breach with Horne and Townsend, 165-6; elected sheriff, 166; and Junius, 166-7; elected Lord Mayor, 168-71; and his supporters: geographical distribution, 172-6; and George III, 176-7; and the opposition peers, 177-8; and the clergy, 178, 179 n.; and the gentry, 178-9; and the merchants, 179-80; and the county freeholders, 181; and the 'inferior set of people', 181-3; 184-5, 189, 190; elected City Chamberlain, 191; his return to Parliament, 191; his conversion to Toryism, 192; his historical importance, 192-5; and the radical movement, 196-8; 219
Wilkes, Polly, 17, 19, 24, 30, 35, 175 n.
Wilkes, Sarah, 17
'Wilkes and Liberty', 1, 14, 27, 30, 34, 36, 40, 42, 44, 49, 50, 53, 58, 65, 71, 104, 125, 171, 172, 173 n., 174, 181, 190, 191, 192, 197
Wilkites, 'Wilkism', 40, 41, 49, 52, 59, 60, 61, 62, 63, 65, 66, 69,

72 n., 74, 75, 81, 85-87, 88, 103, 112, 145, 153, 154 n., 165, 169 and n., 170 and n., 172, 176, 179, 180, 181, 188-9, 198, 214-16, 219

Williamson, Rev. Joseph, 82, 210

Wilson, Rev. Dr. Thomas, 72 n., 116, 179 n.

Wiltshire, 106; and the petitions of 1769, 115-16, 141, 142, 147, 148 n., 211

Wood, Robert, M.P., 28, 77 n., 209

Worcester 106; and the petitions of 1769, 114, 147, 211; 164, 187

Worcestershire, and the petitions of 1769, 113-15, 142, 147, 211

Wray, Sir Cecil, Bart., M.P., 61, 121 and n., 122, 130, 138

Wrey, Sir Bourchier, Bart., 140

Wyvill, Rev. Christopher, 198 and n.

Wyvill, Sir Marmaduke Asty, 121, 138, 198

Yorke, Hon. Charles, M.P., 23, 77 n., 209

Yorke, Hon. John, M.P., 77 n., 209

Yorkshire, 107, 108; and the petitions of 1769, 112 n., 120-2, 127, 130, 135, 138-9, 145, 147, 198 n., 211; 138, 149, 174, 198